Treaty Series

Treaties and international agreements
registered
or filed and recorded
with the Secretariat of the United Nations

VOLUME 2998

Recueil des Traités

Traités et accords internationaux
enregistrés
ou classés et inscrits au répertoire
au Secrétariat de l'Organisation des Nations Unies

United Nations • Nations Unies
New York, 2021

TABLE OF CONTENTS

I

Treaties and international agreements
registered in August 2014
Nos. 52051 to 52100

No. 52051. International Fund for Agricultural Development and China:

Financing Agreement (Shiyan smallholder agribusiness development project (SSADeP)) between the People's Republic of China and the International Fund for Agricultural Development (with schedules and General Conditions for Agricultural Development Financing dated 29 April 2009, as amended through 17 September 2010). Rome, 30 January 2014 3

No. 52052. International Fund for Agricultural Development and India:

Programme Financing Agreement (Convergence of Agricultural Interventions in Maharashtra's Distressed Districts Programme) between the Republic of India and the International Fund for Agricultural Development (with schedules and General Conditions for Agricultural Development Financing dated 2 December 1998). Rome, 30 September 2009 5

No. 52053. International Fund for Agricultural Development and India:

Programme Loan Agreement (Women's Empowerment and Livelihoods Programme in the Mid-Gangetic Plains) between the Republic of India and the International Fund for Agricultural Development (with schedules and General Conditions for Agricultural Development Financing dated 2 December 1998). Rome, 11 December 2008 7

No. 52054. International Fund for Agricultural Development and Uganda:

Programme Loan Agreement (Community Agricultural Infrastructure Improvement Programme (CAIIP)) between the Republic of Uganda and the International Fund for Agricultural Development (with schedules and General Conditions for Agricultural Development Financing dated 2 December 1998). Rome, 19 September 2007 9

No. 52055. International Fund for Agricultural Development and Liberia:

Financing Agreement (Support to the Farmers Union Network of Liberia (FUN)) between the Republic of Liberia and the International Fund for Agricultural Development (with schedules and General Conditions for Agricultural Development Financing dated 29 April 2009, as amended through 17 September 2010). Rome, 2 July 2013, and Monrovia, 8 September 2013 11

No. 52056. International Fund for Agricultural Development and Nigeria:

Financing Agreement (Value Chain Development Programme (VCDP)) between the Federal Republic of Nigeria and the International Fund for Agricultural Development (with schedules and General Conditions for Agricultural Development Financing dated 29 April 2009, as amended through 17 September 2010). Abuja, 23 August 2012 13

No. 52057. International Fund for Agricultural Development and Benin:

Financing Agreement (Rural Economic Growth Support Project) between the Republic of Benin and the International Fund for Agricultural Development (with schedules and General Conditions for Agricultural Development Financing dated 2 December 1998). Rome, 21 July 2009 15

No. 52058. International Fund for Agricultural Development and Burkina Faso:

Financing Agreement (Programme for the support and promotion of the private sector in rural areas) between Burkina Faso and the International Fund for Agricultural Development (with schedules and General Conditions for Agricultural Development Financing dated 2 December 1998). Rome, 23 September 2009 17

No. 52059. International Fund for Agricultural Development and Seychelles:

Financing Agreement (Competitive Local Innovations for Small-Scale Agriculture Project (CLISSA)) between the Republic of Seychelles and the International Fund for Agricultural Development (with schedules and General Conditions for Agricultural Development Financing dated 29 April 2009, as amended through 17 September 2010). Rome, 22 May 2013 19

No. 52060. International Fund for Agricultural Development and Niger:

Financing Agreement (Agricultural and Rural Rehabilitation and Development Initiative – Institutional Capacity Strengthening) between the Republic of the Niger and the International Fund for Agricultural Development (with schedules and General Conditions for Agricultural Development Financing dated 2 December 1998). Rome, 15 January 2009 21

No. 52061. International Fund for Agricultural Development and Mauritius:

Programme Financing Agreement (Marine and Agricultural Resources Support Programme) between the Republic of Mauritius and the International Fund for Agricultural Development (with schedules and General Conditions for Agricultural Development Financing dated 2 December 1998). Port Louis, 5 March 2009 23

No. 52062. International Fund for Agricultural Development and Guatemala:

Financing Agreement (Sustainable Rural Development Programme for the Northern Region) between the Republic of Guatemala and the International Fund for Agricultural Development (with schedules and General Conditions for Agricultural

Development Financing dated 2 December 1998). Guatemala City, 13 December 2011, and Rome, 13 December 2011 25

No. 52063. International Fund for Agricultural Development and Dominican Republic:

Loan Agreement (Development Project for Economic Organizations for the Rural Poor in the Border Region) between the Dominican Republic and the International Fund for Agricultural Development (with schedule and General Conditions for Agricultural Development Financing dated 2 December 1998). Rome, 29 June 2009, and Santo Domingo, 29 June 2009 27

No. 52064. International Fund for Agricultural Development and Philippines:

Programme Financing Agreement (Rapid Food Production Enhancement Programme) between the Republic of the Philippines and the International Fund for Agricultural Development (with schedules and General Conditions for Agricultural Development Financing dated 2 December 1998). Manila, 2 September 2009 29

No. 52065. International Fund for Agricultural Development and Bosnia and Herzegovina:

Project Loan Agreement (Rural Livelihoods Development Project) between Bosnia and Herzegovina and the International Fund for Agricultural Development (with schedules and General Conditions for Agricultural Development Financing dated 2 December 1998). Sarajevo, 9 December 2009 31

No. 52066. International Fund for Agricultural Development and El Salvador:

Financing Agreement (Rural Development and Modernization Project for the Central and Paracentral Regions (PRODEMOR-Central) – Extension) between the Republic of El Salvador and the Spanish Food Security Cofinancing Facility Trust Fund acting through the International Fund for Agricultural Development in its capacity as Trustee of the Fund (with schedules and General Conditions for Agricultural Development Financing dated 29 April 2009, as amended through 17 September 2010). Rome, 25 April 2012, and San Salvador, 4 May 2012 33

No. 52067. International Fund for Agricultural Development and Georgia:

Financing Agreement (Agricultural Support Project) between Georgia and the International Fund for Agricultural Development (with schedules and General Conditions for Agricultural Development Financing dated 29 April 2009). Rome, 24 June 2010, and Tbilisi, 8 July 2010 35

No. 52068. International Fund for Agricultural Development and Ethiopia:

Project Financing Agreement (Community-based Integrated Natural Resources Management Project) between the Federal Democratic Republic of Ethiopia and the International Fund for Agricultural Development (with schedules and General

Conditions for Agricultural Development Financing dated 2 December 1998). Rome, 19 June 2009 37

No. 52069. International Fund for Agricultural Development and Ethiopia:

Financing Agreement (Pastoral Community Development Project II) between the Federal Democratic Republic of Ethiopia and the International Fund for Agricultural Development (with schedules and General Conditions for Agricultural Development Financing dated 29 April 2009). Rome, 26 November 2009 39

No. 52070. International Fund for Agricultural Development and Brazil:

Guarantee Agreement (Rural Business for small producers project (Dom Távora) (Projeto de desenvolvimento de negócios rurais para pequenos produtores – Dom Távora)) between the Federative Republic of Brazil and the International Fund for Agricultural Development (with General Conditions for Agricultural Development Financing dated 29 April 2009, as amended through 17 September 2010). Rome, 20 August 2013, and Brasília, 30 August 2013 41

No. 52071. International Fund for Agricultural Development and Viet Nam:

Agreement between the Government of the Socialist Republic of Viet Nam and the International Fund for Agricultural Development concerning the Fund's country office. Hanoi, 16 January 2008 43

No. 52072. United Nations and Mauritius:

Exchange of letters constituting an Agreement between the United Nations and the Government of the Republic of Mauritius on the hosting of the "Regional workshop on fossil fuel and renewable energy (FFRE)" to be held in Port Louis, Mauritius, from 12 to 16 May 2014. New York, 25 February 2014 and 13 May 2014 71

No. 52073. International Development Association and United Republic of Tanzania:

Financing Agreement (Eleventh Poverty Reduction Support Development Policy Financing) between the United Republic of Tanzania and the International Development Association (with schedules, appendix and International Development Association General Conditions for Credits and Grants, dated 31 July 2010). Washington, 10 April 2014 73

No. 52074. International Development Association and United Republic of Tanzania:

Financing Agreement (Second Power and Gas Sector Development Policy Financing) between the United Republic of Tanzania and the International Development Association (with schedules, appendix and International Development Association General Conditions for Credits and Grants, dated 31 July 2010). Washington, 10 April 2014 75

No. 52075. International Development Association and Lesotho:

Financing Agreement (Public Financial Management Reform Support Project) between the Kingdom of Lesotho and the International Development Association (with schedules, appendix and International Development Association General Conditions for Credits and Grants, dated 31 July 2010). Maseru, 24 February 2014.................. 77

No. 52076. International Bank for Reconstruction and Development and The former Yugoslav Republic of Macedonia:

Loan Agreement (Second Programmatic Competitiveness Development Policy Loan) between The former Yugoslav Republic of Macedonia (the Borrower) and the International Bank for Reconstruction and Development (the Bank) (with schedules, appendix and International Bank for Reconstruction and Development General Conditions for Loans, dated 12 March 2012). Skopje, 23 July 2014......................... 79

No. 52077. International Development Association and Senegal:

Financing Agreement (Casamance Development Pole Project) between the Republic of Senegal and the International Development Association (with schedules, appendix and International Development Association General Conditions for Credits and Grants, dated 31 July 2010). Dakar, 22 November 2013 81

No. 52078. International Development Association and Kyrgyzstan:

Financing Agreement (Second Development Policy Operation) between the Kyrgyz Republic and the International Development Association (with schedules, appendix and International Development Association General Conditions for Credits and Grants, dated 31 July 2010). Bishkek, 16 June 2014.. 83

No. 52079. Turkey and Georgia:

Memorandum of Understanding between the Government of the Republic of Turkey and the Government of Georgia on cooperation in combating crime. Tbilisi, 22 February 2012.. 85

No. 52080. Turkey and Hungary:

Cooperation Programme between the Government of the Republic of Turkey and the Government of Hungary in the fields of education and science for the years 2014-2016. Ankara, 18 December 2013 103

No. 52081. Turkey and Peru:

Exchange of notes constituting an agreement regarding the suppression of visas in diplomatic passports and service passports (or special passports) between the Government of the Republic of Turkey and the Government of the Republic of Peru. Vienna, 28 May 1996 and 17 September 1996 135

No. 52082. International Bank for Reconstruction and Development and Russian Federation:

Loan Agreement (Second National Hydromet Modernization Project) between the Russian Federation and the International Bank for Reconstruction and Development (with schedules, appendix and International Bank for Reconstruction and Development General Conditions for Loans, dated 12 March 2012). Moscow, 17 January 2014 137

No. 52083. International Development Association and India:

Financing Agreement (Third Elementary Education Project) between India and the International Development Association (with schedules, appendix and International Development Association General Conditions for Credits and Grants, dated 31 July 2010). New Delhi, 29 May 2014 139

No. 52084. Turkey and Japan:

Agreement between the Government of the Republic of Turkey and the Government of Japan for cooperation in the use of nuclear energy for peaceful purposes (with annexes). Tokyo, 26 April 2013, and Ankara, 3 May 2013 141

No. 52085. Turkey and China:

Memorandum of Understanding on cooperation in the energy sector between the Ministry of Energy and Natural Resources of the Republic of Turkey and the National Energy Administration of the People's Republic of China. Beijing, 25 June 2009 211

No. 52086. International Development Association and India:

Financing Agreement (Accelerating Universal Access to early and effective tuberculosis care project) between India and the International Development Association (with schedules, appendix and International Development Association General Conditions for Credits and Grants, dated 31 July 2010). New Delhi, 30 May 2014 221

No. 52087. Belgium and Malta:

Agreement between the Government of the Kingdom of Belgium and the Government of Malta on police cooperation. Brussels, 1 December 2005 223

No. 52088. Belgium and St. Lucia:

Agreement between the Kingdom of Belgium and Saint Lucia for the exchange of information relating to tax matters. Brussels, 7 December 2009 255

No. 52089. Belgium, Luxembourg, Netherlands and South Africa:

Agreement between the Governments of the Benelux States and the Government of the Republic of South Africa on the exemption of visa requirements for holders of diplomatic, official and/or service passports. Pretoria, 22 February 2013 273

No. 52090. International Bank for Reconstruction and Development and Croatia:

Loan Agreement (Second Economic Recovery Development Policy Loan) between the Republic of Croatia and the International Bank for Reconstruction and Development (with schedules, appendix and International Bank for Reconstruction and Development General Conditions for Loans, dated 12 March 2012). Zagreb, 30 April 2014 293

No. 52091. International Bank for Reconstruction and Development and Morocco:

Loan Agreement (First Capital Market Development and small and medium-sized enterprise finance development policy loan) between the Kingdom of Morocco and the International Bank for Reconstruction and Development (with schedules, appendix and International Bank for Reconstruction and Development General Conditions for Loans, dated 12 March 2012). Rabat, 27 May 2014 295

No. 52092. United Nations and Fiji:

Exchange of letters constituting an Agreement between the United Nations and the Government of the Republic of Fiji regarding the hosting of the "Regional Workshop on gender statistics and human rights reporting statistics" to be held in Nadi, Fiji, from 4 to 8 August 2014. New York, 28 July 2014 and 31 July 2014 297

No. 52093. Poland and India:

Agreement between the Government of the Polish People's Republic and the Government of the Republic of India for the avoidance of double taxation and the prevention of fiscal evasion with respect to taxes on income. Warsaw, 21 June 1989 299

No. 52094. International Bank for Reconstruction and Development and Indonesia:

Loan Agreement (Coral Reef Rehabilitation and Management Program – Coral Triangle Initiative (COREMAP-CTI) Project) between the Republic of Indonesia and the International Bank for Reconstruction and Development (with schedules, appendix and International Bank for Reconstruction and Development General Conditions for Loans, dated 12 March 2012). Jakarta, 17 March 2014 433

No. 52095. International Bank for Reconstruction and Development and Indonesia:

Global Environment Facility Grant Agreement (Coral Reef Rehabilitation and Management Program – Coral Triangle Initiative (COREMAP-CTI) Project) between the Republic of Indonesia and the International Bank for Reconstruction and Development (acting as an implementing agency of the global environment facility) (with schedules, appendix and Standard Conditions for Grants made by the World Bank out of various funds, dated 15 February 2012). Jakarta, 17 March 2014 435

No. 52096. International Development Association and Gambia:

Financing Agreement (Maternal and Child Nutrition and Health Results Project) between the Republic of the Gambia and the International Development Association (with schedules, appendix and International Development Association General Conditions for Credits and Grants, dated 31 July 2010). Washington, 9 April 2014 437

No. 52097. World Bank (International Bank for Reconstruction and Development and International Development Association) and Gambia:

Multi-donor Trust Fund for Health Results Innovation Grant Agreement (Maternal and Child Nutrition and Health Results Project) between the Republic of the Gambia and the International Bank for Reconstruction and Development and the International Development Association, acting as Administrator of the Multi-Donor Trust Fund for Health Results Innovation (with schedules, appendix and Standard Conditions for Grants made by the World Bank out of various funds, dated 15 February 2012). Washington, 9 April 2014... 439

No. 52098. Argentina and Ecuador:

Exchange of notes constituting an Agreement between the Government of the Argentine Republic and the Government of the Republic of Ecuador on recognition of primary and secondary education (with annex). Quito, 13 May 1993 441

No. 52099. International Development Association and Senegal:

Financing Agreement (Health and Nutrition Financing Project) between the Republic of Senegal and the International Development Association (with schedules, appendix and International Development Association General Conditions for Credits and Grants, dated 31 July 2010). Dakar, 28 March 2014 443

No. 52100. World Bank (International Bank for Reconstruction and Development and International Development Association) and Senegal:

Multi-donor Trust Fund for Health Results Innovation Grant Agreement (Health and Nutrition Financing Project) between the Republic of Senegal and the International Bank for Reconstruction and Development and the International Development Association, both acting as Administrator of the Multi-Donor Trust Fund for Health Results Innovation (with schedules, appendix and International Development Association General Conditions for Credits and Grants, dated 31 July 2010). Dakar, 28 March 2014 445

TABLE DES MATIÈRES

I

*Traités et accords internationaux
enregistrés en août 2014
Nᵒˢ 52051 à 52100*

Nᵒ 52051. Fonds international de développement agricole et Chine :

Accord de financement (Projet relatif au développement de l'agro-industrie pour les petits cultivateurs de Shiyan) entre la République populaire de Chine et le Fonds international de développement agricole (avec annexes et Conditions générales applicables au financement du développement agricole, en date du 29 avril 2009, telles qu'amendées au 17 septembre 2010). Rome, 30 janvier 2014.......................... 3

Nᵒ 52052. Fonds international de développement agricole et Inde :

Accord de financement relatif au programme (Programme de convergence d'interventions agricoles dans les districts en difficulté de Maharashtra) entre la République de l'Inde et le Fonds international de développement agricole (avec annexes et Conditions générales applicables au financement du développement agricole, en date du 2 décembre 1998). Rome, 30 septembre 2009........................... 5

Nᵒ 52053. Fonds international de développement agricole et Inde :

Accord de prêt relatif au programme (Programme d'autonomisation des femmes et des moyens de subsistance dans les plaines du Gange) entre la République de l'Inde et le Fonds international de développement agricole (avec annexes et Conditions générales applicables au financement du développement agricole, en date du 2 décembre 1998). Rome, 11 décembre 2008 7

Nᵒ 52054. Fonds international de développement agricole et Ouganda :

Accord de prêt relatif au programme (Programme communautaire visant à l'amélioration de l'infrastructure agricole) entre la République de l'Ouganda et le Fonds international de développement agricole (avec annexes et Conditions générales applicables au financement du développement agricole, en date du 2 décembre 1998). Rome, 19 septembre 2007... 9

Nᵒ 52055. Fonds international de développement agricole et Libéria :

Accord de financement (Appui au Réseau de l'Union de Fermiers du Libéria) entre la République du Libéria et le Fonds international de développement agricole (avec annexes et Conditions générales applicables au financement du développement agricole, en date du 29 avril 2009, telles qu'amendées au 17 septembre 2010). Rome, 2 juillet 2013, et Monrovia, 8 septembre 2013... 11

N° **52056. Fonds international de développement agricole et Nigéria :**

Accord de financement (Programme de développement de la chaîne de valeur) entre la République fédérale du Nigéria et le Fonds international de développement agricole (avec annexes et Conditions générales applicables au financement du développement agricole, en date du 29 avril 2009, telles qu'amendées au 17 septembre 2010). Abuja, 23 août 2012 13

N° **52057. Fonds international de développement agricole et Bénin :**

Accord de financement (Projet d'appui à la croissance économique rurale (PACER)) entre la République du Bénin et le Fonds international de développement agricole (avec annexes et Conditions générales applicables au financement du développement agricole, en date du 2 décembre 1998). Rome, 21 juillet 2009 15

N° **52058. Fonds international de développement agricole et Burkina Faso :**

Accord de financement (Programme d'appui et de promotion du secteur privé en milieu rural (PASPRU)) entre le Burkina Faso et le Fonds international de développement agricole (avec annexes et Conditions générales applicables au financement du développement agricole, en date du 2 décembre 1998). Rome, 23 septembre 2009... 17

N° **52059. Fonds international de développement agricole et Seychelles :**

Accord de financement (Projet pour les innovations locales concurrentielles pour l'agriculture à petite échelle) entre la République des Seychelles et le Fonds international de développement agricole (avec annexes et Conditions générales applicables au financement du développement agricole, en date du 29 avril 2009, telles qu'amendées au 17 septembre 2010). Rome, 22 mai 2013.............................. 19

N° **52060. Fonds international de développement agricole et Niger :**

Accord de financement (Initiative de réhabilitation et de développement agricole et rural – Renforcement des capacités institutionnelles (IRDAR-RCI)) entre la République du Niger et le Fonds international de développement agricole (avec annexes et Conditions générales applicables au financement du développement agricole, en date du 2 décembre 1998). Rome, 15 janvier 2009.............................. 21

N° **52061. Fonds international de développement agricole et Maurice :**

Accord de financement relatif au programme (Programme d'appui aux ressources marines et agricoles) entre la République de Maurice et le Fonds international de développement agricole (avec annexes et Conditions générales applicables au financement du développement agricole, en date du 2 décembre 1998). Port-Louis, 5 mars 2009.. 23

N° **52062. Fonds international de développement agricole et Guatemala :**

Accord de financement (Programme de développement rural durable dans la région du Nord) entre la République du Guatemala et le Fonds international de développement agricole (avec annexes et Conditions générales applicables au financement du développement agricole, en date du 2 décembre 1998). Guatemala, 13 décembre 2011, et Rome, 13 décembre 2011 25

N° 52063. Fonds international de développement agricole et République dominicaine :

Accord de prêt (Projet de développement pour les organisations économiques pour les ruraux pauvres de la région frontalière) entre la République dominicaine et le Fonds international de développement agricole (avec annexe et Conditions générales applicables au financement du développement agricole, en date du 2 décembre 1998). Rome, 29 juin 2009, et Saint-Domingue, 29 juin 2009 27

N° 52064. Fonds international de développement agricole et Philippines :

Accord de financement relatif au programme (Programme d'amélioration de la production alimentaire rapide) entre la République des Philippines et le Fonds international de développement agricole (avec annexes et Conditions générales applicables au financement du développement agricole, en date du 2 décembre 1998). Manille, 2 septembre 2009 29

N° 52065. Fonds international de développement agricole et Bosnie-Herzégovine :

Accord de prêt relatif au projet (Projet de développement des moyens d'existence ruraux) entre la Bosnie-Herzégovine et le Fonds international de développement agricole (avec annexes et Conditions générales applicables au financement du développement agricole, en date du 2 décembre 1998). Sarajevo, 9 décembre 2009 31

N° 52066. Fonds international de développement agricole et El Salvador :

Accord de financement (Projet de développement et de modernisation rurale des régions centrales et paracentrales – Extension) entre la République d'El Salvador et le Fonds fiduciaire du mécanisme de co-financement espagnol pour la sécurité alimentaire, agissant par l'intermédiaire du Fonds international de développement agricole, en sa qualité de fiduciaire du Fonds (avec annexes et Conditions générales applicables au financement du développement agricole, en date du 29 avril 2009, telles qu'amendées au 17 septembre 2010). Rome, 25 avril 2012, et San Salvador, 4 mai 2012 33

N° 52067. Fonds international de développement agricole et Géorgie :

Accord de financement (Projet d'aide à l'agriculture) entre la Géorgie et le Fonds international de développement agricole (avec annexes et Conditions générales applicables au financement du développement agricole, en date du 29 avril 2009). Rome, 24 juin 2010, et Tbilissi, 8 juillet 2010 35

N° 52068. Fonds international de développement agricole et Éthiopie :

Accord de financement relatif au projet (Projet de gestion de ressources naturelles intégré au niveau de la communauté) entre la République fédérale démocratique d'Éthiopie et le Fonds international de développement agricole (avec annexes et Conditions générales applicables au financement du développement agricole, en date du 2 décembre 1998). Rome, 19 juin 2009 37

Nº **52069. Fonds international de développement agricole et Éthiopie :**

Accord de financement (Projet II de développement des communautés pastorales) entre la République fédérale démocratique d'Éthiopie et le Fonds international de développement agricole (avec annexes et Conditions générales applicables au financement du développement agricole, en date du 29 avril 2009). Rome, 26 novembre 2009 39

Nº **52070. Fonds international de développement agricole et Brésil :**

Accord de garantie (Projet de développement rural pour les petits producteurs (Dom Távora) (Projeto de desenvolvimento de negócios rurais para pequenos produtores – Dom Távora)) entre la République fédérative du Brésil et le Fonds international de développement agricole (avec Conditions générales applicables au financement du développement agricole, en date du 29 avril 2009, telles qu'amendées au 17 septembre 2010). Rome, 20 août 2013, et Brasilia, 30 août 2013   41

Nº **52071. Fonds international de développement agricole et Viet Nam :**

Accord entre le Gouvernement de la République socialiste du Viet Nam et le Fonds international de développement agricole concernant le bureau de pays du Fonds. Hanoï, 16 janvier 2008 43

Nº **52072. Organisation des Nations Unies et Maurice :**

Échange de lettres constituant un accord entre l'Organisation des Nations Unies et le Gouvernement de la République de Maurice relatif à l'organisation de « l'Atelier régional sur les combustibles fossiles et les énergies renouvelables » qui se tiendra à Port-Louis, Maurice, du 12 au 16 mai 2014. New York, 25 février 2014 et 13 mai 2014 71

Nº **52073. Association internationale de développement et République-Unie de Tanzanie :**

Accord de financement (Onzième financement pour la politique de développement à l'appui de la réduction de la pauvreté) entre la République-Unie de Tanzanie et l'Association internationale de développement (avec annexes, appendice et Conditions générales applicables aux crédits et aux dons de l'Association internationale de développement, en date du 31 juillet 2010). Washington, 10 avril 2014 73

N° **52074. Association internationale de développement et République-Unie de Tanzanie :**

Accord de financement (Deuxième Financement de la politique de développement de l'énergie et du secteur à gaz) entre la République-Unie de Tanzanie et l'Association internationale de développement (avec annexes, appendice et Conditions générales applicables aux crédits et aux dons de l'Association internationale de développement, en date du 31 juillet 2010). Washington, 10 avril 2014 75

N° **52075. Association internationale de développement et Lesotho :**

Accord de financement (Projet d'appui à la réforme de la gestion des finances publiques) entre le Royaume du Lesotho et l'Association internationale de développement (avec annexes, appendice et Conditions générales applicables aux crédits et aux dons de l'Association internationale de développement, en date du 31 juillet 2010). Maseru, 24 février 2014 77

N° **52076. Banque internationale pour la reconstruction et le développement et Ex-République yougoslave de Macédoine :**

Accord de prêt (Deuxième prêt programmatique des politiques de développement sur la compétitivité) entre l'ex-République yougoslave de Macédoine (l'Emprunteur) et la Banque internationale pour la reconstruction et le développement (la Banque) (avec annexes, appendice et Conditions générales applicables aux prêts de la Banque internationale pour la reconstruction et le développement, en date du 12 mars 2012). Skopje, 23 juillet 2014 79

N° **52077. Association internationale de développement et Sénégal :**

Accord de financement (Projet du Pôle de développement de la Casamance) entre la République du Sénégal et l'Association internationale de développement (avec annexes, appendice et Conditions générales applicables aux crédits et aux dons de l'Association internationale de développement, en date du 31 juillet 2010). Dakar, 22 novembre 2013 81

N° **52078. Association internationale de développement et Kirghizistan :**

Accord de financement (Deuxième opération de politique de développement) entre la République kirghize et l'Association internationale de développement (avec annexes, appendice et Conditions générales applicables aux crédits et aux dons de l'Association internationale de développement, en date du 31 juillet 2010). Bichkek, 16 juin 2014 83

N° **52079. Turquie et Géorgie :**

Mémorandum d'accord entre le Gouvernement de la République turque et le Gouvernement de la Géorgie relatif à la coopération en matière de lutte contre la criminalité. Tbilissi, 22 février 2012 85

Nº **52080. Turquie et Hongrie :**

Programme de coopération entre le Gouvernement de la République turque et le Gouvernement de la Hongrie dans les domaines de l'éducation et de la science pour les années 2014 à 2016. Ankara, 18 décembre 2013 103

Nº **52081. Turquie et Pérou :**

Échange de notes constituant un accord relatif à la suppression des visas dans les passeports diplomatiques et les passeports de service (ou les passeports spéciaux) entre le Gouvernement de la République turque et le Gouvernement de la République du Pérou. Vienne, 28 mai 1996 et 17 septembre 1996.................... 135

Nº **52082. Banque internationale pour la reconstruction et le développement et Fédération de Russie :**

Accord de prêt (Deuxième Projet national de modernisation hydrométallurgique) entre la Fédération de Russie et la Banque internationale pour la reconstruction et le développement (avec annexes, appendice et Conditions générales applicables aux prêts de la Banque internationale pour la reconstruction et le développement, en date du 12 mars 2012). Moscou, 17 janvier 2014.................... 137

Nº **52083. Association internationale de développement et Inde :**

Accord de financement (Troisième Projet d'enseignement primaire) entre l'Inde et l'Association internationale de développement (avec annexes, appendice et Conditions générales applicables aux crédits et aux dons de l'Association internationale de développement, en date du 31 juillet 2010). New Delhi, 29 mai 2014.................... 139

Nº **52084. Turquie et Japon :**

Accord de coopération entre le Gouvernement de la République turque et le Gouvernement du Japon relatif à l'utilisation de l'énergie nucléaire à des fins pacifiques (avec annexes). Tokyo, 26 avril 2013, et Ankara, 3 mai 2013.................... 141

Nº **52085. Turquie et Chine :**

Mémorandum d'accord relatif à la coopération dans le domaine de l'énergie entre le Ministère de l'énergie et des ressources naturelles de la République turque et l'Administration nationale de l'énergie de la République populaire de Chine. Beijing, 25 juin 2009 211

Nº **52086. Association internationale de développement et Inde :**

Accord de financement (Projet d'accélération vers l'accès universel aux soins précoces et efficaces contre la tuberculose) entre l'Inde et l'Association internationale de développement (avec annexes, appendice et Conditions générales applicables aux crédits et aux dons de l'Association internationale de développement, en date du 31 juillet 2010). New Delhi, 30 mai 2014.................... 221

Nᵒ 52087. Belgique et Malte :

Convention entre le Gouvernement du Royaume de Belgique et le Gouvernement de Malte relative à la coopération policière. Bruxelles, 1ᵉʳ décembre 2005.................... 223

Nᵒ 52088. Belgique et Sainte-Lucie :

Accord entre le Royaume de Belgique et Sainte-Lucie relatif à l'échange de renseignements en matière fiscale. Bruxelles, 7 décembre 2009.............................. 255

Nᵒ 52089. Belgique, Luxembourg, Pays-Bas et Afrique du Sud :

Accord entre les Gouvernements des États du Benelux et le Gouvernement de la République d'Afrique du Sud relatif à l'exemption de l'obligation de visa pour les titulaires de passeports diplomatiques, officiels et/ou de service. Pretoria, 22 février 2013.. 273

Nᵒ 52090. Banque internationale pour la reconstruction et le développement et Croatie :

Accord de prêt (Deuxième Prêt relatif à la politique de développement pour la relance économique) entre la République de Croatie et la Banque internationale pour la reconstruction et le développement (avec annexes, appendice et Conditions générales applicables aux prêts de la Banque internationale pour la reconstruction et le développement, en date du 12 mars 2012). Zagreb, 30 avril 2014 293

Nᵒ 52091. Banque internationale pour la reconstruction et le développement et Maroc :

Accord de prêt (Premier prêt d'appui à une politique de développement visant l'approfondissement du marché des capitaux et le financement de petites et moyennes entreprises) entre le Royaume du Maroc et la Banque internationale pour la reconstruction et le développement (avec annexes, appendice et Conditions générales applicables aux prêts de la Banque internationale pour la reconstruction et le développement, en date du 12 mars 2012). Rabat, 27 mai 2014............................ 295

Nᵒ 52092. Organisation des Nations Unies et Fidji :

Échange de lettres constituant un accord entre l'Organisation des Nations Unies et le Gouvernement de la République des Fidji relatif à l'organisation de « l'Atelier régional sur les statistiques en matière de genre et de rapports sur les droits de l'homme » qui se tiendra à Nadi, Fidji, du 4 au 8 août 2014. New York, 28 juillet 2014 et 31 juillet 2014.. 297

Nᵒ 52093. Pologne et Inde :

Accord entre le Gouvernement de la République populaire de Pologne et le Gouvernement de la République de l'Inde tendant à éviter la double imposition et à prévenir l'évasion fiscale en matière d'impôts sur le revenu. Varsovie, 21 juin 1989. 299

Nᵒ 52094. Banque internationale pour la reconstruction et le développement et Indonésie :

Accord de prêt (Programme de réhabilitation et de gestion des récifs coralliens – Projet concernant l'initiative du triangle de corail) entre la République d'Indonésie et la Banque internationale pour la reconstruction et le développement (avec annexes, appendice et Conditions générales applicables aux prêts de la Banque internationale pour la reconstruction et le développement, en date du 12 mars 2012). Jakarta, 17 mars 2014 433

Nᵒ 52095. Banque internationale pour la reconstruction et le développement et Indonésie :

Accord de don du Fonds pour l'environnement mondial (Programme de réhabilitation et de gestion des récifs coralliens – Projet concernant l'initiative du triangle de corail) entre la République d'Indonésie et la Banque internationale pour la reconstruction et le développement (agissant en qualité d'agence d'exécution du Fonds pour l'environnement mondial) (avec annexes, appendice et Conditions standard pour les dons consentis par la Banque mondiale sur divers fonds, en date du 15 février 2012). Jakarta, 17 mars 2014 435

Nᵒ 52096. Association internationale de développement et Gambie :

Accord de financement (Projet concernant les résultats de santé et la nutrition maternelle et infantile) entre la République de Gambie et l'Association internationale de développement (avec annexes, appendice et Conditions générales applicables aux crédits et aux dons de l'Association internationale de développement, en date du 31 juillet 2010). Washington, 9 avril 2014 437

Nᵒ 52097. Banque mondiale (Banque internationale pour la reconstruction et le développement et Association internationale de développement) et Gambie :

Accord de don du Fonds fiduciaire multidonateurs pour l'innovation en matière de résultats sanitaires (Projet concernant les résultats de santé et de nutrition maternelle et infantile) entre la République de Gambie et la Banque internationale pour la reconstruction et le développement et l'Association internationale de développement, agissant en tant qu'administrateur du Fonds fiduciaire multidonateurs pour l'innovation en matière de résultats sanitaires (avec annexes, appendice et Conditions standard pour les dons consentis par la Banque mondiale sur divers fonds, en date du 15 février 2012). Washington, 9 avril 2014 439

Nᵒ 52098. Argentine et Équateur :

Échange de notes constituant un accord entre le Gouvernement de la République argentine et le Gouvernement de la République de l'Équateur sur la reconnaissance de l'enseignement primaire et secondaire (avec annexe). Quito, 13 mai 1993 441

Nº 52099. Association internationale de développement et Sénégal :

Accord de financement (Projet de financement pour la santé et la nutrition) entre la République du Sénégal et l'Association internationale de développement (avec annexes, appendice et Conditions générales applicables aux crédits et aux dons de l'Association internationale de développement, en date du 31 juillet 2010). Dakar, 28 mars 2014.. 443

Nº 52100. Banque mondiale (Banque internationale pour la reconstruction et le développement et Association internationale de développement) et Sénégal :

Accord de don du Fonds fiduciaire multidonateurs pour l'innovation en matière de résultats sanitaires (Projet de financement pour la santé et la nutrition) entre la République du Sénégal et la Banque internationale pour la reconstruction et le développement et l'Association internationale de développement, agissant en tant qu'administrateur du Fonds fiduciaire multidonateurs pour l'innovation en matière de résultats sanitaires (avec annexes, appendice et Conditions générales applicables aux crédits et aux dons de l'Association internationale de développement, en date du 31 juillet 2010). Dakar, 28 mars 2014 445

NOTE BY THE SECRETARIAT

Under Article 102 of the Charter of the United Nations, every treaty and every international agreement entered into by any Member of the United Nations after the coming into force of the Charter shall, as soon as possible, be registered with the Secretariat and published by it. Furthermore, no party to a treaty or international agreement subject to registration which has not been registered may invoke that treaty or agreement before any organ of the United Nations. The General Assembly, by resolution 97 (I), established regulations to give effect to Article 102 of the Charter (see text of the regulations, vol. 859, p. VIII; https://treaties.un.org/Pages/Resource.aspx?path=Publication/Regulation/Page1_en.xml).

The terms "treaty" and "international agreement" have not been defined either in the Charter or in the regulations, and the Secretariat follows the principle that it acts in accordance with the position of the Member State submitting an instrument for registration that, so far as that party is concerned, the instrument is a treaty or an international agreement within the meaning of Article 102. Registration of an instrument submitted by a Member State, therefore, does not imply a judgement by the Secretariat on the nature of the instrument, the status of a party or any similar question. It is the understanding of the Secretariat that its acceptance for registration of an instrument does not confer on the instrument the status of a treaty or an international agreement if it does not already have that status, and does not confer upon a party a status which it would not otherwise have.

*
* *

Disclaimer: All authentic texts in the present Series are published as submitted for registration by a party to the instrument. Unless otherwise indicated, the translations of these texts have been made by the Secretariat of the United Nations, for information.

NOTE DU SECRÉTARIAT

Aux termes de l'Article 102 de la Charte des Nations Unies, tout traité ou accord international conclu par un Membre des Nations Unies après l'entrée en vigueur de la Charte sera, le plus tôt possible, enregistré au Secrétariat et publié par lui. De plus, aucune partie à un traité ou accord international qui aurait dû être enregistré mais ne l'a pas été ne pourra invoquer ledit traité ou accord devant un organe de l'Organisation des Nations Unies. Par sa résolution 97 (I), l'Assemblée générale a adopté un règlement destiné à mettre en application l'Article 102 de la Charte (voir texte du règlement, vol. 859, p. IX; https://treaties.un.org/Pages/Resource.aspx?path=Publication/Regulation/Page1_fr.xml).

Les termes « traité » et « accord international » n'ont été définis ni dans la Charte ni dans le règlement, et le Secrétariat a pris comme principe de s'en tenir à la position adoptée à cet égard par l'État Membre qui a présenté l'instrument à l'enregistrement, à savoir que, en ce qui concerne cette partie, l'instrument constitue un traité ou un accord international au sens de l'Article 102. Il s'ensuit que l'enregistrement d'un instrument présenté par un État Membre n'implique, de la part du Secrétariat, aucun jugement sur la nature de l'instrument, le statut d'une partie ou toute autre question similaire. Le Secrétariat considère donc que son acceptation pour enregistrement d'un instrument ne confère pas audit instrument la qualité de traité ou d'accord international si ce dernier ne l'a pas déjà, et qu'il ne confère pas à une partie un statut que, par ailleurs, elle ne posséderait pas.

*
* *

Déni de responsabilité : Tous les textes authentiques du présent Recueil sont publiés tels qu'ils ont été soumis pour enregistrement par l'une des parties à l'instrument. Sauf indication contraire, les traductions de ces textes ont été établies par le Secrétariat de l'Organisation des Nations Unies, à titre d'information.

I

Treaties and international agreements

registered in

August 2014

Nos. 52051 to 52100

Traités et accords internationaux

enregistrés en

août 2014

Nos 52051 à 52100

No. 52051

International Fund for Agricultural Development
and
China

Financing Agreement (Shiyan smallholder agribusiness development project (SSADeP)) between the People's Republic of China and the International Fund for Agricultural Development (with schedules and General Conditions for Agricultural Development Financing dated 29 April 2009, as amended through 17 September 2010). Rome, 30 January 2014

Entry into force: *30 January 2014, in accordance with the General Conditions*

Authentic text: *English*

Registration with the Secretariat of the United Nations: *International Fund for Agricultural Development, 12 August 2014*

Not published in print, in accordance with article 12(2) of the General Assembly regulations to give effect to Article 102 of the Charter of the United Nations, as amended.

Fonds international de développement agricole
et
Chine

Accord de financement (Projet relatif au développement de l'agro-industrie pour les petits cultivateurs de Shiyan) entre la République populaire de Chine et le Fonds international de développement agricole (avec annexes et Conditions générales applicables au financement du développement agricole, en date du 29 avril 2009, telles qu'amendées au 17 septembre 2010). Rome, 30 janvier 2014

Entrée en vigueur : *30 janvier 2014, conformément aux Conditions générales*

Texte authentique : *anglais*

Enregistrement auprès du Secrétariat de l'Organisation des Nations Unies : *Fonds international de développement agricole, 12 août 2014*

Non disponible en version imprimée, conformément au paragraphe 2 de l'article 12 du règlement de l'Assemblée générale destiné à mettre en application l'Article 102 de la Charte des Nations Unies, tel qu'amendé.

No. 52052

International Fund for Agricultural Development
and
India

Programme Financing Agreement (Convergence of Agricultural Interventions in Maharashtra's Distressed Districts Programme) between the Republic of India and the International Fund for Agricultural Development (with schedules and General Conditions for Agricultural Development Financing dated 2 December 1998). Rome, 30 September 2009

Entry into force: *4 December 2009, in accordance with the General Conditions*

Authentic text: *English*

Registration with the Secretariat of the United Nations: *International Fund for Agricultural Development, 12 August 2014*

Not published in print, in accordance with article 12(2) of the General Assembly regulations to give effect to Article 102 of the Charter of the United Nations, as amended.

Fonds international de développement agricole
et
Inde

Accord de financement relatif au programme (Programme de convergence d'interventions agricoles dans les districts en difficulté de Maharashtra) entre la République de l'Inde et le Fonds international de développement agricole (avec annexes et Conditions générales applicables au financement du développement agricole, en date du 2 décembre 1998). Rome, 30 septembre 2009

Entrée en vigueur : *4 décembre 2009, conformément aux Conditions générales*

Texte authentique : *anglais*

Enregistrement auprès du Secrétariat de l'Organisation des Nations Unies : *Fonds international de développement agricole, 12 août 2014*

Non disponible en version imprimée, conformément au paragraphe 2 de l'article 12 du règlement de l'Assemblée générale destiné à mettre en application l'Article 102 de la Charte des Nations Unies, tel qu'amendé.

No. 52053

International Fund for Agricultural Development
and
India

Programme Loan Agreement (Women's Empowerment and Livelihoods Programme in the Mid-Gangetic Plains) between the Republic of India and the International Fund for Agricultural Development (with schedules and General Conditions for Agricultural Development Financing dated 2 December 1998). Rome, 11 December 2008

Entry into force: *4 December 2009, in accordance with the General Conditions*

Authentic text: *English*

Registration with the Secretariat of the United Nations: *International Fund for Agricultural Development, 12 August 2014*

Not published in print, in accordance with article 12(2) of the General Assembly regulations to give effect to Article 102 of the Charter of the United Nations, as amended.

Fonds international de développement agricole
et
Inde

Accord de prêt relatif au programme (Programme d'autonomisation des femmes et des moyens de subsistance dans les plaines du Gange) entre la République de l'Inde et le Fonds international de développement agricole (avec annexes et Conditions générales applicables au financement du développement agricole, en date du 2 décembre 1998). Rome, 11 décembre 2008

Entrée en vigueur : *4 décembre 2009, conformément aux Conditions générales*

Texte authentique : *anglais*

Enregistrement auprès du Secrétariat de l'Organisation des Nations Unies : *Fonds international de développement agricole, 12 août 2014*

Non disponible en version imprimée, conformément au paragraphe 2 de l'article 12 du règlement de l'Assemblée générale destiné à mettre en application l'Article 102 de la Charte des Nations Unies, tel qu'amendé.

No. 52054

International Fund for Agricultural Development
and
Uganda

Programme Loan Agreement (Community Agricultural Infrastructure Improvement Programme (CAIIP)) between the Republic of Uganda and the International Fund for Agricultural Development (with schedules and General Conditions for Agricultural Development Financing dated 2 December 1998). Rome, 19 September 2007

Entry into force: *9 January 2008, in accordance with the General Conditions*

Authentic text: *English*

Registration with the Secretariat of the United Nations: *International Fund for Agricultural Development, 12 August 2014*

Not published in print, in accordance with article 12(2) of the General Assembly regulations to give effect to Article 102 of the Charter of the United Nations, as amended.

Fonds international de développement agricole
et
Ouganda

Accord de prêt relatif au programme (Programme communautaire visant à l'amélioration de l'infrastructure agricole) entre la République de l'Ouganda et le Fonds international de développement agricole (avec annexes et Conditions générales applicables au financement du développement agricole, en date du 2 décembre 1998). Rome, 19 septembre 2007

Entrée en vigueur : *9 janvier 2008, conformément aux Conditions générales*

Texte authentique : *anglais*

Enregistrement auprès du Secrétariat de l'Organisation des Nations Unies : *Fonds international de développement agricole, 12 août 2014*

Non disponible en version imprimée, conformément au paragraphe 2 de l'article 12 du règlement de l'Assemblée générale destiné à mettre en application l'Article 102 de la Charte des Nations Unies, tel qu'amendé.

No. 52055

International Fund for Agricultural Development
and
Liberia

Financing Agreement (Support to the Farmers Union Network of Liberia (FUN)) between the Republic of Liberia and the International Fund for Agricultural Development (with schedules and General Conditions for Agricultural Development Financing dated 29 April 2009, as amended through 17 September 2010). Rome, 2 July 2013, and Monrovia, 8 September 2013

Entry into force: *8 September 2013, in accordance with the General Conditions*

Authentic text: *English*

Registration with the Secretariat of the United Nations: *International Fund for Agricultural Development, 12 August 2014*

Not published in print, in accordance with article 12(2) of the General Assembly regulations to give effect to Article 102 of the Charter of the United Nations, as amended.

Fonds international de développement agricole
et
Libéria

Accord de financement (Appui au Réseau de l'Union de Fermiers du Libéria) entre la République du Libéria et le Fonds international de développement agricole (avec annexes et Conditions générales applicables au financement du développement agricole, en date du 29 avril 2009, telles qu'amendées au 17 septembre 2010). Rome, 2 juillet 2013, et Monrovia, 8 septembre 2013

Entrée en vigueur : *8 septembre 2013, conformément aux Conditions générales*

Texte authentique : *anglais*

Enregistrement auprès du Secrétariat de l'Organisation des Nations Unies : *Fonds international de développement agricole, 12 août 2014*

Non disponible en version imprimée, conformément au paragraphe 2 de l'article 12 du règlement de l'Assemblée générale destiné à mettre en application l'Article 102 de la Charte des Nations Unies, tel qu'amendé.

No. 52056

International Fund for Agricultural Development
and
Nigeria

Financing Agreement (Value Chain Development Programme (VCDP)) between the Federal Republic of Nigeria and the International Fund for Agricultural Development (with schedules and General Conditions for Agricultural Development Financing dated 29 April 2009, as amended through 17 September 2010). Abuja, 23 August 2012

Entry into force: *14 October 2013, in accordance with the General Conditions*

Authentic text: *English*

Registration with the Secretariat of the United Nations: *International Fund for Agricultural Development, 12 August 2014*

Not published in print, in accordance with article 12(2) of the General Assembly regulations to give effect to Article 102 of the Charter of the United Nations, as amended.

Fonds international de développement agricole
et
Nigéria

Accord de financement (Programme de développement de la chaîne de valeur) entre la République fédérale du Nigéria et le Fonds international de développement agricole (avec annexes et Conditions générales applicables au financement du développement agricole, en date du 29 avril 2009, telles qu'amendées au 17 septembre 2010). Abuja, 23 août 2012

Entrée en vigueur : *14 octobre 2013, conformément aux Conditions générales*

Texte authentique : *anglais*

Enregistrement auprès du Secrétariat de l'Organisation des Nations Unies : *Fonds international de développement agricole, 12 août 2014*

Non disponible en version imprimée, conformément au paragraphe 2 de l'article 12 du règlement de l'Assemblée générale destiné à mettre en application l'Article 102 de la Charte des Nations Unies, tel qu'amendé.

No. 52057

International Fund for Agricultural Development
and
Benin

Financing Agreement (Rural Economic Growth Support Project) between the Republic of Benin and the International Fund for Agricultural Development (with schedules and General Conditions for Agricultural Development Financing dated 2 December 1998). Rome, 21 July 2009

Entry into force: *1 October 2010, in accordance with the General Conditions*

Authentic text: *French*

Registration with the Secretariat of the United Nations: *International Fund for Agricultural Development, 12 August 2014*

Not published in print, in accordance with article 12(2) of the General Assembly regulations to give effect to Article 102 of the Charter of the United Nations, as amended.

Fonds international de développement agricole
et
Bénin

Accord de financement (Projet d'appui à la croissance économique rurale (PACER)) entre la République du Bénin et le Fonds international de développement agricole (avec annexes et Conditions générales applicables au financement du développement agricole, en date du 2 décembre 1998). Rome, 21 juillet 2009

Entrée en vigueur : *1er octobre 2010, conformément aux Conditions générales*

Texte authentique : *français*

Enregistrement auprès du Secrétariat de l'Organisation des Nations Unies : *Fonds international de développement agricole, 12 août 2014*

Non disponible en version imprimée, conformément au paragraphe 2 de l'article 12 du règlement de l'Assemblée générale destiné à mettre en application l'Article 102 de la Charte des Nations Unies, tel qu'amendé.

No. 52058

International Fund for Agricultural Development
and
Burkina Faso

Financing Agreement (Programme for the support and promotion of the private sector in rural areas) between Burkina Faso and the International Fund for Agricultural Development (with schedules and General Conditions for Agricultural Development Financing dated 2 December 1998). Rome, 23 September 2009

Entry into force: *8 December 2010, in accordance with the General Conditions*

Authentic text: *French*

Registration with the Secretariat of the United Nations: *International Fund for Agricultural Development, 12 August 2014*

Not published in print, in accordance with article 12(2) of the General Assembly regulations to give effect to Article 102 of the Charter of the United Nations, as amended.

Fonds international de développement agricole
et
Burkina Faso

Accord de financement (Programme d'appui et de promotion du secteur privé en milieu rural (PASPRU)) entre le Burkina Faso et le Fonds international de développement agricole (avec annexes et Conditions générales applicables au financement du développement agricole, en date du 2 décembre 1998). Rome, 23 septembre 2009

Entrée en vigueur : *8 décembre 2010, conformément aux Conditions générales*

Texte authentique : *français*

Enregistrement auprès du Secrétariat de l'Organisation des Nations Unies : *Fonds international de développement agricole, 12 août 2014*

Non disponible en version imprimée, conformément au paragraphe 2 de l'article 12 du règlement de l'Assemblée générale destiné à mettre en application l'Article 102 de la Charte des Nations Unies, tel qu'amendé.

No. 52059

International Fund for Agricultural Development
and
Seychelles

Financing Agreement (Competitive Local Innovations for Small-Scale Agriculture Project (CLISSA)) between the Republic of Seychelles and the International Fund for Agricultural Development (with schedules and General Conditions for Agricultural Development Financing dated 29 April 2009, as amended through 17 September 2010). Rome, 22 May 2013

Entry into force: *14 November 2013, in accordance with the General Conditions*

Authentic text: *English*

Registration with the Secretariat of the United Nations: *International Fund for Agricultural Development, 12 August 2014*

Not published in print, in accordance with article 12(2) of the General Assembly regulations to give effect to Article 102 of the Charter of the United Nations, as amended.

Fonds international de développement agricole
et
Seychelles

Accord de financement (Projet pour les innovations locales concurrentielles pour l'agriculture à petite échelle) entre la République des Seychelles et le Fonds international de développement agricole (avec annexes et Conditions générales applicables au financement du développement agricole, en date du 29 avril 2009, telles qu'amendées au 17 septembre 2010). Rome, 22 mai 2013

Entrée en vigueur : *14 novembre 2013, conformément aux Conditions générales*

Texte authentique : *anglais*

Enregistrement auprès du Secrétariat de l'Organisation des Nations Unies : *Fonds international de développement agricole, 12 août 2014*

Non disponible en version imprimée, conformément au paragraphe 2 de l'article 12 du règlement de l'Assemblée générale destiné à mettre en application l'Article 102 de la Charte des Nations Unies, tel qu'amendé.

No. 52060

International Fund for Agricultural Development
and
Niger

Financing Agreement (Agricultural and Rural Rehabilitation and Development Initiative – Institutional Capacity Strengthening) between the Republic of the Niger and the International Fund for Agricultural Development (with schedules and General Conditions for Agricultural Development Financing dated 2 December 1998). Rome, 15 January 2009

Entry into force: *22 September 2009, in accordance with the General Conditions*

Authentic text: *French*

Registration with the Secretariat of the United Nations: *International Fund for Agricultural Development, 12 August 2014*

Not published in print, in accordance with article 12(2) of the General Assembly regulations to give effect to Article 102 of the Charter of the United Nations, as amended.

Fonds international de développement agricole
et
Niger

Accord de financement (Initiative de réhabilitation et de développement agricole et rural – Renforcement des capacités institutionnelles (IRDAR-RCI)) entre la République du Niger et le Fonds international de développement agricole (avec annexes et Conditions générales applicables au financement du développement agricole, en date du 2 décembre 1998). Rome, 15 janvier 2009

Entrée en vigueur : *22 septembre 2009, conformément aux Conditions générales*

Texte authentique : *français*

Enregistrement auprès du Secrétariat de l'Organisation des Nations Unies : *Fonds international de développement agricole, 12 août 2014*

Non disponible en version imprimée, conformément au paragraphe 2 de l'article 12 du règlement de l'Assemblée générale destiné à mettre en application l'Article 102 de la Charte des Nations Unies, tel qu'amendé.

No. 52061

International Fund for Agricultural Development
and
Mauritius

Programme Financing Agreement (Marine and Agricultural Resources Support Programme) between the Republic of Mauritius and the International Fund for Agricultural Development (with schedules and General Conditions for Agricultural Development Financing dated 2 December 1998). Port Louis, 5 March 2009

Entry into force: *6 October 2009, in accordance with the General Conditions*

Authentic text: *English*

Registration with the Secretariat of the United Nations: *International Fund for Agricultural Development, 12 August 2014*

Not published in print, in accordance with article 12(2) of the General Assembly regulations to give effect to Article 102 of the Charter of the United Nations, as amended.

Fonds international de développement agricole
et
Maurice

Accord de financement relatif au programme (Programme d'appui aux ressources marines et agricoles) entre la République de Maurice et le Fonds international de développement agricole (avec annexes et Conditions générales applicables au financement du développement agricole, en date du 2 décembre 1998). Port-Louis, 5 mars 2009

Entrée en vigueur : *6 octobre 2009, conformément aux Conditions générales*

Texte authentique : *anglais*

Enregistrement auprès du Secrétariat de l'Organisation des Nations Unies : *Fonds international de développement agricole, 12 août 2014*

Non disponible en version imprimée, conformément au paragraphe 2 de l'article 12 du règlement de l'Assemblée générale destiné à mettre en application l'Article 102 de la Charte des Nations Unies, tel qu'amendé.

No. 52062

International Fund for Agricultural Development
and
Guatemala

Financing Agreement (Sustainable Rural Development Programme for the Northern Region) between the Republic of Guatemala and the International Fund for Agricultural Development (with schedules and General Conditions for Agricultural Development Financing dated 2 December 1998). Guatemala City, 13 December 2011, and Rome, 13 December 2011

Entry into force: *27 January 2012, in accordance with the General Conditions*

Authentic text: *Spanish*

Registration with the Secretariat of the United Nations: *International Fund for Agricultural Development, 12 August 2014*

Fonds international de développement agricole
et
Guatemala

Accord de financement (Programme de développement rural durable dans la région du Nord) entre la République du Guatemala et le Fonds international de développement agricole (avec annexes et Conditions générales applicables au financement du développement agricole, en date du 2 décembre 1998). Guatemala, 13 décembre 2011, et Rome, 13 décembre 2011

Entrée en vigueur : *27 janvier 2012, conformément aux Conditions générales*

Texte authentique : *espagnol*

Enregistrement auprès du Secrétariat de l'Organisation des Nations Unies : *Fonds international de développement agricole, 12 août 2014*

No. 52063

International Fund for Agricultural Development
and
Dominican Republic

Loan Agreement (Development Project for Economic Organizations for the Rural Poor in the Border Region) between the Dominican Republic and the International Fund for Agricultural Development (with schedule and General Conditions for Agricultural Development Financing dated 2 December 1998). Rome, 29 June 2009, and Santo Domingo, 29 June 2009

Entry into force: *26 May 2010, in accordance with the General Conditions*

Authentic text: *Spanish*

Registration with the Secretariat of the United Nations: *International Fund for Agricultural Development, 12 August 2014*

Not published in print, in accordance with article 12(2) of the General Assembly regulations to give effect to Article 102 of the Charter of the United Nations, as amended.

Fonds international de développement agricole
et
République dominicaine

Accord de prêt (Projet de développement pour les organisations économiques pour les ruraux pauvres de la région frontalière) entre la République dominicaine et le Fonds international de développement agricole (avec annexe et Conditions générales applicables au financement du développement agricole, en date du 2 décembre 1998). Rome, 29 juin 2009, et Saint-Domingue, 29 juin 2009

Entrée en vigueur : *26 mai 2010, conformément aux Conditions générales*

Texte authentique : *espagnol*

Enregistrement auprès du Secrétariat de l'Organisation des Nations Unies : *Fonds international de développement agricole, 12 août 2014*

Non disponible en version imprimée, conformément au paragraphe 2 de l'article 12 du règlement de l'Assemblée générale destiné à mettre en application l'Article 102 de la Charte des Nations Unies, tel qu'amendé.

No. 52064

International Fund for Agricultural Development
and
Philippines

Programme Financing Agreement (Rapid Food Production Enhancement Programme) between the Republic of the Philippines and the International Fund for Agricultural Development (with schedules and General Conditions for Agricultural Development Financing dated 2 December 1998). Manila, 2 September 2009

Entry into force: *9 November 2009, in accordance with the General Conditions*

Authentic text: *English*

Registration with the Secretariat of the United Nations: *International Fund for Agricultural Development, 12 August 2014*

Not published in print, in accordance with article 12(2) of the General Assembly regulations to give effect to Article 102 of the Charter of the United Nations, as amended.

Fonds international de développement agricole
et
Philippines

Accord de financement relatif au programme (Programme d'amélioration de la production alimentaire rapide) entre la République des Philippines et le Fonds international de développement agricole (avec annexes et Conditions générales applicables au financement du développement agricole, en date du 2 décembre 1998). Manille, 2 septembre 2009

Entrée en vigueur : *9 novembre 2009, conformément aux Conditions générales*

Texte authentique : *anglais*

Enregistrement auprès du Secrétariat de l'Organisation des Nations Unies : *Fonds international de développement agricole, 12 août 2014*

Non disponible en version imprimée, conformément au paragraphe 2 de l'article 12 du règlement de l'Assemblée générale destiné à mettre en application l'Article 102 de la Charte des Nations Unies, tel qu'amendé.

No. 52065

International Fund for Agricultural Development
and
Bosnia and Herzegovina

Project Loan Agreement (Rural Livelihoods Development Project) between Bosnia and Herzegovina and the International Fund for Agricultural Development (with schedules and General Conditions for Agricultural Development Financing dated 2 December 1998). Sarajevo, 9 December 2009

Entry into force: *28 May 2010, in accordance with the General Conditions*

Authentic text: *English*

Registration with the Secretariat of the United Nations: *International Fund for Agricultural Development, 12 August 2014*

Not published in print, in accordance with article 12(2) of the General Assembly regulations to give effect to Article 102 of the Charter of the United Nations, as amended.

Fonds international de développement agricole
et
Bosnie-Herzégovine

Accord de prêt relatif au projet (Projet de développement des moyens d'existence ruraux) entre la Bosnie-Herzégovine et le Fonds international de développement agricole (avec annexes et Conditions générales applicables au financement du développement agricole, en date du 2 décembre 1998). Sarajevo, 9 décembre 2009

Entrée en vigueur : *28 mai 2010, conformément aux Conditions générales*

Texte authentique : *anglais*

Enregistrement auprès du Secrétariat de l'Organisation des Nations Unies : *Fonds international de développement agricole, 12 août 2014*

Non disponible en version imprimée, conformément au paragraphe 2 de l'article 12 du règlement de l'Assemblée générale destiné à mettre en application l'Article 102 de la Charte des Nations Unies, tel qu'amendé.

No. 52066

International Fund for Agricultural Development
and
El Salvador

Financing Agreement (Rural Development and Modernization Project for the Central and Paracentral Regions (PRODEMOR-Central) – Extension) between the Republic of El Salvador and the Spanish Food Security Cofinancing Facility Trust Fund acting through the International Fund for Agricultural Development in its capacity as Trustee of the Fund (with schedules and General Conditions for Agricultural Development Financing dated 29 April 2009, as amended through 17 September 2010). Rome, 25 April 2012, and San Salvador, 4 May 2012

Entry into force: *23 January 2014, in accordance with the General Conditions*

Authentic text: *Spanish*

Registration with the Secretariat of the United Nations: *International Fund for Agricultural Development, 12 August 2014*

Not published in print, in accordance with article 12(2) of the General Assembly regulations to give effect to Article 102 of the Charter of the United Nations, as amended.

Fonds international de développement agricole
et
El Salvador

Accord de financement (Projet de développement et de modernisation rurale des régions centrales et paracentrales – Extension) entre la République d'El Salvador et le Fonds fiduciaire du mécanisme de co-financement espagnol pour la sécurité alimentaire, agissant par l'intermédiaire du Fonds international de développement agricole, en sa qualité de fiduciaire du Fonds (avec annexes et Conditions générales applicables au financement du développement agricole, en date du 29 avril 2009, telles qu'amendées au 17 septembre 2010). Rome, 25 avril 2012, et San Salvador, 4 mai 2012

Entrée en vigueur : *23 janvier 2014, conformément aux Conditions générales*

Texte authentique : *espagnol*

Enregistrement auprès du Secrétariat de l'Organisation des Nations Unies : *Fonds international de développement agricole, 12 août 2014*

Non disponible en version imprimée, conformément au paragraphe 2 de l'article 12 du règlement de l'Assemblée générale destiné à mettre en application l'Article 102 de la Charte des Nations Unies, tel qu'amendé.

No. 52067

International Fund for Agricultural Development
and
Georgia

Financing Agreement (Agricultural Support Project) between Georgia and the International Fund for Agricultural Development (with schedules and General Conditions for Agricultural Development Financing dated 29 April 2009). Rome, 24 June 2010, and Tbilisi, 8 July 2010

Entry into force: *8 July 2010, in accordance with the General Conditions*

Authentic text: *English*

Registration with the Secretariat of the United Nations: *International Fund for Agricultural Development, 12 August 2014*

Not published in print, in accordance with article 12(2) of the General Assembly regulations to give effect to Article 102 of the Charter of the United Nations, as amended.

Fonds international de développement agricole
et
Géorgie

Accord de financement (Projet d'aide à l'agriculture) entre la Géorgie et le Fonds international de développement agricole (avec annexes et Conditions générales applicables au financement du développement agricole, en date du 29 avril 2009). Rome, 24 juin 2010, et Tbilissi, 8 juillet 2010

Entrée en vigueur : *8 juillet 2010, conformément aux Conditions générales*

Texte authentique : *anglais*

Enregistrement auprès du Secrétariat de l'Organisation des Nations Unies : *Fonds international de développement agricole, 12 août 2014*

Non disponible en version imprimée, conformément au paragraphe 2 de l'article 12 du règlement de l'Assemblée générale destiné à mettre en application l'Article 102 de la Charte des Nations Unies, tel qu'amendé.

No. 52068

International Fund for Agricultural Development
and
Ethiopia

Project Financing Agreement (Community-based Integrated Natural Resources Management Project) between the Federal Democratic Republic of Ethiopia and the International Fund for Agricultural Development (with schedules and General Conditions for Agricultural Development Financing dated 2 December 1998). Rome, 19 June 2009

Entry into force: *17 March 2010, in accordance with the General Conditions*

Authentic text: *English*

Registration with the Secretariat of the United Nations: *International Fund for Agricultural Development, 12 August 2014*

Not published in print, in accordance with article 12(2) of the General Assembly regulations to give effect to Article 102 of the Charter of the United Nations, as amended.

Fonds international de développement agricole
et
Éthiopie

Accord de financement relatif au projet (Projet de gestion de ressources naturelles intégré au niveau de la communauté) entre la République fédérale démocratique d'Éthiopie et le Fonds international de développement agricole (avec annexes et Conditions générales applicables au financement du développement agricole, en date du 2 décembre 1998). Rome, 19 juin 2009

Entrée en vigueur : *17 mars 2010, conformément aux Conditions générales*

Texte authentique : *anglais*

Enregistrement auprès du Secrétariat de l'Organisation des Nations Unies : *Fonds international de développement agricole, 12 août 2014*

Non disponible en version imprimée, conformément au paragraphe 2 de l'article 12 du règlement de l'Assemblée générale destiné à mettre en application l'Article 102 de la Charte des Nations Unies, tel qu'amendé.

No. 52069

International Fund for Agricultural Development
and
Ethiopia

Financing Agreement (Pastoral Community Development Project II) between the Federal Democratic Republic of Ethiopia and the International Fund for Agricultural Development (with schedules and General Conditions for Agricultural Development Financing dated 29 April 2009). Rome, 26 November 2009

Entry into force: *14 July 2010, in accordance with the General Conditions*

Authentic text: *English*

Registration with the Secretariat of the United Nations: *International Fund for Agricultural Development, 12 August 2014*

Not published in print, in accordance with article 12(2) of the General Assembly regulations to give effect to Article 102 of the Charter of the United Nations, as amended.

Fonds international de développement agricole
et
Éthiopie

Accord de financement (Projet II de développement des communautés pastorales) entre la République fédérale démocratique d'Éthiopie et le Fonds international de développement agricole (avec annexes et Conditions générales applicables au financement du développement agricole, en date du 29 avril 2009). Rome, 26 novembre 2009

Entrée en vigueur : *14 juillet 2010, conformément aux Conditions générales*

Texte authentique : *anglais*

Enregistrement auprès du Secrétariat de l'Organisation des Nations Unies : *Fonds international de développement agricole, 12 août 2014*

Non disponible en version imprimée, conformément au paragraphe 2 de l'article 12 du règlement de l'Assemblée générale destiné à mettre en application l'Article 102 de la Charte des Nations Unies, tel qu'amendé.

No. 52070

International Fund for Agricultural Development
and
Brazil

Guarantee Agreement (Rural Business for small producers project (Dom Távora) (Projeto de desenvolvimento de negócios rurais para pequenos produtores – Dom Távora)) between the Federative Republic of Brazil and the International Fund for Agricultural Development (with General Conditions for Agricultural Development Financing dated 29 April 2009, as amended through 17 September 2010). Rome, 20 August 2013, and Brasília, 30 August 2013

Entry into force: *30 August 2013, in accordance with the General Conditions*

Authentic text: *English*

Registration with the Secretariat of the United Nations: *International Fund for Agricultural Development, 12 August 2014*

Not published in print, in accordance with article 12(2) of the General Assembly regulations to give effect to Article 102 of the Charter of the United Nations, as amended.

Fonds international de développement agricole
et
Brésil

Accord de garantie (Projet de développement rural pour les petits producteurs (Dom Távora) (Projeto de desenvolvimento de negócios rurais para pequenos produtores – Dom Távora)) entre la République fédérative du Brésil et le Fonds international de développement agricole (avec Conditions générales applicables au financement du développement agricole, en date du 29 avril 2009, telles qu'amendées au 17 septembre 2010). Rome, 20 août 2013, et Brasilia, 30 août 2013

Entrée en vigueur : *30 août 2013, conformément aux Conditions générales*

Texte authentique : *anglais*

Enregistrement auprès du Secrétariat de l'Organisation des Nations Unies : *Fonds international de développement agricole, 12 août 2014*

Non disponible en version imprimée, conformément au paragraphe 2 de l'article 12 du règlement de l'Assemblée générale destiné à mettre en application l'Article 102 de la Charte des Nations Unies, tel qu'amendé.

No. 52071

International Fund for Agricultural Development
and
Viet Nam

Agreement between the Government of the Socialist Republic of Viet Nam and the International Fund for Agricultural Development concerning the Fund's country office. Hanoi, 16 January 2008

Entry into force: *16 January 2008 by signature, in accordance with article 14*

Authentic texts: *English and Vietnamese*

Registration with the Secretariat of the United Nations: *International Fund for Agricultural Development, 1 August 2014*

Fonds international de développement agricole
et
Viet Nam

Accord entre le Gouvernement de la République socialiste du Viet Nam et le Fonds international de développement agricole concernant le bureau de pays du Fonds. Hanoï, 16 janvier 2008

Entrée en vigueur : *16 janvier 2008 par signature, conformément à l'article 14*

Textes authentiques : *anglais et vietnamien*

Enregistrement auprès du Secrétariat de l'Organisation des Nations Unies : *Fonds international de développement agricole, 1er août 2014*

[ENGLISH TEXT – TEXTE ANGLAIS]

AGREEMENT

BETWEEN

THE GOVERNMENT OF THE SOCIALIST REPUBLIC OF VIET NAM

AND

THE INTERNATIONAL FUND FOR AGRICULTURAL DEVELOPMENT

CONCERNING

THE FUND'S COUNTRY OFFICE

Dated 16 January 2008

AGREEMENT

WHEREAS the International Fund for Agricultural Development wishes to establish a Country Office in Viet Nam to support its operations, including supervision of projects; consolidate its cooperation and linkages; be close to its partners and programmes; and manage knowledge; and the Government of the Socialist Republic of Viet Nam agrees to permit the establishment of such an office;

NOW, THEREFORE, the Government of the Socialist Republic of Viet Nam and the International Fund for Agricultural Development (IFAD) hereby agree as follows:

Article 1
Definitions

For the purpose of this Agreement:

(a) "Government" means the Government of the Socialist Republic of Viet Nam;

(b) "The Fund" or "IFAD" means the International Fund for Agricultural Development;

(c) "Office" means the International Fund for Agricultural Development's Country Office located in the Socialist Republic of Viet Nam;

(d) "IFAD officials" means the Country Representative and all other officials as specified by IFAD in accordance with Article VI, Section 18 of the Convention on the Privileges and Immunities of the Specialized Agencies.

Article 2
Juridical Personality of the Fund

1. The Government recognizes the juridical personality of the Fund, and in particular its capacity:

(a) To contract;

(b) To acquire and dispose of movable and immovable property in accordance with the laws of Viet Nam; and

(c) To be a party to judicial proceedings.

2. The Government shall permit the Fund to rent premises to serve as its Office.

3. The Office shall be authorised to display the emblem of the Fund on its premises and vehicles.

Article 3
Inviolability of the Office

1. The property and assets of the Office, wherever located and by whomsoever held, shall be immune from search, requisition, confiscation, expropriation and any other form of interference, whether by executive, administrative, judicial or legislative action.

2. The archives of the Office, and in general all documents belonging to it or held by it, shall be inviolable, wherever located.

3. The Office and its property and assets, wherever located and by whomsoever held, shall enjoy immunity from every form of legal process except in so far as in any particular case the Fund has expressly waived its immunity. No waiver of immunity shall extend to any measure of execution.

4. The Office shall not allow its premises to serve as a refuge for any person wanted for a criminal offence or in respect of whom a warrant, conviction or expulsion order has been issued by the competent authorities of the Socialist Republic of Viet Nam.

5. The authorities, officials and agents of the Socialist Republic of Viet Nam shall not enter the Office in an official capacity unless at the request or with the authorisation of the Office, granted by the Country Representative or his or her delegate. In the event of *force majeure*, fire or any other calamity requiring urgent measures of protection, the consent of the Country Representative or his or her representative shall be considered to have been given. However, if requested by the Country Representative, any person who has entered the Office with his or her presumed consent shall leave the Office immediately.

6. The competent authorities of the Socialist Republic of Viet Nam shall, to the extent possible, take all necessary measures to protect the Office against any intrusion or damage, to ensure that their tranquillity is not disturbed and to preserve their dignity.

7. The residences of IFAD officials who are not citizens or permanent residents of the Socialist Republic of Viet Nam shall be entitled to the same inviolability and protection as the Office.

Article 4
Public Services

1. The Government shall ensure that the Office is supplied with necessary public services on equitable terms. The Office shall bear the cost of these services.

2. In the case of interruption or threatened interruption of any such services, the competent authorities shall consider the Office's need for such services as important as that of the State's public services, and shall therefore take the necessary measures to ensure that the Office's activities are not impaired by such a situation.

Article 5
Communications

No censorship shall be applied to the official correspondence and other official communications of the Office. The Office shall have the right to use codes and to dispatch and receive correspondence by courier or in sealed bags, which shall have the same immunities and privileges as diplomatic couriers and bags.

Article 6
Tax Exemption

The Office, its assets, income and other property shall be exempt from:

(a) All direct and indirect taxes, it being understood, however, that no claim of exemption will be made from taxes which are, in fact, no more than charges for public utility services;

(b) Customs duties or other taxes, and all prohibitions or restrictions on imports and exports in respect of articles imported or exported by the Office for its official use in accordance with the functions of the Office. It is understood, however, that articles imported under such exemption will not be sold in the Socialist Republic of Viet Nam except under conditions agreed with the Government; and

(c) Customs duties or other taxes and all prohibitions or restrictions on imports and exports in respect of its publications.

Article 7
Financial Facilities

1. In connection with its official activities permitted under the laws of Viet Nam, the Office may freely:

(a) Acquire currencies and funds, hold them, use them, and have accounts in Dong or any other currency and convert any currency held by it into any other currency;

(b) Transfer Dong within the territory of the Socialist Republic of Viet Nam and transfer other currencies to or from the Socialist Republic of Viet Nam.

2. The Office shall enjoy the same exchange facilities as other international organisations represented in the Socialist Republic of Viet Nam.

Article 8
Social Security

Since IFAD officials are covered by the Fund's social security scheme, the Office shall not be required to contribute to any social security scheme in the Socialist Republic of Viet Nam, and the Government shall not require any member of the Office staff to join such a scheme.

Article 9
Entry, Travel and Sojourn

1. The Government shall recognize and accept the United Nations laissez-passer issued to officials of IFAD as valid travel documents.

2. Applications for visas, where required, from officials of IFAD holding United Nations laissez-passer, when accompanied by a certificate that they are travelling on the business of IFAD, shall be dealt with as speedily as possible. In addition, such persons shall be granted facilities for speedy travel.

3. Similar facilities to those specified in paragraph 2 shall be accorded to experts and other persons who, though not the holders of United Nations laissez-passer, have a certificate that they are travelling on the business of IFAD.

4. The Government shall in no way obstruct the entry into or departure from the Socialist Republic of Viet Nam, when travelling to or from the Office, of persons exercising official functions at the Office or invited by it.

5. The Government undertakes to facilitate the following persons and their dependants to enter into the Socialist Republic of Viet Nam and sojourn in the country throughout the duration of their assignment or missions to the Office:

(a) The Country Representative and other IFAD officials;

(b) All other persons invited by the Office.

6. Without prejudice to the specific immunities to which they may be entitled, the persons referred to in paragraph 5 above shall not, during their assignment or missions, be required by the authorities of the Socialist Republic of Viet Nam to leave the territory of the Socialist Republic of Viet Nam unless it is established, in accordance with the provisions of Article 12 paragraph 6 hereof, that they have abused the privileges to which they are entitled by pursuing an activity unrelated to their official functions or missions.

Article 10
Identity Cards

1. The Country Representative shall communicate to the Government a list of the IFAD officials (including spouses and other dependants) and inform it of any changes in this list.

2. Upon notification of their appointment, the Government shall issue to all persons referred to in paragraph 1 a card bearing the photograph of its holder in accordance with the procedures applied to the staff of the representative offices of international and diplomatic organizations in Viet Nam.

Article 11
Privileges and Immunities of IFAD Officials

1. IFAD officials shall enjoy the following privileges and immunities in the Socialist Republic of Viet Nam:

(a) Immunity from legal process, even after the termination of their functions, in respect of all acts, including words spoken or written, performed by them in their official capacity;

(b) Exemption from any form of taxation in respect of the salaries and emoluments pertaining to their work for the Office, and for IFAD officials who are not citizens or permanent residents of Viet Nam, any other income from sources outside the Socialist Republic of Viet Nam;

(c) Exemption, together with their spouses and other dependents, from immigration restrictions and alien registration;

(d) Exemption, together with their spouses and other dependents, from national service obligations and any other compulsory service;

(e) Exemption from import duty and other levies on their imported household and personal effects and the temporary import or purchase of a vehicle in accordance with the local rules and procedures applied to the staff of international and diplomatic organizations;

(f) In the event of international crisis, the same repatriation facilities as members of the diplomatic corps accredited to the Government, for themselves, their spouses and other dependents;

(g) The same exchange facilities as those accorded to officials of comparable rank of diplomatic missions accredited to the Government.

2. Throughout the duration of his or her functions, the Country Representative shall enjoy the privileges and immunities accorded to the heads of diplomatic missions. The other senior members of the Office designated from time to time by the Country Representative on the basis of the positions of responsibility which they fill shall be accorded the privileges granted to diplomatic agents.

3. IFAD officials who are Vietnamese citizens shall enjoy such privileges and immunities similar to those enjoyed by the national staff of the other United Nations organizations in accordance with the agreements signed by Viet Nam and these organizations, including, but not limited to, immunity from legal process in connection with acts performed in their official capacity. Nationals and permanent residents of the Socialist Republic of Viet Nam employed by the Office shall not enjoy the privileges and immunities mentioned in this Article.

Article 12
General Provisions

1. The Government shall make every effort to ensure that the Office and IFAD officials enjoy treatment not less favourable than that granted to other intergovernmental, international and regional organisations represented in the Socialist Republic of Viet Nam.

2. The privileges and immunities provided for in this Agreement are not designed to secure personal advantage for their beneficiaries; they are designed exclusively to ensure that the Office may operate freely in all circumstances, and to safeguard the complete independence of the persons to whom they are granted.

3. Without prejudice to the privileges and immunities granted under this Agreement, the Office and all persons who enjoy these privileges and immunities have the duty to respect the laws and regulations of the Socialist Republic of Viet Nam. They also have the duty not to interfere in the internal affairs of the Socialist Republic of Viet Nam.

4. The President of the Fund has the right and duty to waive the immunity of any official when he or she considers that such immunity would impede the course of justice and can be waived without prejudice to the interests of the Office.

5. The Country Representative shall take all measures necessary to prevent any abuse of the privileges and immunities granted under this Agreement; to this end, he or she shall issue such regulations, applicable to IFAD officials and others concerned, as may be deemed necessary and appropriate.

6. Should the Government consider that there has been an abuse of a privilege or immunity granted under this Agreement, consultations shall take place, at its request, between the Country Representative and the competent authorities with a view to determining whether such an abuse took place. Should such consultations not produce a result which is satisfactory to the Government and the Country Representative, the matter shall be settled in accordance with the procedure described in Article 13.

7. Nothing in this Agreement shall be construed as limiting the right of the Government to take such measures as are necessary to safeguard the security of the Socialist Republic of Viet Nam.

8. Should the Government find it necessary to apply paragraph 7 of this Article, it shall enter into contact with the Country Representative as soon as circumstances permit with a view to determining by mutual agreement the measures required to protect the interests of the Fund.

9. The provisions of this Agreement are applicable to all persons covered by the Agreement, regardless of whether the Government maintains diplomatic relations with the State of which such persons are nationals, or whether such State grants similar privileges and immunities to the diplomatic officials and nationals of the Socialist Republic of Viet Nam.

10. Whenever this Agreement imposes obligations on the competent authorities, the Government shall be ultimately responsible for ensuring the fulfilment of such obligations.

Article 13
Interpretation and Settlement of Disputes

1. This Agreement shall be interpreted in accordance with the customary rules of treaty interpretation, in particular in the light of its principal objective, which is to enable the Office to carry out its activities fully and efficiently.

2. Any dispute between the Government and the Office concerning the interpretation or application of this Agreement, or of any supplementary arrangement, which is not settled by negotiation shall, unless the parties agree otherwise, be referred for final decision to a tribunal of three (3) arbitrators, one to be named by the Government, one to be named by the President of the Fund, and the third, who shall chair the tribunal, to be chosen by mutual agreement by the other two arbitrators.

3. Should the first two arbitrators fail to agree on the choice of the third within six months following their appointment, the third arbitrator shall be named by the President of the International Court of Justice, unless he or she is a national of the Socialist Republic of Viet Nam, in which case the third arbitrator shall be named by the Vice-President.

4. The decisions of the tribunal of arbitrators shall be fully binding and not subject to appeal.

Article 14
Entry into force and Revision

1. The provisions of this Agreement shall come into force upon signature by both parties.

2. This Agreement will remain in force while the Office remains established in the Socialist Republic of Viet Nam.

3. The obligations assumed by the Government under this Agreement shall survive its termination to the extent necessary to permit orderly withdrawal of the property, funds and assets of the Fund and the officials and other persons performing services on behalf of the Fund.

4. This Agreement may only be amended by mutual agreement of the Parties in writing.

5. This Agreement is prepared in the Vietnamese and English languages, both being equally authentic. In the event a difference is found between the versions, the English version shall have precedence.

In witness whereof the undersigned duly authorised representatives of the Government and the Fund respectively have, on behalf of both parties, signed the present Agreement in Hanoi on 16 January 2008, in four copies, two in each language.

FOR THE GOVERNMENT OF THE
SOCIALIST REPUBLIC OF VIETNAM

FOR THE INTERNATIONAL FUND FOR
AGRICULTURAL DEVELOPMENT

_____(Pham Binh Minh)_____
Standing Deputy Minister of Foreign Affairs

_____(Lennart Båge)_____
President

[Vietnamese text – Texte vietnamien]

HIỆP ĐỊNH

GIỮA

CHÍNH PHỦ NƯỚC CỘNG HÒA XÃ HỘI CHỦ NGHĨA VIỆT NAM

VÀ

QUỸ QUỐC TẾ VỀ PHÁT TRIỂN NÔNG NGHIỆP

VỀ

VĂN PHÒNG ĐẠI DIỆN CỦA QUỸ TẠI VIỆT NAM

Ngày 16 tháng 01 năm 2008

HIỆP ĐỊNH

Xét rằng Quỹ Quốc tế về Phát triển Nông nghiệp (IFAD) mong muốn lập Văn phòng Đại diện tại Việt Nam để hỗ trợ các hoạt động của mình, trong đó có việc giám sát dự án; củng cố hoạt động và các mối liên hệ; gần gũi với các đối tác và các chương trình; và quản lý tri thức; và Chính phủ nước Cộng hòa xã hội chủ nghĩa Việt Nam đồng ý cho phép lập một Văn phòng Đại diện như vậy,

Chính phủ nước Cộng hòa xã hội chủ nghĩa Việt Nam và Quỹ Quốc tế về Phát triển Nông nghiệp (IFAD) thỏa thuận như sau:

Điều 1
Định nghĩa

Vì mục đích của Hiệp định này:

a) "Chính phủ" là Chính phủ nước Cộng hòa xã hội chủ nghĩa Việt Nam;

b) "Quỹ" hoặc "IFAD" là Quỹ Quốc tế về Phát triển Nông nghiệp;

c) "Văn phòng" là Văn phòng Đại diện của Quỹ Quốc tế về Phát triển Nông nghiệp đóng tại Việt Nam;

d) "Quan chức IFAD" là Trưởng Đại diện và tất cả các quan chức khác được IFAD chỉ định theo điều VI, Mục 18 Công ước về Quyền Ưu đãi Miễn trừ đối với các Cơ quan Chuyên môn.

Điều 2
Tư cách pháp nhân của Quỹ

1. Chính phủ công nhận tư cách pháp nhân của Quỹ, cụ thể là năng lực của Quỹ trong việc:

a) Ký kết hợp đồng;

b) Được có và được định đoạt về động sản và bất động sản phù hợp với pháp luật Việt Nam;

c) Là một bên tham gia các thủ tục tố tụng.

55

2. Chính phủ sẽ cho phép Quỹ thuê trụ sở để làm Văn phòng.

3. Văn phòng sẽ được quyền trương biểu tượng của Quỹ tại trụ sở và trên phương tiện đi lại của Quỹ.

Điều 3
Quyền bất khả xâm phạm của Văn phòng

1. Các tài sản của Văn phòng, dù ở đâu và do ai giữ, đều được miễn khám xét, trưng dụng, tịch thu, xung công và các hình thức can thiệp khác, dù bằng hành động hành pháp, hành chính, pháp lý hay lập pháp.

2. Hồ sơ của Văn phòng và nói chung tất cả các tài liệu của Văn phòng hoặc do Văn phòng giữ được hưởng quyền bất khả xâm phạm, dù được để ở đâu.

3. Quỹ và các tài sản của Quỹ, dù được để ở đâu và do ai giữ, được miễn các thủ tục pháp lý, trừ trường hợp cụ thể mà Quỹ đã tuyên bố từ bỏ quyền miễn trừ của mình. Quyền miễn trừ sẽ không bị khước từ đối với bất kỳ biện pháp thi hành án nào.

4. Văn phòng sẽ không cho phép trụ sở của mình làm nơi tị nạn cho bất kỳ ai bị truy nã vì phạm tội hình sự hoặc là đối tượng bị truy nã, đã bị kết tội hoặc trục xuất theo lệnh của nhà chức trách có thẩm quyền của Việt Nam.

5. Nhà chức trách, các quan chức và nhân viên của nước Cộng hoà xã hội chủ nghĩa Việt Nam không được vào Văn phòng trừ khi có yêu cầu hoặc được Trưởng Đại diện hoặc người được uỷ quyền của Văn phòng cho phép. Trong trường hợp bất khả kháng, hoả hoạn hoặc thiên tai khác đòi hỏi phải có các biện pháp bảo vệ khẩn cấp thì việc vào Văn phòng được coi như đã có sự chấp thuận của Trưởng Đại diện hoặc người được uỷ quyền.Tuy nhiên, nếu được Trưởng Đại diện yêu cầu, bất kỳ người nào đã vào Văn phòng sẽ phải rời khỏi Văn phòng ngay lập tức.

6. Nhà chức trách Việt Nam sẽ, trong chừng mực có thể, sẽ có những biện pháp cần thiết để bảo vệ Văn phòng, ngăn chặn các hành vi xâm nhập hoặc làm hư hại, nhằm đảm bảo an ninh và tôn nghiêm của Văn phòng.

7. Nơi ở của quan chức IFAD, không phải là công dân hoặc người thường trú tại Việt Nam, sẽ được hưởng quyền bất khả xâm phạm và quyền được bảo vệ như Văn phòng.

Điều 4
Các dịch vụ tiện ích công

1. Chính phủ sẽ đảm bảo rằng Văn phòng được cung cấp một cách bình đẳng các dịch vụ tiện ích công. Văn phòng sẽ chịu mọi chi phí đối với các dịch vụ tiện ích công này.

2. Trong trường hợp bị ngưng trệ hoặc đe doạ bị ngưng trệ bất kỳ dịch vụ tiện ích công nào, nhà chức trách có thẩm quyền sẽ coi nhu cầu của Văn phòng về các dịch vụ này cũng quan trọng như đối với các cơ quan của Nhà nước, và sẽ có các biện pháp cần thiết để đảm bảo rằng các hoạt động của Văn phòng không bị đình trệ do tình hình như thế gây ra.

Điều 5
Thông tin liên lạc

Thư từ chính thức và các phương tiện thông tin liên lạc chính thức khác của Văn phòng không bị kiểm duyệt. Văn phòng có quyền sử dụng mật mã và chuyển/nhận thư tín bằng giao liên hoặc túi thư được dán kín và được hưởng các quyền ưu đãi miễn trừ như giao thông viên và túi thư ngoại giao.

Điều 6
Miễn thuế

Văn phòng, các tài sản, thu nhập và các tài sản khác sẽ được miễn:

a) Tất cả các loại thuế trực thu và gián thu; mặc dù vậy, cần hiểu rằng Văn phòng sẽ không yêu cầu được miễn các khoản thuế mà thực chất chỉ là các khoản phí đối với các dịch vụ tiện ích công;

b) Thuế hải quan hoặc các loại thuế khác cũng như tất cả các quy định cấm hoặc hạn chế đối với các vật dụng được Văn phòng nhập khẩu hoặc xuất khẩu vì mục đích sử dụng chính thức phù hợp với chức năng hoạt động của Văn phòng. Tuy nhiên, cần hiểu rằng các mặt hàng nhập khẩu miễn thuế như vậy sẽ không được bán ở nước Cộng hòa xã hội chủ nghĩa Việt Nam, trừ trường hợp phù hợp với các điều kiện được thỏa thuận với Chính phủ; và

c) Thuế hải quan hoặc các loại thuế khác cũng như các quy định cấm hoặc hạn chế đối với việc nhập khẩu và xuất khẩu các ấn phẩm của Văn phòng.

Điều 7
Tài chính

1. Liên quan đến các hoạt động chính thức phù hợp với pháp luật và quy định của Việt Nam, Văn phòng có thể tự do:

a) Có tiền và các quỹ, giữ và sử dụng chúng và có tài khoản tiền Đồng hoặc bất kỳ loại tiền nào và chuyển đổi bất kỳ loại tiền nào mà Văn phòng giữ sang bất kỳ loại tiền nào khác;

b) Chuyển tiền Đồng trong lãnh thổ nước Cộng hòa xã hội chủ nghĩa Việt Nam và chuyển các loại tiền khác tới hoặc ra khỏi nước Cộng hòa xã hội chủ nghĩa Việt Nam.

2. Văn phòng sẽ được hưởng cùng tỉ giá hối đoái như các tổ chức quốc tế khác có đại diện tại Việt Nam.

Điều 8
An sinh xã hội

Vì các quan chức IFAD được hưởng bảo hiểm an sinh xã hội theo chương trình của Quỹ, Văn phòng sẽ không bị yêu cầu đóng bất kỳ chế độ an sinh xã hội nào ở nước Cộng hòa xã hội chủ nghĩa Việt Nam, và Chính phủ sẽ không yêu cầu bất kỳ quan chức IFAD nào tham gia chế độ bảo hiểm như vậy.

Điều 9
Nhập cảnh, đi lại và lưu trú tại Việt Nam

1. Chính phủ sẽ công nhận và chấp thuận giấy thông hành do Liên hợp quốc cấp cho các quan chức của IFAD là giấy tờ đi lại có giá trị.

2. Đơn xin visa, khi được yêu cầu, của các quan chức IFAD mang giấy thông hành Liên hợp quốc, khi được kèm theo giấy chứng nhận rằng họ đi làm công việc của IFAD, sẽ được giải quyết nhanh nhất có thể. Ngoài ra những người này sẽ được tạo thuận lợi để có thể đi lại một cách nhanh chóng.

3. Các điều kiện tương tự đối với những người nêu tại khoản 2 sẽ được dành cho các chuyên gia và những người khác, dù không mang giấy thông hành Liên hợp quốc, nhưng có giấy chứng nhận rằng họ đi làm công việc của IFAD.

4. Chính phủ sẽ không ngăn cản việc nhập cảnh và xuất cảnh nước Cộng hòa xã hội chủ nghĩa Việt Nam để đến hoặc rời khỏi Văn phòng đối với những người thực hiện các nhiệm vụ chính thức tại Văn phòng hoặc được Văn phòng mời.

5. Chính phủ sẽ tạo điều kiện thuận lợi cho những người sau đây và những người phụ thuộc của họ được nhập cảnh và xuất cảnh nước Cộng hòa xã hội chủ nghĩa Việt Nam trong thời gian thực hiện nhiệm vụ hoặc công việc ở Văn phòng:

a) Trưởng Đại diện và các quan chức IFAD khác;

b) Tất cả những người khác được Văn phòng mời.

6. Không phương hại tới các quyền miễn trừ cụ thể mà họ có thể được hưởng, những người nêu tại khoản 5 ở trên, trong thời gian thực thi nhiệm vụ hoặc công việc, sẽ không bị nhà chức trách nước Cộng hòa xã hội chủ nghĩa Việt Nam yêu cầu rời khỏi lãnh thổ nước Cộng hòa xã hội chủ nghĩa Việt Nam, trừ khi được xác định, phù hợp với các quy định ở khoản 6, Điều 12 của Hiệp định này, rằng họ đã lạm dụng các quyền ưu đãi mà họ được hưởng để làm những việc không liên quan tới nhiệm vụ và công việc chính thức của họ.

Điều 10
Thẻ chứng minh

1. Trưởng Đại diện sẽ thông báo cho Chính phủ danh sách các quan chức IFAD của Văn phòng (kể cả vợ, chồng và những người phụ thuộc) và thông báo cập nhật những thay đổi trong danh sách này.

2. Sau khi được thông báo việc họ được cử, Chính phủ sẽ cấp cho tất cả những người nêu tại khoản 1 một giấy chứng minh có dán ảnh của người được cấp tương tự như áp dụng với các quan chức cùng cấp của các Văn phòng đại diện các tổ chức quốc tế và của các cơ quan đại diện ngoại giao.

Điều 11
Các quyền ưu đãi và miễn trừ của các quan chức IFAD

1. Các quan chức IFAD được hưởng các quyền ưu đãi và miễn trừ sau đây tại nước Cộng hòa xã hội chủ nghĩa Việt Nam:

a) Miễn trừ xem xét pháp lý, kể cả sau khi họ đã kết thúc nhiệm vụ, đối với các hành động, kể cả các phát ngôn bằng văn bản hay lời nói, mà họ đã thực hiện trong khi thực hiện chức năng chính thức của mình;

b) Miễn trừ bất kỳ hình thức thuế nào đối với lương bổng có được do làm việc cho Văn phòng, và đối với các quan chức IFAD không phải là công dân hoặc người thường trú tại Việt Nam, bất kỳ khoản thu nhập nào khác từ các nguồn bên ngoài nước Cộng hòa xã hội chủ nghĩa Việt Nam;

c) Được miễn, cùng với vợ/chồng và người phụ thuộc khác, không bị hạn chế xuất nhập cảnh và đăng ký ngoại kiều;

d) Được miễn, cùng với vợ/chồng và người phụ thuộc khác, đối với các nghĩa vụ quốc gia và bất kỳ nghĩa vụ bắt buộc nào khác;

e) Được miễn thuế nhập khẩu và các lệ phí khác đối với đồ dùng gia đình và cá nhân nhập khẩu; được tạm nhập, hoặc mua xe ô tô phù hợp với các quy định và thủ tục trong nước được áp dụng đối với các quan chức cùng cấp của các Văn phòng đại diện các tổ chức quốc tế và của các cơ quan đại diện ngoại giao;

f) Trong trường hợp có khủng hoảng quốc tế, các quan chức IFAD, vợ/chồng và người phụ thuộc sẽ được hưởng các điều kiện thuận lợi để hồi hương như các thành viên đoàn ngoại giao bên cạnh Chính phủ;

g) Được hưởng các điều kiện thuận lợi về tỉ giá hối đoái như các quan chức cùng cấp của các phái đoàn ngoại giao bên cạnh Chính phủ Việt Nam.

2. Trong suốt thời gian công tác, Trưởng Đại diện sẽ được hưởng các quyền ưu đãi và miễn trừ được dành cho người đứng đầu các cơ quan đại diện ngoại giao. Các quan chức cao cấp khác của Văn phòng, được người Đại diện chỉ định trên cơ sở vị trí và trách nhiệm mà họ đảm nhận, sẽ được dành cho các quyền ưu đãi như các các bộ ngoại giao khác được hưởng.

3. Các quan chức IFAD là công dân Việt Nam được hưởng các quyền ưu đãi, miễn trừ tương tự như các quyền dành cho các quan chức mang quốc tịch Việt Nam của các cơ quan của Liên hợp quốc phù hợp với các hiệp định về quyền ưu đãi và miễn trừ Việt Nam đã ký kết với các tổ chức này, bao gồm, nhưng không bị giới hạn, miễn trừ các thủ tục pháp lý liên quan đến các hành vi mà họ thực hiện với tư cách công vụ. Công dân và người thường trú tại nước Cộng hòa xã hội chủ nghĩa Việt Nam được Văn phòng thuê làm việc sẽ không được hưởng các quyền ưu đãi và miễn trừ nêu tại Điều này.

Điều 12
Các điều khoản chung

1. Chính phủ sẽ hết sức nỗ lực để đảm bảo cho Văn phòng và cán bộ Văn phòng được hưởng sự đối xử không kém thuận lợi hơn sự đối xử đã dành cho các tổ chức khu vực, quốc tế và liên chính phủ khác có mặt tại nước Cộng hòa xã hội chủ nghĩa Việt Nam.

2. Những quyền ưu đãi và miễn trừ được quy định trong Hiệp định này không nhằm tạo thuận lợi cho các hoạt động cá nhân của các đối tượng hưởng các quyền này mà chỉ nhằm đảm bảo cho Văn phòng có thể hoạt động thuận lợi trong mọi hoàn cảnh, và đảm bảo sự độc lập hoàn toàn của những người được hưởng các quyền lợi này.

3. Không gây phương hại tới các quyền ưu đãi và miễn trừ được quy định trong Hiệp định này, Văn phòng và mọi cá nhân được hưởng các quyền ưu đãi và miễn trừ này có nghĩa vụ tôn trọng các quy định và pháp luật của nước Cộng hòa xã hội chủ nghĩa Việt Nam. Họ cũng có trách nhiệm không được can thiệp vào các công việc nội bộ của nước Cộng hòa xã hội chủ nghĩa Việt Nam.

4. Chủ tịch của Quỹ có quyền và trách nhiệm bãi bỏ quyền miễn trừ của bất kỳ quan chức nào khi thấy rằng quyền miễn trừ này gây cản trở cho việc thực hiện công lý và có thể được bãi bỏ mà không gây phương hại tới lợi ích của Văn phòng.

5. Trưởng Đại diện sẽ tiến hành mọi biện pháp cần thiết để ngăn cản bất cứ sự lạm dụng các quyền về ưu đãi miễn trừ nào được quy định trong Hiệp định này; nhằm mục đích này, Trưởng Đại diện sẽ đưa ra các quy định, được áp dụng đối với các quan chức IFAD và những người liên quan khác, nếu thấy cần thiết và phù hợp.

6. Nếu Chính phủ thấy có sự lạm dụng về quyền ưu đãi miễn trừ được quy định trong Hiệp định này, Trưởng Đại diện và các cơ quan có thẩm quyền sẽ tiến hành tham vấn, theo yêu cầu của Chính phủ, để xác định xem có hành vi lạm dụng đó không. Nếu các cuộc tham vấn đó không mang lại kết quả thoả đáng đối với Chính phủ và Trưởng Đại diện thì vấn đề sẽ được giải quyết theo các thủ tục nêu tại Điều 13.

7. Không điều nào trong Hiệp định này được hiểu là hạn chế quyền của Chính phủ được tiến hành các biện pháp được coi là cần thiết để bảo vệ an ninh của nước Cộng hòa xã hội chủ nghĩa Việt Nam.

8. Nếu thấy cần áp dụng khoản 7 Điều này, Chính phủ sẽ liên hệ với Trưởng Đại diện ngay khi hoàn cảnh cho phép để thoả thuận về các biện pháp cần thiết nhằm bảo vệ các quyền lợi của Quỹ.

9. Các điều khoản của Hiệp định này được áp dụng đối với tất cả những người thuộc phạm vi điều chỉnh của Hiệp định, dù Chính phủ có quan hệ ngoại giao với quốc gia mà những người đó mang quốc tịch hay không, hoặc dù quốc gia đó có dành các quyền về ưu đãi và miễn trừ tương tự cho các quan chức ngoại giao và công dân của nước Cộng hòa xã hội chủ nghĩa Việt Nam hay không.

10. Trong trường hợp các nhà chức trách có thẩm quyền phải thực hiện nghĩa vụ theo quy định của Hiệp định này, Chính phủ sẽ có trách nhiệm cuối cùng nhằm đảm bảo việc hoàn thành các nghĩa vụ đó.

Điều 13
Giải thích Hiệp định và giải quyết tranh chấp

1. Hiệp định này được giải thích phù hợp với các quy tắc tập quán về giải thích điều ước quốc tế, đặc biệt là phù hợp với mục đích chủ đạo cho phép Văn phòng thực hiện các hoạt động của mình một cách đầy đủ và hiệu quả.

2. Mọi tranh chấp giữa Chính phủ và Văn phòng liên quan tới việc giải thích và áp dụng Hiệp định này, hoặc bất cứ sự dàn xếp bổ sung nào, mà không giải quyết được bằng thương lượng, trừ khi có thoả thuận khác, được chuyển cho một tòa trọng tài đưa ra quyết định cuối cùng. Tòa trọng tài này gồm ba (3) trọng tài, một do Chính phủ đề nghị, một do Chủ tịch Quỹ đề nghị, và trọng tài thứ ba, là chủ toạ, sẽ được chọn lựa theo thỏa thuận giữa hai trọng tài kia.

3. Nếu hai trọng tài do Chủ tịch Quỹ và Chính phủ đề cử không thỏa thuận được việc chọn lựa trọng tài thứ ba trong vòng sáu tháng sau khi họ được đề cử, thì trọng tài thứ ba sẽ do Chủ tịch Tòa án Quốc tế đề cử, trừ khi Chủ tịch Tòa án Quốc tế là công dân của nước Cộng hòa xã hội chủ nghĩa Việt Nam; trong trường hợp đó, trọng tài thứ ba sẽ do Phó Chủ tịch đề cử.

4. Các quyết định của tòa trọng tài phải được thực hiện đầy đủ và có giá trị chung thẩm.

Điều 14
Hiệu lực thi hành và sửa đổi Hiệp định

1. Các điều khoản của Hiệp định này sẽ có hiệu lực kể từ ngày ký.

2. Hiệp định này sẽ còn hiệu lực chừng nào Văn phòng còn được duy trì tại nước Cộng hòa xã hội chủ nghĩa Việt Nam.

3. Các nghĩa vụ đã được Chính phủ chấp nhận trong Hiệp định này sẽ tiếp tục được thực hiện sau khi Hiệp định này chấm dứt hiệu lực trong khoảng thời gian cần thiết nhằm cho phép việc rút có trật tự các tài sản, các quỹ, và trang thiết bị của Quỹ và các quan chức IFAD cũng như các nhân viên khác đang thực thi công vụ với tư cách đại diện cho Quỹ.

4. Thỏa thuận này chỉ có thể được sửa đổi bổ sung theo thỏa thuận bằng văn bản của hai bên.

5. Hiệp định này được làm bằng tiếng Việt và tiếng Anh; các văn bản có giá trị như nhau. Trong trường hợp có sự giải thích khác nhau, văn bản tiếng Anh sẽ được dùng làm cơ sở.

Để làm bằng, các đại diện được sự ủy quyền hợp thức của Chính phủ và Quỹ, thay mặt cho hai bên ký Hiệp định này tại Hà Nội, ngày 16 tháng 01 năm 2008, làm bốn văn bản, mỗi ngôn ngữ hai văn bản.

ĐẠI DIỆN CHÍNH PHỦ
NƯỚC CỘNG HÒA XÃ HỘI CHỦ NGHĨA
VIỆT NAM

Phạm Bình Minh
Thứ trưởng thường trực Bộ Ngoại giao

ĐẠI DIỆN QUỸ QUỐC TẾ
VỀ PHÁT TRIỂN NÔNG NGHIỆP

Len-na Ba-giờ
Chủ tịch

ACCORD ENTRE LE GOUVERNEMENT DE LA RÉPUBLIQUE SOCIALISTE DU VIET NAM ET LE FONDS INTERNATIONAL DE DÉVELOPPEMENT AGRICOLE CONCERNANT LE BUREAU DE PAYS DU FONDS

Attendu que le Fonds international de développement agricole souhaite établir un bureau de pays au Viet Nam afin d'appuyer ses opérations, y compris la supervision des projets, de renforcer sa coopération et ses relations, de se rapprocher de ses partenaires et de ses programmes et de gérer les connaissances, et que le Gouvernement de la République socialiste du Viet Nam accepte d'autoriser l'établissement d'un tel bureau,

Le Gouvernement de la République socialiste du Viet Nam et le Fonds international de développement agricole (FIDA) conviennent de ce qui suit :

Article premier. Définitions

Aux fins du présent Accord :

a) Le terme « Gouvernement » désigne le Gouvernement de la République socialiste du Viet Nam;

b) Les termes « Fonds » ou « FIDA » désignent le Fonds international de développement agricole;

c) Le terme « Bureau » désigne le bureau de pays du Fonds international de développement agricole situé dans la République socialiste du Viet Nam;

d) L'expression « Fonctionnaires du FIDA » désigne le représentant du FIDA dans le pays et tous les autres fonctionnaires déterminés par le FIDA conformément à l'article VI, section 18 de la Convention sur les privilèges et immunités des institutions spécialisées.

Article 2. Personnalité juridique du Fonds

1. Le Gouvernement reconnaît la personnalité juridique du Fonds et en particulier sa capacité :

a) De contracter;

b) D'acquérir et de vendre des biens meubles et immeubles conformément à la législation du Viet Nam; et

c) D'ester en justice.

2. Le Gouvernement permet au Fonds de louer des locaux qui serviront de siège à son Bureau.

3. Le Bureau est autorisé à afficher l'emblème du Fonds sur ses locaux et ses véhicules.

Article 3. Inviolabilité du Bureau

1. Les biens et les avoirs du Bureau, en quelque endroit qu'ils se trouvent et quel qu'en soit le détenteur, sont exempts de toute perquisition, réquisition, confiscation, expropriation ou de toute autre forme de contrainte exécutive, administrative, judiciaire ou législative.

2. Les archives du Bureau et, d'une manière générale, tous les documents lui appartenant ou en sa possession, sont inviolables, où qu'ils se trouvent.

3. Le Bureau, ses biens et ses avoirs, en quelque endroit qu'ils se trouvent et quel qu'en soit le détenteur, jouissent de l'immunité à l'égard de toute forme d'action judiciaire, à moins que, dans un cas particulier, le Fonds n'y ait renoncé expressément. La levée de l'immunité ne s'étend à aucune mesure d'exécution.

4. Le Bureau ne permet pas que ses locaux servent de refuge à toute personne recherchée pour une infraction pénale ou contre laquelle un mandat a été délivré, une condamnation prononcée ou un arrêté d'expulsion pris par les autorités compétentes de la République socialiste du Viet Nam.

5. Les autorités, les fonctionnaires et les agents de la République socialiste du Viet Nam ne peuvent pénétrer dans le Bureau dans le cadre de leurs fonctions officielles qu'à la demande ou avec l'autorisation du Bureau, accordée par le représentant dans le pays ou par son délégué. En cas de force majeure, d'incendie ou de toute autre catastrophe exigeant des mesures urgentes de protection, le consentement du représentant dans le pays ou de son délégué est présumé avoir été donné. Toutefois, à la demande du représentant dans le pays, toute personne ayant pénétré dans le Bureau sur la base d'une telle présomption doit le quitter immédiatement.

6. Dans la mesure du possible, les autorités compétentes de la République socialiste du Viet Nam prennent toutes les mesures nécessaires pour protéger le Bureau contre toute intrusion ou tout dommage, afin d'en assurer la tranquillité et d'en préserver la dignité.

7. Les résidences des fonctionnaires du FIDA qui ne sont ni ressortissants ni résidents permanents de la République socialiste du Viet Nam bénéficient de la même inviolabilité et de la même protection que celle accordée au Bureau.

Article 4. Services publics

1. Le Gouvernement veille à ce que le Bureau dispose des services publics nécessaires dans des conditions d'équité. Les coûts de ces services sont à la charge du Bureau.

2. En cas d'interruption ou de menace d'interruption de l'un de ces services, les autorités compétentes considèrent que les besoins du Bureau pour ces services sont aussi importants que ceux des services publics de l'État et prennent par conséquent les mesures nécessaires pour veiller à ce que les activités du Bureau ne soient pas affectées par une telle situation.

Article 5. Communications

Aucune censure n'est appliquée aux courriers officiels et aux autres communications officielles du Bureau. Le Bureau a le droit d'employer des codes ainsi que d'expédier et de recevoir sa correspondance par courrier ou par valises scellées, qui bénéficient des mêmes immunités et privilèges que les courriers et les valises diplomatiques.

Article 6. Exonération fiscale

Le Bureau, ses avoirs, ses revenus et autres biens sont exonérés :

a) De tout impôt direct et indirect, étant entendu toutefois qu'aucune exonération ne sera demandée à l'égard des taxes qui ne correspondent en réalité qu'à la simple rémunération de services d'utilité publique;

b) De droits de douane ou d'autres taxes et de toutes les interdictions ou restrictions d'importation et d'exportation à l'égard des articles importés ou exportés par le Bureau destinés à un usage officiel dans le cadre de ses activités. Toutefois, il est entendu que les articles importés bénéficiant d'une telle exonération ne seront pas revendus dans la République socialiste du Viet Nam, sauf si les conditions de cette vente sont convenues avec le Gouvernement; et

c) De droits de douane ou d'autres taxes et de toutes interdictions ou restrictions relatifs à l'importation et l'exportation de ses publications.

Article 7. Facilités financières

1. Dans le cadre de ses activités officielles en vertu de la législation du Viet Nam, le Bureau peut librement :

a) Acquérir, détenir et utiliser des devises et des fonds ainsi que gérer des comptes en dong ou en toute autre monnaie et convertir toute devise qu'elle détient en une autre monnaie;

b) Transférer des dong sur le territoire de la République socialiste du Viet Nam et transférer d'autres devises vers ou depuis la République socialiste du Viet Nam.

2. Le Bureau jouit, en matière de change, des mêmes facilités que celles accordées à d'autres organisations internationales représentées dans la République socialiste du Viet Nam.

Article 8. Sécurité sociale

Compte tenu du fait que les fonctionnaires du FIDA sont couverts par le régime de sécurité sociale du Fonds, le Bureau n'est tenu de contribuer à aucun régime de sécurité sociale dans la République socialiste du Viet Nam et le Gouvernement ne peut exiger qu'un membre du personnel du Bureau s'affilie à ce régime.

Article 9. Entrée, voyage et séjour

1. Le Gouvernement reconnaît et accepte le laissez-passer délivré par l'Organisation des Nations Unies aux fonctionnaires du FIDA comme un titre de voyage valable.

2. Le cas échéant, les demandes de visas émanant de fonctionnaires du FIDA titulaires d'un laissez-passer de l'Organisation des Nations Unies, accompagnées d'un certificat attestant que le voyage est en rapport avec les activités du FIDA, doivent être traitées le plus rapidement possible. En outre, ces personnes bénéficient de facilités pour les voyages urgents.

3. Des facilités analogues à celles prévues au paragraphe 2 sont accordées aux experts et autres personnes qui, bien que n'étant pas titulaires d'un laissez-passer de l'Organisation des Nations Unies, détiennent un certificat attestant qu'ils voyagent pour le compte du FIDA.

4.   Le Gouvernement ne fait en aucun cas obstacle à l'entrée dans la République socialiste du Viet Nam ou au départ de celle-ci, lors de déplacements à destination ou en provenance du Bureau, de personnes exerçant des fonctions officielles au Bureau ou invitées par ce dernier.

5.   Le Gouvernement s'engage à faciliter l'entrée et le séjour des personnes ci-après et de leurs personnes à charge dans la République socialiste du Viet Nam pendant toute la durée de leurs fonctions ou missions auprès du Bureau :

a)   Le représentant dans le pays et d'autres fonctionnaires du FIDA;

b)   Toute autre personne invitée par le Bureau.

6.   Sans préjudice des immunités spécifiques dont elles peuvent bénéficier, les personnes visées au paragraphe 5 ci-dessus ne peuvent, pendant toute la durée de leurs fonctions ou missions, être contraintes par les autorités de la République socialiste du Viet Nam à quitter le territoire de la République socialiste du Viet Nam que dans le cas où il est établi, conformément aux dispositions du paragraphe 6 de l'article 12 ci-après, qu'elles ont abusé des privilèges qui leur sont accordés en exerçant une activité sans rapport avec leurs fonctions ou missions officielles.

Article 10. Cartes d'identité

1.   Le représentant dans le pays communique au Gouvernement une liste des fonctionnaires du FIDA (y compris les conjoints et autres personnes à charge) et l'informe de tout changement apporté à cette liste.

2.   Dès qu'il est avisé de la nomination des fonctionnaires, le Gouvernement délivre à toutes les personnes visées au paragraphe 1 une carte portant la photographie de son titulaire, conformément aux procédures appliquées au personnel des bureaux de représentation des organisations internationales et diplomatiques au Viet Nam.

Article 11. Privilèges et immunités accordés aux fonctionnaires du FIDA

1.   Les fonctionnaires du FIDA bénéficient des privilèges et immunités ci-après dans la République socialiste du Viet Nam :

a)   L'immunité de juridiction, même après qu'ils ont cessé d'exercer leurs fonctions, pour les actes, y compris les paroles ou les écrits, accomplis par eux dans l'exercice de leurs fonctions;

b)   L'exonération de l'impôt sur les traitements et émoluments perçus dans le cadre de leurs fonctions auprès du Bureau et pour les fonctionnaires du FIDA qui ne sont ni ressortissants ni résidents permanents du Viet Nam, ainsi que sur d'autres revenus provenant de sources extérieures à la République socialiste du Viet Nam;

c)   L'exemption, pour eux, leur conjoint et autres personnes à charge, des restrictions en matière d'immigration et des formalités d'enregistrement des étrangers;

d)   L'exemption, pour eux, leur conjoint et autres personnes à charge, des obligations de service national et de tout autre service obligatoire;

e)   L'exonération des droits d'importation et autres prélèvements sur leur mobilier et effets personnels importés, et d'importation ou d'achat temporaire d'un véhicule conformément aux règles et procédures locales applicables au personnel des organisations internationales et diplomatiques;

f) En cas de crise internationale, les mêmes facilités de rapatriement, pour eux, leur conjoint et autres personnes à charge que celles des membres des missions diplomatiques accréditées auprès du Gouvernement;

g) Les mêmes facilités en ce qui concerne le change que celles accordées aux fonctionnaires de missions diplomatiques de rang comparable accréditées auprès du Gouvernement.

2. Pendant toute la durée de ses fonctions, le représentant dans le pays bénéficie des privilèges et immunités accordés aux chefs de missions diplomatiques. Les autres fonctionnaires de rang supérieur du Bureau désignés de temps à autre par le représentant dans le pays, sur la base des postes de responsabilité qu'ils occupent, bénéficient des privilèges accordés aux agents diplomatiques.

3. Les fonctionnaires du FIDA ressortissants vietnamiens jouissent des privilèges et immunités analogues à ceux dont jouissent les agents nationaux des autres organismes des Nations Unies conformément aux accords signés entre le Viet Nam et ces organismes, y compris, mais sans s'y limiter, l'immunité de juridiction en lien avec des actes accomplis dans l'exercice de leurs fonctions. Les ressortissants et les résidents permanents de la République socialiste du Viet Nam employés par le Bureau ne jouissent pas des privilèges et immunités mentionnés dans le présent article.

Article 12. Dispositions générales

1. Le Gouvernement met tout en œuvre pour que le Bureau et les fonctionnaires du FIDA jouissent d'un traitement qui ne soit pas moins favorable que celui accordé aux autres organisations intergouvernementales, internationales ou régionales représentées dans la République socialiste du Viet Nam.

2. Les privilèges et immunités prévus dans le présent Accord n'ont pas pour objet d'assurer un avantage personnel à leurs bénéficiaires; ils ont pour but exclusif d'assurer au Bureau la possibilité de fonctionner librement en toutes circonstances et de préserver la totale indépendance des personnes auxquelles ces privilèges et immunités sont accordés.

3. Sans préjudice des privilèges et immunités accordés en vertu du présent Accord, le Bureau et toutes les personnes jouissant de ces privilèges et immunités sont tenus de respecter les lois et règlements de la République socialiste du Viet Nam. Ils sont également tenus de s'abstenir de s'ingérer dans les affaires internes de la République socialiste du Viet Nam.

4. Le Président du Fonds a le droit et le devoir de lever l'immunité de tout fonctionnaire lorsqu'il estime que cette immunité peut entraver le cours de la justice et qu'elle peut être levée sans porter préjudice aux intérêts du Bureau.

5. Le représentant dans le pays prend toutes les mesures nécessaires pour prévenir tout abus des privilèges et immunités accordés en vertu du présent Accord; à cette fin, il édicte les règlements applicables aux fonctionnaires du FIDA et aux autres personnes concernées qui sont jugés nécessaires et appropriés.

6. Si le Gouvernement estime qu'une utilisation abusive a été faite de l'un des privilèges ou immunités accordés en vertu du présent Accord, des consultations ont lieu à sa demande entre le représentant dans le pays et les autorités compétentes en vue de déterminer l'existence d'une telle utilisation abusive. Si l'issue de telles consultations ne satisfait pas tant le Gouvernement que le représentant dans le pays, la question est réglée conformément à la procédure décrite à l'article 13 du présent Accord.

7. Aucune disposition du présent Accord ne peut être interprétée comme limitant le droit du Gouvernement de prendre les mesures nécessaires à la sauvegarde de la sécurité de la République socialiste du Viet Nam.

8. Si le Gouvernement estime nécessaire d'appliquer le paragraphe 7 du présent article, il entre en contact avec le représentant dans le pays dès que les circonstances le permettent, afin de déterminer d'un commun accord les mesures nécessaires pour protéger les intérêts du Fonds.

9. Les dispositions du présent Accord s'appliquent à toutes les personnes couvertes par l'Accord, que le Gouvernement entretienne ou non des relations diplomatiques avec l'État dont ces personnes sont ressortissantes ou que cet État accorde ou non des privilèges et immunités analogues aux fonctionnaires diplomatiques et aux ressortissants de la République socialiste du Viet Nam.

10. Chaque fois que le présent Accord impose des obligations aux autorités compétentes, c'est au Gouvernement qu'il appartient, en dernier ressort, de s'assurer de la satisfaction de ces obligations.

Article 13. Interprétation et règlement des différends

1. Le présent Accord est interprété conformément aux règles coutumières d'interprétation des traités, notamment à la lumière de son principal objectif qui est de permettre au Bureau de mener ses activités de manière pleine et efficace.

2. Tout différend entre le Gouvernement et le Bureau au sujet de l'interprétation ou de l'application du présent Accord ou de tout arrangement complémentaire, s'il n'a pas été réglé par voie de négociation, sauf si les Parties en décident autrement, est soumis à la décision définitive d'un tribunal composé de trois arbitres dont l'un est désigné par le Gouvernement, un autre par le Président du Fonds et le troisième, qui préside le tribunal, est choisi d'un commun accord par les deux autres arbitres.

3. Si les deux premiers arbitres ne parviennent pas à s'entendre sur le choix du troisième arbitre dans les six mois qui suivent leur nomination, le troisième arbitre est désigné par le Président de la Cour internationale de Justice, à moins qu'il ne soit un ressortissant de la République socialiste du Viet Nam, auquel cas le troisième arbitre est désigné par le Vice-président.

4. Les décisions du tribunal arbitral ont force obligatoire et ne peuvent faire l'objet d'un appel.

Article 14. Entrée en vigueur et révision

1. Les dispositions du présent Accord entrent en vigueur à la date de sa signature par les deux Parties.

2. Le présent Accord reste en vigueur tant que le Bureau demeure établi dans la République socialiste du Viet Nam.

3. Les obligations contractées par le Gouvernement en vertu du présent Accord ne survivent après son expiration qu'au terme de la période nécessaire pour permettre un retrait ordonné des biens, des fonds et des avoirs du Fonds et des fonctionnaires et autres personnes qui assurent des services au nom du Fonds.

4. Le présent Accord ne peut être modifié que par accord mutuel écrit entre les Parties.

5. Le présent Accord est établi en langues anglaise et vietnamienne, les deux textes faisant également foi. En cas de divergence d'interprétation entre les deux versions, le texte anglais prévaut.

EN FOI DE QUOI, les soussignés, représentants dûment autorisés du Gouvernement et du Fonds respectivement, ont signé, au nom des deux Parties, le présent Accord à Hanoï le 16 janvier 2008, en quatre exemplaires, deux dans chaque langue.

Pour le Gouvernement de la République socialiste du Viet Nam :

PHAM BINH MINH
Vice-ministre permanent aux affaires étrangères

Pour le Fonds international de développement agricole :

LENNART BÅGE
Président

No. 52072

United Nations
and
Mauritius

Exchange of letters constituting an Agreement between the United Nations and the Government of the Republic of Mauritius on the hosting of the "Regional workshop on fossil fuel and renewable energy (FFRE)" to be held in Port Louis, Mauritius, from 12 to 16 May 2014. New York, 25 February 2014 and 13 May 2014

Entry into force: *13 May 2014 and with retroactive effect from 12 May 2014, in accordance with the provisions of the said letters*

Authentic text: *English*

Registration with the Secretariat of the United Nations: *ex officio, 1 August 2014*

Not published in print, in accordance with article 12(2) of the General Assembly regulations to give effect to Article 102 of the Charter of the United Nations, as amended.

Organisation des Nations Unies
et
Maurice

Échange de lettres constituant un accord entre l'Organisation des Nations Unies et le Gouvernement de la République de Maurice relatif à l'organisation de « l'Atelier régional sur les combustibles fossiles et les énergies renouvelables » qui se tiendra à Port-Louis, Maurice, du 12 au 16 mai 2014. New York, 25 février 2014 et 13 mai 2014

Entrée en vigueur : *13 mai 2014 et avec effet rétroactif à compter du 12 mai 2014, conformément aux dispositions desdites lettres*

Texte authentique : *anglais*

Enregistrement auprès du Secrétariat de l'Organisation des Nations Unies : *d'office, 1er août 2014*

Non disponible en version imprimée, conformément au paragraphe 2 de l'article 12 du règlement de l'Assemblée générale destiné à mettre en application l'Article 102 de la Charte des Nations Unies, tel qu'amendé.

No. 52073

International Development Association
and
United Republic of Tanzania

Financing Agreement (Eleventh Poverty Reduction Support Development Policy Financing) between the United Republic of Tanzania and the International Development Association (with schedules, appendix and International Development Association General Conditions for Credits and Grants, dated 31 July 2010). Washington, 10 April 2014

Entry into force: *9 June 2014 by notification*

Authentic text: *English*

Registration with the Secretariat of the United Nations: *International Development Association, 26 August 2014*

Not published in print, in accordance with article 12(2) of the General Assembly regulations to give effect to Article 102 of the Charter of the United Nations, as amended.

Association internationale de développement
et
République-Unie de Tanzanie

Accord de financement (Onzième financement pour la politique de développement à l'appui de la réduction de la pauvreté) entre la République-Unie de Tanzanie et l'Association internationale de développement (avec annexes, appendice et Conditions générales applicables aux crédits et aux dons de l'Association internationale de développement, en date du 31 juillet 2010). Washington, 10 avril 2014

Entrée en vigueur : *9 juin 2014 par notification*

Texte authentique : *anglais*

Enregistrement auprès du Secrétariat de l'Organisation des Nations Unies : *Association internationale de développement, 26 août 2014*

Non disponible en version imprimée, conformément au paragraphe 2 de l'article 12 du règlement de l'Assemblée générale destiné à mettre en application l'Article 102 de la Charte des Nations Unies, tel qu'amendé.

No. 52074

International Development Association
and
United Republic of Tanzania

Financing Agreement (Second Power and Gas Sector Development Policy Financing) between the United Republic of Tanzania and the International Development Association (with schedules, appendix and International Development Association General Conditions for Credits and Grants, dated 31 July 2010). Washington, 10 April 2014

Entry into force: *9 June 2014 by notification*

Authentic text: *English*

Registration with the Secretariat of the United Nations: *International Development Association, 26 August 2014*

Not published in print, in accordance with article 12(2) of the General Assembly regulations to give effect to Article 102 of the Charter of the United Nations, as amended.

Association internationale de développement
et
République-Unie de Tanzanie

Accord de financement (Deuxième Financement de la politique de développement de l'énergie et du secteur à gaz) entre la République-Unie de Tanzanie et l'Association internationale de développement (avec annexes, appendice et Conditions générales applicables aux crédits et aux dons de l'Association internationale de développement, en date du 31 juillet 2010). Washington, 10 avril 2014

Entrée en vigueur : *9 juin 2014 par notification*

Texte authentique : *anglais*

Enregistrement auprès du Secrétariat de l'Organisation des Nations Unies : *Association internationale de développement, 26 août 2014*

Non disponible en version imprimée, conformément au paragraphe 2 de l'article 12 du règlement de l'Assemblée générale destiné à mettre en application l'Article 102 de la Charte des Nations Unies, tel qu'amendé.

No. 52075

International Development Association
and
Lesotho

Financing Agreement (Public Financial Management Reform Support Project) between the Kingdom of Lesotho and the International Development Association (with schedules, appendix and International Development Association General Conditions for Credits and Grants, dated 31 July 2010). Maseru, 24 February 2014

Entry into force: *25 July 2014 by notification*

Authentic text: *English*

Registration with the Secretariat of the United Nations: *International Development Association, 26 August 2014*

Not published in print, in accordance with article 12(2) of the General Assembly regulations to give effect to Article 102 of the Charter of the United Nations, as amended.

Association internationale de développement
et
Lesotho

Accord de financement (Projet d'appui à la réforme de la gestion des finances publiques) entre le Royaume du Lesotho et l'Association internationale de développement (avec annexes, appendice et Conditions générales applicables aux crédits et aux dons de l'Association internationale de développement, en date du 31 juillet 2010). Maseru, 24 février 2014

Entrée en vigueur : *25 juillet 2014 par notification*

Texte authentique : *anglais*

Enregistrement auprès du Secrétariat de l'Organisation des Nations Unies : *Association internationale de développement, 26 août 2014*

Non disponible en version imprimée, conformément au paragraphe 2 de l'article 12 du règlement de l'Assemblée générale destiné à mettre en application l'Article 102 de la Charte des Nations Unies, tel qu'amendé.

No. 52076

International Bank for Reconstruction and Development
and
The former Yugoslav Republic of Macedonia

Loan Agreement (Second Programmatic Competitiveness Development Policy Loan) between The former Yugoslav Republic of Macedonia (the Borrower) and the International Bank for Reconstruction and Development (the Bank) (with schedules, appendix and International Bank for Reconstruction and Development General Conditions for Loans, dated 12 March 2012). Skopje, 23 July 2014

Entry into force: *30 July 2014 by notification*

Authentic text: *English*

Registration with the Secretariat of the United Nations: *International Bank for Reconstruction and Development, 26 August 2014*

Not published in print, in accordance with article 12(2) of the General Assembly regulations to give effect to Article 102 of the Charter of the United Nations, as amended.

Banque internationale pour la reconstruction et le développement
et
Ex-République yougoslave de Macédoine

Accord de prêt (Deuxième prêt programmatique des politiques de développement sur la compétitivité) entre l'ex-République yougoslave de Macédoine (l'Emprunteur) et la Banque internationale pour la reconstruction et le développement (la Banque) (avec annexes, appendice et Conditions générales applicables aux prêts de la Banque internationale pour la reconstruction et le développement, en date du 12 mars 2012). Skopje, 23 juillet 2014

Entrée en vigueur : *30 juillet 2014 par notification*

Texte authentique : *anglais*

Enregistrement auprès du Secrétariat de l'Organisation des Nations Unies : *Banque internationale pour la reconstruction et le développement, 26 août 2014*

Non disponible en version imprimée, conformément au paragraphe 2 de l'article 12 du règlement de l'Assemblée générale destiné à mettre en application l'Article 102 de la Charte des Nations Unies, tel qu'amendé.

No. 52077

_____

International Development Association
and
Senegal

Financing Agreement (Casamance Development Pole Project) between the Republic of Senegal and the International Development Association (with schedules, appendix and International Development Association General Conditions for Credits and Grants, dated 31 July 2010). Dakar, 22 November 2013

Entry into force: *20 May 2014 by notification*

Authentic text: *English*

Registration with the Secretariat of the United Nations: *International Development Association, 26 August 2014*

Not published in print, in accordance with article 12(2) of the General Assembly regulations to give effect to Article 102 of the Charter of the United Nations, as amended.

_____

Association internationale de développement
et
Sénégal

Accord de financement (Projet du Pôle de développement de la Casamance) entre la République du Sénégal et l'Association internationale de développement (avec annexes, appendice et Conditions générales applicables aux crédits et aux dons de l'Association internationale de développement, en date du 31 juillet 2010). Dakar, 22 novembre 2013

Entrée en vigueur : *20 mai 2014 par notification*

Texte authentique : *anglais*

Enregistrement auprès du Secrétariat de l'Organisation des Nations Unies : *Association internationale de développement, 26 août 2014*

Non disponible en version imprimée, conformément au paragraphe 2 de l'article 12 du règlement de l'Assemblée générale destiné à mettre en application l'Article 102 de la Charte des Nations Unies, tel qu'amendé.

No. 52078

International Development Association
and
Kyrgyzstan

Financing Agreement (Second Development Policy Operation) between the Kyrgyz Republic and the International Development Association (with schedules, appendix and International Development Association General Conditions for Credits and Grants, dated 31 July 2010). Bishkek, 16 June 2014

Entry into force: *11 July 2014 by notification*

Authentic text: *English*

Registration with the Secretariat of the United Nations: *International Development Association, 26 August 2014*

Not published in print, in accordance with article 12(2) of the General Assembly regulations to give effect to Article 102 of the Charter of the United Nations, as amended.

Association internationale de développement
et
Kirghizistan

Accord de financement (Deuxième opération de politique de développement) entre la République kirghize et l'Association internationale de développement (avec annexes, appendice et Conditions générales applicables aux crédits et aux dons de l'Association internationale de développement, en date du 31 juillet 2010). Bichkek, 16 juin 2014

Entrée en vigueur : *11 juillet 2014 par notification*

Texte authentique : *anglais*

Enregistrement auprès du Secrétariat de l'Organisation des Nations Unies : *Association internationale de développement, 26 août 2014*

Non disponible en version imprimée, conformément au paragraphe 2 de l'article 12 du règlement de l'Assemblée générale destiné à mettre en application l'Article 102 de la Charte des Nations Unies, tel qu'amendé.

No. 52079

———

Turkey
and
Georgia

Memorandum of Understanding between the Government of the Republic of Turkey and the Government of Georgia on cooperation in combating crime. Tbilisi, 22 February 2012

Entry into force: *1 September 2012, in accordance with article 12*

Authentic texts: *English, Georgian and Turkish*

Registration with the Secretariat of the United Nations: *Turkey, 14 August 2014*

———

Turquie
et
Géorgie

Mémorandum d'accord entre le Gouvernement de la République turque et le Gouvernement de la Géorgie relatif à la coopération en matière de lutte contre la criminalité. Tbilissi, 22 février 2012

Entrée en vigueur : *1er septembre 2012, conformément à l'article 12*

Textes authentiques : *anglais, géorgien et turc*

Enregistrement auprès du Secrétariat de l'Organisation des Nations Unies : *Turquie, 14 août 2014*

[ENGLISH TEXT – TEXTE ANGLAIS]

**Memorandum of Understanding
Between
The Government of the Republic of Turkey
And
The Government of Georgia
On Cooperation in Combating Crime**

The Government of the Republic of Turkey and the Government of Georgia, hereinafter referred to as the "Parties",

Desiring to develop and strengthen the existing friendship and partnership relations between their States and particularly to take into consideration common will to strengthen the police cooperation between them,

Concerned by the increasing scale and trends of the crime especially the forms of organized crime,

Being aware that any form of crime endangers international peace, law and order, rule of law, security, stability and territorial integrity of their States, impedes development of economy, establishment of investment environment, democratic values and justice,

Stemming from the desire to provide reliable protection of life, rights and legal interests of human, interests of the society and the State from crime,

Recognizing the importance of international cooperation in the fight against crime,

Based on the provisions of the "Agreement between the Government of the Republic of Turkey and the Government of the Republic of Georgia on cooperation in the field of security", signed at Ankara on 13 January 1994; the "Agreement between the Republic of Turkey, Georgia and the Republic of Azerbaijan, on cooperation in the fight against terrorism, organized crime and other serious crimes", signed at Trabzon on 30 April 2002; and the "Protocol between the Republic of Turkey and Georgia on the implementation of the Article 9 to the Agreement between the Republic of Turkey, Georgia and the Republic of Azerbaijan on cooperation in the fight against terrorism, organized crime and other serious crimes", signed at Ankara on 10 March 2005,

Considering the basic principles of international law and the international conventions to which their States are parties and which concern the scope of the present MoU,

Agreed as follows:

**Article 1
Fields and Forms of Cooperation**

1. The Parties shall cooperate and provide mutual assistance in the following fields:

a) combating international terrorism;

b) combating organized crime;

c) combating illicit trafficking in narcotic drugs, psychotropic substances and their precursors;

d) combating migrant smuggling, human trafficking and illegal migration;

e) combating illegal acts related to arms, ammunition, explosives, nuclear, chemical and biological materials;

f) combating illegal crossing of state border and falsification of travel documents;

g) combating cybercrime;

h) combating other crimes falling within the competence of the Parties.

2. The cooperation between the two Parties shall be realized in following forms:

a) provision of crime-related information and personal data on persons committing crime;

b) assistance in searching of persons accused or convicted in commission of crime;

c) exchange of legal information, documentation, publications and results of scientific research;

d) organization of trainings, seminars and workshops and cooperation in the field of improving the qualification of personnel of the Parties;

e) provision of police equipment.

3. Parties will cooperate and share criminal intelligence information between their competent authorities on counter-terrorism so as to trail and dismantle terrorist acts and the members of the terrorist groups.

4. The Parties shall realize the cooperation under the present MoU in accordance with the national legislation in force in their States and the norms of international law.

Article 2
Provision of Information on Detained Persons

Each Party shall provide the other Party with details on the citizens of the State of the other Party who may be under detention in the respective country, in accordance with the national legislation in force in its State and international norms on protection of personal data.

Article 3
Cooperation in Searching of Persons

The Parties, in accordance with the national legislation in force in their States, shall conduct all necessary measures in order to find, detain, arrest or provide information on wanted persons.

Article 4
Holding of Expert Meetings

The Parties shall hold expert meetings within the framework of their competence, whenever they both agree that there is a need to face urgent or special matters relating to the fields of cooperation.

Article 5
Realization of Cooperation

1. The cooperation within the frames of the present MoU is realized in English language, or in the state language of either Parties.

2. Requests on provision of information or rendering assistance within the frames of the present MoU are made by the Parties in written form. In urgent cases, request may be made verbally, which shall be confirmed in written form within reasonable time.

Article 6
Non-fulfillment of Request

Request may be wholly of partially refused, if the receiving Party considers, that it may threaten sovereignty, security, national interests of its State, public order, human health, or other important interests of its State or if it might contradict the national legislation in force in its State.

Article 7
Limits on the Use of Information and Document

1. The Parties agree that the information and personal data transmitted under the present MoU shall be used exclusively for the purposes envisaged by it, in conformity with the provisions of the international conventions on human rights and shall be protected in accordance with the national legislation in force in their States.

2. The Parties shall aim to conclude an agreement on cooperation in the exchange and mutual protection of classified information.

3. Under the present MoU any information and documents will not be disclosed to any third Parties without the prior consent of the competent authority that provided them.

Article 8
Competent Authorities for the Implementation of the present MoU

1. The competent Authorities for the implementation of the present MoU shall be:

- for the Turkish Party: the Ministry of the Interior of the Republic of Turkey;
- for the Georgian Party: the Ministry of Internal Affairs of Georgia.

2. For the purposes of effective realization of the present MOU, the Competent Authorities of the Parties shall provide each other their contact information and inform each other any changes to their names, competences and contact information.

Article 9
Relation to Other International Agreements

The provisions of the present MoU do not affect the rights and obligations of the Parties arising from other bilateral or multilateral international agreements to which their States are parties.

Article 10
Settlement of Disputes

Disputes arising during implementation and interpretation of the present MoU shall be settled through consultations between the Parties or negotiations via diplomatic channels.

Article 11
Amendments and Supplements

The present MoU may be amended and supplemented in written form upon a mutual consent of the Parties. Such amendments and supplements shall be drawn up as a Single Protocol and be the integral part of the present MoU. The Protocol shall enter into force in accordance with the procedure provided by the Paragraph 1 of the Article 12 of the present MoU.

Article 12
Final Provisions

1. The present MoU shall enter into force on the first day of the following month from the date of the receipt of the last written notification by which the Parties notify each other, through diplomatic channels, of the completion of their internal legal procedures required for the entry into force of the present MoU.

2. The present MoU shall be concluded for an indefinite period of time. Either Party may terminate the application of the present MoU by a written notification to the other Party communicated through diplomatic channels. The termination shall become effective 6 (six) months from the date of the receipt of the notification of termination.

Done in Tbilisi, on 22/02/2012, in two equally valid original copies, each in Turkish, Georgian and English languages. In case of divergence in the interpretation of the present MoU by the Parties, the English text shall prevail.

For the Government of the Republic of Turkey	**For the Government of Georgia**
İdris Naim ŞAHİN Minister of the Interior	**Ivane MERABISHVILI Minister of Internal Affairs**

[GEORGIAN TEXT – TEXTE GÉORGIEN]

ურთიერთგაკების მემორანდუმი
თურქეთის რესპუბლიკის მთავრობასა და საქართველოს მთავრობას
შორის დანაშაულთან ბრძოლაში თანამშრომლობის შესახებ

თურქეთის რესპუბლიკის მთავრობა და საქართველოს მთავრობა, შემდგომში წოდებულნი როგორც „მხარეები",

გამოთქვამენ რა ხვრეილს, განაეთიათარონ და გააძლიერონ თავიანთ ხახელმწიფოებს შორის არსებული მეგობრული და პარტნიორული ურთიერთობები და განსაკუთრებით, მხედველობაში მიიღონ მათ შორის პოლიციის სფეროში თანამშრომლობის გაძლიერების საერთო ნება,

გამოთქვამენ რა შეშფოთებას დანაშაული, განსაკუთრებით ორგანიზებული დანაშაულის ფორმების მზარდი მასშტაბისა და ტენდენციების გამო,

გაცნობიერებული აქეთ რა, რომ ნებისმიერი ფორმის დანაშაული საფრთხეს უქმნის საერთაშორისო მშვიდობას, მართლწესრიგს, კანონის უზენაესობას, უსაფრთხოებას, სტაბილურობას და თავიანთი სახელმწიფოების ტერიტორიულ მთლიანობას, ხელს უშლის ეკონომიკის განვითარებას, საინვესტიციო გარემოს შექმნას, დემოკრატიული ღირებულებებისა და კანონიერების დამკვიდრებას,

გამომდინარეობენ რა ხურვილიდან, უზრუნველყონ ადამიანის სიცოცხლის, უფლებებისა და ,კანონიერი ინტერესის, საზოგადოების და სახელმწიფოს ინტერესების სამე დაცვა დანაშაულისაგან,

აღიარებენ რა, დანაშაულის წინააღმდეგ ბრძოლაში საერთაშორისო თანამშრომლობის მნიშვნელობას,

ეყუდნებიან რა, ქ. ანკარაში 1994 წლის 13 იანვარს ხელმოწერილი ,თურქეთის რესპუბლიკის მთავრობასა და საქართველოს რესპუბლიკის მთავრობას შორის უსაფრთხოების დარგში თანამშრომლობის შესახებ" შეთანხმების, ქ. ტრაპიზონში 2002 წლის 30 აპრილს ხელმოწერილი ,თურქეთის რესპუბლიკას, საქართველოსა და აზერბაიჯანის რესპუბლიკას შორის ტერორიზმის, ორგანიზებული დანაშაულისა და სხვა მნიშვნელოვანი დანაშაულების წინააღმდეგ ბრძოლაში თანამშრომლობის შესახებ" შეთანხმების და ქ. ანკარაში 2005 წლის 10 მარტს ხელმოწერილი ,თურქეთის რესპუბლიკასა და საქართველოს შორის თურქეთის რესპუბლიკას, და აზერბაიჯანის რესპუბლიკას შორის ტერორიზმის, ორგანიზებული დანაშაულისა და სხვა მნიშვნელოვანი დანაშაულების წინააღმდეგ ბრძოლაში თანამშრომლობის შესახებ შეთანხმების მე-9 მუხლის შესრულების შესახებ" ოქმის დებულებებს,

ითვალისწინებენ რა, საერთაშორისო სამართლის ძირითად პრინციპებს და იმ საერთაშორისო კონვენციებს, რომელთა წევრებადაც არიან მათი სახელმწიფოები და რომლებიც ეხება წინამდებარე ურთიერთგაკების მემორანდუმის ხვერილს,

შეთანხმდნენ შემდეგ ზე:

მუხლი 1
თანამშრომლობის სფეროები და ფორმები

1. მხარეები თიანამშრომლოვებენ და დაეხმარებიან ერთმანეთს შემდეგ სფეროებში:

a) საერთაშორისო ტერორიზმთან ბრძოლა;

b) ორგანიზებულ დანაშაულთან ბრძოლა;

c) ნარკოტიკების, ფსიქოტროპული ნივთიერებებისა და მათი პრეკურსორების უკანონო ბრუნვასთან ბრძოლა;

d) საზღვარზე მიგრანტის უკანონო გადაყვანის, ადამიანებით ვაჭრობისა და უკანონო მიგრაციის წინააღმდეგ ბრძოლა;

e) იარაღთან, საბრძოლო მასალებთან, ფეთქებად ნივთიერებებთან, ბირთვულ, ქიმიურ და ბიოლოგიურ მასალებთან დაკავშირებული უკანონო ქმედებების წინააღმდეგ ბრძოლა;

f) სახელმწიფო საზღვრის უკანონო გადაკვეთასა და სამგზავრო დოკუმენტების გაყალბებასთან ბრძოლა;

g) კიბერდანაშაულის წინააღმდეგ ბრძოლა;

h) მხარეების კომპეტენციის სფეროში შემავალი სხვა დანაშაულების წინააღმდეგ ბრძოლა.

2. მხარეებს შორის თანამშრომლობა განხორციელდება შემდეგი ფორმებით:

a) დანაშაულთან დაკავშირებული ინფორმაციისა და დანაშაულის ჩამდენ პირთა პირადი მონაცემების მიწოდება;

b) დანაშაულის ჩადენაში ბრალდებული ან მსჯავრდებული პირების ძებნაში დახმარება;

c) საჭიროებისამებრ ინფორმაციის, დოკუმენტაციის, პუბლიკაციებისა და სამეცნიერო კვლევების მედეგების გაცვლა;

d) ტრენინგების, სემინარების და სამუშაო შეხვედრების ორგანიზება და თანამშრომლობა მხარეების პერსონალის კვალიფიკაციის ამაღლების სფეროში;

e) საპოლიციო აღჭურვილობის მიწოდება.

3. მხარეები ითანამშრომლებენ და თავიანთ კომპეტენტურ ორგანოებს შორის გაცვლიან ოპერატიულ-სამძებრო ინფორმაციას კონტრტერორიზმის შესახებ იმ მიზნით, რათა გამოავლინონ და აღკვეთონ ტერორისტული აქტები და ტერორისტული ჯგუფების წევრები.

4. მხარეები წინამდებარე ურთიერთგაცების მემორანდუმით გათვალისწინებულ თანამშრომლობას განახორციელებენ თავიანთ სახელმწიფოებში მოქმედი შიდასახელმწიფოებრივი კანონმდებლობისა და საერთაშორისო სამართლის ნორმების შესაბამისად.

მუხლი 2
დაკავებულ პირებზე ინფორმაციის მიწოდება

თითოეული მხარე მიაწვდის მეორე მხარეს დეტალებს მეორე მხარის სახელმწიფოს მოქალაქის შესახებ, რომელიც მესახელოა დაკავებული იმ ჯერ შესაბამის ქვეყანაში, პირადი მონაცემების დაცვის შესახებ თავის სახელმწიფოში

მოქმედ შიდასახელმწიფოებრივი კანონდებლობისა და საერთაშორისო სამართლის ნორმების შესაბამისად.

მუხლი 3
პირების ძებნაში თანამშრომლობა

მხარეები თავიანთ სახელმწიფოებში მოქმედი შიდასახელმწიფოებრივი კანონდებლობის შესაბამისად კათგარებენ გეელა აუცილებელ ღონისხიებას ძებნას დაქვემდებარებული პირების აღმოჩენის, დაკავების, დასამისრების ან მათ შესახებ ინფორმაციის მიწოდების მიზნით.

მუხლი 4
ექსპერტთა მსხვერების გაძართვა

მხარეები გაძართავენ ექსხერტების მსხვერებს, მათი კომპეტენციის ფარგლებში, როდესაც ორივე მხარე მეთანხმდება, რომ თანამშრომლობის სფერებში არსებობს გადაუდებელი და სპეციალური საჭიროების განხილეის საჭიროება.

მუხლი 5
თანამშრომლობის განხორციელება

1. წინამდებარე ურთიერთიკკების მემორანდის ფარგლებში თანამშრომლობა ხორციელდება ინგლისურ ენაზე, ან ერთ-ერთი მხარის სახელმწიფოს ენაზე.

2. მოთხოენები ინფორმაციის მიწოდებაზე ან დახმარების აღმჩენაზე წინამდებარე ურთიერთიკკების მემორანდის ფარგლებში იგზავნება მხარეების მიერ წერილობითი ფორმით. გადაუდებელ შემთხვევებში, დასამუშია მოთხოენის ზეპირი ფორმით წარდგენა, რომელიც გონივრულ ვადაში უნდა დადასტურდეს წერილობითი ფორმით.

მუხლი 6
მოთხოენის შეესრულებლობა

მოთხოენაზე შეიძლება ითქვას უარი მთლიანად ან ნაწილობრივ, თუ მოთხოენის მიმღები მხარე მიიჩნევს, რომ მან შესაძლებელია საფრთხის მუქყნას თაით სახელმწიფოს სუვერენიტეტს, უსაფრთხოებას, ჯოოებულ ინტერესებს, საზოგადოებრივ წესრიგს, მოხსელლიის ჯამარ თავლობას ან თავისი სახელმწიფოს სხვა არსებითლაგ ინტერესებს ან შესაძლებელია იგი ეწინააღმდეგებოდეს თავის სახელმწიფოში მოქმედ შიდასახელმწიფოებრივ კანონდებლობას.

მუხლი 7
შეზღუდვები ინფორმაციისა და დოკუმენტების გამოყენებაზე

1. მხარეები თანხმდებიან, რომ წინამდებარე ურთიერთგაკების მემორანდუმის ფარგლებში გადაცემული ინფორმაცია და პერსონალური მონაცემები გამოყენებული იქნება ადამიანის უფლებების შესახებ საერთაშორისო კონვენციების დებულებების მესაბამისად მხოლოდ იმ მიზნებით, რომლებსაც ის ითვალისწინებს და დაცული იქნება თავიანთ სახელმწიფოებში მოქმედი მიღახასხელმწიფოებრივი კანონმდებლობის შესაბამისად.

2. მხარეები მიზნად ისახავენ, დაღონ შეთანხმება საღგუშული ინფორმაციის გაცვლისა და ორმხრივად დაცული ხერხომში თანამშრომლობის შესახებ.

3. წინამღებარე ურთიერთგაკების მემორანდუმის ფარგლებში გადაცემული ნებისმიერი ინფორმაცია და დოკუმენტი არ უნდა გაგცეს არცერთ მესამე მხარეს მათი მიმწოდებელი კომპეტენტური ორგანოს წინასწარი თანხმობის გარეშე.

მუხლი 8
წინამღებარე ურთიერთგაკების მემორანდუმის შესრულებაზე კომპეტენტური ორგანოები

1. წინამდებარე ურთიერთოგაკების მემორანდუმის შესრულებაზე კომპეტენტური ორგანოები არიან:

* თურქეთის მხრიდან: თურქეთის რესპუბლიკის შინაგან საქმეთა სამინისტრო;
* საქართველოს მხრიდან: საქართველოს შინაგან საქმეთა სამინისტრო.

2. წინამდებარე ურთიერთგაკების მემორანდუმის ეფექტურად განხორციელების მიზნით მხარეების კომპეტენტური ორგანოები მაუწდას ერთმანეთს თავიანთ საკონტაქტო ინფორმაციას და აჯრთავ აცნობებენ ერთმანეთს თავიანთ დასახელებაში, კომპეტენციასა და საკონტაქტო ინფორმაციაში ნებისმიერი ცვლილების შეტანის შესახებ.

მუხლი 9
ურთიერთობა სხვა საერთაშორისო შეთანხმებებთან

წინამღებარე ურთიერთგაკების მემორანდუმის დებულებები ზეგავლენას არ ახდუს მხარედა უფლებებსა და გალღებულებებზე, რომლებიც გამომდინარეობენ იმ სხვა ორმხრივი ან მრავალმხრივი საერთაშორისი შეთანხმებებიდან, რომლთა მონაწილენიც მათი სახელმწიფოები არიან.

მუხლი 10
დავების გადაწყვეტა

წინამდებარე ურთიერთგაკების მემორანდუმის განხორციელებისა და განმარტების დროს წარმოშობილი დავები გადაწყდება მხარეებს შორის კონსულტაციების ან დიალოგმატური არხების-მოლაპარაკების გზით.

მუხლი 11
ცვლილებები და დამატებები

წინამდებარე ურთიერთგაგების მემორანდუმში წერილობითი ფორმით შეიძლება შეტანილ იქნეს ცვლილებები და დამატებები მხარეთა ურთიერთშეთანხმებით. ასეთი ცვლილებები და დამატებები გაფორმდება ცალკე ოქმის სახით და წინამდებარე ურთიერთგაგების მემორანდუმის განუყოფელი ნაწილი იქნება. აღნიშნული ოქმი ძალაში შევა წინამდებარე ურთიერთგაგების მემორანდუმის მე-12 მუხლის პირველი პუნქტით გათვალისწინებული პროცედურის შესაბამისად.

მუხლი 12
დასკვნითი დებულებები

1. წინამდებარე ურთიერთგაგების მემორანდუმი ძალაში შედის მხარეთა მიერ ამ ურთიერთგაგების მემორანდუმის ძალაში შესვლისთვის აუცილებელი შიდასახელმწიფოებრივი პროცედურების დასრულების შესახებ დიპლომატიური არხების მეშვეობით უკანასკნელი წერილობითი შეტყობინების მიღების დღიდან მომდევნო თვის პირველ დღეს.

2. წინამდებარე ურთიერთგაგების მემორანდუმი იდება განუსაზღვრელი ვადით. თითოეულ მხარეს შეუძლია წინამდებარე ურთიერთგაგების მემორანდუმის მოქმედების შეწყვეტა მეორე მხარისათვის დიპლომატიური არხებით გაგზავნილი წერილობითი შეტყობინების გზით. მოქმედების შეწყვეტა ძალაში შევა მოქმედების შეწყვეტის შესახებ შეტყობინების მიღების დღიდან 6 (ექვსი) თვის გასვლის შემდეგ.

შესრულებულია ქ. თბილისში 22/02/2012, თანაბარი ძალის მქონე ორ დედანად, თითოეული თურქულ, ქართულ და ინგლისურ ენებზე. მხარეთა მიერ წინამდებარე ურთიერთგაგების მემორანდუმის დებულებათა განმარტებისას უთანხმოების შემთხვევაში, უპირატესობა ენიჭება ტექსტს ინგლისურ ენაზე.

თურქეთის რესპუბლიკის მთავრობის   საქართველოს მთავრობის
სახელით   სახელით

იდრის ნაიმ შაჰინი   ივანე მერაბიშვილი
შინაგან საქმეთა მინისტრი   შინაგან საქმეთა მინისტრი

[Turkish text – Texte turc]

**Türkiye Cumhuriyeti Hükümeti
ile
Gürcistan Hükümeti
Arasında
Suçla Mücadelede İşbirliği Konulu
Mutabakat Zaptı**

Bundan böyle 'Taraflar' olarak anılacak olan Türkiye Cumhuriyeti Hükümeti ve Gürcistan Hükümeti,

Devletleri arasındaki mevcut dostluk ve ortaklık ilişkilerini geliştirmeyi ve güçlendirmeyi arzu ederek ve özellikle de aralarındaki polis işbirliğini güçlendirmeye yönelik ortak isteklerini göz önünde bulundurarak,

Özellikle organize suç türleri olmak üzere, suçların artmakta olan oran ve eğilimlerinden endişe duyarak,

Her türdeki suçların Devletlerindeki uluslararası barışı, kanun ve nizamı, hukukun üstünlüğünü, güvenliği, istikrarı ve toprak bütünlüğünü tehlikeye attığının ve ekonominin gelişimini, yatırım ortamının oluşturulmasını, demokratik değerleri ve adaleti sekteye uğrattığının farkında olarak,

İnsanların hayatlarının, haklarının ve yasal menfaatlerinin, toplum çıkarlarının ve Devletlerin, suçtan güvenilir bir şekilde korunmasını sağlamak isteğinden hareketle,

Suçla mücadelede uluslararası işbirliğinin önemini fark ederek,

Türkiye Cumhuriyeti Hükümeti ile Gürcistan Cumhuriyeti Hükümeti arasında 13 Ocak 1994 tarihinde Ankara'da imzalanan Güvenlik alanında işbirliği konulu Anlaşma; Türkiye Cumhuriyeti, Gürcistan ve Azerbaycan Cumhuriyeti arasında 30 Nisan 2002 tarihinde Trabzon'da imzalanan Terörizm, Organize Suçlar ve Diğer Ağır Suçlar ile Mücadelede İşbirliği konulu Anlaşma ve Türkiye Cumhuriyeti, Gürcistan ve Azerbaycan Cumhuriyeti arasında imzalanan Terörizm, Organize Suçlar ve diğer ağır suçlar ile mücadelede İşbirliği konulu Anlaşmanın 9. Maddesinin uygulanmasına yönelik olarak 10 Mart 2005 tarihinde Türkiye Cumhuriyeti ve Gürcistan arasında imzalanan Protokolün hükümlerine dayanarak,

Devletlerin Taraf oldukları ve işbu Mutabakat Zaptının kapsamı ile ilgili olan uluslararası hukuk ve uluslararası konvansiyonların temel ilkelerini göz önünde bulundurarak,

Aşağıda yer alan hususlarda anlaşmaya varmışlardır:

**Madde 1
İşbirliğinin Alanları ve Şekilleri**

1. Taraflar, aşağıdaki alanlarda işbirliğinde bulunacak ve karşılıklı yardım sağlayacaktır:

a) Uluslararası terörizmle mücadele;

b) Organize suçlarla mücadele;

c) Narkotik maddeler, psikotrop maddeler ve bunların ara kimyasallarının yasadışı ticareti ile mücadele;

d) Göçmen kaçakçılığı, insan ticareti ve yasadışı göç ile mücadele;

e) Silahlar, mühimmat, patlayıcılar, nükleer, kimyasal ve biyolojik materyallere ilişkin yasadışı eylemler ile mücadele,

f) Sınırların yasadışı geçişi ve seyahat evraklarında sahtecilik ile mücadele,

g) Siber suçlarla mücadele;

h) Tarafların yetkileri dâhilinde bulunan diğer suçlar ile mücadele;

2. Taraflar arasındaki işbirliği aşağıda yer alan şekillerde gerçekleştirilecektir:

a) Suçla ilgili bilginin ve suç işleyen şahıslara ilişkin kişisel verilerin sağlanması;

b) Suç işlemekle itham edilen ya da mahkûm edilen kişilerin aranmasında yardım sağlanması;

c) Yasal bilgi, belge, yayın ve bilimsel araştırma sonuçlarının mübadele edilmesi;

d) Eğitim, seminer ve çalıştayların düzenlenmesi ve Tarafların personelinin niteliklerinin artırılması alanında işbirliği yapılması;

e) Polis ekipmanı tedarik edilmesi.

3. Taraflar, terörist grupların faaliyetlerinin takibi ve deşifresi amacıyla, bu grupların üyelerine ve faaliyetlerine yönelik, terörle mücadele alanında yetkili birimleri arasında işbirliği ve suçla ilgili istihbari bilgi paylaşımı faaliyetlerinde bulunurlar.

4. Taraflar, Devletlerinde yürürlükte bulunan ulusal mevzuatlar ve uluslararası hukuk normları ile uyumlu olarak işbu Mutabakat Zaptı uyarınca işbirliğini gerçekleştireceklerdir.

Madde 2
Gözaltına Alınan Şahıslara İlişkin Bilginin Temin Edilmesi

Taraflardan her biri, Devletinde yürürlükte olan ulusal mevzuat ve kişisel verilerin korunmasına ilişkin uluslararası normlar uyarınca, ülkesinde gözaltında olabilecek diğer Taraf vatandaşlarına ilişkin ayrıntıları diğer Tarafa bildirecektir.

Madde 3
Şahısların Aranmasında İşbirliği

Taraflar, Devletlerinde yürürlükte olan ulusal mevzuatları uyarınca aranan şahısların bulunmasını, gözaltına alınmasını, tutuklanmasını sağlamak amacıyla ya da bu şahıslara ilişkin bilgi sağlanması için tüm gerekli önlemleri alacaklardır.

Madde 4
Uzman Toplantılarının Düzenlenmesi

Tarafların her ikisi de işbirliği alanlarına yönelik ivedi ya da özel konuların ele alınmasına ihtiyaç olduğu hususunda fikir birliğine vardığında yetki alanları çerçevesinde uzman toplantıları düzenleyecektir.

Madde 5
İşbirliğinin Gerçekleştirilmesi

1. İşbu Mutabakat Zaptı çerçevesindeki işbirliği, İngilizce lisanında ya da Taraflardan herhangi birinin resmi lisanında gerçekleştirilecektir.

2. İşbu Mutabakat Zaptı uyarınca bilgi ya da yardım sağlanmasına ilişkin talepler Taraflarca yazılı şekilde iletilecektir. Talepler, acil durumlarda, makul bir zaman içerisinde yazılı bir şekilde teyit edilmesi şartıyla, sözlü olarak da iletilebilir.

Madde 6
Talebin Yerine Getirilmemesi

Talebi alan Taraf talebin, Devletinin egemenliğini, güvenliğini, ulusal menfaatlerini, kamu düzenini, insan sağlığını ya da diğer önemli çıkarlarını tehdit ettiği ya da yürürlükte olan ulusal mevzuatına ters düştüğü görüşünde ise talebi tamamen ya da kısmen reddedebilir.

Madde 7
Bilgi ve Evrakın Kullanımına İlişkin Kısıtlamalar

1. Taraflar, işbu Mutabakat Zaptı kapsamında iletilen bilgi ve kişisel verilerin sadece Mutabakat Zaptının amaçları doğrultusunda ve uluslararası insan hakları sözleşmelerinin hükümleri uyarınca kullanılacağını ve Devletlerin yürürlükteki ulusal mevzuatı uyarınca korunacağını kabul eder.

2. Taraflar, gizli bilgilerin teatisinde ve korunmasında işbirliğine ilişkin bir anlaşma imzalayacaklardır.

3. İşbu Mutabakat Zaptı kapsamında yetkili bir merci tarafından sağlanan bilgi ve evrak, bu bilgi ve evrakı ileten yetkili merciin rızası olmadan üçüncü kişilere verilemez.

Madde 8
İşbu Mutabakat Zaptının Uygulanmasında Yetkili Kurumlar

1. İşbu Mutabakat Zaptını uygulama yetkisine sahip olan kurumlar:

- Türk Tarafı için: Türkiye Cumhuriyeti İçişleri Bakanlığı;
- Gürcü Tarafı için: Gürcistan İçişleri Bakanlığı.

2. İşbu Mutabakat Zaptının etkili bir şekilde uygulanması amacına yönelik olarak Tarafların Yetkili Makamları, birbirlerine irtibat bilgilerini verecekler, isimlerindeki, yetki alanlarındaki ve irtibat bilgilerindeki her türlü değişikliği birbirlerine bildireceklerdir.

Madde 9
Diğer Uluslararası Anlaşmalarla Olan İlgi

İşbu Mutabakat Zaptının hükümleri, Tarafların taraf oldukları diğer ikili ya da çok taraflı uluslararası anlaşmalardan doğan hak ve yükümlülüklerini etkilemez.

Madde 10
Anlaşmazlıkların Çözülmesi

İşbu Mutabakat Zaptının uygulanması ya da yorumlanması sırasında ortaya çıkan anlaşmazlıklar, Taraflar arasındaki istişareler ya da diplomatik kanallar aracılığıyla yapılan müzakereler yoluyla çözülecektir.

Madde 11
Düzeltmeler ve Ekler

İşbu Mutabakat Zaptında, Tarafların karşılıklı rızaları ile yazılı bir şekilde düzeltmeler ya da eklemeler yapılabilir. Bu gibi düzeltme ve eklemeler Tekli Protokol halinde tanzim edilecek ve işbu Mutabakat Zaptının ayrılmaz bir parçası olacaktır. Bahse konu Protokol, işbu Mutabakat Zaptının 12. Maddesinin 1.bendinde belirtilen prosedür uyarınca yürürlüğe girecektir.

Madde 12
Nihai Hükümler

1. İşbu Mutabakat Zaptı, Tarafların, işbu Mutabakat Zaptının yürürlüğe girmesi için gerekli yasal usullerin tamamlandığını birbirlerine diplomatik yollarla bildirdikleri son yazılı bildirimin alındığı tarihten sonraki ayın ilk günü yürürlüğe girecektir.

2. İşbu Mutabakat Zaptı süresiz olarak imzalanacaktır. Taraflardan herhangi birisi, işbu Mutabakat Zaptının uygulanmasını diğer Tarafa diplomatik kanallar aracılığıyla gönderilen bir yazılı bildirim ile feshedebilir. Fesih, fesih bildiriminin alındığı tarihten sonraki 6 (altı) ay içerisinde geçerli olacaktır.

İşbu Mutabakat Zaptı, Tiflis'te, 22/02/2012 tarihinde, her biri eşit derecede geçerli olacak şekilde Türkçe, Gürcüce ve İngilizce lisanlarında iki orijinal nüsha halinde tanzim edilmiştir. Taraflarca işbu Mutabakat Zaptının hükümlerinin yorumlanmasında anlaşmazlık olması halinde İngilizce metin esas alınacaktır.

Türkiye Cumhuriyeti **Hükümeti adına**	**Güreistan Hükümeti** **adına**
İdris Naim ŞAHİN İçişleri Bakanı	**Ivane MERABISHVILI** İçişleri Bakanı

MÉMORANDUM D'ACCORD ENTRE LE GOUVERNEMENT DE LA RÉPUBLIQUE TURQUE ET LE GOUVERNEMENT DE LA GÉORGIE RELATIF À LA COOPÉRATION EN MATIÈRE DE LUTTE CONTRE LA CRIMINALITÉ

Le Gouvernement de la République turque et le Gouvernement de la Géorgie, ci-après dénommés les « Parties »,

Souhaitant développer et renforcer leurs relations d'amitié et de partenariat et, en particulier, réaffirmer leur volonté commune de renforcer leur coopération policière,

Préoccupés par l'ampleur croissante et l'évolution de la criminalité, en particulier des différentes formes de criminalité organisée,

Conscients que toute forme de criminalité met en péril la paix internationale, l'ordre public et l'état de droit ainsi que la sécurité, la stabilité et l'intégrité territoriale de leurs États et nuit au développement économique, à l'instauration de conditions propices à l'investissement, aux valeurs démocratiques et à la justice,

Désireux de protéger efficacement la vie, les droits et les intérêts des êtres humains, les intérêts de la société et l'État contre la criminalité,

Reconnaissant l'importance de la coopération internationale en matière de lutte contre la criminalité,

Se référant aux dispositions de l'Accord entre le Gouvernement de la République turque et le Gouvernement de la République de Géorgie en matière de coopération dans le domaine de la sécurité, signé à Ankara le 13 janvier 1994, de l'Accord entre la République turque, la Géorgie et la République d'Azerbaïdjan concernant la coopération en matière de lutte contre le terrorisme, la criminalité organisée et d'autres crimes graves, signé à Trabzon le 30 avril 2002, et du Protocole entre la République turque et la Géorgie sur la mise en œuvre de l'article 9 de l'Accord entre la République turque, la Géorgie et la République d'Azerbaïdjan concernant la coopération en matière de lutte contre le terrorisme, la criminalité organisée et d'autres crimes graves, signé à Ankara le 10 mars 2005,

Considérant les principes fondamentaux du droit international et les conventions internationales auxquelles leurs États sont parties et qui concernent l'objet du présent Mémorandum d'accord,

Sont convenus de ce qui suit :

Article premier. Domaines et formes de coopération

1. Les Parties coopèrent et s'accordent une assistance mutuelle pour combattre :
    a) Le terrorisme international;
    b) La criminalité organisée;
    c) Le trafic illicite de stupéfiants, de substances psychotropes et de leurs précurseurs;
    d) Le trafic de migrants, la traite d'êtres humains et la migration illégale;
    e) Les actes illégaux liés aux armes, aux munitions, aux explosifs et aux matières nucléaires, chimiques et biologiques;

f) Le passage illégal de frontières internationales et la falsification de documents de voyage;

g) La cybercriminalité;

h) D'autres crimes relevant de la compétence des Parties.

2. La coopération entre les deux Parties prend les formes suivantes :

a) Transmission de renseignements en matière de criminalité et de données à caractère personnel sur les personnes qui commettent un crime;

b) Assistance en matière de recherche de personnes accusées ou reconnues coupables d'un crime;

c) Échange d'informations juridiques, de documents, de publications et de résultats de recherches scientifiques;

d) Organisation de formations, séminaires et ateliers et coopération concernant le perfectionnement professionnel des membres du personnel des Parties;

e) Fourniture d'équipement de police.

3. Les autorités antiterroristes compétentes des Parties coopéreront et échangeront des renseignements en matière criminelle de manière à repérer et déjouer les actes de terrorisme et à traquer et démanteler les groupes terroristes.

4. La coopération des Parties en exécution du présent Mémorandum d'accord est conforme à leur législation interne et aux normes du droit international.

Article 2. *Fourniture de renseignements sur les personnes détenues*

Chaque Partie fournit à l'autre des informations sur les citoyens de l'État de l'autre Partie qui peuvent être détenus sur le territoire respectif, conformément à la législation interne en vigueur dans cet État et aux normes internationales applicables à la protection des données à caractère personnel.

Article 3. *Coopération en matière de recherche de personnes*

Conformément à la législation interne en vigueur dans leur État, les Parties prennent toute mesure nécessaire pour trouver, appréhender ou arrêter des personnes recherchées, ou pour fournir des renseignements sur lesdites personnes.

Article 4. *Tenue de réunions d'experts*

Les Parties tiennent des réunions d'experts, dans leur domaine de compétence, à chaque fois qu'elles reconnaissent toutes deux la nécessité de traiter une question urgente ou particulière ayant trait aux domaines visés par la coopération.

Article 5. *Modalités de coopération*

1. Dans le cadre du présent Mémorandum d'accord, les activités de coopération sont menées en anglais ou dans la langue officielle de l'une ou l'autre des Parties.

2.   Dans le cadre du présent Mémorandum d'accord, toute demande d'information ou d'assistance est soumise par écrit par les Parties. En cas d'urgence, une demande peut être formulée oralement, puis confirmée par écrit dans un délai raisonnable.

Article 6. Non-exécution d'une demande

Une demande peut être refusée, en totalité ou en partie, si la Partie destinataire considère que ladite demande risque de porter atteinte à sa souveraineté, sa sécurité ou ses intérêts nationaux, ou à l'ordre public, la santé publique ou à d'autres intérêts importants de son État, ou que ladite demande risque d'être contraire à sa législation interne en vigueur.

Article 7. Limites restreignant l'utilisation de renseignements et de documents

1.   Les Parties conviennent que toutes informations et données à caractère personnel transmises en vertu du présent Mémorandum d'accord sont utilisées exclusivement aux fins qui y sont prévues et conformément aux dispositions des conventions internationales relatives aux droits de la personne, et sont protégées conformément à la législation interne en vigueur dans leur État.

2.   Les Parties s'engagent à conclure un accord de coopération régissant l'échange et la protection réciproque d'informations classifiées.

3.   En vertu du présent Mémorandum d'accord, aucun renseignement ou document ne peut être divulgué à une tierce partie sauf consentement préalable de l'autorité compétente ayant fourni ledit renseignement ou document.

Article 8. Autorités compétentes aux fins de l'application du présent Mémorandum d'accord

1.   Les autorités compétentes aux fins de l'exécution du présent Mémorandum d'accord sont :

- Pour la Partie turque : le Ministère de l'intérieur de la République turque;

- Pour la Partie géorgienne : le Ministère des affaires intérieures de la Géorgie.

2.   Aux fins de la bonne exécution du présent Mémorandum d'accord, les autorités compétentes de chacune des Parties échangent leurs coordonnées respectives et s'informent de toute modification relative à leur dénomination, leurs compétences ou leurs coordonnées.

Article 9. Rapports avec d'autres accords internationaux

Les dispositions du présent Mémorandum d'accord ne portent pas atteinte aux droits et obligations des Parties découlant d'autres accords internationaux bilatéraux ou multilatéraux auxquels elles sont parties.

Article 10. Règlement de différends

Tout différend relatif à l'application ou à l'interprétation du présent Mémorandum d'accord est réglé par voie de consultations ou de négociations entre les Parties, par la voie diplomatique.

Article 11. Modifications et suppléments

Le présent Mémorandum d'accord peut faire l'objet de modifications et de suppléments, par écrit, sous réserve de l'accord mutuel des Parties. Ces modifications et suppléments forment un seul protocole et font partie intégrante du présent Mémorandum d'accord. Le Protocole entre en vigueur conformément à la procédure prévue au paragraphe 1 de l'article 12 du présent Mémorandum d'accord.

Article 12. Dispositions finales

1. Le présent Mémorandum d'accord entre en vigueur le premier jour du mois suivant la date de réception de la dernière notification écrite des Parties, transmise par la voie diplomatique, confirmant l'accomplissement des procédures juridiques internes nécessaires à son entrée en vigueur.

2. Le présent Mémorandum d'accord est conclu pour une durée indéterminée. Chacune des Parties peut dénoncer ledit Mémorandum d'accord moyennant une notification écrite adressée par la voie diplomatique à l'autre Partie. La dénonciation prend effet six mois après la date de réception de cette notification.

FAIT à Tbilissi, le 22 février 2012, en deux exemplaires originaux, en langues anglaise, géorgienne et turque. En cas de divergence d'interprétation du présent Mémorandum d'accord entre les Parties, le texte anglais prévaut.

Pour le Gouvernement de la République turque :

İDRIS NAIM ŞAHIN
Ministre de l'intérieur

Pour le Gouvernement de la Géorgie :

IVANE MERABISHVILI
Ministre des affaires intérieures

No. 52080

———

Turkey
and
Hungary

Cooperation Programme between the Government of the Republic of Turkey and the Government of Hungary in the fields of education and science for the years 2014-2016. Ankara, 18 December 2013

Entry into force: *7 May 2014 by notification, in accordance with article 12*

Authentic texts: *English, Hungarian and Turkish*

Registration with the Secretariat of the United Nations: *Turkey, 20 August 2014*

———

Turquie
et
Hongrie

Programme de coopération entre le Gouvernement de la République turque et le Gouvernement de la Hongrie dans les domaines de l'éducation et de la science pour les années 2014 à 2016. Ankara, 18 décembre 2013

Entrée en vigueur : *7 mai 2014 par notification, conformément à l'article 12*

Textes authentiques : *anglais, hongrois et turc*

Enregistrement auprès du Secrétariat de l'Organisation des Nations Unies : *Turquie, 20 août 2014*

[ENGLISH TEXT – TEXTE ANGLAIS]

COOPERATION PROGRAMME
BETWEEN
THE GOVERNMENT OF THE REPUBLIC OF TURKEY
AND
THE GOVERNMENT OF HUNGARY
IN THE FIELDS OF EDUCATION AND SCIENCE
FOR THE YEARS 2014-2016

The Government of the Republic of Turkey and the Government of Hungary (hereinafter: the Parties) desiring to further develop their relations and cooperation in the fields of education and science, in the spirit of the Agreement between the Government of the Republic of Turkey and the Government of the Hungarian People's Republic on Cooperation in the Fields of Education and Culture, signed in Ankara, on 5th June, 1989, have adopted the following Programme of Cooperation for the years 2014-2016.

I. EDUCATION AND SCIENCE

Scholarships

ARTICLE 1

1.1 The Parties in accordance with their respective scholarship programmes shall mutually offer scholarships on the basis of reciprocity.

1.2 The Parties shall communicate annually through diplomatic channels, specifications of various categories of scholarships to be awarded to the citizens of the other Party along with conditions for eligibility.

1.3 Turkish Scholarships: The Turkish Party, in the framework of the "Türkiye Scholarships Programme", shall offer scholarships to Hungarian students for undergraduate, graduate, PhD studies in the Turkish universities. The Turkish Party shall also offer short-term (maximum 8 months) scholarships for research and Turkish Language summer courses.

1.3.1 The financial scope of the scholarships, allocation, requirements for eligibility and selection of students shall be carried out under the provisions of the Türkiye Scholarships Programme.

1.3.2 The information about the scholarship programs shall be annually communicated through diplomatic channels and shall be published on the website http://www.trscholarships.org.

1.4 The Hungarian Party shall invite the Turkish Party to the new governmental scholarship program, which aims to provide scholarships for the students of excellence.

1.4.1 The Hungarian Party shall offer scholarships for 150 Turkish students per year to pursue studies in Hungary in the Hungarian or the English language according to the following framework:

- 50 places for full BA/BSc study programmes in the field of agriculture, natural sciences and sustainable development.
- 50 places for full MA/MSc study programmes in the field of technology, engineering and economics, international relations, EU studies, Central European Studies.
- altogether 200 man-month scholarship for short term studies. One course or training shall last for 1-5 months in the above mentioned field of studies.
- furthermore, the Hungarian Party offers 30 scholarships for full PhD studies in the English language in any field of interest.

1.4.2 Prior to commencing higher education studies in Hungarian, students shall take part in a one-year preparatory course at Balassi Institute. Students applying for programmes in the English language shall have an appropriate knowledge of English on a certain level that is defined by the host institution.

Cooperation in Higher Education

ARTICLE 2

2.1 The Parties shall promote the development of direct relationships between their higher education institutions.

2.2 The Parties shall exchange - in case of demand - through diplomatic channels, consolidated lists containing the public data of their respective institutions of higher education as well as institutions dealing with scientific research and technology.

2.3 The Parties - in case of demand - shall inform each other on their foreign language study programmes offered by their universities and polytechnics in the given academic year. The Parties shall enhance the mobility of self-financed students to each other's country.

2.4 The Parties shall encourage the participation of their higher education institutions at international education fair and symposiums.

Higher Education and Scientific Research

ARTICLE 3

3.1 The Parties shall continue to promote and strengthen in various fields of mutual interest, direct contacts and cooperation between universities and other institutions of higher education as well as between institutions dealing with scientific research and technology in their respective countries.

3.2 The Parties shall continue to encourage, in the fields of higher education and university research, the enhancement of cooperation between the respective institutions of the Black Sea Economic Cooperation (BSEC) States.

3.3 The Parties shall promote activities of academic cooperation and scientific research between their respective institutions, in particular through the interchange of:

-university professors and other academicians or experts engaged in scientific research, as guest professors and researchers;

-visitors to scientific laboratories and related institutions;

-delegations wishing to study systems, programmes, methodologies and documents as well as infrastructure and to share experiences;

-scientific books and other publications.

3.4 During the validity of the present Programme of Cooperation the Parties shall exchange 3 (three) university professors and/or researchers for up to 10 (ten) days visits in order to establish contacts with their counterparts with a view to identifying research fields of common interest, including literature and history, architecture and conservation of cultural heritage.

3.5 The Parties shall encourage contacts between the Higher Education Council (YOK) of the Republic of Turkey and the Hungarian Higher Education and Scientific Council (HESC), as well as the relations between the accreditation committees and the higher education civil organizations of the two countries, such as the Hungarian Rectors' Conference and Inter University Board of Turkey.

Mutual Promotion of Respective Languages and Cultures

ARTICLE 4

4.1 The Parties shall mutually promote knowledge of the language, literature and culture of one another, within the limits of available means. In order to achieve this objective, the Parties shall appoint lecturers to the universities of one another in conformity with their respective legislation.

4.2 The Hungarian Party shall receive Turkish lecturers, one in the Eotvos Lorand University in Budapest, and one in the University of Szeged.

4.3 The Turkish Party shall receive one Hungarian native speaker lecturer in the Department of Hungarian Studies of the Faculty of Language and History-Geography of the University of Ankara.

4.4 The Parties shall collaborate for the teaching of the Turkish language and culture at the levels of primary and secondary education to students belonging to the Turkish community residing in Hungary, where the possibilities are given for this.

4.5 The Parties shall provide, within the limits of available means, books and other educational materials to one another in order to assist in the teaching of their respective language, literature and culture.

Equivalence of degrees and diplomas

ARTICLE 5

5.1 The Parties shall consult and cooperate, as necessary, for better international comparability in higher education degree systems as well as the acceptance of diplomas of the other country, taking into consideration the basis of the Bologna Process too.

II. CONTACTS BETWEEN PEOPLE AND ACTIVITIES IN THE FRAMEWORK OF THE EUROPEAN UNION'S PROGRAMMES

ARTICLE 6

6.1 The Parties shall continue to encourage and facilitate the establishment and conduct of twinning relations between interested municipalities of the two countries.

6.2. The Parties shall support the cooperation between the Turkish-Hungarian Friendship Associations in Turkey and the Hungarian-Turkish Friendship Association in Hungary.

6.3. The Parties shall consult and cooperate, as appropriate, under the relevant programmes of the European Union, including regional development programmes.

6.4. The Parties shall consult and cooperate, as appropriate, for joint activities under EU programmes for education and training, including the relevant aspects of the current regional development and Information Society programmes, also the "integrated Action Programme in Lifelong Learning".

6.5. The Parties shall cooperate in organizing workshops and enhancing consultation between the prospective partners for joint EU project, especially within the framework of Erasmus+ Program (Action 2 and 3).

6.6 The Parties shall encourage the cooperation of the relevant Hungarian and Turkish institutions with the European Study Centers.

6.7 The Parties shall consult and cooperate, for joint activities under EU Programmes for education and training, as appropriate and when applicable.

6.8 The Hungarian Party shall organize courses on EU cooperation, project management and experience regarding the implementation of the educational programs in English language for Turkish experts.

III. GENERAL AND FINANCIAL PROVISIONS IN THE FIELD OF EDUCATION AND SCIENCE

Exchange of Experts

ARTICLE 7

7.1. The sending Party shall nominate the persons to be exchanged and shall notify the receiving Party, at least 3 (three) months prior to the planned date of the visit.

7.2 The sending Party shall forward to the receiving Party a file with information about the persons to be exchanged. The file shall include short curriculum vitae, professional qualifications, academic degrees and titles, languages spoken (the language of the host country or English or French), the purpose of the visit, the proposed work programme and the duration of stay.

7.3 The receiving Party shall convey to the sending Party its consent to the proposed visit at least 6 (six) weeks prior to the planned date of arrival.

7.4 The sending Party shall notify the receiving Party of the exact date of arrival and departure at least 3 (three) weeks prior to the planned date of arrival.

7.5 The sending Party shall cover the cost of the international travel to and from the capital of the receiving country for the experts of short-term visits (at least for 15 days).

The Receiving Party shall provide to the extent it is possible:

- appropriate means of travel within the country, according to the approved programme of stay;
- appropriate meals and accommodation;
- in case of emergency, medical care at a public hospital.

Exchange of Scholarship-holders

ARTICLE 8

8.1 Based on Article 1.4 of the present Cooperation Programme the Hungarian Party shall provide to the Turkish scholarships holders:
- tuition-free course;
- the higher education institutions may offer dormitory places - according to the dormitory capacity of the given institution;
- medical insurance;
- monthly allowance (The stipend per month will be granted by the host institution. The amount of the scholarship in the year 2013 - according to the actual laws in force - is HUF 40 460 stipend per month in case of BA/BSc, MA/MSc programs, and HUF 100.000 stipend per month for PhD students).

8.2 Application forms and additional information (actual monthly allowance, fees, accommodation, travel expenses, health insurance etc.) will be provided by the Hungarian Scholarship Board.

Exchange of Lecturers

ARTICLE 9

9.1 The Parties with the aim of promoting the knowledge of each other's language and culture, on the basis of the Article 4.1, shall receive and send lecturers. The Hungarian Party shall delegate and the Turkish Party shall host a tutor of Hungarian language and literature at Ankara University for the full duration of this exchange programme. The circumstances of hosting should be settled in the agreement between Ankara University in Ankara and the Balassi Institute, which is an integral part of the co-operation programme.

Issuance of Visas and Residence Permits, Temporary Importation/Exportation of Materials

ARTICLE 10

10.1 Nothing in this Programme shall be deemed to affect the obligation of any person to comply with the laws and regulations in force in the territory of either Party concerning the entry, residence and departure of foreigners.

10.2 The Parties shall mutually facilitate and expedite, as far as its national law permits, the issuance of visas for individuals and ensembles to be exchanged under this Programme, also of residence permits, as necessary.

10.2.1 The Parties shall issue the necessary visas gratis and as soon as practicable for individuals and ensembles to be exchanged under this Programme, upon submission of the Letter of invitation, and of the Diplomatic Note of the Ministry of Foreign Affairs of the sending Party, as necessary.

10.2.2 The Parties shall issue the necessary residence permits gratis and as soon as practicable for persons (lecturers, scholars, experts, etc.) to be exchanged for long-term under this Programme.

10.3 The Parties shall mutually facilitate and expedite, as far as its national law permits, the temporary importation/exportation of objects and materials necessary to carry out missions or activities under this Programme.

IV. FINAL PROVISIONS

ARTICLE 11

11.1 For the purpose of the application of the present Programme, the Parties may convene in the form of a Joint Commission, alternately in Turkey and in Hungary.

11.2 For the implementation of this Programme, the Parties may conclude Action Plans in the future.

11.3 The Parties shall implement this Programme in line with the international agreements of which they are both contracting Parties and on the basis of their respective national legislation, as applicable.

11.4 This Programme shall be implemented through diplomatic or other channels to be mutually agreed upon.

11.5 This Programme does not preclude the possibility of undertaking any other activity to be agreed by the Parties through diplomatic channels.

11.6 This Programme may be amended by mutual consent of the Parties at any time. The amendments shall enter into force in accordance with the same legal procedures prescribed under the Paragraph 1 of Article 12.

ARTICLE 12

The present Programme will enter into force on the date of the receipt of the notification of the Turkish Party through diplomatic channels that all the necessary internal procedures for the entry into force have been fulfilled by the Parties.

The present Programme shall remain valid for three years from the date of its entry into force, renewable automatically for successive periods; of one year unless either side terminates it 6 (six) months before the date of expiry of the Programme by notification through diplomatic channels.

Done in Ankara on 18 December 2013, in two original copies in Turkish, Hungarian and English languages. In case of difference in interpretation, the English text shall prevail.

On Behalf of the Government of
the Republic of Turkey

On Behalf of the Government of
Hungary

Nabi AVCI

Minister of National Education

Balog ZOLTÁN

Minister of Human Resources

EGYÜTTMŰKÖDÉSI MEGÁLLAPODÁS A TÖRÖK KÖZTÁRSASÁG KORMÁNYA ÉS MAGYARORSZÁG KORMÁNYA KÖZÖTT AZ OKTATÁS ÉS TUDOMÁNY TERÜLETÉN A 2014-2016 ÉVEKRE

A Török Köztársaság Kormánya és Magyarország Kormánya (a továbbiakban: a Felek) attól a szándéktól vezérelve, hogy továbbfejlesszék kapcsolataikat és együttműködésüket az oktatás és tudomány területén, a Török Köztársaság Kormánya és a Magyar Népköztársaság Kormánya között 1989. június 5-én Ankarában aláírt Oktatási és Tudományos Megállapodás szellemében eljárva a következő Együttműködési Programot fogadták el a 2014-2016-os évekre.

I. OKTATÁS ÉS TUDOMÁNY

Ösztöndíjak

1. CIKK

1.1 A Felek saját ösztöndíj-programjaikkal összhangban ösztöndíjakat ajánlanak fel egymás részére a kölcsönösség elve alapján.

1.2 A Felek diplomáciai csatornákon keresztül évente értesítik egymást a másik Fél állampolgárai számára rendelkezésre álló különféle típusú ösztöndíjak részleteiről és a jelentkezési feltételekről.

1.3 Török Ösztöndíjak: a török Fél a "Türkiye Ösztöndíjprogram" keretei között ösztöndíjakat ajánl fel magyar hallgatók számára török felsőoktatási intézményekben alapszintű, mesterszintű és PhD tanulmányokhoz. A török Fél felajánl továbbá rövid távú (legfeljebb 8 hónapos) ösztöndíjakat kutatási célra és nyári török nyelvtanfolyamok céljára.

1.3.1 Az ösztöndíjak pénzügyi mértéke, azok elosztása, a jelentkezési feltételek és a hallgatók kiválasztása megfelelnek a Türkiye Ösztöndíjprogram szabályzatának.

1.3.2 Az ösztöndíjprogramokkal kapcsolatos információkról a török Fél évente, diplomáciai csatornákon keresztül nyújt tájékoztatást, valamint közzéteszi a http://www.trscholarships.org oldalon.

1.4 A magyar Fél meghívja a török Felet új kormányzati ösztöndíjprogramjába, amelynek célja a kiváló hallgatók számára ösztöndíjak nyújtása.

1.4.1 A magyar Fél évente 150 török hallgató számára ajánl fel ösztöndíjakat magyarországi magyar vagy angol nyelvű tanulmányok folytatása céljából, az alábbiak szerint:

- 50 ösztöndíjat teljes BA/BSc szintű képzésre agrár-, természettudományi és fenntartható fejlődés területeken,
- 50 ösztöndíjat teljes MA/MSc szintű képzésre műszaki, mérnöki, gazdasági, nemzetközi kapcsolatok, EU tanulmányok és Közép-Európa tanulmányok területeken,
- összesen 200 emberhónap ösztöndíjat rövid távú tanulmányokhoz. Egy képzés időtartama egy- öt hónap lehet, a fent felsorolt területeken.
- A magyar fél felajánl továbbá 30 ösztöndíjat teljes PhD szintű tanulmányok folytatására angol nyelven, bármely, érdeklődésre számot tartó területen.

1.4.2 A magyar nyelvű tanulmányok megkezdése előtt a hallgatók egy egyéves előkészítő programon vesznek részt a Balassi Intézet szervezésében. Az angol nyelvű programokra jelentkező hallgatóknak a fogadó intézmény által meghatározott szintű angol nyelvtudással kell rendelkezniük.

Felsőoktatási együttműködés

2. CIKK

2.1 A Felek ösztönzik a közvetlen kapcsolatok létrejöttét egymás felsőoktatási intézményeik között.

2.2 A Felek igény esetén diplomáciai csatornákon keresztül felsőoktatási intézményeik, valamint tudományos és műszaki kutatóintézeteik nyilvános adatait tartalmazó listákat cserélnek ki egymás között.

2.3 A Felek igény esetén tájékoztatják egymást az egyetemeik és főiskoláik az adott tanévben indított idegen nyelvű képzési programjairól. A Felek elősegítik az önköltséges hallgatók mobilitását egymás országaiba.

2.4 A Felek ösztönzik felsőoktatási intézményeik részvételét nemzetközi oktatási vasarokon és kiállításokon.

Felsőoktatás és tudományos kutatás

3. CIKK

3.1 A Felek továbbra is elősegítik és erősítik a közvetlen kapcsolatokat és együttműködést egyetemeik és más felsőoktatási intézményeik, valamint tudományos és műszaki kutatóintézeteik között a különféle, kölcsönös érdeklődésre számot tartó területeken.

3.2 A Felek továbbra is ösztönzik az együttműködést a felsőoktatás és egyetemi kutatás területén a Fekete-Tengeri Gazdasági Együttműködés országainak intézményei között.

3.3 A Felek támogatják az oktatói együttműködést és tudományos kutatást egymás intézményei között, különösen a módokon:

- felsőoktatási intézményi oktatók és más tudományos kutatók, valamint tudományos kutatásokban részt vevő szakértők küldése és fogadása vendégoktatóként és vendégkutatóként;
- kölcsönös látogatások kutatólaboratóriumokban és kapcsolódó intézményekben;
- delegációk cseréje tanulmányi rendszerek, programok, módszerek, dokumentumok és az infrastruktúra tanulmányozása, valamint tapasztalatcsere céljából;
- könyvek és egyéb tudományos publikációk cseréje.

3.4 Jelen Együttműködési Program hatálya alatt a Felek 3 (három) felsőoktatási intézményi oktató vagy kutató cseréjét teszik lehetővé legfeljebb 10 (tíz) napos látogatásra abból a célból, hogy felvegyék a kapcsolatot fogadó országbeli kollégáikkal és közös érdeklődésre számot tartó kutatási témákat határozzanak meg, többek között az irodalom és történelem, építészet és kulturális örökségvédelem területén.

3.5 A Felek ösztönzik a kapcsolatok létrejöttét a Török Köztársaság Felsőoktatási Tanácsa (YOK) és a magyar Felsőoktatási és Tudományos Tanács (FTT), továbbá a két ország akkreditációs bizottságai és felsőoktatási civil szervezetei, csakúgy mint a Magyar Rektori Konferencia és Törökország Egyetemközi Tanácsa között.

Egymás nyelvének és kultúrájának kölcsönös megismertetése

4. CIKK

4.1 A Felek kölcsönösen ösztönzik egymás nyelvének, irodalmának és kultúrájának megismerését a rendelkezésre álló lehetőségeik keretei között. Ebből a célból a Felek oktatókat küldenek egymás felsőoktatási intézményeibe, a másik Fél vonatkozó jogszabályaival összhangban.

4.2 A magyar Fél egy-egy török lektort fogad az Eötvös Loránd Tudományegyetemen, Budapesten, és a Szegedi Tudományegyetemen.

4.3 A török Fél egy magyar anyanyelvű lektort fogad az Ankarai Egyetem Nyelv és Történeti Földrajz Karának Magyar Tanulmányok Tanszékén.

4.4 A Felek együttműködnek a török nyelv és kultúra általános és középiskolai szintű oktatásában a Magyarországon élő török közösséghez tartozó diákok részére ott, ahol erre adottak a lehetőségek.

4.5 A Felek a rendelkezésre álló lehetőségeik keretei között tankönyveket és más oktatási segédanyagokat biztosítanak egymás számára saját nyelvük, irodalmuk és kultúrájuk oktatásához.

Diplomák és végzettségek egyenértékűsége

5. CIKK

5.1 A Felek szükség szerint egyezetnek és együttműködnek egymással a felsőoktatási rendszer tudományos fokozatainak nemzetközi összehasonlíthatásának elősegítése, valamint a másik fél diplomáinak elismerése érdekében, figyelembe véve a Bolognai Folyamat alapjait.

II. A NÉPEK KÖZÖTTI KAPCSOLAT ÉS AZ EURÓPAI UNIÓ PROGRAMJAINAK KERETÉBEN VÉGZETT TEVÉKENYSÉGEK

6. CIKK

6.1 A Felek a továbbiakban is ösztönözni fogják, illetve megkönnyítik ikerintézményi (twinning) kapcsolatok létrehozását és fenntartását a két ország érdekelt önkormányzatai között.

6.2. A Felek támogatják a törökországi Török–Magyar Baráti Társaságok és a magyarországi Magyar–Török Baráti Társaság közötti együttműködést.

6.3 A Felek egyeztetnek és együttműködnek egymással, amennyiben szükséges, az Európai Unió vonatkozó programjainak keretében, a regionális fejlesztési programokat is beleértve.

6.4 A Felek egyeztetnek és együttműködnek egymással, amennyiben szükséges, az EU oktatási és képzési programjainak keretében folytatott közös tevékenységükkel kapcsolatban, az aktuális regionális fejlesztési és információs társadalmat fejlesztő programokat, valamint az integrált Élethosszig Tartó Tanulás Integrált Akcióprogramot is beleértve.

6.5 A Felek együttműködnek a közös EU projektek leendő partnerei közötti műhelyek szervezése és közöttük folyó konzultáció elősegítése kapcsán, különösen az Erasmus+ Program keretei között (2. és 3. Akció).

6.6 A Felek ösztönzik az érdekelt magyar és török intézmények együttműködését az Európai Oktatási Központokkal.

6.7 A Felek egyeztetnek és együttműködnek egymással, amennyiben szükséges, az EU oktatási és képzési programjainak keretei között folytatott közös tevékenységükkel kapcsolatban, amennyiben ez lehetséges.

6.8 A magyar Fél angol nyelvű kurzusokat szervez török szakértőknek az Európai Uniós együttműködésről, projektmenedzsmentről, és oktatási programok megvalósításának tapasztalatairól.

III. ÁLTALÁNOS ÉS PÉNZÜGYI RENDELKEZÉSEK AZ OKTATÁS ÉS TUDOMÁNY TERÜLETÉN

Szakértők cseréje

7. CIKK

7.1 A küldő Fél megnevezi a delegáció tagjait és a fogadó Felet erről legalább három (3) hónappal a látogatás tervezett kezdete előtt tájékoztatja.

7.2 A küldő Fél tájékoztatja a fogadó Felet az utazó személyekkel kapcsolatos információkról. A dokumentáció tartalmazza kiutazók rövid életrajzát, szakmai végzettségét, tudományos címeit, fokozatait és diplomáit, az általuk beszélt nyelveket (a fogadó ország nyelve, vagy angol vagy francia), látogatásuk célját, a javasolt munkaprogramot és a tartózkodás tervezett időtartamát.

7.3   A fogadó Fél legkésőbb 6 (hat) héttel az érkezés tervezett időpontja előtt jelzi egyetértését a tervezett látogatással kapcsolatban a küldő Fél számára.

7.4   A küldő Fél értesíti a fogadó Felet az érkezés és a visszautazás pontos időpontjáról legkésőbb 3 (három) héttel az érkezés tervezett időpontja előtt.

7.5   A küldő Fél fedezi az utazási nemzetközi költségeit a fogadó Fél fővárosába és onnan vissza a szakértők rövid idejű látogatása (legalább 15 nap) esetén.

A fogadó Fél biztosítja a rendelkezésére álló lehetőségeinek megfelelően:
- megfelelő közlekedési lehetőséget az országon belül, a látogatás elfogadott programjának megfelelően;
- megfelelő étkezést és szállást;
- vészhelyzet esetére orvosi ellátást az állami kórházakban.

Ösztöndíjasok cseréje

8. CIKK

8.1   Jelen Együttműködési Program 1.4 cikke alapján a magyar Fél a következőket biztosítja a török ösztöndíjasok számára:
- tandíjmentes képzés
- kollégiumi   elhelyezés   az   adott   felsőoktatási   intézmény   kollégiumi kapacitásának függvényében
- egészségbiztosítás
- havi ösztöndíj (A havi ösztöndíjat a fogadó intézmény utalja át. A 2013-as évben a jogszabályoknak megfelelően a hallgatói ösztöndíj mértéke alap- és mesterképzésben havi 40 460 forint, PhD hallgatók számára havi 100 000 forint).

8.2 A jelentkezési lapot és további információt (aktuális havi juttatás, díjak, lakhatás, utazási költség, egészségbiztosítás, stb.) a Magyar Ösztöndíj Bizottság nyújt.

Lektorok cseréje

9. CIKK

9.1 A Felek, abból a célból, hogy elősegítsék egymás nyelvének és kultúrájának megismerését, lektorokat küldenek és fogadnak a 4.1 cikknek megfelelően. A török Fél fogadja a magyar Fél által delegált, magyar nyelv és irodalom oktatására szakosodott oktatót az Ankarai Egyetemen a program teljes időtartamára. A fogadás pontos körülményeit az Ankarai Egyetem és a Balassi Intézet közötti megállapodás szabályozza, amely jelen együttműködési program szerves része.

Vízumok és tartózkodási engedélyek kiállítása, eszközök és anyagok ideiglenes behozatala és kivitele

10. CIKK

10.1 Jelen Program egyetlen rendelkezése sem érinti a résztvevő személyek azon kötelezettségét, amely szerint meg kell felelniük az egyes Felek területén hatályos, a külföldieknek az ország területére való belépését, ott-tartózkodását és annak elhagyását szabályozó jogszabályoknak.

10.2 A Felek kölcsönösen törekszenek rá, hogy jogszabályaik adta keretek között egyszerűsítsék és meggyorsítsák a jelen Program keretei között küldött és fogadott személyek számára a vízumok, illetve szükség szerint a tartózkodási engedélyek kiállítását.

10.2.1 A Felek a meghívóleveleket és a küldő Fél Külügyminisztériuma diplomáciai jegyzékének kézhezvételét követően, amennyiben ezek szükségesek, a lehető legrövidebb időn belül és térítésmentesen állítják ki a vízumot a jelen Program keretei között küldött és fogadott személyek és csoportok számára.

10.2.2 A Felek a lehető legrövidebb időn belül és térítésmentesen állítják ki a szükséges tartózkodási engedélyeket a jelen Program keretei között, hosszú távra küldött, illetve fogadott személyek (oktatók, ösztöndíjasok, szakértők, stb.) számára.

10.3 A Felek kölcsönösen törekszenek rá, hogy jogszabályaik adta keretek között egyszerűsítsék és meggyorsítsák a jelen Program keretei között folytatott feladathoz vagy tevékenységhez szükséges eszközök és anyagok ideiglenes behozatalát és kivitelét.

IV. ZÁRÓ RENDELKEZÉSEK

11. CIKK

11.1 Jelen Program megvalósításának céljából a Felek Vegyes Bizottságot alakíthatnak, amely felváltva ülésezik Törökországban és Magyarországon.

11.2 Jelen program megvalósításának céljából a Felek a jövőben akcióterveket hozhatnak létre.

11.3 A Felek nemzeti jogszabályaikkal és azon nemzetközi egyezményekkel összhangban valósítják meg jelen Programot, amelyeknek mindketten részeseik.

11.4 Jelen Program diplomáciai vagy egyéb, kölcsönösen elfogadott csatornákon keresztül kerül megvalósításra.

11.5 Jelen Program nem zárja ki annak a lehetőségét, hogy a Felek diplomáciai csatornákon keresztül történt egyeztetését követően bármilyen egyéb közös tevékenységet folytassanak.

11.6 Jelen Program a Felek kölcsönös egyetértése esetén bármikor módosítható. A módosítások azon jogi eljárásnak megfelelően lépnek hatályba, amelyet a 12. cikk 1. bekezdése tartalmaz.

12. CIKK

Jelen Program azt követően lép hatályba, hogy a magyar Fél diplomáciai csatornákon keresztül kézhez kapta a török Fél jegyzékét arról, hogy a hatályba lépéshez szükséges jogi lépések teljesültek.

Jelen Program a hatályba lépés dátumától számított három évig marad hatályban, ezt követően egyéves periódusokra automatikusan meghosszabbodik, amennyiben a Felek valamelyike nem jelzi felmondási szándékát diplomáciai csatornákon keresztül, 6 (hat) hónappal a Program hatályának lejárta előtt.

Készült Ankarában 2013. december hónap ..... napján, kettő eredeti példányban, angol, török és magyar nyelven. A Program rendelkezéseinek esetlegesen eltérő értelmezése esetén az angol nyelvű szöveg az irányadó.

A Török Köztársaság Kormánya nevében   Magyarország Kormánya nevében

Nabi Avci   Balog Zoltán

Nemzeti Oktatási Minisztérium   Emberi Erőforrások Minisztérium

TÜRKİYE CUMHURİYETİ HÜKÜMETİ
İLE
MACARİSTAN HÜKÜMETİ
ARASINDA
2014-2016 YILLARI İÇİN
EĞİTİM VE BİLİM ALANLARINDA
İŞBİRLİĞİ PROGRAMI

Türkiye Cumhuriyeti Hükümeti ve Macaristan Hükümeti (bundan sonra Taraflar olarak anılacaktır), eğitim ve bilim alanlarındaki ilişkilerini ve işbirliğini daha da geliştirmek arzusuyla, Türkiye Cumhuriyeti Hükümeti ile Macaristan Halk Cumhuriyeti Hükümeti arasında 5 Haziran 1989 tarihinde Ankara'da imzalanan Eğitim ve Kültür Alanlarında İşbirliği Anlaşması'nın ruhuna uygun olacak şekilde, aşağıdaki 2014-2016 yılları için İşbirliği Programını kabul etmişlerdir.

I. EĞİTİM VE BİLİM

Burslar

MADDE 1

1.1. Taraflar, kendi burs programları ile uyumlu olacak şekilde mütekabiliyet temelinde karşılıklı olarak burs verirler.

1.2. Taraflar, her yıl diğer Tarafın vatandaşlarına verilecek olan çeşitli bursların kategori özelliklerinin yanı sıra seçilebilme şartlarını da diplomatik yollardan birbirlerine bildirirler.

1.3. Türk Bursları: Türk Tarafı, "Türkiye Bursları Programı" çerçevesinde, Türk üniversitelerinde lisans, lisansüstü ve doktora öğrenimi gören Macar öğrencilere burs verir. Türk Tarafı, araştırma ve Türk Dili yaz kursları için kısa dönem (en fazla 8 ay) burslar da verir.

1.3.1. Bursların mali kapsamı, tahsisi, öğrencilerin seçilmesine ilişkin gereklilikler ve öğrencilerin seçilmeleri Türkiye Bursları Programı hükümlerine dayalı olarak gerçekleştirilir.

1.3.2. Burs programları ile ilgili bilgiler diplomatik yollardan her yıl iletilir ve http://www.trscholarships.org web sitesinde yayınlanır.

1.4. Macaristan Tarafı, üstün başarılı öğrencilere burs sağlamayı hedefleyen yeni hükümet bursu programına Türk Tarafını davet eder.

1.4.1. Macaristan Tarafı, yılda 150 Türk öğrenciye Macaristan'da Macarca veya İngilizce dillerinde eğitim almaları için aşağıdaki çerçeveye uygun olacak şekilde burs verir:

- Tarım, tabiat bilimleri ve sürdürülebilir kalkınma alanlarında Edebiyat Fakültesi/Fen Fakültesi sosyal bilimler lisansı/fen bilimleri lisansı öğrenim programlarının tamamı için 50 yer.
- Teknoloji, mühendislik ve ekonomi, uluslararası ilişkiler, AB çalışmaları, Orta Avrupa çalışmaları alanlarında sosyal bilimler yüksek lisansı/fen bilimleri yüksek lisansı eğitim programlarının tamamı için 50 yer.
- Kısa dönem çalışmalar için toplam 200 kişi-ay karşılığı burs. Yukarıda belirtilen çalışma alanlarında bir kurs veya eğitim 1 ila 5 ay sürmektedir.
- Bunlara ek olarak, Macaristan Tarafı herhangi bir konuda İngilizce doktora öğrenimi için tüm programı kapsayacak şekilde 30 burs verir.

1.4.2. Macarca yükseköğretime başlamadan önce, öğrenciler Balassi Enstitüsü'nde bir yıllık hazırlık kursuna katılırlar. İngilizce dilindeki programlar için başvuruda bulunan öğrenciler, ilgili eğitim kurumu tarafından belirlenen düzeyde İngilizce bilgisine sahip olmalıdır.

Yüksek Öğretimde İşbirliği

MADDE 2

2.1. Taraflar, yükseköğretim kurumları arasında doğrudan ilişkilerin geliştirilmesini teşvik ederler.

2.2. Talep olması durumunda, Taraflar her birinin yüksek öğretim kurumlarının yanı sıra bilimsel araştırma ve teknoloji ile ilgilenen kurumları hakkında kamuya açık verileri içeren konsolide listeleri diplomatik yollardan teati ederler.

2.3. Talep olması durumunda, Taraflar, söz konusu akademik yıl içinde üniversiteleri ile yüksek teknik okulları tarafından sunulan yabancı dilde eğitim programlarından birbirlerini haberdar ederler. Taraflar, eğitim masraflarını kendileri karşılayan öğrencilerin birbirlerinin ülkelerine yönelik hareketliliğini arttırlar.

2.4. Taraflar, yükseköğretim kurumlarının uluslararası eğitim fuarlarına ve sempozyumlarına katılımlarını teşvik ederler.

Yüksek Öğretim ve Bilimsel Araştırma

MADDE 3

3.1. Taraflar, üniversiteleri ve diğer yükseköğretim kurumlarının yanı sıra kendi ülkelerinde bilimsel araştırma ve teknoloji alanında çalışan kurumları arasında çeşitli ortak ilgi alanlarında doğrudan temasları ve işbirliğini teşvik etmeye ve güçlendirmeye devam ederler.

3.2. Taraflar, yükseköğretim ve üniversite araştırması alanlarında Karadeniz Ekonomik İşbirliği (KEİ) ülkelerinin ilgili kurumları arasında işbirliğinin geliştirilmesini teşvik etmeye devam ederler.

3.3. Taraflar, ilgili kurumları arasında, akademik işbirliği ve bilimsel araştırma faaliyetlerini özellikle aşağıdakilerin değişimi yoluyla destekleyeceklerdir:

-üniversite öğretim görevlilerinin ve bilimsel araştırma ile uğraşan diğer akademisyen ve uzmanların misafir öğretim üyesi ve araştırmacı olarak değişimi;

-bilimsel laboratuvar ve ilgili kurumlara yönelik ziyaretçilerin değişimi;

-sistemler, programlar, metodolojiler ve belgeler ile altyapıyı tetkik etmeyi ve tecrübe paylaşımı yapmayı amaçlayan heyetlerin değişimi;

-bilimsel kitap ve diğer yayınların değişimi.

3.4. İşbu İşbirliği Programının geçerlilik süresi boyunca, Taraflar, edebiyat ve tarih, mimari ve kültürel mirasın korunması dahil, araştırma için ortak ilgi alanları belirlemek amacıyla, meslektaşları ile temas kurmak üzere 10 (on) güne kadar olan ziyaretlerde bulunacak 3 (üç) üniversite öğretim üyesi ve/veya araştırmacısının değişimini gerçekleştirir.

3.5. Taraflar, Türkiye Cumhuriyeti Yüksek Öğretim Kurulu (YÖK) ile Macaristan Yükseköğretim ve Bilimsel Konseyi (MYBK) arasındaki temasların yanı sıra Macaristan Rektörler Konferansı ve Türkiye Üniversitelerarası Kurul Başkanlığı ve iki ülkenin akreditasyon komiteleri ve yükseköğretime yönelik sivil toplum örgütleri arasındaki ilişkileri teşvik ederler.

Dillerin ve Kültürlerin Karşılıklı Olarak Teşvik Edilmesi

MADDE 4

4.1. Taraflar, diğer Tarafın dil, edebiyat ve kültürünün öğrenilmesini, imkânlar ölçüsünde, karşılıklı olarak desteklerler. Taraflar bu hedefin gerçekleştirilmesi için, kendi mevzuatlarına uygun olacak şekilde birbirlerinin üniversitelerinde okutmanlar görevlendirirler.

4.2. Macaristan Tarafı, biri Budapeşte'deki Eötvos Lörand Üniversitesi'nde, biri de Szeged Üniversitesi'nde olmak üzere Türk okutmanları kabul eder.

4.3. Tarafı, Ankara Üniversitesi Dil ve Tarih-Coğrafya Fakültesi Hungaroloji Anabilim Dalı'na ana dili Macarca olan bir okutmanı kabul eder.

4.4. Olanak sağlandığı durumlarda, Taraflar Macaristan'da ikamet eden Türk toplumu mensubu öğrencilere ilk ve orta öğretim düzeylerinde Türk dili ve kültürünün öğretilmesi için işbirliği yaparlar.

4.5. Taraflar, kendi dil, edebiyat ve kültürlerinin öğretilmesine yardım etmek amacıyla, imkânları ölçüsünde, birbirlerine kitap ve diğer eğitim malzemeleri sağlarlar.

Derece ve Diplomaların Denkliği

MADDE 5

5.1. Taraflar, gerekli görüldüğünde, yükseköğretim derece sistemlerinin uluslararası düzeyde daha iyi kıyaslanabilir olmasının yanı sıra diğer ülkenin diplomalarının kabul edilmesini sağlamak amacıyla, Bologna Sürecini de temel alarak danışma ve işbirliğinde bulunurlar.

II. AVRUPA BİRLİĞİ PROGRAMLARI ÇERÇEVESİNDE HALKLARARASI TEMASLAR VE FAALİYETLER

MADDE 6

6.1. Taraflar, iki ülkenin konuya ilgi duyan belediyeleri arasında kardeş şehir ilişkileri kurulmasını ve yürütülmesini teşvik etmeye ve kolaylaştırmaya devam ederler.

6.2. Taraflar, Türkiye'deki Türk-Macar Dostluk Dernekleri ile Macaristan'daki Macar-Türk Dostluk Derneklerinin işbirliğini desteklerler.

6.3. Taraflar, bölgesel kalkınma programları da dahil olmak üzere ilgili Avrupa Birliği programları çerçevesinde, uygun olduğu ölçüde, istişare ve işbirliğinde bulunurlar.

6.4. Taraflar, uygun olduğu ölçüde, "Hayatboyu Öğrenim için Entegre Eylem Programı"nın yanısıra mevcut Bölgesel Kalkınma ve Bilgi Toplumu programları da dâhil olmak üzere eğitim ve öğretim ile ilgili AB Programları kapsamında ortak etkinlikler için istişare ve işbirliğinde bulunurlar.

6.5. Taraflar özellikle Erasmus+ Programı (Eylem 2 ve 3) çerçevesinde ortak AB projelerinin olası ortakları arasında istişareleri arttırma ve çalıştay düzenleme konularında işbirliği yaparlar.

6.6. Taraflar ilgili Macar ve Türk kuruluşlarını Avrupa Öğrenim Merkezleri ile işbirliğine teşvik ederler.

6.7. Taraflar, uygun olduğu ve uygulanabildiği ölçüde, eğitim ve öğrenimle ilgili AB Programları kapsamında ortak etkinlikler için istişare ve işbirliğinde bulunurlar.

6.8. Macar Tarafı Türk uzmanlar için İngilizce olarak AB işbirliği, eğitim programlarının yürütülmesi, proje yönetimi ve deneyimi alanlarında kurslar düzenler.

III. EĞİTİM VE BİLİM ALANINDA GENEL VE MALİ HÜKÜMLER

Uzman Değişimi

MADDE 7

7.1. Gönderen Taraf değişime konu olacak kişileri belirler ve kabul eden Tarafı, planlanan ziyaret tarihinden en az 3 (üç) ay önceden bilgilendirir.

7.2. Gönderen Taraf kabul eden Tarafa değişime konu kişilerin bilgilerini içeren bir dosyayı iletir. Dosyada kısa özgeçmiş, mesleki nitelikler, akademik dereceler ve unvanlar, konuşulan diller (ev sahibi ülkenin dili veya İngilizce ya da Fransızca), ziyaret amacı, önerilen çalışma programı ve kalma süresine ilişkin bilgileri kapsar.

7.3. Kabul eden Taraf, önerilen ziyarete ilişkin onayını, planlanan varış tarihinden en az altı (6) hafta önce gönderen Tarafa iletir.

7.4. Gönderen Taraf, kabul eden Tarafa, kesin varış ve ayrılış tarihlerini, planlanan varış tarihinden en az üç (3) hafta önce bildirecektir.

7.5. Gönderen Taraf kısa-dönemli (en az 15 günlük) ziyarette bulunan uzmanların kabul eden ülkenin başkentine uluslararası gidiş-dönüş yolculuk masraflarını karşılar.

Kabul eden Taraf mümkün olduğu ölçüde:

-onaylanan kalış programına uygun olarak ülke içerisindeki seyahatler için uygun ulaşım araçları;

-uygun yeme-içme ve konaklama;

-acil bir durumda, devlet hastanesinde tedavi sağlar.

Bursiyer Mübadelesi

MADDE 8

8.1. Mevcut İşbirliği Programının 1.4. maddesine dayanarak Macaristan Tarafı Türk bursiyerlere aşağıdakileri sağlar:

-ücretsiz eğitim;

-yükseköğretim kurumları, kurumun yurt kapasitesine bağlı olarak yurtta kalma imkânı sağlayabilir;

-sağlık sigortası;

-aylık burs (Aylık burs ev sahibi kurum tarafından ödenecektir. 2013 yılı için belirlenen burs miktarı - yürürlükteki yasalara göre - lisans ve yüksek lisans öğrencileri için aylık 40.460 Macar Forinti, doktora öğrencileri için 100.000 Macar Forintidir).

8.2. Başvuru formları ve ek bilgi (güncel burs miktarı, ücretler, konaklama, ulaşım masrafları, sağlık sigortası vb.) Macaristan Burs Komisyonu tarafından sağlanacaktır.

Okutman Mübadelesi

MADDE 9

9.1. Taraflar 4.1. maddeye dayanarak birbirlerinin dil ve kültürlerine hakkında bilgiyi desteklenmesi amacıyla okutman gönderir ve kabul ederler. Macaristan Tarafı, bir Macaristan dili ve edebiyatı okutmanını Türkiye Tarafından konuk edilmek üzere işbu değişim programının süresi boyunca Ankara Üniversitesinde görevlendirir. Konuk etme koşulları işbirliği programının tamamlayıcı bir parçasını teşkil eden Ankara Üniversitesi ve Balassi Enstitüsü arasında yapılacak anlaşma ile belirlenmelidir.

Vize ve İkamet İzinlerinin Verilmesi, Malzemelerin Geçici İthalatı/İhracatı

MADDE 10

10.1. Bu Programda yer alan hiçbir husus, herhangi bir kişinin, Taraflardan her birinin ülkesinde yürürlükte olan yabancıların ülkeye girişi, ülkede ikameti ve ülkeden çıkışına ilişkin yasa ve yönetmeliklere uyma yükümlülüğünü etkilediği şeklinde yorumlanamaz.

10.2. Taraflar, gerektiğinde, milli mevzuatları izin verdiği ölçüde, bu Program kapsamında mübadele edilecek kişi ve topluluklara vize itasını, ayrıca ikamet izni verilmesini karşılıklı olarak kolaylaştırır ve hızlandırırlar.

10.2.1. Taraflar, gerektiğinde bu program kapsamında mübadele edilecek olan kişi ve topluluklar için davet mektubunun ve gönderen Tarafın Dışişleri Bakanlığının Notasının sunulmasının ardından gerekli vizeleri ücretsiz olarak ve mümkün olan en kısa sürede verirler.

10.2.2. Taraflar, bu Program kapsamında uzun süreli olarak mübadele edilecek olan kişiler (okutmanlar, akademisyenler, uzmanlar vb.) için gerekli ikamet izinlerini ücretsiz olarak ve mümkün olan en kısa sürede verirler.

10.3. Taraflar, milli mevzuatları izin verdiği ölçüde, bu Program kapsamında öngörülen görev ve etkinlikleri gerçekleştirmek için gerekli mal ve malzemelerin geçici ithalini/ihracını karşılıklı olarak kolaylaştırır ve hızlandırırlar.

IV. NİHAİ HÜKÜMLER

MADDE 11

11.1. Bu Programın uygulanması amacıyla, Taraflar dönüşümlü olarak Türkiye ve Macaristan'da Ortak Komisyon bünyesinde bir araya gelebilirler.

11.2. Bu Programın uygulanması için, Taraflar gelecekte Eylem Planları akdedebilir.

11.3. Taraflar, bu Programı, ikisinin de taraf olduğu uluslararası anlaşmalara uygun olarak ve duruma göre, milli mevzuatları temelinde uygular.

11.4. Bu program diplomatik kanallar ya da üzerinde mutabık kalınacak diğer kanallar üzerinden uygulanır.

11.5. Bu Program Tarafların diplomatik kanallarla mutabık kalacağı başka bir etkinliğin yürütülmesine halel getirmez.

11.6. Bu Program, Tarafların karşılıklı rızasıyla her zaman değiştirilebilir. Değişiklikler 12. maddenin 1. fıkrasında belirtilen hukuki sürecin aynısı uyarınca yürürlüğe girer.

MADDE 12

İşbu Program, yürürlüğe girmesi için gerekli tüm iç usullerin, Taraflarca yerine getirildiğinin diplomatik kanallarla Türk tarafınca yapılan bildirimin alındığı tarih itibariyle yürürlüğe girer.

İşbu Program, yürürlüğe girmesinden itibaren üç yıl boyunca geçerli olup, Programın sona erme süresine 6 (altı) ay kalana kadar taraflardan biri diplomatik kanallarla anlaşmayı sonlandırdığına ilişkin bildirimde bulunmadığı sürece, Program bunu takip eden bir yıllık süreler için otomatik olarak yenilenir.

18 Aralık 2013 tarihinde Ankara'da Türkçe, Macarca ve İngilizce dillerinde iki orijinal nüsha halinde yapılmıştır. Yorumunda farklılık olması halinde, İngilizce metin esas alınır.

Türkiye Cumhuriyeti Hükümeti   Macaristan Hükümeti

Adına   Adına

Nabi AVCI   Balog ZOLTÁN

Milli Eğitim Bakanı   İnsan Kaynakları Bakanı

[TRANSLATION – TRADUCTION]

PROGRAMME DE COOPÉRATION ENTRE LE GOUVERNEMENT DE LA RÉPUBLIQUE TURQUE ET LE GOUVERNEMENT DE LA HONGRIE DANS LES DOMAINES DE L'ÉDUCATION ET DE LA SCIENCE POUR LES ANNÉES 2014 À 2016

Le Gouvernement de la République turque et le Gouvernement de la Hongrie (ci-après dénommés les « Parties »), désireux de renforcer leurs relations et leur coopération dans les domaines de l'éducation et de la science, dans l'esprit de l'Accord entre le Gouvernement de la République turque et le Gouvernement de la République populaire hongroise relatif à la coopération dans les domaines de l'éducation et de la culture, signé à Ankara le 5 juin 1989, ont adopté le Programme de coopération ci-après pour les années 2014 à 2016.

I. ÉDUCATION ET SCIENCE

Article premier. Bourses d'études

1.1 Les Parties, conformément à leurs programmes de bourses d'études respectifs, s'engagent à s'offrir mutuellement des bourses d'études, sur la base de la réciprocité.

1.2 Les Parties se communiquent annuellement, par la voie diplomatique, les caractéristiques des diverses catégories de bourses d'études à accorder aux citoyens de l'autre Partie, ainsi que les conditions d'admissibilité.

1.3 Bourses d'études de la Turquie : la Partie turque offre, dans le cadre du Programme de bourses d'études de la Turquie, des bourses aux étudiants hongrois aux fins d'études de premier cycle, de second cycle et de doctorat dans les universités turques. La Partie turque offre également des bourses d'études de courte durée (d'un maximum de huit mois) aux fins de cours d'été de langue turque et de recherches.

1.3.1 L'étendue financière des bourses d'études, leur attribution, les conditions d'admissibilité et la sélection des étudiants sont déterminées conformément aux dispositions du Programme de bourses d'études de la Turquie.

1.3.2 Les Parties se communiquent annuellement, par la voie diplomatique, les renseignements sur leurs programmes de bourses d'études et les publient sur le site Web http ://www.trscholarships.org.

1.4 La Partie hongroise invite la Partie turque à participer au nouveau programme gouvernemental de bourses d'études, qui vise à procurer des bourses d'études aux étudiants ayant fait preuve d'excellence.

1.4.1 La Partie hongroise offre annuellement des bourses d'études à 150 étudiants turcs afin qu'ils poursuivent leurs études en Hongrie, en langues hongroise ou anglaise, selon la répartition suivante :

- 50 places dans des programmes intégraux d'études en vue de l'obtention d'un B. A. ou d'un B. Sc. en agriculture, en sciences naturelles ou en développement durable;

- 50 places dans des programmes intégraux d'études en vue de l'obtention d'un M. A. ou d'un M. Sc. en technologie, en génie, en sciences économiques, en relations internationales, en études sur l'Union européenne, ou en études sur l'Europe centrale;

- Bourses d'études de courte durée représentant un total de 200 personnes-mois, pour des cours ou formations d'un à cinq mois chacun dans les domaines susmentionnés;

- En outre, 30 bourses pour des études intégrales de doctorat, en langue anglaise, dans tout domaine d'intérêt.

1.4.2 Avant d'entamer des études supérieures en langue hongroise, les étudiants participent à un cours préparatoire d'un an à l'Institut Balassi. Les étudiants présentent une demande de participation à un programme en langue anglaise ont une connaissance de l'anglais se situant au niveau que détermine l'établissement visé.

Article 2. Coopération en études supérieures

2.1 Les Parties favorisent le développement de relations directes entre leurs établissements d'enseignement supérieur.

2.2 Les Parties échangent, sur demande, par la voie diplomatique, des listes récapitulatives contenant les données publiques de leurs établissements d'enseignement supérieur et établissements de recherche scientifique et de technologie respectifs.

2.3 Les Parties s'informent mutuellement, sur demande, des programmes d'études en langues étrangères offerts par leurs universités et écoles polytechniques au cours d'une année universitaire donnée. Chacune des Parties facilite l'entrée dans son pays des étudiants autofinancés de l'autre Partie.

2.4 Les Parties encouragent la participation de leurs établissements d'enseignement supérieur aux foires et aux colloques internationaux sur l'éducation.

Article 3. Enseignement supérieur et recherche scientifique

3.1 Les Parties continuent de favoriser et de renforcer, dans divers domaines d'intérêt commun, les contacts directs et la coopération entre les universités et les autres établissements d'enseignement supérieur ainsi qu'entre les établissements de recherche scientifique et de technologie de leurs pays respectifs.

3.2 Les Parties continuent d'encourager, dans les domaines de l'enseignement supérieur et de la recherche universitaire, le renforcement de la coopération entre les établissements des États membres de la Coopération économique de la mer Noire (CEMN).

3.3 Les Parties favorisent les activités de coopération universitaire et de recherche scientifique entre leurs établissements respectifs, notamment par :

- L'échange de professeurs et autres universitaires ou experts se consacrant à la recherche scientifique, comme professeurs et chercheurs invités;

- La visite réciproque de laboratoires scientifiques et d'établissements connexes;

- L'envoi réciproque de délégations souhaitant étudier les systèmes, programmes, méthodologies et documents ainsi que les infrastructures et partager leurs données expériences;

- L'échange d'ouvrages scientifiques et d'autres publications.

3.4 Pendant la durée du présent Programme de coopération, les Parties s'échangent trois professeurs d'université ou chercheurs pour une durée maximale de dix jours afin qu'ils établissent des contacts avec leurs homologues dans le but de trouver des domaines de recherche d'intérêt commun, notamment en littérature, en histoire, en architecture et en conservation du patrimoine culturel.

3.5 Les Parties encouragent les échanges entre le Conseil de l'enseignement supérieur de la République turque (YOK) et le Conseil hongrois de l'enseignement supérieur et scientifique (HESC) ainsi que les relations entre les comités d'attestation et les organisations civiles d'enseignement supérieur des deux pays, comme la Conférence hongroise des recteurs et le Conseil interuniversitaire de la Turquie.

Article 4. Promotion réciproque des langues et cultures respectives

4.1 Chacune des Parties veille à favoriser la connaissance de la langue, de la littérature et de la culture de l'autre Partie, dans la limite des moyens disponibles. Pour atteindre cet objectif, chacune des Parties nomme des maîtres de conférences aux universités de l'autre Partie conformément à sa législation.

4.2 La Partie hongroise reçoit des maîtres de conférences turcs, un à l'Université Eotvos Lorand, à Budapest, et un à l'Université de Szeged.

4.3 La Partie turque reçoit un maître de conférences de langue maternelle hongroise au Département d'études hongroises de la Faculté des langues, d'histoire et de géographie de l'Université d'Ankara.

4.4 Les Parties collaborent à l'enseignement de la langue et de la culture turques aux élèves du primaire et du secondaire de la communauté turque résidant en Hongrie, là où les possibilités existent.

4.5 Les Parties se procurent réciproquement, dans la limite des moyens disponibles, des livres et d'autres matériels pédagogiques afin de faciliter l'enseignement de leurs langues, littératures et cultures respectives.

Article 5. Équivalence des diplômes et titres

5.1 Les Parties se consultent et coopèrent au besoin en vue d'améliorer la comparabilité internationale des systèmes d'octroi de diplômes d'études supérieures ainsi que la reconnaissance des diplômes de l'autre pays, tout en tenant compte des bases du processus de Bologne.

II. LIENS ENTRE PERSONNES ET ACTIVITÉS DANS LE CADRE DES PROGRAMMES DE L'UNION EUROPÉENNE

Article 6

6.1 Les Parties continuent d'encourager et de faciliter l'établissement et le maintien de relations de jumelage entre les municipalités intéressées des deux pays.

6.2 Les Parties appuient la coopération entre l'Association des amitiés turques et hongroises en Turquie et l'Association des amitiés hongroises et turques en Hongrie.

6.3 Les Parties se consultent et coopèrent, s'il y a lieu, dans le cadre des programmes pertinents de l'Union européenne (UE), y compris les programmes de développement régional.

6.4 Les Parties se consultent et coopèrent, s'il y a lieu, en vue d'activités conjointes dans le cadre des programmes de l'UE en matière d'éducation et de formation, y compris à l'égard des aspects pertinents des programmes actuels de développement régional et de la société de l'information, ainsi que du « Programme d'action intégré dans le domaine de la formation tout au long de la vie ».

6.5 Les Parties coopèrent à l'organisation d'ateliers et au renforcement des consultations entre les partenaires potentiels de projets communs de l'UE, particulièrement dans le cadre du programme Erasmus+ (actions 2 et 3).

6.6 Les Parties encouragent la coopération entre les établissements hongrois et turcs compétents et les Centres d'études européennes.

6.7 Les Parties se consultent et coopèrent en vue d'activités conjointes dans le cadre des programmes de l'UE en matière d'éducation et de formation, s'il y a lieu.

6.8 La Partie hongroise organise des cours sur la coopération, la gestion de projets et l'expérience au sein de l'UE aux fins de la mise en œuvre des programmes d'études en langue anglaise à l'intention des experts turcs.

III. DISPOSITIONS GÉNÉRALES ET FINANCIÈRES DANS LES DOMAINES DE L'ÉDUCATION ET DE LA SCIENCE

Article 7. Échange d'experts

7.1 La Partie d'envoi désigne les personnes visées par l'échange et en informe la Partie d'accueil au moins trois mois avant la date prévue de la visite.

7.2 La Partie d'envoi fait parvenir à la Partie d'accueil un dossier d'information sur les personnes visées par l'échange. Le dossier comprend un curriculum vitæ condensé, les compétences professionnelles, les diplômes et titres universitaires, les langues parlées (la langue du pays d'accueil ou l'anglais ou le français), le but de la visite, le programme de travail proposé et la durée du séjour.

7.3 La Partie d'accueil informe la Partie d'envoi qu'elle consent à la visite proposée six semaines au moins avant la date d'arrivée prévue.

7.4 La Partie d'envoi informe la Partie d'accueil de la date d'arrivée et de la date de départ exactes trois semaines au moins avant la date d'arrivée prévue.

7.5 La Partie d'envoi prend à sa charge les frais des déplacements internationaux des experts à destination et à partir de la capitale du pays d'accueil pour les visites de courte durée (d'au moins 15 jours).

La Partie d'accueil fournit, dans la mesure possible :

- Des moyens de déplacement appropriés à l'intérieur du pays, conformément au programme de séjour approuvé;

- Des repas et un hébergement appropriés;

- En cas d'urgence, des soins médicaux dans un hôpital public.

Article 8. Échange de boursiers

8.1 En vertu du paragraphe 1.4 de l'article premier du présent Programme de coopération, la Partie hongroise offre aux boursiers turcs :

- Des cours sans frais de scolarité;

- Des places en dortoir, dans le cas des établissements d'enseignement supérieur, sous réserve de leur capacité d'accueil;

- Une assurance maladie;

- Une allocation mensuelle (L'allocation mensuelle est versée par l'établissement d'accueil. La bourse d'études pour l'année 2013, selon la législation en vigueur, est constituée d'une allocation mensuelle de 40 460 forints hongrois pour les étudiants des programmes de B. A. ou B. Sc. et de M. A. ou M. Sc. et de 100 000 forints hongrois pour les étudiants des programmes de doctorat).

8.2 Le Conseil hongrois des bourses d'études fournit les formulaires de demande et les renseignements supplémentaires (le montant de l'allocation mensuelle, les frais, l'hébergement, les frais de déplacement, l'assurance maladie, etc.).

Article 9. Échange de maîtres de conférences

9.1 Chacune des Parties, dans le but de favoriser la connaissance de la langue et de la culture de l'autre Partie, conformément au paragraphe 4.1 de l'article 4, accueille et envoie des maîtres de conférences. La Partie hongroise délègue et la Partie turque accueille un tuteur de langue et de littérature hongroises à l'Université d'Ankara pour toute la durée du programme d'échange visé par les présentes. Les conditions d'accueil devraient être établies dans l'accord entre l'Université d'Ankara à Ankara et l'Institut Balassi, lequel fait partie intégrante du Programme de coopération.

Article 10. Délivrance de visas et de permis de séjour,
importation et exportation temporaires de matériel

10.1 Aucune disposition du présent Programme ne peut être réputée dispenser toute personne de se conformer aux lois et règlements en vigueur sur le territoire de l'une ou l'autre des Parties concernant l'entrée, le séjour et le départ des étrangers.

10.2 Chacune des Parties facilite et accélère pour l'autre Partie, dans la mesure où sa législation nationale le permet, la délivrance de visas pour les personnes et les groupes de l'autre Partie visés par les échanges prévus par le présent Programme, ainsi que de permis de séjour, au besoin.

10.2.1 Les Parties délivrent les visas nécessaires à titre gracieux et dès que possible pour les personnes et les groupes visés par les échanges prévus par le présent Programme, sur présentation de la lettre d'invitation et, au besoin, de la note diplomatique du Ministère des affaires étrangères de la Partie d'envoi.

10.2.2 Les Parties délivrent les permis de séjour nécessaires à titre gracieux et dès que possible pour les personnes (maîtres de conférences, universitaires, experts ou autres) visées par un échange à long terme conformément au présent Programme.

10.3 Chacune des Parties facilite et accélère pour l'autre Partie, dans la mesure où sa législation nationale le permet, l'importation et l'exportation temporaires des objets et du matériel nécessaires à l'exécution des missions ou activités faisant partie du présent Programme.

IV. DISPOSITIONS FINALES

Article 11

11.1 Aux fins de l'application du présent Programme, les Parties peuvent se réunir en commission mixte alternativement en Turquie et en Hongrie.

11.2 Aux fins de la mise en œuvre du présent Programme, les Parties peuvent dresser des plans d'action à l'avenir.

11.3 Les Parties mettent en œuvre le présent Programme en conformité avec les accords internationaux dont elles sont toutes deux Parties contractantes et sur la base de leurs législations nationales applicables respectives.

11.4 Le présent Programme est mis en œuvre par la voie diplomatique ou toute autre voie convenue d'un commun accord.

11.5 Le présent Programme n'exclut pas la possibilité d'entreprendre toute autre activité dont conviennent les Parties par la voie diplomatique.

11.6 Le présent Programme peut être modifié en tout temps d'un commun accord entre les Parties. Toute modification apportée entre en vigueur conformément aux modalités énoncées au premier paragraphe de l'article 12.

Article 12

Le présent Programme entre en vigueur à la date de réception de la notification par la Partie turque, par la voie diplomatique, de l'accomplissement par les Parties de toutes les procédures internes nécessaires à son entrée en vigueur.

Le présent Programme a une durée de validité de trois ans à compter de la date de son entrée en vigueur et est renouvelable tacitement pour des périodes successives d'un an, à moins que l'une ou l'autre des Parties ne le dénonce six mois avant sa date d'expiration moyennant une notification adressée par la voie diplomatique.

FAIT à Ankara, le 18 décembre 2013, en deux exemplaires originaux en langues anglaise, hongroise et turque. En cas de divergence d'interprétation, le texte anglais prévaut.

Pour le Gouvernement de la République turque :
NABI AVCI
Ministre de l'éducation nationale

Pour le Gouvernement de la Hongrie :
BALOG ZOLTÁN
Ministre des ressources humaines

No. 52081

Turkey
and
Peru

Exchange of notes constituting an agreement regarding the suppression of visas in diplomatic passports and service passports (or special passports) between the Government of the Republic of Turkey and the Government of the Republic of Peru. Vienna, 28 May 1996 and 17 September 1996

Entry into force: *19 February 1997, in accordance with article 8*

Authentic texts: *English and Turkish*

Registration with the Secretariat of the United Nations: *Turkey, 20 August 2014*

Not published in print, in accordance with article 12(2) of the General Assembly regulations to give effect to Article 102 of the Charter of the United Nations, as amended.

Turquie
et
Pérou

Échange de notes constituant un accord relatif à la suppression des visas dans les passeports diplomatiques et les passeports de service (ou les passeports spéciaux) entre le Gouvernement de la République turque et le Gouvernement de la République du Pérou. Vienne, 28 mai 1996 et 17 septembre 1996

Entrée en vigueur : *19 février 1997, conformément à l'article 8*

Textes authentiques : *anglais et turc*

Enregistrement auprès du Secrétariat de l'Organisation des Nations Unies : *Turquie, 20 août 2014*

Non disponible en version imprimée, conformément au paragraphe 2 de l'article 12 du règlement de l'Assemblée générale destiné à mettre en application l'Article 102 de la Charte des Nations Unies, tel qu'amendé.

No. 52082

International Bank for Reconstruction and Development
and
Russian Federation

Loan Agreement (Second National Hydromet Modernization Project) between the Russian Federation and the International Bank for Reconstruction and Development (with schedules, appendix and International Bank for Reconstruction and Development General Conditions for Loans, dated 12 March 2012). Moscow, 17 January 2014

Entry into force: *8 May 2014 by notification*

Authentic text: *English*

Registration with the Secretariat of the United Nations: *International Bank for Reconstruction and Development, 26 August 2014*

Not published in print, in accordance with article 12(2) of the General Assembly regulations to give effect to Article 102 of the Charter of the United Nations, as amended.

Banque internationale pour la reconstruction et le développement
et
Fédération de Russie

Accord de prêt (Deuxième Projet national de modernisation hydrométallurgique) entre la Fédération de Russie et la Banque internationale pour la reconstruction et le développement (avec annexes, appendice et Conditions générales applicables aux prêts de la Banque internationale pour la reconstruction et le développement, en date du 12 mars 2012). Moscou, 17 janvier 2014

Entrée en vigueur : *8 mai 2014 par notification*

Texte authentique : *anglais*

Enregistrement auprès du Secrétariat de l'Organisation des Nations Unies : *Banque internationale pour la reconstruction et le développement, 26 août 2014*

Non disponible en version imprimée, conformément au paragraphe 2 de l'article 12 du règlement de l'Assemblée générale destiné à mettre en application l'Article 102 de la Charte des Nations Unies, tel qu'amendé.

No. 52083

International Development Association
and
India

Financing Agreement (Third Elementary Education Project) between India and the International Development Association (with schedules, appendix and International Development Association General Conditions for Credits and Grants, dated 31 July 2010). New Delhi, 29 May 2014

Entry into force: *10 July 2014 by notification*

Authentic text: *English*

Registration with the Secretariat of the United Nations: *International Development Association, 26 August 2014*

Not published in print, in accordance with article 12(2) of the General Assembly regulations to give effect to Article 102 of the Charter of the United Nations, as amended.

Association internationale de développement
et
Inde

Accord de financement (Troisième Projet d'enseignement primaire) entre l'Inde et l'Association internationale de développement (avec annexes, appendice et Conditions générales applicables aux crédits et aux dons de l'Association internationale de développement, en date du 31 juillet 2010). New Delhi, 29 mai 2014

Entrée en vigueur : *10 juillet 2014 par notification*

Texte authentique : *anglais*

Enregistrement auprès du Secrétariat de l'Organisation des Nations Unies : *Association internationale de développement, 26 août 2014*

Non disponible en version imprimée, conformément au paragraphe 2 de l'article 12 du règlement de l'Assemblée générale destiné à mettre en application l'Article 102 de la Charte des Nations Unies, tel qu'amendé.

No. 52084

——

Turkey
and
Japan

Agreement between the Government of the Republic of Turkey and the Government of Japan for cooperation in the use of nuclear energy for peaceful purposes (with annexes). Tokyo, 26 April 2013, and Ankara, 3 May 2013

Entry into force: *29 June 2014, in accordance with article 15*

Authentic texts: *English, Japanese and Turkish*

Registration with the Secretariat of the United Nations: *Turkey, 14 August 2014*

Turquie
et
Japon

Accord de coopération entre le Gouvernement de la République turque et le Gouvernement du Japon relatif à l'utilisation de l'énergie nucléaire à des fins pacifiques (avec annexes). Tokyo, 26 avril 2013, et Ankara, 3 mai 2013

Entrée en vigueur : *29 juin 2014, conformément à l'article 15*

Textes authentiques : *anglais, japonais et turc*

Enregistrement auprès du Secrétariat de l'Organisation des Nations Unies : *Turquie, 14 août 2014*

[ENGLISH TEXT – TEXTE ANGLAIS]

AGREEMENT
BETWEEN
THE GOVERNMENT OF THE REPUBLIC OF TURKEY
AND
THE GOVERNMENT OF JAPAN
FOR CO-OPERATION IN THE USE OF NUCLEAR ENERGY
FOR PEACEFUL PURPOSES

The Government of the Republic of Turkey and the Government of Japan (hereinafter referred to as the "Parties");

Based on the friendly relations existing between the Republic of Turkey and Japan;

Recognising that both the Republic of Turkey and Japan are members of the International Atomic Energy Agency (hereinafter referred to as "the Agency");

Considering that both the Republic of Turkey and Japan are parties to the Treaty on the Non-Proliferation of Nuclear Weapons, done on 1 July 1968;

Noting that safeguards by the Agency are applied in Japan in accordance with the Agreement between the Government of Japan and the International Atomic Energy Agency in Implementation of Article III. 1 and 4 of the Treaty on the Non-Proliferation of Nuclear Weapons, done on 4 March 1977 as supplemented by the Protocol additional to the said Agreement, done on 4 December 1998 (hereinafter referred to as "the Safeguards Agreement for Japan");

Noting that safeguards by the Agency are applied in the Republic of Turkey in accordance with the Agreement between the Government of the Republic of Turkey and the International Atomic Energy Agency for the Application of Safeguards in Connection with the Treaty on the Non-Proliferation of Nuclear Weapons, done on 30 June 1981 as supplemented by the Protocol additional to the said Agreement, done on 6 July 2000 (hereinafter referred to as "the Safeguards Agreement for the Republic of Turkey");

Reaffirming the commitment of the Parties to pursue peaceful uses of nuclear energy in a manner ensuring nuclear safety, nuclear security and nuclear non-proliferation; and

Emphasising the importance of co-operation in the use of nuclear energy for peaceful purposes and assurance of nuclear safety;

Have agreed as follows:

ARTICLE 1

For the purposes of this Agreement:

(a)   The term "authorised person" means any individual or entity within the jurisdiction of the State of a Party and authorised by that Party to cooperate under this Agreement, including to supply or receive nuclear material, material, equipment and technology, and to perform or receive services, but does not include the Parties;

(b)   The term "nuclear material" means:

    (i)   source material, namely, uranium containing the mixture of isotopes occurring in nature; uranium depleted in the isotope 235; thorium; any of the foregoing in the form of metal, alloy, chemical compound or concentrate; any other substance containing one or more of the foregoing in such concentration as may be determined by the Parties; and such other substances as may be determined by the Parties; and

    (ii)   special fissionable material, namely, plutonium; uranium-233; uranium enriched in the isotope 233 or 235; any substance containing one or more of the foregoing; and such other substances as may be determined by the Parties. Special fissionable material does not include source material;

(c)   The term "material" means substances for use in a nuclear reactor which are specified in Part A of Annex A to this Agreement, but does not include nuclear material;

(d)   The term "equipment" means major items of machinery, plant or instrumentation, or major components thereof, which are specially designed or prepared for use in nuclear activities, and which are specified in Part B of Annex A to this Agreement;

(e)   The term "technology" means specific information required for the development, production or use of any nuclear material, material or equipment, excluding information which has been made available without restrictions upon its further dissemination. Basic scientific research information may also be excluded, if specified and determined by the Parties. This specific information may take the form of technical data which includes blueprints, plans, diagrams, models, formulae, engineering designs and specifications, manuals and instructions written or recorded on other media or devices such as disk, tape and read-only memories. It may also take the form of technical assistance which includes instruction, skills, training, working knowledge and consulting services;

(f)   The term "development" referred to in paragraph (e) of this Article means all phases before production such as design, design research, design analysis, design concepts, assembly and testing of prototypes, pilot production schemes, design data, process of transforming design data into a product, configuration design, integration design and layouts;

(g)   The term "production" referred to in paragraphs (e) and (f) of this Article means all activities for producing nuclear material, material or equipment such as construction, production engineering, manufacture, integration, assembly (mounting), inspection, testing and quality assurance;

(h)   The term "use" referred to in paragraph (e) of this Article means operation, installation including on-site installation, maintenance, checking, repair, overhaul and refurbishing;

(i)   The term "equipment based on technology" means equipment which the Parties jointly determine as produced from the use of technology transferred pursuant to this Agreement; and

(j)   The term "nuclear material recovered or produced as a by-product" means:

    (i)   nuclear material derived from nuclear material transferred pursuant to this Agreement;

    (ii)   nuclear material derived by one or more processes from the use of material or equipment transferred pursuant to this Agreement; and

    (iii)   nuclear material which the Parties jointly determine as derived from the use of technology transferred pursuant to this Agreement.

ARTICLE 2

1.   Co-operation under this Agreement may be undertaken in the following ways:

(a)   exchange of experts and trainees;

(b)   exchange of information other than that which is classified for national security reasons, on such terms as may be determined by the Parties, by authorised persons of the Parties, or by either Party and authorised persons of the other Party;

(c)   supply from a Party or its authorised persons to the other Party or its authorised persons of nuclear material, material, equipment and technology on such terms as may be determined by the supplier and the recipient;

(d)   provision of services by a Party or its authorised persons and receipt of services by the other Party or its authorised persons on matters within the scope of this Agreement on such terms as may be determined by the supplier and the recipient; and

(e)   other ways as may be agreed by the Parties.

2.   Co-operation as specified in paragraph 1 of this Article may be undertaken in the following areas:

(a)   exploration and exploitation of source material which occurs in nature;

(b)   design, construction, operation and decommissioning of nuclear reactors agreed upon by the Parties;

(c)   production of nuclear fuel and equipment thereof;

(d)   nuclear safety including radiation protection and environmental monitoring;

(e)   nuclear security;

(f)   spent fuel and radioactive waste management;

(g)   study on and application of radio-isotopes and radiation;

(h)   research and development on areas within the scope of this Agreement; and

(i)   other areas as may be agreed by the Parties.

3.   Technology and equipment for uranium enrichment, spent nuclear fuel reprocessing, conversion of plutonium and production of material including those items listed in Part C of Annex A, as well as plutonium may be transferred under this Agreement only when this Agreement is amended for that purpose in accordance with paragraph 1 of Article 14.

ARTICLE 3

1.   Co-operation under this Agreement shall be carried out only for peaceful non-explosive purposes.

2.   Nuclear material, material, equipment and technology transferred pursuant to this Agreement, equipment based on technology and nuclear material recovered or produced as a by-product shall not be used other than for peaceful purposes; nor shall they be used for any nuclear explosive device, for research on or for development of any such device.

ARTICLE 4

1.   Co-operation specified in Article 2 of this Agreement shall be subject to the provisions of this Agreement and the laws and regulations in force in the respective States. Co-operation envisaged in particular in sub-paragraph (c) of paragraph 1 of the said Article shall require the application of safeguards by the Agency with respect to all nuclear material in all nuclear activities within the respective States in accordance with the Safeguards Agreement for the Republic of Turkey and the Safeguards Agreement for Japan respectively.

2.   To ensure the fulfilment of the obligations arising under Article 3 of this Agreement, nuclear material transferred pursuant to this Agreement and nuclear material recovered or produced as a by-product:

(a)   while within Japan, shall be subject to the Safeguards Agreement for Japan; and

(b)   while within the Republic of Turkey, shall be subject to the Safeguards Agreement for the Republic of Turkey.

3.   In the exceptional event that for any reason the Agency does not apply safeguards as required by paragraph 2 of this Article, the Parties shall, in view of the vital importance for nuclear material transferred pursuant to this Agreement and nuclear material recovered or produced as a by-product to remain permanently subject to safeguards, forthwith consult jointly with the Agency to take rectifying measures and, in the absence of such rectifying measures, shall immediately enter into arrangements which conform to safeguards principles and procedures of the Agency and provide effectiveness and coverage equivalent to that intended to be provided by the safeguards of the Agency specified in paragraph 2 of this Article.

ARTICLE 5

1.   In implementing the provisions of this Agreement, the Republic of Turkey and Japan shall act in conformity with the existing obligations of each State under the provisions of the Convention on Early Notification of a Nuclear Accident, adopted on 26 September 1986, the Convention on Assistance in the Case of a Nuclear Accident or Radiological Emergency, adopted on 26 September 1986, and the Convention on Nuclear Safety, adopted on 17 June 1994.

2.   Japan shall act in conformity with the provisions of the Joint Convention on the Safety of Spent Fuel Management and on the Safety of Radioactive Waste Management, done on 5 September 1997. Upon the conclusion of the said Convention, the Republic of Turkey shall act in conformity with its provisions.

3.   In respect of facilities in which nuclear material, material, equipment or technology transferred pursuant to this Agreement, equipment based on technology or nuclear material recovered or produced as a by-product is located or used, the Parties may make mutually satisfactory arrangements for the implementation of measures to ensure the safety of such facilities.

4.   The Parties may hold periodic bilateral consultations for the purpose of enhancing nuclear safety including preparedness and response to nuclear incidents.

ARTICLE 6

1.   In respect of nuclear material transferred pursuant to this Agreement and nuclear material recovered or produced as a by-product, the Parties shall apply measures of physical protection according to their respective criteria which bring about, as a minimum, protection at levels set out in Annex B to this Agreement.

2.   In respect of international transport of nuclear material transferred pursuant to this Agreement and nuclear material recovered or produced as a by-product, the Republic of Turkey and Japan shall act in conformity with the existing obligations of each State under the provisions of the Convention on the Physical Protection of Nuclear Material, opened for signature on 3 March 1980.

3.   Either Party may consult with the other Party for the purpose of reviewing the adequacy of measures of physical protection related to nuclear material transferred pursuant to this Agreement prior to the transfer and nuclear material recovered or produced as a by-product.

4.   The Parties shall act in conformity with the existing obligations of each State under the provisions of the International Convention for the Suppression of Acts of Nuclear Terrorism, opened for signature on 14 September 2005.

ARTICLE 7

Nuclear material, material, equipment and technology transferred pursuant to this Agreement, equipment based on technology and nuclear material recovered or produced as a by-product shall not be transferred or retransferred beyond the jurisdiction of the State of the receiving Party, except into the jurisdiction of the State of the supplying Party, unless the prior written consent of the supplying Party is obtained.

ARTICLE 8

Nuclear material transferred pursuant to this Agreement and nuclear material recovered or produced as a by-product may be enriched or reprocessed within the jurisdiction of the Republic of Turkey, only if the Parties agree in writing.

ARTICLE 9

1.   Nuclear material, material, equipment and technology transferred between the two States, whether directly or through a third State, shall become subject to this Agreement upon their entry into the jurisdiction of the State of the receiving Party, only if the supplying Party has notified the receiving Party in writing and in advance of the intended transfer.   Prior to the notified transfer of such nuclear material, material, equipment or technology, the supplying Party shall obtain from the receiving Party a written confirmation that the transferred nuclear material, material, equipment or technology will be held subject to this Agreement and that the proposed recipient, if other than the receiving Party, will be an authorised person of the receiving Party.

2.   Nuclear material, material, equipment and technology transferred pursuant to this Agreement, equipment based on technology and nuclear material recovered or produced as a by-product shall no longer be subject to this Agreement if:

(a)   such nuclear material, material or equipment has been transferred beyond the jurisdiction of the State of the receiving Party in accordance with the relevant provisions of this Agreement;

(b)   the Parties jointly determine that such nuclear material, material, equipment or technology shall no longer be subject to this Agreement; or

(c)   in the case of nuclear material, the Agency determines, in accordance with the provisions for the termination of safeguards in the relevant agreement referred to in Article 4 of this Agreement, that the nuclear material has been consumed, or has been diluted in such a way that it is no longer usable for any nuclear activity relevant from the point of view of safeguards, or has become practicably irrecoverable.

ARTICLE 10

1.   Neither Party shall use the provisions of this Agreement for the purpose of seeking commercial or industrial advantages over the other Party or its authorised persons, or for the purpose of interfering with the commercial or industrial interests of

the other Party or its authorised persons, or for the purpose of hindering the development of the peaceful uses of nuclear energy.

2.   For the effective implementation of this Agreement, the Parties shall exchange annually the then current inventories of nuclear material, material, equipment and technology transferred pursuant to this Agreement and equipment based on technology and nuclear material recovered or produced as a by-product based upon the national system of accounting for and control of nuclear material.

3.   Nuclear material transferred pursuant to this Agreement and nuclear material recovered or produced as a by-product may be handled based on the principles of fungibility and proportionality when they are used in mixing processes where they lose their identity, or are deemed to lose it, in the process of conversion, fuel fabrication, enrichment or reprocessing.

ARTICLE 11

The Parties shall ensure the adequate and effective protection of intellectual property and technology created or transferred pursuant to the co-operation under this Agreement in accordance with the relevant international agreements to which the Republic of Turkey and Japan are parties and the laws and regulations in force in the respective States.

ARTICLE 12

1.   The Parties shall, at the request of either of them, consult with each other, if any question arises concerning the interpretation or application of this Agreement.

2.   If any dispute arising out of the interpretation or application of this Agreement is not settled by consultations, such dispute shall, at the request of either Party, be submitted to an arbitral tribunal which shall be composed of three arbitrators appointed in accordance with the following provisions:

(a)   Each Party shall designate one arbitrator who may be a national of its State and the two arbitrators so designated shall designate by mutual agreement a third arbitrator, a national of a third State, who shall be the Chairman;

(b)   If, within thirty days of the request for arbitration, either Party has not designated an arbitrator, either Party may request the President of the International Court of Justice (hereinafter referred to as "ICJ") to appoint an arbitrator. If the President of the ICJ is a national of the State of either Party or is prevented from making the appointments for any other reason, the Vice-President of the ICJ or, if the Vice-President is a national of the State of either Party or is similarly prevented from acting, the most senior judge of the ICJ who is not a national of the State of either Party, and is not prevented similarly may be requested to make the appointments;

(c)   The same procedure set out in the sub-paragraph (b) above shall apply if, within thirty days of the designation or appointment of the second arbitrator, the third arbitrator has not been elected, provided that the third arbitrator so appointed shall not be a national of the State of either Party;

(d)   A majority of the members of the arbitral tribunal shall constitute a quorum, and all decisions shall require the concurrence of a majority of the members of the tribunal;

(e)   The arbitral procedure shall be fixed by decisions of the tribunal. The decisions of the tribunal shall be binding on the Parties; and

(f)   Each Party shall bear the cost of its own arbitrator and its representation in the arbitral proceedings. The cost of the Chairman of the arbitral tribunal in discharging the duties and the remaining costs of the arbitral tribunal shall be borne equally by the Parties.

ARTICLE 13

1.   If Japan or the Republic of Turkey at any time following entry into force of this Agreement:

(a)   acts in violation of the provisions of Article 3, 4, 5, 6, 7, or 8 of this Agreement, or the decisions of the arbitral tribunal referred to in Article 12 of this Agreement; or

(b)   terminates or materially violates its Safeguards Agreement with the Agency referred to in Article 4 of this Agreement,

the Government of the Republic of Turkey or the Government of Japan respectively shall have the right to cease co-operation under this Agreement in whole or in part, or to terminate this Agreement and to require the return of any nuclear material, material and equipment transferred pursuant to this Agreement.

2.   If Japan or the Republic of Turkey detonates a nuclear explosive device, the Government of the Republic of Turkey or the Government of Japan respectively shall have the right specified in paragraph 1 of this Article.

3.   Before either Party takes steps to cease co-operation under this Agreement in whole or in part or to terminate this Agreement, the Parties shall consult for the purpose of taking corrective measures and shall, where appropriate, carefully consider the following, taking into account the need to make such other appropriate arrangements as may be required:

(a)   the effects of taking such steps; and

(b)   whether the facts which gave rise to considering such steps were caused deliberately.

4.   The right under this Article to require the return of any nuclear material, material, or equipment transferred pursuant to this Agreement shall be exercised in accordance with terms, conditions and procedures mutually acceptable to the Parties.

5.   Following the consultations referred to in paragraph 3 of this Article, the right under this Article shall be exercised by either Party:

(a)   In the case referred to in paragraph 1 of this Article, only if the other Party fails to take corrective measures within an appropriate period of time; and

(b)   In the case referred to in paragraph 2 of this Article, if it determines that no corrective measures can be found.

ARTICLE 14

1.   The Parties shall, at the request of either Party, consult each other on amendments to this Agreement.   This Agreement may be amended by a written agreement between the Parties.   Amendments to this Agreement shall enter into force in accordance with the same procedure as set out in paragraph 1 of Article 15.

2.   The Annexes to this Agreement form an integral part of this Agreement.   The Annexes may be modified by a written agreement between the Parties without amendment of this Agreement.   Modifications of Annexes shall enter into force on the date of receipt by the Government of Japan of the written notification from the Government of the Republic of Turkey of the completion of its necessary internal procedures.

ARTICLE 15

1.   Each Party shall send through diplomatic channels to the other Party the notification by which the Party informs the other Party of the completion of its internal procedures required for the entry into force of this Agreement.   This Agreement shall enter into force on the thirtieth day after the date of the receipt of the latter notification.

2.   This Agreement shall remain in force for a period of fifteen years, and shall be automatically extended for five-year periods thereafter unless either Party notifies the other Party through diplomatic channels in writing of its intention to terminate this Agreement not later than six months prior to the expiry date.

3.   Notwithstanding the termination of this Agreement, Article 1, Article 3, paragraphs 2 and 3 of Article 4, Articles 5 to 8, paragraph 2 of Article 9 and Articles 10 to 13 of this Agreement shall continue in effect.

In witness whereof, the undersigned, being duly authorised by their respective Governments, have signed this Agreement.

Done in duplicate, each in Turkish, Japanese and English, each being equally authentic, and signed at Ankara on the third day of May, 2013, and at Tokyo on the twenty-sixth day of April, 2013.   Should any dispute concerning the interpretation of the texts arise, the English version shall prevail.

For the Government
of the Republic of Turkey:

Taner Yıldız
Minister of Energy and
Natural Resources

For the Government
of Japan:

Fumio Kishida
Minister for Foreign Affairs

Annex A

Part A

1.   Deuterium and heavy water:

Deuterium, heavy water (deuterium oxide) and any other deuterium compound in which the ratio of deuterium to hydrogen atoms exceeds 1:5000 for use in a nuclear reactor as defined in paragraph 1 of Part B below, in quantities exceeding 200 kg of deuterium atoms in any period of 12 months.

2.   Nuclear grade graphite:

Graphite having a purity level better than 5 parts per million boron equivalent and with a density greater than $1.50g/cm^3$ for use in a nuclear reactor as defined in paragraph 1 of Part B below, in quantities exceeding 30 metric tons in any period of 12 months.

Part B

1.   Complete nuclear reactors:

Nuclear reactors capable of operation so as to maintain a controlled self-sustaining fission chain reaction, excluding zero energy reactors, the latter being defined as reactors with a designed maximum rate of production of plutonium not exceeding 100 grams per year.

2.   Nuclear reactor vessels:

Metal vessels, or major shop-fabricated parts therefor, especially designed or prepared to contain the core of a nuclear reactor as defined in paragraph 1 above, as well as relevant nuclear reactor internals as defined in paragraph 8 below.

3.   Nuclear reactor fuel charging and discharging machines:

Manipulative equipment especially designed or prepared for inserting or removing fuel in a nuclear reactor as defined in paragraph 1 above.

4.   Nuclear reactor control rods and equipment:

Especially designed or prepared rods, support or suspension structures therefor, rod drive mechanisms or rod guide tubes to control the fission process in a nuclear reactor as defined in paragraph 1 above.

5.   Nuclear reactor pressure tubes:

Tubes which are especially designed or prepared to contain fuel elements and the primary coolant in a nuclear reactor as defined in paragraph 1 above at an operating pressure in excess of 50 atmospheres.

6. Zirconium tubes:

Zirconium metal and alloys in the form of tubes or assemblies of tubes, and in quantities exceeding 500 kg in any period of 12 months, especially designed or prepared for use in a nuclear reactor as defined in paragraph 1 above, and in which the relation of hafnium to zirconium
is less than 1:500 parts by weight.

7. Primary coolant pumps:

Pumps especially designed or prepared for circulating the primary coolant for a nuclear reactor as defined in paragraph 1 above.

8. Nuclear reactor internals:

Nuclear reactor internals especially designed or prepared for use in a nuclear reactor as defined in paragraph 1 above, including support columns for the core, fuel channels, thermal shields, baffles, core grid plates and diffuser plates.

9. Heat exchangers:

Heat exchangers (steam generators) especially designed or prepared for use in the primary coolant circuit of a nuclear reactor as defined in paragraph 1 above.

10. Neutron detection and measuring instruments:

Especially designed or prepared neutron detection and measuring instruments for determining neutron flux levels within the core of a nuclear reactor as defined in paragraph 1 above.

11. Plants for the fabrication of nuclear reactor fuel elements, and equipment especially designed or prepared therefor.

12. Plants for the conversion of uranium for use in the fabrication of fuel elements and the separation of uranium isotopes, and equipment especially designed or prepared therefor.

Part C

1. Plants for the conversion of plutonium for use in the fabrication of fuel elements and the separation of uranium isotopes, and equipment especially designed or prepared therefor.

2. Plants for the reprocessing of irradiated fuel elements, and equipment especially designed or prepared therefor.

3. Plants for the separation of isotopes of natural uranium, depleted uranium or special fissionable material and equipment, other than analytical instruments, especially designed or prepared therefor.

4. Plants for the production or concentration of heavy water, deuterium and deuterium compounds and equipment especially designed or prepared therefor.

Annex B
Levels of physical protection

CATEGORY III
(as defined in the attached table)

Use and storage within an area to which access is controlled.

Transportation under special precautions including prior arrangements among sender, recipient and carrier,
and prior agreement between entities subject to the jurisdiction and regulation of supplier and recipient States, respectively, in case of international transport, specifying time, place and procedures for transferring transport responsibility.

CATEGORY II
(as defined in the attached table)

Use and storage within a protected area to which access is controlled, i.e., an area under constant surveillance by guards or electronic devices, surrounded by a physical barrier with a limited number of points of entry under appropriate control, or any area with an equivalent level of physical protection.

Transportation under special precautions including prior arrangements among sender, recipient and carrier,
and prior agreement between entities subject to the jurisdiction and regulation of supplier and recipient States, respectively, in case of international transport, specifying time, place and procedures for transferring transport responsibility.

CATEGORY I
(as defined in the attached table)

Nuclear material in this category shall be protected with highly reliable systems against unauthorised use as follows:

Use and storage within a highly protected area, i.e., a protected area as defined for Category II above, to which, in addition, access is restricted to persons whose trustworthiness has been determined, and which is under surveillance by guards who are in close communication with appropriate response authorities. Specific measures taken in this context should have as their objective the detection and prevention of any assault, unauthorised access or unauthorized removal of the nuclear material concerned.

Transportation under special precautions as identified above for transportation of Category II and III nuclear material and, in addition, under constant surveillance by escorts and under conditions which assure close communication with appropriate response authorities.

TABLE: CATEGORIZATION OF NUCLEAR MATERIAL

Nuclear Material	Form	Category I	Category II	Category III[c]
1. Plutonium[a]	Unirradiated[b]	2kg or more	Less than 2kg but more than 500g	500g or less but more than 15g
2. Uranium-235	Unirradiated[b] -uranium enriched to 20% 235U or more -uranium enriched to 10% 235U but less than 20% 235U -uranium enriched above natural, but less than 10% 235U	5kg or more	Less than 5kg but more than 1kg 10kg or more	1kg or less but more than 15g Less than 10kg but more than 1kg 10kg or more
3. Uranium-233	Unirradiated[b]	2kg or more	Less than 2kg but more than 500g	500g or less but more than 15g
4. Irradiated Fuel			Depleted or natural uranium, thorium or low-enriched fuel (less than 10% fissile content)[d]/[e]	

154

(a)   All plutonium except that with isotopic concentration exceeding 80% in plutonium-238.

(b)   Nuclear material not irradiated in a reactor or nuclear material irradiated in a reactor but with a radiation level equal to or less than 1 Gy/hr (100 rads/hr) at one meter unshielded.

(c)   Quantities not falling in Category III and natural uranium, depleted uranium and thorium should be protected at least in accordance with prudent management practice.

(d)   Although this level of protection is recommended, it would be open to the Parties, upon evaluation of the specific circumstances, to assign a different category of physical protection.

(e)   Other fuel which by virtue of its original fissile material content is classified as Category I or II before irradiation may   be reduced one category level while the radiation level from the fuel exceeds 1 Gy/hr (100 rads/hr) at one meter unshielded.

注a　全てのプルトニウム（プルトニウム二三八の同位体濃度が八〇パーセントを超えるプルトニウムを除く。）

注b　原子炉内で照射されていない核物質、又は原子炉内で照射された核物質であって当該核物質からの放射線の吸収線量率が遮蔽のない距離一メートルの地点において一グレイ毎時（一〇〇ラド毎時）以下であるもの

注c　第三群に掲げる量未満のもの並びに天然ウラン、劣化ウラン及びトリウムは、少なくとも管理についての慎重な慣行に従って防護するものとする。

注d　第二群に属する核物質としての防護の水準が望ましいが、いずれの締約国政府も、具体的な状況についての評価に基づき、これと異なる区分の防護の水準を指定することができる。

注e　他の燃料であって当初の核分裂性成分含有量により照射前に第一群又は第二群に分類されるものについては、当該燃料からの放射線の吸収線量率が遮蔽のない距離一メートルの地点において一グレイ毎時（一〇〇ラド毎時）を超える間においては、防護の水準をそれぞれ一群ずつ下げることができる。

付表　核物質の区分

核物質	形態	第一群	第二群	第三群（注c）
1 プルトニウム（注a）	未照射（注b）	二キログラム以上	五〇〇グラムを超え二キログラム未満	一五グラムを超え五〇〇グラム以下
2 ウラン二三五	未照射ウラン二三五濃度が〇・二〇以上のウラン（注b）パーセント	五キログラム以上	一キログラムを超え五キログラム未満	一五グラムを超え一キログラム以下
	未照射ウラン二三五濃度が〇・一〇以上〇・二〇未満のウラン（注b）パーセント		一〇キログラム以上	一キログラムを超え一〇キログラム未満
	未照射ウラン二三五濃度が天然ウランを超え〇・一〇未満のウラン（注b）パーセント			一〇キログラム以上
3 ウラン二三三	未照射（注b）	二キログラム以上	五〇〇グラムを超え二キログラム未満	一五グラムを超え五〇〇グラム以下
4 照射済燃料	（注b）		劣化ウラン、天然ウラン、トリウム又は一〇パーセント未満の核分裂性成分を含有する低濃縮燃料（注d）（注e）	

合にあっては供給国及び受領国それぞれの管轄権及び規制に服する者の間の事前の合意であって、輸送に係る責任の移転する日時、場所及び手続を明記したものを締結することを含む。）の下に行うこと。

第一群（付表の定義による。）

この群に属する核物質は、次に定める信頼性の高い方式により、許可なしに使用される危険から防護されるものとする。

使用及び貯蔵に当たっては、高度に防護された区域（第二群に属する核物質について定める防護区域であって、さらに、信頼性につき確認を受けた者にのみ出入が許可され、かつ、適当な関係当局との緊密な連絡の下にある警備員により監視されるものをいう。）内において行うこと。この関連においてとられる具体的な措置は、攻撃、許可されない出入又は許可されない関係核物質の除去を探知し、及び防止することを、その目的とすべきものである。

輸送に当たっては、第二群及び第三群に属する核物質の輸送について定める特別の予防措置の下において、さらに、護送者により常時監視され、及び適当な関係当局との緊密な連絡が確保される状況の下で行うこと。

附属書B　防護の水準

第三群（付表の定義による。）

使用及び貯蔵に当たっては、出入が規制されている区域内において行うこと。

輸送に当たっては、特別の予防措置（荷送人、荷受人及び運送人の間の事前の取決め並びに国際輸送の場合にあっては供給国及び受領国それぞれの管轄権及び規制に服する者の間の事前の合意であって、輸送に係る責任の移転する日時、場所及び手続を明記したものを締結することを含む。）の下に行うこと。

第二群（付表の定義による。）

使用及び貯蔵に当たっては、出入が規制されている防護区域（警備員又は電子装置により常時監視される区域であって、適切な管理の下にある限定された箇所においてのみ出入が可能な物理的障壁により囲い込まれたものをいう。）内において又は防護の水準がこれと同等の水準にある区域内において行うこと。

輸送に当たっては、特別の予防措置（荷送人、荷受人及び運送人の間の事前の取決め並びに国際輸送の場

C部

1 原子炉燃料要素の加工又はウラン同位元素の分離に使用するためのプルトニウムの転換プラント及び当該プルトニウムの転換のために特に設計し、又は製作した設備

2 照射済原子炉燃料要素の再処理プラント及び照射済原子炉燃料要素の再処理のために特に設計し、又は製作した設備

3 天然ウラン、劣化ウラン又は特殊核分裂性物質の同位元素の分離プラント及び当該プラントのために特に設計し、又は製作した設備であって分析機器以外のもの

4 重水、重水素及び重水素化合物の生産又は濃縮のためのプラント並びに重水、重水素及び重水素化合物の生産又は濃縮のために特に設計し、又は製作した設備

7　一次冷却材ポンプ　1に規定する原子炉における一次冷却材の循環のために特に設計し、又は製作した
ポンプ

8　原子炉内装物　炉心支持柱、燃料チャネル、熱遮蔽体、調節板、炉心格子板、拡散板等1に規定する原子炉の内部において使用するために特に設計し、又は製作した原子炉内装物

9　熱交換器　1に規定する原子炉の一次冷却材回路において使用するために特に設計し、又は製作した熱交換器（蒸気発生器）

10　中性子検出機器及び中性子計測機器　1に規定する原子炉の炉心内部の中性子束を測定するために特に設計し、又は製作した中性子検出機器及び中性子計測機器

11　原子炉燃料要素の加工プラント及び原子炉燃料要素の加工のために特に設計し、又は製作した設備

12　原子炉燃料要素の加工又はウラン同位元素の分離に使用するためのウランの転換プラント及び当該ウランの転換のために特に設計し、又は製作した設備

の供給を行う場合に限る。）

B部

1　原子炉　制御された自己維持的核分裂連鎖反応を維持する運転能力を有する原子炉（ゼロ出力炉を除く。ゼロ出力炉とは、設計上の最大プルトニウム生成量が年間百グラムを超えない炉をいう。）

2　原子炉容器　1に規定する原子炉の炉心及び8に規定する原子炉内装物を収納するために特に設計し、又は製作した金属容器又はその主要な工作部品

3　原子炉燃料交換機　1に規定する原子炉についての燃料の挿入又は取出しのために特に設計し、又は製作した操作用設備

4　原子炉制御棒及び原子炉制御設備　1に規定する原子炉における核分裂過程の制御のために特に設計し、又は製作した棒、その支持体若しくは懸架体、制御棒駆動機構又は制御棒案内管

5　原子炉圧力管　1に規定する原子炉の内部に燃料要素及び一次冷却材を五十気圧を超える運転圧力下において収容するために特に設計し、又は製作した管

6　ジルコニウム管　ジルコニウム金属若しくはジルコニウム合金の管又はこれらの管の集合体であって、1に規定する原子炉の内部において使用するために特に設計し、又は製作し、かつ、ハフニウムとジルコニウムとの重量比が一対五百未満のもの（いずれかの十二箇月の期間において五百キログラムを超える量

附属書A

A部

1　重水素及び重水　B部の1に規定する原子炉において使用する重水素、重水（酸化重水素）及び重水素原子と水素原子との比が一対五千を超える他の重水素化合物（いずれかの十二箇月の期間において重水素原子の量につき二百キログラムを超える量の供給を行う場合に限る。）

2　原子炉級黒鉛　ほう素当量百万分の五の純度を超える純度及び一・五〇グラム毎立方センチメートルを超える密度を有する黒鉛であって、B部の1に規定する原子炉において使用するもの（いずれかの十二箇月の期間において三十メートル・トンを超える量の供給を行う場合に限る。）

ひとしく正文であるトルコ語、日本語及び英語により本書二通を作成し、二千十三年五月三日にアンカラ

で、及び二千十三年四月二十六日に東京で署名した。これらの言語の本文の解釈に関し紛争が生ずる場合に

は、英語の本文による。

トルコ共和国政府のために

日本国政府のために

岸田文雄

る合意により、この協定の改正によることなく修正することができる。附属書の修正は、日本国政府がト

ルコ共和国政府から必要な国内手続が完了した旨の書面による通告を受領した日に効力を生ずる。

第十五条

1　各締約国政府は、他方の締約国政府に対し、外交上の経路を通じて、この協定の効力発生のために必要

とされる国内手続が完了したことを通告する。この協定は、遅い方の通告が受領された日の後三十日目の

日に効力を生ずる。

2　この協定は、十五年間効力を有するものとし、その後は、いずれか一方の締約国政府がこの協定の有効

期間の満了する日の遅くとも六箇月前までに他方の締約国政府に対し、外交上の経路を通じて、この協定

を終了させる意思を書面により通告しない限り、自動的に五年間ずつ延長されるものとする。

3　この協定の終了の後においても、第一条、第三条、第四条2及び3、第五条から第八条まで、第九条2

並びに第十条から第十三条までの規定は、引き続き効力を有する。

以上の証拠として、下名は、各自の政府から正当に委任を受けてこの協定に署名した。

(b) 当該行動を検討することの原因となった事情が故意にもたらされたものであるか否か。

4 この協定に基づいて移転された核物質、資材又は設備の返還を要求するこの条の規定に基づく権利は、両締約国政府が相互に受け入れることができる条件及び手続に従って行使される。

5 いずれか一方の締約国政府は、3に規定する協議の後、次の場合にはこの条の規定に基づく権利を行使するものとする。

(a) 1に規定する場合において、適当な期間内に他方の締約国政府が是正措置をとらなかったとき。

(b) 2に規定する場合において、当該一方の締約国政府が是正措置を見いだすことができないと判断するとき。

　　第十四条

1 両締約国政府は、いずれか一方の締約国政府の要請に基づき、この協定の改正について、相互に協議する。この協定は、両締約国政府の書面による合意によって改正することができる。この協定の改正は、次条1に規定する手続と同様の手続に従い、効力を生ずる。

2 この協定の附属書は、この協定の不可分の一部を成す。この協定の附属書は、両締約国政府の書面によ

166

本国又はトルコ共和国について次の(a)又は(b)に規定する事情が生じた場合には、この協定の下での協力の全部若しくは一部を停止し、又はこの協定を終了させ、並びにこの協定に基づいて移転された核物質、資材及び設備の返還を要求する権利を有する。

(a) 第三条から第八条までのいずれかの規定又は前条に規定する仲裁裁判所の決定に対する違反をする場合

(b) 第四条に規定する機関との間の保障措置協定を終了させ、又はこれに対する重大な違反をする場合

2 トルコ共和国政府又は日本国政府は、それぞれ、日本国又はトルコ共和国が核爆発装置を爆発させる場合には、1に規定する権利と同じ権利を有する。

3 いずれか一方の締約国政府がこの協定の下での協力の全部若しくは一部を停止し、又はこの協定を終了させるに先立ち、両締約国政府は、他の適当な取極を行うことが必要となる場合のあることを考慮しつつ、是正措置をとることを目的として協議を行うものとし、適当な場合には、次の事項について慎重に検討する。

(a) 当該行動の影響

167

司法裁判所における先任の裁判官であって、いずれの一方の締約国政府の国の国民でもなく、かつ、そ

の任命を行うことができるもの）に対して、一人の仲裁裁判官を任命するよう要請することができる。

(c) 第二の仲裁裁判官の指名又は任命が行われてから三十日以内に第三の仲裁裁判官が選任されなかった

場合には、(b)に規定する手続と同様の手続が適用される。ただし、任命される第三の仲裁裁判官は、両

国のうちのいずれの国民であってもならない。

(d) 仲裁裁判には、仲裁裁判所の構成員の過半数が出席していなければならず、全ての決定には、過半数

の仲裁裁判官の同意を必要とする。

(e) 仲裁裁判の手続は、仲裁裁判所が定める。仲裁裁判所の決定は、両締約国政府を拘束する。

(f) 各締約国政府は、自らが指名した仲裁裁判官に係る費用及び自らが仲裁に参加する費用をそれぞれ負

担する。仲裁裁判長がその職務を遂行するための費用及び仲裁裁判所の残余の費用は、両締約国政府が

均等に負担する。

　　第十三条

1　トルコ共和国政府又は日本国政府は、この協定の効力発生後のいずれかの時点において、それぞれ、日

第十二条

1　この協定の解釈又は適用に関して問題が生じた場合には、両締約国政府は、いずれか一方の締約国政府の要請により、相互に協議を行う。

2　この協定の解釈又は適用から生ずる紛争が協議によって解決されない場合には、当該紛争は、いずれか一方の締約国政府の要請により、次の規定に従って選定される三人の仲裁裁判官によって構成される仲裁裁判所に付託される。

(a)　各締約国政府は、一人の仲裁裁判官を指名し（自国民を指名することができる。）、指名された二人の仲裁裁判官は、相互の合意により第三国の国民で裁判長となる第三の仲裁裁判官を指名する。

(b)　仲裁裁判の要請が行われてから三十日以内にいずれか一方の締約国政府が仲裁裁判官を指名しなかった場合には、いずれか一方の締約国政府は、国際司法裁判所長に対して、一人の仲裁裁判官を任命するよう要請することができる。国際司法裁判所長が一方の締約国政府の国の国民である場合又はその他の理由によりその任命を行うことができない場合には、国際司法裁判所次長（同次長がいずれか一方の締約国政府の国の国民である場合又はその他の理由によりその任命を行うことができない場合には、国際

169

優位を追求するため、他方の締約国政府若しくは産業上の利益を損なうため又は原子力の平和的利用の進展を妨げるためにこの協定の規定を利用してはならない。

2　両締約国政府は、この協定の効果的な実施のため、国内の核物質計量管理制度に基づき、この協定に基づいて移転された核物質、資材、設備及び技術、技術に基づく設備並びに回収され又は副産物として生産された核物質の最新の在庫目録を毎年交換する。

3　転換、燃料加工、濃縮又は再処理の工程において他の核物質と混合されることにより、この協定に基づいて移転された核物質及び回収され又は副産物として生産された核物質の特定性が失われた場合又は失われたと認められる場合には、この協定の下での当該核物質の特定については、代替可能性の原則及び構成比率による比例の原則により行うことができるものとする。

第十一条

両締約国政府は、この協定の下での協力に基づいて生じ、又は移転された知的財産及び技術の適切かつ効果的な保護を、トルコ共和国及び日本国が当事国である関係する国際協定並びにそれぞれの国において効力を有する法令に従って確保する。

2 この協定に基づいて移転された核物質、資材、設備及び技術、技術に基づく設備並びに回収され又は副産物として生産された核物質は、次のいずれかの場合には、この協定の適用を受けないこととなるものとする。

(a) そのような核物質、資材又は設備がこの協定の関係する規定に従って受領締約国政府の国の管轄の外に移転された場合

(b) そのような核物質、資材、設備又は技術がこの協定の適用を受けないこととなることを両締約国政府が共同で決定する場合

(c) 核物質について、機関が、第四条に規定する関係する保障措置協定の保障措置の終了に係る規定に従い、当該核物質が消耗したこと、保障措置の適用が相当とされるいかなる原子力活動にも使用することができないような態様で希釈されたこと又は実際上回収不可能となったことを決定する場合

第十条

1 いずれの締約国政府も、他方の締約国政府若しくはその認められた者に対する商業上若しくは産業上の

171

物として生産された核物質は、供給締約国政府の書面による事前の同意が得られる場合を除くほか、受領締約国政府の国の管轄の外（供給締約国政府の国の管轄内を除く。）に移転され、又は再移転されない。

第八条

この協定に基づいて移転された核物質及び回収され又は副産物として生産された核物質は、両締約国政府が書面により合意する場合に限り、トルコ共和国の管轄内において、濃縮し、又は再処理することができる。

第九条

1　直接であると第三国を経由してであるとを問わず、両国の間において移転される核物質、資材、設備及び技術は、予定されるこれらの移転を供給締約国政府が受領締約国政府に対して書面により事前に通告した場合に限り、かつ、これらが受領締約国政府の国の管轄に入る時から、この協定の適用を受ける。供給締約国政府は、通告された核物質、資材、設備又は技術の移転に先立ち、移転される当該核物質、資材、設備又は技術がこの協定の適用を受けることとなること及び予定される受領者が受領締約国政府でない場合には当該受領者が受領締約国政府の認められた者であることの書面による確認を受領締約国政府から得

約国政府は、それぞれの基準（少なくともこの協定の附属書Bに定める水準の防護を実現するものに限る。）に従って防護の措置をとる。

2　この協定に基づいて移転される核物質及び回収され又は副産物として生産された核物質の国際輸送について、トルコ共和国及び日本国は、千九百八十年三月三日に署名のために開放された核物質の防護に関する条約に基づくそれぞれの国の既存の義務に適合するように行動する。

3　一方の締約国政府は、この協定に基づいて移転される核物質に関係する防護措置の妥当性について検討するため、その移転が行われる前に、他方の締約国政府と協議を行うことができる。また、一方の締約国政府は、回収され又は副産物として生産された核物質に関係する防護措置の妥当性について検討するため、他方の締約国政府と協議を行うことができる。

4　両締約国政府は、二千五年九月十四日に署名のために開放された核によるテロリズムの行為の防止に関する国際条約に基づくそれぞれの国の既存の義務に適合するように行動する。

第七条

この協定に基づいて移転された核物質、資材、設備及び技術、技術に基づく設備並びに回収され又は副産

力事故の早期通報に関する条約、千九百八十六年九月二十六日に採択された原子力事故又は放射線緊急事態の場合における援助に関する条約及び千九百九十四年六月十七日に採択された原子力の安全に関する条約に基づくそれぞれの国の既存の義務に適合するように行動する。

2　日本国は、千九百九十七年九月五日に作成された使用済燃料管理及び放射性廃棄物管理の安全に関する条約に適合するように行動する。トルコ共和国は、同条約の締結の時から同条約に適合するように行動する。

3　両締約国政府は、この協定に基づいて移転された核物質、資材、設備若しくは技術、技術に基づく設備又は回収され又は副産物として生産された核物質が置かれ、又は用いられる施設について、当該施設の安全性を確保するための措置の実施に関する相互に満足する取極を行うことができる。

4　両締約国政府は、原子力事故に係る準備及び対応を含む原子力の安全を向上させるため、定期的に両締約国政府間で協議を行うことができる。

　　第六条

1　この協定に基づいて移転された核物質及び回収され又は副産物として生産された核物質について、両締

されていることを要件とする。

2　前条の規定に基づく義務の履行を確保するため、この協定に基づいて移転された核物質及び回収され又は副産物として生産された核物質は、

（a）　日本国内においては、日本国に関する保障措置協定の適用を受ける。

（b）　トルコ共和国内においては、トルコ共和国に関する保障措置協定の適用を受ける。

3　機関が何らかの理由により2の規定の下で必要とされる保障措置を適用しない例外的な場合には、この協定に基づいて移転された核物質及び回収され又は副産物として生産された核物質に常に保障措置が適用されていることが極めて重要であることに鑑み、両締約国政府は、是正措置をとるため直ちに共同で機関と協議するものとし、また、そのような是正措置がとられないときは、機関の保障措置の原則及び手続に適合する取極であって、2に規定する機関の保障措置が意図するところと同等の効果及び適用範囲を有するものを速やかに締結する。

第五条

1　トルコ共和国及び日本国は、この協定の実施に当たり、千九百八十六年九月二十六日に採択された原子

175

3 ウランの濃縮、使用済核燃料の再処理、プルトニウムの転換及び資材の生産のための技術及び設備（これらの3の規定において、「設備」には、この協定の附属書AのC部に掲げるものを含む。）並びにプルトニウムは、第十四条1の規定に従ってこれらを移転することを可能にするような改正が行われた場合に限り、この協定の下で移転することができる。

第三条

1 この協定の下での協力は、平和的非爆発目的に限って行う。

2 この協定に基づいて移転された核物質、資材、設備及び技術、技術に基づく設備並びに回収され又は副産物として生産された核物質は、平和的目的以外の目的で使用してはならず、また、いかなる核爆発装置のためにも又はいかなる核爆発装置の研究若しくは開発のためにも使用してはならない。

第四条

1 第二条に規定する協力は、この協定及びそれぞれの国において効力を有する法令に従う。特に、同条1(c)に規定する協力については、それぞれの国内で行われる全ての原子力活動に係る全ての核物質について、トルコ共和国に関する保障措置協定及び日本国に関する保障措置協定に従って機関の保障措置が適用

176

国政府又はその認められた者が役務を提供し、及び他方の締約国政府又はその認められた者がこれを受

領すること。

(e) 両締約国政府により合意されるその他の方法

2
1に規定する協力は、次の分野において行うことができる。

(a) 原料物質であって天然に存在するものの探鉱及び採掘

(b) 原子炉（両締約国政府が合意するものに限る。）の設計、建設、運転及び廃止

(c) 核燃料の生産及びそのための設備の製作

(d) 原子力の安全（放射線防護及び環境の監視を含む。）

(e) 核セキュリティ

(f) 使用済燃料及び放射性廃棄物の管理

(g) 放射性同位元素及び放射線の研究及び応用

(h) この協定の範囲内の分野に関する研究及び開発

(i) 両締約国政府により合意されるその他の分野

(ii) この協定に基づいて移転された資材又は設備を用いて行う一又は二以上の処理によって得られた核

物質

(iii) この協定に基づいて移転された技術を用いて得られたものとして両締約国政府が共同で決定する核

物質

第二条

1 この協定の下での協力は、次の方法により行うことができる。

(a) 専門家及び研修生を交換すること。

(b) 両締約国政府、両締約国政府の認められた者又は一方の締約国政府と他方の締約国政府の認められた者とによって決定される条件で、国家安全保障上の理由により秘密とされた情報以外の情報を交換すること。

(c) 供給者と受領者との間の決定によって定める条件で、一方の締約国政府又はその認められた者から他方の締約国政府又はその認められた者に対し、核物質、資材、設備及び技術を供給すること。

(d) この協定の範囲内の事項について、提供者と受領者との間の決定によって定める条件で、一方の締約

178

は、技術援助の形式をとることができ、そのような形式には、指導、技能の養成、訓練、実用的な知識の提供及び諮問サービスを含む。

(e)にいう「開発」とは、設計、設計の研究、設計の解析、設計の概念、試作体の組立て及び試験、試験生産に係る計画、設計用の資料、設計用の資料から製品化を検討する過程、外形的な設計、統合的な設計、配置計画等の生産前の全ての段階をいう。

(e)及び(f)にいう「生産」とは、建設、生産工学、製造、統合、組立て（取付けを含む。）、検査、試験、品質保証等の核物質若しくは資材を生産し、又は設備を製作するための全ての活動をいう。

(e)にいう「使用」とは、運転、据付け（現場への据付けを含む。）、保守、点検、修理、整備及び補修をいう。

(h)

(i) 「技術に基づく設備」とは、この協定に基づいて移転された技術を用いて製作されたものとして両締約国政府が共同で決定する設備をいう。

(j) 「回収され又は副産物として生産された核物質」とは、次の核物質をいう。

(i) この協定に基づいて移転された核物質から得られた核物質

前記の物質の一又は二以上を含有する物質

両締約国政府により決定されるその他の物質

特殊核分裂性物質には、原料物質を含まない。

(c) 「資材」とは、原子炉において使用する物質であってこの協定の附属書Aの A 部に掲げるものをい、核物質を含まない。

(d) 「設備」とは、原子力活動における使用のために特に設計し、又は製作した主要な機械、プラント若しくは器具又はこれらの主要な構成部分であって、この協定の附属書Aの B 部に掲げるものをいう。

(e) 「技術」とは、核物質、資材又は設備の開発、生産又は使用のために必要とされる特定の情報をいう。ただし、利用可能な情報であって、更に提供することが制限されていないものを除く。両締約国政府が特定し、及び決定する場合には、基礎科学的研究に関する情報についても除くことができる。当該特定の情報は、技術的資料の形式をとることができ、そのような形式には、青写真、計画書、図面、模型、数式、工学的な設計図及び仕様書、説明書並びに指示書であって、書面による又は他の媒体若しくは装置（ディスク、テープ、読取専用のメモリー等）に記録されたものを含む。また、当該特定の情報

(b) 「核物質」とは、次に規定する原料物質又は特殊核分裂性物質をいう。

(i) 原料物質とは、次の物質をいう。

ウランの同位元素の天然の混合率から成るウラン

同位元素ウラン二三五の劣化ウラン

トリウム

金属、合金、化合物又は高含有物の形状において前記のいずれかの物質を含有する物質

他の物質であって両締約国政府により決定される含有率において前記の物質の一又は二以上を含有するもの

両締約国政府により決定されるその他の物質

(ii) 特殊核分裂性物質とは、次の物質をいう。

プルトニウム

ウラン二三三

同位元素ウラン二三三又は二三五の濃縮ウラン

の不拡散に関連する条約に関連する保障措置の適用のためのトルコ共和国政府と国際原子力機関との間の協定

（以下「トルコ共和国に関する保障措置協定」という。）に従い、トルコ共和国において機関による保障措

置が適用されていることに留意し、

原子力の安全、核セキュリティ及び核不拡散が確保される方法で原子力の平和的利用を追求するという両

締約国政府の誓約を再確認し、

平和的目的のための原子力の利用及び原子力の安全の保証についての協力の重要性を強調して、

次のとおり協定した。

　　第一条

この協定の適用上、

(a)　「認められた者」とは、一方の締約国政府の国の管轄内にある個人又は団体であって、当該一方の締

約国政府により、この協定の下での協力（核物質、資材、設備及び技術を供給し、又は受領すること並

びに役務を提供し、又は受領することを含む。）を行うことを認められたものをいう。ただし、両締約

国政府を含まない。

[JAPANESE TEXT – TEXTE JAPONAIS]

平和的目的のための原子力の利用における協力のためのトルコ共和国政府と日本国政府との間の協定

トルコ共和国政府及び日本国政府（以下「両締約国政府」という。）は、

トルコ共和国と日本国との間に存在する友好関係に基づき、

トルコ共和国及び日本国の双方が国際原子力機関（以下「機関」という。）の加盟国であることを認識し、

トルコ共和国及び日本国の双方が千九百六十八年七月一日に作成された核兵器の不拡散に関する条約の当事国であることを考慮し、

千九百九十八年十二月四日に作成された追加議定書により補足された千九百七十七年三月四日に作成された日本国政府と国際原子力機関との間の核兵器の不拡散に関する条約第三条1及び4の規定の実施に関する日本国政府と国際原子力機関との間の協定（以下「日本国に関する保障措置協定」という。）に従い、日本国において機関による保障措置が適用されていることに留意し、

二千年七月六日に作成された追加議定書により補足された千九百八十一年六月三十日に作成された核兵器

TÜRKİYE CUMHURİYETİ HÜKÜMETİ İLE JAPONYA HÜKÜMETİ ARASINDA NÜKLEER ENERJİNİN BARIŞÇIL AMAÇLARLA KULLANIMINA DAİR İŞBİRLİĞİ ANLAŞMASI

Türkiye Cumhuriyeti Hükümeti ve Japonya Hükümeti (bundan böyle "Taraflar" olarak anılacaklardır);

Türkiye Cumhuriyeti ile Japonya arasında mevcut olan dostane ilişkiler temelinde;

Hem Türkiye Cumhuriyeti'nin hem de Japonya'nın Uluslararası Atom Enerjisi Ajansına (bundan böyle "Ajans" olarak anılacaktır) üye olduğu gerçeğini idrak ederek;

Hem Türkiye Cumhuriyeti hem de Japonya'nın 1 Temmuz 1968 tarihinde imzalanan Nükleer Silahların Yayılmasının Önlenmesi Antlaşmasına taraf olduklarını göz önüne alarak;

Ajans tarafından uygulanan güvence denetiminin, Japonya Hükümeti ile Uluslararası Atom Enerjisi Ajansı arasında 4 Aralık 1998 tarihinde Ek Protokolü imzalanan 4 Mart 1977 tarihli Nükleer Silahların Yayılmasının Önlenmesi Antlaşmasının III/1 ve 4. Maddelerinin Uygulanmasına yönelik Anlaşma (bundan böyle "Japonya için Güvence Denetimi Anlaşması" olarak anılacaktır) uyarınca Japonya'da uygulanmakta olduğunu dikkate alarak,

Ajans tarafından uygulanan güvence denetiminin, Türkiye Cumhuriyeti ile Uluslararası Atom Enerjisi Ajansı arasında 6 Temmuz 2000 tarihinde Ek Protokolü imzalanan Nükleer Silahların Yayılmasının Önlenmesi Antlaşmasına İlişkin Olarak Güvence Denetimi Uygulanmasına dair 30 Haziran 1981 tarihli Anlaşma (bundan böyle "Türkiye Cumhuriyeti için Güvence Denetimi Anlaşması" olarak anılacaktır) uyarınca Türkiye Cumhuriyeti'nde uygulanmakta olduğunu dikkate alarak;

Tarafların nükleer güvenliği ve nükleer emniyeti ve nükleer silahların yayılmasının önlenmesini sağlayacak şekilde nükleer enerjinin barışçıl kullanımı yönündeki taahhütlerini yeniden teyit ederek; ve

Nükleer enerjinin barışçıl amaçlarla kullanımında ve nükleer güvenliğin güvence altına alınmasında işbirliğinin önemini vurgulayarak;

aşağıdaki hususlarda anlaşmaya varmışlardır:

MADDE 1

İşbu Anlaşmanın amaçları doğrultusunda:

(a) "Yetkili kişi" Taraflardan birinin temsil ettiği Devletin yetki alanı içerisinde olan ve söz konusu Tarafça bu Anlaşma çerçevesinde nükleer madde, madde, ekipman ve teknoloji temin etmek veya almak ve hizmet ifa etmek veya almak dahil olmak üzere işbirliği yapmakla yetkilendirilmiş olan ancak Tarafları içermeyen gerçek veya tüzel kişi anlamına gelir;

(b)   "Nükleer madde":

(i)   doğada var olan izotopların karışımını içeren uranyum; uranyum 235 izotopu içeriği doğal düzeyin altına düşmüş tüketilmiş uranyum; toryum; bunlardan herhangi birinin metal, alaşım, kimyasal bileşik veya konsantre edilmiş şekli; Tarafların belirleyeceği oranda yukarıdakilerden birini veya daha fazlasını içeren diğer maddeler; ve Taraflarca belirlenen diğer benzer maddeler olarak tanımlanan kaynak maddeler; ve

(ii)   Plütonyum, uranyum-233, uranyum-235 izotopları bakımından zenginleştirilmiş uranyum veya uranyum-233 izotopları bakımından zenginleştirilmiş uranyum; bunlardan birini veya birden fazlasını içeren herhangi bir madde; ve Taraflarca belirlenecek diğer benzeri maddeler şeklinde tanımlanan özel bölünebilir maddeler anlamına gelir. Özel bölünebilir madde, kaynak maddeyi içermez;

(c)   "Madde" bir nükleer reaktörde kullanılmak üzere bu Anlaşma EK A Kısım A'da belirtilen ancak nükleer maddeyi içermeyen maddeler anlamına gelir;

(d)   "Ekipman" işbu Anlaşmada Ek A Kısım B altında belirtilen ve nükleer faaliyetlerde kullanılmak üzere özel olarak hazırlanmış veya tasarlanmış olan başlıca makine, tesis veya enstrümantasyon öğeleri veya bunların başlıca bileşenleri anlamına gelir;

(e)   "Teknoloji" herhangi bir nükleer madde, madde veya ekipmanın geliştirilmesi, üretimi veya kullanımı için gerekli olan özel bilgi anlamında olup, dağıtımına kısıtlama getirilmeksizin emre amade kılınmış olan bilgiler bu kapsama girmez. Taraflarca belirtilmişse ve kararlaştırılmışsa, temel bilimsel araştırmalara ilişkin bilgiler de kapsam dışında tutulabilir. Bu özel bilgi yazılı ortamlara ya da disk, bant ve salt-okunur bellekler gibi diğer ortam veya cihazlara yazılmış veya kaydedilmiş kroki, plan, diyagram, model, formül, mühendislik tasarımları ve şartnameleri, el kitapları ve talimatlar dâhil teknik veri biçiminde olabilir. Bu bilgiler ayrıca talimatlar, beceriler, eğitim, pratik bilgi ve danışmanlık hizmetini içerecek şekilde teknik yardım biçimini de alabilir;

(f)   Bu Maddede paragraf (e)de sözü edilen "geliştirme" ifadesi tasarım, tasarım araştırması, tasarım analizi, tasarım konseptleri, prototiplerin montajı ve test edilmesi, pilot üretim programları, tasarım verileri, tasarım verilerinin ürüne dönüştürülmesi süreci, konfigürasyon tasarımı, entegrasyon tasarımı ve yerleşim düzenleri gibi üretim öncesinde gerçekleşen tüm aşamalar anlamına gelir;

(g)   Bu Maddede paragraf (e) ve (f)de kullanılan "üretim" ifadesi inşaat, üretim mühendisliği, imalat, entegrasyon, montaj, muayene, test ve kalite güvencesi gibi, nükleer madde, madde veya ekipman üretimine yönelik tüm faaliyetler anlamına gelir;

(h)   Bu maddede paragraf (e)de kullanılan "kullanma" ifadesi işletme, sahada kurulum dahil kurulum, bakım, kontrol, onarım, revizyon ve yenileme anlamına gelir;

(i)   "Teknolojiye dayalı ekipman" ifadesi bu Anlaşma uyarınca transfer edilen teknoloji kullanılarak üretildiği, Taraflarca ortaklaşa belirlenen ekipman anlamına gelir; ve

(j) "Geri kazanılan veya yan ürün olarak üretilen nükleer madde" ifadesi aşağıdaki anlamdadır:

(i) Bu Anlaşma uyarınca transfer edilen nükleer maddeden türetilen nükleer madde;

(ii) Bu Anlaşma uyarınca transfer edilen madde veya ekipmanların kullanımı sonucu bir veya daha fazla süreçten türetilen nükleer madde; ve

(iii) Bu Anlaşma uyarınca transfer edilen teknolojinin kullanımından türetildiği, Taraflarca ortaklaşa belirlenen nükleer madde.

MADDE 2

1.   Bu Anlaşma kapsamında işbirliği aşağıdaki şekillerde gerçekleştirilebilir:

(a) uzman ve kursiyer değişimi;

(b) Taraflarca, Tarafların yetkili kişileri ya da Taraflardan herhangi biri ve diğer Tarafın yetkili kişileri tarafından belirlenen şartlar esasında,ulusal güvenlik sebepleriyle gizli olarak sınıflandırılmış bilgiler hariç olmak üzere, bilgi alışverişi;

(c) bir Taraf veya yetkili kişileri tarafından diğer Tarafa veya yetkili kişilerine, tedarikçi ve alıcı tarafından belirlenen şartlar esasında nükleer madde, madde, ekipman ve teknoloji tedariki;

(d) bu Anlaşmanın kapsamına giren konularda ve tedarikçi ile alıcının belirlediği şartlar esasında, bir Taraf veya yetkili kişilerince hizmet sağlanması ve diğer Taraf veya yetkili kişilerince hizmet alınması şeklinde; ve

(e) Taraflarca üzerinde anlaşmaya varılabilecek diğer şekillerde

2.   İşbu Maddede paragraf 1'de açıklandığı şekliyle işbirliği aşağıdaki alanlarda gerçekleşebilir:

(a) doğada var olan kaynak maddelerin keşif ve kullanımı;

(b) Taraflarca üzerinde anlaşmaya varılan nükleer reaktörlerin tasarımı, inşası, işletilmesi ve işletmeden çıkarılması;

(c) nükleer yakıt ve bununla ilgili ekipman üretimi;

(d) radyasyondan korunma ve çevre izleme dâhil nükleer güvenlik;

(e) nükleer emniyet;

(f) kullanılmış yakıt ve radyoaktif atık yönetimi;

(g) radyoizotop ve radyasyona ilişkin çalışmalar ve uygulamalar;

(h) işbu Anlaşma kapsamındaki alanlarda araştırma ve geliştirme; ve

(i)   Taraflarca üzerinde anlaşmaya varılabilecek diğer alanlar.

3.   Uranyum zenginleştirmeye, kullanılmış nükleer yakıtın yeniden işlenmesine, plütonyum dönüştürmeye ve Ek A Kısım C'de sıralananlar dahil maddelerin üretimine yönelik teknoloji ve ekipman ve plütonyum, ancak işbu Anlaşma'nın 14. Maddesi'nin 1. paragrafı uyarınca söz konusu amaç için tadil edildiği takdirde işbu Anlaşma kapsamında transfer edilebilir.

MADDE 3

1.   İşbu Anlaşma kapsamında sadece barışçıl, patlayıcı nitelikte olmayan amaçlar için işbirliği yürütülecektir.

2.   İşbu Anlaşma uyarınca transfer edilen nükleer madde, madde, ekipman ve teknoloji, teknolojiye dayalı ekipman ve Geri kazanılan veya yan ürün olarak üretilen nükleer madde, barışçıl amaçlar dışındaki herhangi bir amaç için kullanılmayacağı gibi, herhangi bir nükleer patlayıcı cihaz için veya böyle bir cihaza yönelik araştırma veya geliştirme çalışmaları için de kullanılmayacaktır.

MADDE 4

1.   İşbu Anlaşma'nın 2. Maddesi'nde açıklanan işbirliği, bu Anlaşmanın hükümlerine ve Taraf devletlerde yürürlükte olan mevzuata tabi olacaktır. Özellikle sözkonusu Madde'nin 1. paragrafının (c)bendinde öngörülen işbirliği, Türkiye Cumhuriyeti için Güvenlik Tedbirleri Anlaşması ve Japonya için Güvenlik Tedbirleri Anlaşmasına uygun olarak ilgili Devletlerin sınırları içinde gerçekleştirilen tüm nükleer faaliyetlerdeki tüm nükleer maddelerle ilgili olarak Ajans tarafından güvence denetiminin uygulanmasını gerektirecektir.

2.   Bu Anlaşmanın 3. maddesinden doğan yükümlülüklerin yerine getirilmesini sağlamak için, bu Anlaşma uyarınca transfer edilen nükleer madde ve Geri kazanılan veya yan ürün olarak üretilen nükleer madde:

        (a)   Japonya sınırları içerisindeyken, Japonya için Güvenlik Tedbirleri Anlaşmasına tabi olacaktır; ve

        (b)   Türkiye Cumhuriyeti sınırları içerisindeyken, Türkiye Cumhuriyeti için Güvenlik Tedbirleri Anlaşmasına tabi olacaktır.

3.   Ajansın herhangi bir sebeple işbu maddenin 2. paragrafında şart koşulan güvence denetimlerini uygulamadığı istisnai bir durumda, Taraflar, işbu Anlaşma uyarınca transfer edilen nükleer maddenin ve Geri kazanılan veya yan ürün olarak üretilen nükleer maddenin daima güvence denetimine tabi kalmasının taşıdığı hayati önemi göz önüne alarak, düzeltici önlemleri alması için hemen müştereken Ajansla görüşecek, söz konusu düzeltici önlemlerin alınmaması durumunda Ajansın güvence denetimi esas ve usullerine uygun olan düzenlemeleri derhal yapacak ve Ajansın işbu maddenin 2. paragrafında belirtilen güvence denetimiyle sağlanması amaçlanana eş etkinliği ve kapsamı sağlayacaktır.

MADDE 5

1.   Bu Anlaşmanın hükümlerinin uygulanmasında, Türkiye Cumhuriyeti ve Japonya 26 Eylül 1986 tarihli Nükleer Kaza Halinde Erken Bildirim Sözleşmesi, 26

Eylül 1986 tarihli Nükleer Kaza veya Radyolojik Acil Hallerde Yardımlaşma Sözleşmesi ve 17 Haziran 1994 tarihli Nükleer Güvenlik Sözleşmesi hükümleri çerçevesinde her bir Devlete düşen mevcut yükümlülüklere uygun olarak hareket edeceklerdir.

2.   Japonya, 5 Eylül 1997 tarihinde imzalanan Kullanılmış Yakıt İdaresinin ve Radyoaktif Atık İdaresinin Güvenliği Üzerine Birleşik Sözleşme hükümlerine uygun hareket edecektir. Söz konusu Sözleşmenin akdedilmesiyle birlikte, Türkiye Cumhuriyeti de bunun hükümlerine uygun olarak hareket edecektir.

3.   İşbu Anlaşma uyarınca transfer edilen nükleer madde, madde, ekipman veya teknoloji, teknolojiye dayalı ekipman veya Geri kazanılan veya yan ürün olarak üretilen nükleer maddenin bulunduğu veya kullanıldığı tesislerle ilgili olarak, Taraflar bu tür tesislerin güvenliğini sağlamaya yönelik tedbirlerin uygulanması için karşılıklı tatmin edici düzenlemeler yapabilirler.

4.   Taraflar, nükleer hadiselere hazırlıklı olma ve müdahale dâhil olmak üzere nükleer güvenliği arttırmak amacıyla dönemsel iki taraflı istişare toplantıları yapabilirler.

MADDE 6

1.   İşbu Anlaşma uyarınca transfer edilen nükleer madde ve Geri kazanılan veya yan ürün olarak üretilen nükleer maddeyle ilgili olarak, Taraflar kendi kriterlerine göre, asgari olarak işbu Anlaşma'nın EK B'sinde belirlenen düzeylerde koruma sağlayan fiziksel koruma tedbirleri uygulayacaktır.

2.   İşbu Anlaşma uyarınca transfer edilen nükleer maddelerin ve Geri kazanılan veya yan ürün olarak üretilen nükleer maddenin uluslararası taşınması ile ilgili olarak, Türkiye Cumhuriyeti ve Japonya 3 Mart 1980 tarihinde imzaya açılan Nükleer Maddenin Fiziksel Korunması Hakkında Sözleşmenin hükümleri çerçevesinde her bir Devlete düşen mevcut yükümlülüklere uygun olarak hareket edeceklerdir.

3.   Taraflardan herhangi birisi, transferden önce işbu Anlaşma uyarınca transfer edilen nükleer madde ve Geri kazanılan veya yan ürün olarak üretilen nükleer maddeyle ilgili olarak fiziksel koruma tedbirlerinin yeterliliğini gözden geçirmek amacıyla diğer Tarafla görüşebilir.

4.   Taraflar 14 Eylül 2005'te imzaya açılan Nükleer Terör Eylemlerinin Önlenmesine Yönelik Uluslararası Sözleşme hükümleri çerçevesinde her bir Devlete düşen mevcut yükümlülüklere uygun olarak hareket edecektir.

MADDE 7

İşbu Anlaşma uyarınca transfer edilen nükleer madde, madde, ekipman ve teknoloji, teknolojiye dayalı ekipman ve Geri kazanılan veya yan ürün olarak üretilen nükleer madde, tedarik eden Tarafın önceden yazılı rızası alınmadan tedarik eden Tarafın Devletinin yetki alanı hariç olmak üzere alıcı Tarafın Devletinin yetki alanı ötesine transfer veya yeniden transfer edilemez.

MADDE 8

İşbu Anlaşma uyarınca transfer edilen nükleer madde ve Geri kazanılan veya yan ürün olarak üretilen nükleer madde, ancak Tarafların yazılı olarak anlaşmaya varması halinde Türkiye Cumhuriyeti'nin yetki alanı içinde zenginleştirilebilir veya yeniden işlenebilir.

MADDE 9

1.   İki Devlet arasında ister doğrudan ister bir Üçüncü Devlet aracılığıyla transfer edilen nükleer madde, madde, ekipman ve teknoloji, ancak tedarik eden Tarafın alıcı Tarafa planlanan transferi yazılı olarak ve önceden bildirmiş olması halinde, alıcı Tarafın Devletinin yetki alanına girer girmez işbu Anlaşmaya tabi hale gelecektir. Bu tür nükleer madde, madde, ekipman veya teknolojinin önceden bildirilmiş transferinin öncesinde, tedarikçi Taraf transfer edilen nükleer madde, madde, ekipman veya teknolojinin bu Anlaşmaya tabi tutulacağı ve alıcı Taraftan farklı ise önerilen alıcının alıcı Tarafın bir yetkili kişisi olacağı yönünde yazılı bir teyidi alıcı Taraftan alacaktır.

2.   İşbu Anlaşma uyarınca transfer edilen nükleer madde, madde, ekipman ve teknoloji, teknolojiye dayalı ekipman ve Geri kazanılan veya yan ürün olarak üretilen nükleer madde aşağıdaki hallerde işbu Anlaşmaya artık tabi olmayacaklardır:

(a)   Söz konusu nükleer madde, madde veya ekipman, bu Anlaşmanın ilgili hükümlerine uygun olarak alıcı Tarafın Devletinin yetki alanı ötesine transfer edilmişse;

(b)   Taraflar söz konusu nükleer madde, madde, ekipman veya teknolojinin artık bu Anlaşmaya tabi olmayacağı konusunda ortak karara varırsa; veya

(c)   nükleer maddenin söz konusu olduğu hallerde, Ajans, işbu Anlaşma'nın 4. maddesinde sözü edilen ilgili anlaşmada güvence denetiminin sonlandırılmasına ilişkin olarak yer verilen hükümlere uygun olarak, nükleer maddenin tüketildiğini veya güvence denetimi açısından herhangi bir nükleer faaliyette artık kullanılamaz hale gelecek şekilde seyreltilmiş olduğunu veya uygulamada geri kazanılamaz hale geldiğini tespit ederse.

MADDE 10

1.   Taraflardan hiç birisi diğer Tarafın veya yetkili kişilerinin üzerinde ticari veya sınaî bir avantaj elde etme amacıyla veya diğer Tarafın veya yetkili kişisinin ticari veya sınaî menfaatlerine müdahale etme amacıyla veya nükleer enerjinin barışçıl kullanımlarının geliştirilmesini önleme amacıyla bu Anlaşmanın hükümlerini kullanmayacaktır.

2.   İşbu Anlaşmanın etkin bir şekilde uygulanması için, Taraflar yıllık olarak bu Anlaşma uyarınca transfer edilen nükleer madde, madde, ekipman ve teknolojinin ve teknolojiye dayalı ekipmanın ve nükleer maddelerin sayım ve kontrolü için kullanılan ulusal sistem temelinde Geri kazanılan veya yan ürün olarak üretilen nükleer maddelerin güncel envanterlerini birbirlerine sunacaklardır.

3.   İşbu anlaşma uyarınca transfer edilen nükleer madde ve Geri kazanılan veya yan ürün olarak üretilen nükleer madde, kimliklerini kaybettikleri karıştırma süreçlerinde veya kimliklerini kaybetmiş sayıldıkları dönüştürme, yakıt imalat, zenginleştirme veya yeniden işleme süreçlerinde kullanılmaları halinde, ikame edilebilirlik ve orantılılık ilkeleri temelinde işlem görebilir.

MADDE 11

Taraflar, Türkiye Cumhuriyeti ile Japonya'nın taraf oldukları ilgili uluslararası anlaşmalara ve her iki ülkede geçerli olan mevzuata uygun olarak bu Anlaşma çerçevesinde gerçekleştirilen işbirliği uyarınca yaratılan veya transfer edilen fikri mülkiyetin ve teknolojinin yeterli ve etkili bir şekilde korunmasını sağlayacaklardır.

MADDE 12

1.   Taraflar, içlerinden birinin talep etmesi durumunda, işbu Anlaşmanın uygulanmasıyla veya yorumlanmasıyla ilgili olarak ortaya çıkabilecek herhangi bir soruyla ilgili olarak birbirleriyle istişare edeceklerdir.

2.   Bu Anlaşmanın yorumlanmasından veya uygulanmasından doğan herhangi bir ihtilaf istişareler yoluyla çözüme kavuşturulamazsa, söz konusu ihtilaf, Taraflardan herhangi birinin talebi üzerine, aşağıdaki hükümlere uygun olarak atanacak üç hakemden oluşan bir hakem heyetine havale edilecektir:

        (a)   Her bir Taraf, kendi Devletinin vatandaşı olabilecek tek bir hakem atayacak, böylece atanan iki hakem karşılıklı mutabakata varmak yoluyla üçüncü bir Devletin vatandaşı olup heyetin Başkanlığını yapacak olan üçüncü hakemi belirleyecektir;

        (b)   Şayet, tahkim talebinden itibaren otuz gün içinde Taraflardan herhangi birisi henüz bir hakem belirlememişse, Taraflardan herhangi biri Uluslararası Adalet Divanı (bundan böyle "UAD" olarak anılacaktır) Başkanından bir hakem belirlemesini isteyebilir. Şayet UAD Başkanı Taraf Devletlerden herhangi birinin vatandaşı ise veya herhangi başka bir nedenden dolayı atamaları yapmaktan alıkonuyorsa, UAD Başkan yardımcısı veya, Başkan Yardımcısı da Taraf Devletlerden herhangi birinin vatandaşıysa veya benzer şekilde atamaları yapmaktan alıkonuyorsa, UAD'nin Taraf Devletlerden herhangi birinin vatandaşı olmayan ve benzer şekilde engellenmeyen en kıdemli hakiminden, atamaları yapması istenebilir;

        (c)   Yukarıda (b) fıkrasında belirtilen aynı usul, ikinci hakemin belirlenmesini veya görevlendirilmesini müteakip otuz gün içinde üçüncü hakemin seçilmemesi durumunda bu şekilde atanan üçüncü hakemin Taraf Devletlerden herhangi birinin vatandaşı olmaması kaydıyla geçerli olmak üzere, uygulanacaktır;

        (d)   Tahkim heyetinin üye çoğunluğu yeter sayıyı sağlayacak ve tüm kararlarda heyet üyelerinin çoğunluğunun onayı gerekecektir;

        (e)   Tahkim usulü, heyetin kararlarıyla tespit edilecektir. Heyetin kararları Taraflar üzerinde bağlayıcı olacaktır; ve

        (f)   Her bir Taraf, kendi hakeminin ve tahkim sürecindeki temsilinin maliyetlerini üstlenecektir. Vazifeyi icrada hakem heyeti Başkanının sebep olduğu maliyet ve hakem heyetinin diğer maliyetleri taraflarca eşit şekilde üstlenilecektir.

MADDE 13

1.   Şayet Japonya veya Türkiye Cumhuriyeti bu Anlaşmanın yürürlüğe girmesinin ardından herhangi bir zamanda:

(a)   işbu Anlaşmanın 3., 4., 5., 6., 7. veya 8. Maddelerindeki hükümleri veya bu Anlaşmanın 12. maddesinde sözü edilen tahkim heyetinin kararlarını ihlal ederse; ya da

(b)   işbu Anlaşmanın 4. Maddesinde sözü edilen ve Ajansla imzalanmış olan Güvenlik Tedbirleri Anlaşmasını sona erdirir veya maddi olarak ihlal ederse,

Türkiye Cumhuriyeti Hükümeti veya Japonya Hükümeti, bu Anlaşma kapsamındaki işbirliğini tamamen veya kısmen durdurma, ya da bu Anlaşmayı sona erdirme ve bu Anlaşma uyarınca transfer edilmiş olan her türlü nükleer madde, madde ve ekipmanın iadesini isteme hakkına karşılıklı olarak sahip olacaktır.

2.   Japonya veya Türkiye Cumhuriyeti'nin bir nükleer patlayıcı cihaz patlatması durumunda, Türkiye Cumhuriyeti Hükümeti veya Japonya Hükümeti, bu Maddenin birinci paragrafında belirtilen hakka karşılıklı olarak sahip olacaktır.

3.   Taraflardan herhangi birisi bu Anlaşma kapsamındaki işbirliğini tamamen veya kısmen durdurmak ya da bu Anlaşmayı sona erdirmek için harekete geçmeden önce, Taraflar düzeltici tedbirler almak amacıyla birbirlerine danışacak ve, uygun hallerde, gerekli diğer uygun düzenlemeleri yapma ihtiyacını göz önünde bulundurarak aşağıdakileri dikkatle değerlendirmeye alacaktır:

(a)   bu tür adımları atmanın yaratacağı etkiler; ve

(b)   söz konusu adımların dikkate alınmasına neden olan olgulara kasıtlı olarak sebep olunup olunmadığı.

4.   İşbu anlaşma uyarınca transfer edilmiş olan nükleer madde, madde veya ekipmanın bu madde kapsamında iadesini isteme hakkı, Taraflarca karşılıklı kabul edilebilir olan şart, koşul ve usullere uygun olarak kullanılacaktır.

5.   İşbu Maddenin 3. paragrafında sözü edilen istişarelerin ardından, işbu Madde kapsamındaki hak her iki Tarafça aşağıdaki hallerde uygulanacaktır:

(a)   İşbu Maddenin 1. Paragrafında sözü edilen durumda, şayet diğer Taraf uygun bir süre içinde düzeltici tedbirleri alamazsa; ve

(b)   İşbu Maddenin 2. paragrafında sözü edilen durumda, hiçbir düzeltici tedbirin bulunmadığını tespit ederse.

MADDE 14

1.   Taraflar, herhangi bir Tarafın talebi üzerine, işbu Anlaşmada yapılacak değişiklikler konusunda birbirleriyle istişare edecektir. İşbu Anlaşma, Taraflar arasında yapılacak yazılı bir anlaşmayla değiştirilebilir. Bu Anlaşmada yapılacak değişiklikler, Madde 15 paragraf 1'de belirtilen usule uygun olarak yürürlüğe girecektir.

2.   İşbu Anlaşmanın Ekleri işbu Anlaşmanın ayrılmaz bir parçasını oluşturur. Ekler, işbu Anlaşmada herhangi bir değişiklik gerektirmeksizin Taraflar arasında yapılacak yazılı bir anlaşmayla tadil edilebilir. Eklerdeki tadilat, gerekli iç usullerin tamamlandığına dair Türkiye Cumhuriyeti Hükümeti tarafından yapılan yazılı bildirimin Japonya Hükümeti tarafından alındığı tarihte yürürlüğe girer.

MADDE 15

1.   Her bir Taraf, işbu Anlaşmanın yürürlüğe girmesi için gerekli olan iç usulleri tamamladığını diğer tarafa bildirdiği tebligatı diplomatik kanallar yoluyla diğer Tarafa gönderecektir. Bu Anlaşma, son bildirimin alındığı tarihi takip eden otuzuncu günde yürürlüğe girer.

2.   İşbu Anlaşma onbeş yıllık bir süre için yürürlükte kalacak ve Taraflardan herhangi biri bu Anlaşmayı sona erdirme niyetini diğer tarafa yazılı olarak Anlaşmanın sona eriş tarihinden en az altı ay önce diplomatik kanallar aracılığıyla bildirmediği sürece, sona eriş tarihinden itibaren otomatik olarak beşer yıllık dönemlerle uzatılacaktır.

3.   Bu Anlaşmanın sona erdirilmesinden bağımsız olarak, bu Anlaşmadaki Madde 1, Madde 3, Madde 4 paragraf 2 ve 3, Madde 5 ila 8, Madde 9 paragraf 2 ve Madde 10 ila 13 yürürlükte kalmaya devam edecektir.

Yukarıdaki hususları tasdiken, aşağıda imzaları bulunan ve kendi Hükümetlerince usulüne uygun olarak yetkili kılınmış temsilciler bu Anlaşmaya imza atmıştır.

İki nüsha halinde tüm metinler eşit derecede geçerli olmak üzere Türkçe, Japonca ve İngilizce olarak düzenlenmiş ve üç Mayıs 2013 tarihinde Ankara'da ve yirmi altı Nisan 2013 tarihinde Tokyo'da imzalanmıştır. Metinlerin yorumlanmasına ilişkin herhangi bir ihtilaf durumunda, İngilizce metin geçerli olacaktır.

Türkiye Cumhuriyeti
Hükümeti adına:

Taner Yıldız
Enerji ve Tabii Kaynaklar
Bakanı

Japonya
Hükümeti adına:

Fumio Kishida
Dışişleri Bakanı

Ek A

Kısım A

1. Döteryum ve ağır su:

Aşağıda Kısım B paragraf 1'de tanımlandığı gibi bir nükleer reaktörde kullanılmak üzere, 12 aylık bir sürede 200 kg döteryum atomunu aşan miktarlardaki döteryum, ağır su (döteryum oksit) ve döteryum atomlarının hidrojen atomlarına oranı 1:5000'den fazla olan diğer döteryum bileşikleri.

2. Nükleer amaçlı grafit:

Aşağıda Kısım B paragraf 1'de tanımlandığı gibi bir nükleer reaktörde kullanılmak üzere, 12 aylık bir sürede 30 metrik tonu aşan miktarlarda, milyonda 5 boron eşdeğerinden daha iyi saflığa ve $1,50g/cm^3$'den daha yüksek yoğunluğa sahip grafit.

Kısım B

1. Tam nükleer reaktörler:

Maksimum Plütonyum üretimi 100 gram/yıl'dan daha fazla olmayacak şekilde tasarımlanmış reaktörler olarak tanımlanan sıfır enerjili reaktörler hariç olmak üzere, kendiliğinden devam eden fisyon zincirleme reaksiyonunu kontrollü bir şekilde devam ettirerek çalışan nükleer reaktörler.

2. Nükleer reaktör kapları:

Aşağıda 8. paragrafta tanımlandığı gibi nükleer reaktör iç aksamı ile beraber, yukarıda 1. paragrafta tanımlandığı gibi özel olarak nükleer reaktör korunu içermek üzere tasarımlanmış veya hazırlanmış metal kap veya bu kabın başlıca parçaları.

3. Nükleer reaktör yakıtı yükleme ve boşaltma makineleri:

Yukarıda 1. paragrafta tanımlandığı gibi, özel olarak nükleer reaktörlere yakıt koymak veya almak için tasarımlanmış veya hazırlanmış manipülatif ekipmanlar.

4. Nükleer reaktör kontrol çubukları ve ekipmanı:

Yukarıda 1. paragrafta tanımlandığı üzere, nükleer reaktörlerdeki fisyon işlemini kontrol etmek için özel olarak tasarımlanmış veya hazırlanmış çubuklar, bunların destek veya askı sistemleri, çubuk sürme mekanizmaları veya çubuk kılavuz boruları.

5. Nükleer reaktör basınç tüpleri:

Yukarıda 1. paragrafta tanımlandığı gibi bir nükleer reaktörde 50 atmosferin üzerindeki çalışma basıncında yakıt elemanlarını ve birincil soğutucuyu kapsamak üzere özel olarak tasarımlanmış veya hazırlanmış tüpler.

6. Zirkonyum tüpler:

Yukarıda 1. paragrafta tanımlandığı gibi bir nükleer reaktörde kullanılmak üzere özel olarak tasarımlanmış veya hazırlanmış, hafniyum/zirkonyum oranı ağırlıkça 1:500'den az olan ve 12 aylık bir süre zarfında miktarları 500 kg'ı geçen tüp veya tüp demetleri şeklindeki zirkonyum metal ve alaşımları.

7. Birincil devre soğutucu pompaları:

Yukarıda 1. paragrafta tanımlandığı gibi özel olarak bir nükleer reaktör için birincil devre soğutucusunu dolaştırmak amacıyla tasarımlanmış veya hazırlanmış pompalar.

8. Nükleer reaktör iç aksamı:

Yukarıda 1. paragrafta tanımlandığı gibi bir nükleer reaktörde kullanılmak üzere özel olarak tasarımlanmış veya hazırlanmış olup kor destek sütunları, yakıt kanalları, termal zırhlar, deflektör plakaları, kor ızgara plakaları ve yayıcı plakaları dâhil nükleer reaktör iç aksamları.

9. Isı değiştiriciler:

Yukarıda 1. paragrafta tanımlandığı gibi bir nükleer reaktörün birincil soğutucu devresinde kullanılmak üzere özel olarak tasarımlanmış veya hazırlanmış ısı değiştiriciler (buhar jeneratörleri).

10. Nötron tespit ve ölçüm aygıtları:

Yukarıda 1. paragrafta tanımlandığı gibi bir nükleer reaktörde kor içindeki nötron akısı seviyelerini belirlemek için özel olarak tasarımlanmış veya hazırlanmış nötron tespit ve ölçüm aygıtları.

11. Nükleer reaktör yakıt elemanlarının üretimine yönelik tesisler ve bunlar için özel olarak tasarımlanmış veya hazırlanmış ekipmanlar.

12. Yakıt elemanlarının üretiminde ve uranyum izotoplarının ayrıştırılmasında kullanılan uranyumun dönüştürülmesi için kullanılan tesisler ve bunlar için özel olarak tasarımlanmış veya hazırlanmış ekipmanlar.

Kısım C

1. Yakıt elemanlarının üretiminde ve uranyum izotoplarının ayrıştırılmasında kullanılan plütonyumun dönüştürülmesi için kullanılan tesisler ve bunlar için özel olarak tasarımlanmış veya hazırlanmış ekipmanlar.

2. Işınlanmış yakıt elemanlarının yeniden işlenmesine yönelik tesisler ve bunlar için özel olarak tasarımlanmış veya hazırlanmış ekipmanlar.

3. Doğal uranyumun, tükenmiş uranyumun veya özel bölünebilir maddenin izotoplarının ayrıştırılmasına yönelik tesisler ve bunlar için özel olarak tasarımlanmış veya hazırlanmış olan, analitik aygıtlar hariç ekipmanlar.

4. Ağır su, döteryum ve döteryum bileşiklerinin üretimine veya yoğunlaştırılmasına yönelik tesisler ve bunlar için özel olarak tasarımlanmış veya hazırlanmış ekipmanlar.

Ek B
Fiziksel koruma düzeyleri

III. SINIF
(ekli tabloda tanımlandığı üzere)

Erişimin kontrollü olduğu bir alan içerisinde kullanım ve depolama.

Taşıma; gönderici, alıcı ve taşıyıcı arasında önceden yapılan düzenlemeler ile ihraç ve ithal eden Devletlerin yetkisine ve mevzuatına tabi olan gerçek ve tüzel kişiler arasında zaman, yer ve taşıma mesuliyetinin devrine dair muameleleri belirleyen ön anlaşmaları ihtiva eden özel düzenlemeler altında yapılır.

II. SINIF
(ekli tabloda tanımlandığı üzere)

Erişimin kontrollü olduğu, korunan bir alan içerisinde kullanım ve depolama; örneğin, elektronik cihazlarla veya koruma görevlilerince sürekli gözlem altında tutulan, uygun şekilde kontrol altında tutulan sınırlı sayıda giriş noktasının bulunduğu, fiziksel bir bariyerle çevrili alan ya da eşdeğer fiziksel korumaya sahip herhangi bir alan.

Taşıma; gönderici, alıcı ve taşıyıcı arasında önceden yapılan düzenlemeler ile tedarikçi ve alıcı Devletlerin yetkisine ve mevzuatına tabi olan birimler arasında zaman, yer ve taşıma mesuliyetinin devrine dair muameleleri belirleyen ön anlaşmaları ihtiva eden özel düzenlemeler altında yapılır.

I. SINIF
(ekli tabloda tanımlandığı üzere)

Bu kategorideki nükleer madde, izinsiz kullanıma karşı, yüksek güvenilirliğe sahip sistemlerle aşağıdaki gibi korunacaktır:

Yüksek korumalı bir alan içinde kullanım ve depolama;örneğin, yukarıda II. Sınıf için tanımlandığı gibi bir korumalı alana ek olarak, girişi güvenilirlikleri belirlenmiş kişilere sınırlandırılmış ve uygun kolluk kuvvetleriyle yakın irtibat içinde olan koruma görevlilerince sürekli nezaret altında tutulan alan. Bu konuda alınan özel tedbirlerin amacı, söz konusu bir nükleer madde ile ilgili olarak gelebilecek bir saldırıyı, yetkisiz girişleri veya maddenin yetkisiz olarak alınmasını tespit etmek ve önlemek olmalıdır.

Taşıma, yukarıda II. ve III. Sınıf maddeler için tayin edilmiş olan özel tedbirlere ek olarak, taşıma aracına eşlik eden koruma görevlilerinin sürekli nezareti altında ve uygun kolluk kuvvetleriyle yakın iletişimi sağlayacak koşullarda yapılır.

TABLO: NÜKLEER MADDELERİN SINIFLANDIRILMASI

Nükleer Madde	Biçim	I	II	III[c]
1. Plütonyum [a]	Işınlanmamış [b]	2 kg veya daha fazla	2 kg'dan az fakat 500 gr'dan fazla	500 gr veya daha az fakat 15 gr'dan daha fazla
2. Uranyum-235	Işınlanmamış [b] -U-235'i %20 veya daha fazla zenginleştirilmiş uranyum -U-235'i %10 veya daha fazla ancak %20'den daha az zenginleştirilmiş uranyum -Doğal uranyumdan daha zengin fakat %10'dan daha az zenginleştirilmiş U-235 içeren uranyum	5 kg veya daha fazla	5 kg'dan az fakat 1kg'dan daha fazla 10 kg veya daha fazla	1 kg veya daha az fakat 15 gr'dan fazla 10 kg'dan az fakat 1 kg'dan fazla 10 kg veya daha fazla
3. Uranyum-233	Işınlanmamış [b]	2 kg veya daha fazla	2 kg'dan daha az fakat 500 gr'dan daha fazla	500 gr veya daha az fakat 15 gr'dan fazla
4. Işınlanmış Yakıt			Tüketilmiş veya doğal uranyum, toryum veya düşük zenginlikteki yakıt (bölünebilir madde içeriği %10'dan daha az)[d],[e]	

(a)   Plütonyum-238 izotopu %80'i aşan izotopik konsantrasyona sahip plütonyum dışındaki plütonyum.

(b)   Reaktörde ışınlanmamış nükleer madde veya reaktörde ışınlanmış ancak zırhlama olmaksızın bir metre uzaklıkta 1 Gy/saat'e (100 rad/saat)eşit veya daha az radyasyon düzeyi olan nükleer madde.

(c)   III'üncü sınıfa girmeyen miktarlar ve doğal uranyum, tükenmiş uranyum ve toryum asgari olarak ihtiyatlı yönetim uygulamaları gereğince korunmalıdır.

(d)   Her ne kadar bu düzeydeki koruma önerilmişse de, özel durumlar değerlendirilerek farklı fiziksel korunma sınıfına tahsis edilmesi hususu Taraflara bırakılmıştır.

(e)   Işınlanmadan önce bölünebilir madde içeriğinden dolayı diğer yakıtlardan I ve II'nci Sınıf olarak ayrılmış olanlar zırhlama olmaksızın yakıttan bir metre uzaklıktaki radyasyon seviyesinin 100 rad/saati aşması durumunda, bir alt sınıfa geçirilebilir.

[TRANSLATION – TRADUCTION]

ACCORD DE COOPÉRATION ENTRE LE GOUVERNEMENT DE LA RÉPUBLIQUE TURQUE ET LE GOUVERNEMENT DU JAPON RELATIF À L'UTILISATION DE L'ÉNERGIE NUCLÉAIRE À DES FINS PACIFIQUES

Le Gouvernement de la République turque et le Gouvernement du Japon (ci-après dénommés les « Parties »),

Guidés par les relations d'amitié qui unissent la République turque et le Japon,

Considérant que la République turque et le Japon sont tous deux membres de l'Agence internationale de l'énergie atomique (ci-après dénommée « l'Agence »),

Considérant que la République turque et le Japon sont tous deux parties au Traité sur la non-prolifération des armes nucléaires, conclu le 1er juillet 1968,

Notant que les garanties de l'Agence sont appliquées au Japon conformément à l'Accord entre le Gouvernement du Japon et l'Agence internationale de l'énergie atomique en application des paragraphes 1 et 4 de l'article III du Traité sur la non-prolifération des armes nucléaires, conclu le 4 mars 1977, tel que complété par le Protocole additionnel, conclu le 4 décembre 1998 (ci-après dénommé « l'Accord de garanties pour le Japon »),

Notant que les garanties de l'Agence sont appliquées en République turque conformément à l'Accord entre le Gouvernement de la République turque et l'Agence internationale de l'énergie atomique relatif à l'application de garanties dans le cadre du Traité sur la non-prolifération des armes nucléaires, conclu le 30 juin 1981, tel que complété par le Protocole additionnel, conclu le 6 juillet 2000 (ci-après dénommé « l'Accord de garanties pour la République turque »),

Réaffirmant l'engagement des Parties à utiliser l'énergie nucléaire à des fins pacifiques de façon à garantir la sûreté, la sécurité et la non-prolifération nucléaires, et

Soulignant l'importance de la coopération pour l'utilisation de l'énergie nucléaire à des fins pacifiques et l'assurance de la sûreté nucléaire,

Sont convenus de ce qui suit :

Article premier

Aux fins du présent Accord :

a) L'expression « personne autorisée » désigne toute personne physique ou entité relevant de la compétence de l'État d'une Partie et autorisée par celle-ci à mener des activités de coopération au titre du présent Accord, et notamment à fournir ou à recevoir des matières nucléaires, des matières, des équipements et de la technologie, et à fournir ou à recevoir des services, mais n'inclut pas les Parties;

b) L'expression « matière nucléaire » désigne :

i) Une matière brute, à savoir l'uranium contenant le mélange d'isotopes que l'on trouve dans la nature, l'uranium appauvri en isotope 235, le thorium, l'une quelconque des matières précitées sous forme de métal, d'alliage, de composé chimique ou de concentré, toute autre substance contenant une ou plusieurs des matières précitées à une concentration déterminée par les Parties et toute autre substance déterminée par les Parties; et

ii) Un produit fissile spécial, à savoir le plutonium, l'uranium 233, l'uranium enrichi en isotope 233 ou 235, toute substance contenant une ou plusieurs des matières précitées et toute autre substance déterminée par les Parties. Les produits fissiles spéciaux n'incluent pas les matières brutes;

c) Le terme « matière » désigne les substances destinées à être utilisées dans un réacteur nucléaire et visées dans la partie A de l'annexe A du présent Accord, mais n'inclut pas les matières nucléaires;

d) Le terme « équipement » désigne les grands éléments d'installation, les machines ou les instruments, ou leurs principaux composants, spécialement conçus ou préparés pour être utilisés dans des activités nucléaires et visés dans la partie B de l'annexe A du présent Accord;

e) Le terme « technologie » désigne les informations précises nécessaires à la mise au point, à la production ou à l'utilisation d'une matière nucléaire, d'une matière ou d'un équipement, à l'exception des informations qui ont été rendues disponibles sans restriction quant à leur diffusion ultérieure. Les informations provenant de la recherche scientifique fondamentale peuvent également être exclues, sur décision des Parties. Ces informations précises peuvent prendre la forme de données techniques, qui comprennent les schémas, les plans, les diagrammes, les modèles, les formules, les projets et spécifications d'ingénierie, les manuels et les instructions écrites ou enregistrées sur d'autres médias ou dispositifs tels que des disques, des bandes et des dispositifs de stockage en mémoire morte. Elles peuvent également prendre la forme d'une assistance technique, qui comprend les instructions, les compétences, la formation, les connaissances pratiques et les services de conseil;

f) L'expression « mise au point » visée au paragraphe e) du présent article désigne toutes les phases précédant la production, telles que la conception, la recherche et l'analyse en vue de la conception, les concepts, l'assemblage et l'essai des prototypes, la production pilote, les données de conception, la transformation des données de conception en produit, la conception de la configuration, la conception de l'intégration et les plans d'ensemble;

g) Le terme « production » visé aux paragraphes e) et f) du présent article désigne toutes les activités liées à la production d'une matière nucléaire, d'une matière ou d'un équipement, telles que la construction, la technique de production, la fabrication, l'intégration, l'assemblage (montage), l'inspection, les essais et l'assurance qualité;

h) Le terme « utilisation » visé au paragraphe e) du présent article désigne l'exploitation, l'installation, y compris l'installation sur site, l'entretien, la vérification, la réparation, la révision et la rénovation;

i) Le terme « équipement basé sur la technologie » désigne un équipement dont les Parties établissent conjointement qu'il est produit grâce à l'utilisation de la technologie transférée en application du présent Accord; et

j) L'expression « matière nucléaire récupérée ou obtenue sous forme de sous-produit » désigne :

i) Une matière nucléaire obtenue à partir d'une matière nucléaire transférée en application du présent Accord;

ii) Une matière nucléaire obtenue au moyen d'un ou de plusieurs processus provenant de l'utilisation d'une matière ou d'un équipement transféré en application du présent Accord; et

iii) Une matière nucléaire dont les Parties établissent conjointement qu'elle est tirée de l'utilisation de la technologie transférée en application du présent Accord.

Article 2

1. La coopération au titre du présent Accord peut prendre les formes suivantes :

a) L'échange d'experts et de stagiaires;

b) L'échange d'informations autres que des informations classifiées pour des raisons nationales, dans les conditions dont décident les Parties, entre les personnes autorisées des Parties, ou entre l'une des Parties et les personnes autorisées de l'autre;

c) La fourniture, par une Partie ou par les personnes autorisées de celle-ci à l'autre Partie ou aux personnes autorisées de celle-ci, de matières nucléaires, de matières, d'équipements ou de technologies, dans les conditions dont décident le fournisseur et le bénéficiaire;

d) La fourniture de services par une Partie ou par les personnes autorisées de celle-ci et la réception de services par l'autre Partie ou par les personnes autorisées de celle-ci sur des questions relevant du présent Accord, dans les conditions dont décident le fournisseur et le bénéficiaire; et

e) Les autres formes dont conviennent les Parties.

2. La coopération définie au paragraphe 1 du présent article peut être menée dans les domaines suivants :

a) La prospection et l'exploitation des matières brutes que l'on trouve dans la nature;

b) La conception, la construction, l'exploitation et la mise hors service de réacteurs nucléaires dont conviennent les Parties;

c) La production de combustible nucléaire et d'équipements destinés à ces réacteurs;

d) La sûreté nucléaire, y compris la radioprotection et le contrôle de l'environnement;

e) La sécurité nucléaire;

f) La gestion du combustible usé et des déchets radioactifs;

g) L'étude des radio-isotopes et des rayonnements et leurs applications;

h) La recherche et le développement dans des domaines relevant du présent Accord; et

i) Les autres domaines dont conviennent les Parties.

3. La technologie et l'équipement servant à l'enrichissement de l'uranium, au retraitement du combustible nucléaire usé, à la conversion du plutonium et à la production de matières, y compris celles énumérées dans la partie C de l'annexe A, et de plutonium ne peuvent être transférés au titre du présent Accord que lorsque celui-ci est modifié à cet effet conformément au paragraphe 1 de l'article 14.

Article 3

1.   La coopération au titre du présent Accord est menée uniquement à des fins pacifiques et non explosives.

2.   Les matières nucléaires, les matières, les équipements et les technologies transférés en application du présent Accord, les équipements basés sur la technologie et les matières nucléaires récupérées ou obtenues sous forme de sous-produits ne peuvent être utilisés qu'à des fins pacifiques et ne peuvent être utilisés ni dans un dispositif nucléaire explosif quelconque, ni pour des travaux de recherche et développement portant sur un tel dispositif.

Article 4

1.   La coopération définie à l'article 2 du présent Accord doit être conforme aux dispositions du présent Accord ainsi qu'aux lois et règlements en vigueur dans chacun des États. La coopération visée à l'alinéa c) du paragraphe 1 dudit article nécessite l'application des garanties par l'Agence en ce qui concerne toutes les matières nucléaires dans toutes les activités nucléaires menées dans chacun des États conformément à l'Accord de garanties pour la République turque et l'Accord de garanties pour le Japon, selon le cas.

2.   Aux fins de l'accomplissement des obligations découlant de l'article 3 du présent Accord, les matières nucléaires transférées en application du présent Accord et les matières nucléaires récupérées ou obtenues sous forme de sous-produits :

    a)   Sont soumises à l'Accord de garanties pour le Japon tant qu'elles se trouvent dans ce pays; et

    b)   Sont soumises à l'Accord de garanties pour la République turque tant qu'elles se trouvent dans ce pays.

3.   Dans le cas exceptionnel où, pour une quelconque raison, l'Agence n'applique pas les garanties comme prévu au paragraphe 2 du présent article, les Parties, compte tenu du fait qu'il est essentiel que les matières nucléaires transférées en application du présent Accord et les matières nucléaires récupérées ou obtenues sous forme de sous-produits fassent en permanence l'objet de garanties, consultent l'Agence conjointement sans délai afin de prendre des mesures correctives et, en l'absence de telles mesures, concluent immédiatement des arrangements conformes aux principes et aux procédures de garanties de l'Agence et qui assurent une efficacité et une couverture équivalentes à celles qui doivent être fournies par les garanties de l'Agence visées au paragraphe 2 du présent article.

Article 5

1.   En mettant en œuvre les dispositions du présent Accord, la République turque et le Japon se conforment aux obligations qu'imposent à chacun les dispositions de la Convention sur la notification rapide d'un accident nucléaire, adoptée le 26 septembre 1986, de la Convention sur l'assistance en cas d'accident nucléaire ou de situation d'urgence radiologique, adoptée le 26 septembre 1986 et de la Convention sur la sûreté nucléaire, adoptée le 17 juin 1994.

2.   Le Japon se conforme aux dispositions de la Convention commune sur la sûreté de la gestion du combustible usé et sur la sûreté de la gestion des déchets radioactifs, conclue

le 5 septembre 1997. Dès qu'elle aura signé ladite Convention, le République turque agira conformément à ses dispositions.

3. Les Parties peuvent conclure des accords mutuellement satisfaisants aux fins de la mise en œuvre de mesures visant à assurer la sûreté des installations dans lesquelles se trouvent ou sont utilisés les matières nucléaires, les matières, les équipements ou les technologies transférées en application du présent Accord, les équipements basés sur la technologie et les matières nucléaires récupérées ou obtenues sous forme de sous-produits.

4. Les Parties peuvent organiser périodiquement des consultations bilatérales afin de renforcer la sûreté nucléaire, y compris la préparation aux accidents nucléaires et les mesures d'intervention en cas d'accident nucléaire.

Article 6

1. S'agissant des matières nucléaires transférées en application du présent Accord et des matières nucléaires récupérées ou obtenues sous forme de sous-produits, les Parties appliquent des mesures de protection physique conformément à leurs critères respectifs qui offrent, au minimum, les niveaux de protection visés à l'annexe B du présent Accord.

2. S'agissant du transport international des matières nucléaires transférées en application du présent Accord et des matières nucléaires récupérées ou obtenues sous forme de sous-produits, la République turque et le Japon se conforment aux obligations qu'imposent à chacun les dispositions de la Convention sur la protection physique des matières nucléaires, ouverte à la signature le 3 mars 1980.

3. Chacune des Parties peut consulter l'autre Partie aux fins de réexaminer le bien-fondé des mesures de protection physique liées aux matières nucléaires transférées en application du présent Accord avant le transfert et aux matières nucléaires récupérées ou produites sous forme de sous-produits.

4. Les Parties se conforment aux obligations qu'imposent à chaque État les dispositions de la Convention internationale pour la répression des actes de terrorisme nucléaire, ouverte à la signature le 14 septembre 2005.

Article 7

Les matières nucléaires, les matières, les équipements et les technologies transférés en application du présent Accord, les équipements basés sur la technologie et les matières nucléaires récupérées ou obtenues sous forme de sous-produits ne sont ni transférés ni retransférés en dehors du territoire de l'État de la Partie destinataire, sauf vers le territoire de l'État de la Partie expéditrice, à moins que cette dernière n'en ait donné l'autorisation au préalable, par écrit.

Article 8

Les matières nucléaires transférées en application du présent Accord et les matières nucléaires récupérées ou obtenues sous forme de sous-produits ne peuvent faire l'objet d'un enrichissement ou d'un retraitement sur le territoire de la République turque que si les Parties en conviennent par écrit.

Article 9

1.   Les matières nucléaires, les matières, les équipements et les technologies transférés entre les deux États, soit directement soit par l'intermédiaire d'un État tiers, ne sont soumis aux dispositions du présent Accord dès leur entrée sur le territoire de l'État de la Partie destinataire que si la Partie expéditrice a préalablement informé par écrit la Partie destinataire du transfert envisagé. Avant le transfert notifié des matières nucléaires, des matières, des équipements ou des technologies, la Partie expéditrice obtient de la Partie destinataire une confirmation écrite du fait que les matières nucléaires, les matières, les équipements ou les technologies destinés à être transférés seront soumis aux dispositions du présent Accord et du fait que le destinataire proposé, s'il ne s'agit pas de la Partie destinataire, sera une personne autorisée de cette dernière.

2.   Les matières nucléaires, les matières, les équipements et les technologies transférés en application du présent Accord, les équipements basés sur la technologie et les matières nucléaires récupérées ou obtenues sous forme de sous-produits soumis aux dispositions du présent Accord ne le sont plus :

a)   Si ces matières nucléaires, matières ou équipements ont été transférés en dehors du territoire de l'État de la Partie destinataire conformément aux dispositions pertinentes du présent Accord;

b)   Si les Parties décident conjointement que ces matières nucléaires, matières, équipements ou technologies ne sont plus régis par le présent Accord; ou

c)   En ce qui concerne les matières nucléaires, si l'Agence constate, conformément aux dispositions pour la levée des garanties de l'accord pertinent visé à l'article 4 du présent Accord, que lesdites matières ont été consommées, ou ont été diluées de telle manière qu'elles ne sont plus utilisables pour une activité nucléaire pouvant faire l'objet de garanties, ou sont devenues pratiquement irrécupérables.

Article 10

1.   Aucune des Parties n'utilise les dispositions du présent Accord pour rechercher des avantages commerciaux ou industriels sur l'autre Partie ou les personnes autorisées de celle-ci, ni pour s'immiscer dans les intérêts commerciaux ou industriels de l'autre Partie ou des personnes autorisées de celle-ci ou entraver le développement des utilisations pacifiques de l'énergie nucléaire.

2.   Aux fins de la mise en œuvre de du présent Accord, les Parties échangent chaque année les inventaires à jour des matières nucléaires, matières, équipements et technologies transférés en application dudit Accord, des équipements basés sur la technologie et des matières nucléaires récupérées ou obtenues sous forme de sous-produits, établis selon le système national de comptabilité et de contrôle des matières nucléaires.

3.   Les matières nucléaires transférées en application du présent Accord et les matières nucléaires récupérées ou obtenues sous forme de sous-produits peuvent être manipulées sur la base des principes de fongibilité et de proportionnalité lorsqu'elles sont utilisées dans des processus de mélange au cours desquels elles perdent leur identité, ou sont réputées la perdre, lors de la conversion, de la fabrication de combustible, de l'enrichissement ou du retraitement.

Article 11

Les Parties veillent à la protection effective et adéquate de la propriété intellectuelle et de la technologie créée ou transférée dans le cadre de la coopération découlant du présent Accord, conformément aux accords internationaux pertinents auxquels la République turque et le Japon sont parties ainsi qu'aux lois et règlements en vigueur dans chacun des États.

Article 12

1. À la demande de l'une d'elles, les Parties se consultent sur toute question qui se pose à propos de l'interprétation ou de l'application du présent Accord.

2. Dans le cas où un différend lié à l'interprétation ou à l'application du présent Accord n'est pas réglé par la voie de consultations, l'une ou l'autre des Parties peut demander qu'il soit soumis à un tribunal d'arbitrage composé de trois arbitres nommés conformément aux dispositions suivantes :

    a) Chaque Partie désigne un arbitre qui peut être un ressortissant de son État et les deux arbitres ainsi désignés en choisissent un troisième, ressortissant d'un État tiers, qui devient le président du tribunal;

    b) Si l'une des Parties n'a pas désigné son arbitre dans les 30 jours suivant la demande d'arbitrage, l'une ou l'autre peut demander au Président de la Cour internationale de Justice (ci-après dénommée la « CIJ ») de procéder à la nomination. Si le Président de la CIJ est un ressortissant de l'État de l'une ou l'autre Partie ou ne peut procéder aux nominations pour une raison quelconque, le Vice-Président de la CIJ ou, si le Vice-Président est un ressortissant de l'État de l'une ou l'autre Partie, ou s'il est de même empêché d'agir, le plus ancien des juges de la CIJ qui n'est ni un ressortissant d'une Partie ni de même empêché d'agir peut être prié de procéder aux nominations;

    c) La procédure prévue à l'alinéa b) ci-dessus s'applique si le troisième arbitre n'a pas été choisi dans les 30 jours suivant la désignation ou nomination du deuxième arbitre, étant entendu que le troisième arbitre ainsi nommé ne peut être un ressortissant de l'État de l'une ou l'autre des Parties;

    d) Le quorum est constitué par la majorité des membres du tribunal d'arbitrage, qui prend toutes ses décisions à la majorité de ses membres;

    e) Le tribunal définit sa procédure. Les décisions du tribunal sont contraignantes pour les Parties; et

    f) Chacune des Parties contractantes prend à sa charge les frais afférents à l'activité de l'arbitre qu'elle a désigné ainsi que les frais de sa défense dans la procédure arbitrale. Les frais afférents au président du tribunal d'arbitrage dans l'exercice de ses fonctions et les autres coûts du tribunal d'arbitrage sont supportés à parts égales par les deux Parties.

Article 13

1. Si le Japon ou la République turque, à un moment quelconque après l'entrée en vigueur du présent Accord :

    a) Agit en violation des dispositions des articles 3, 4, 5, 6, 7 ou 8 du présent Accord, ou des décisions du tribunal d'arbitrage visé à l'article 12 du présent Accord; ou

b) Dénonce ou viole de façon substantielle son Accord de garanties avec l'Agence, visé à l'article 4 du présent Accord;

Le Gouvernement de l'autre Partie a le droit de cesser toute coopération au titre du présent Accord, en tout ou partie, ou de dénoncer le présent Accord et d'exiger la restitution des matières nucléaires, matières et équipements transférés en application du présent Accord.

2. Si le Japon ou la République turque fait exploser un dispositif explosif nucléaire, le Gouvernement de l'autre Partie a le droit énoncé au paragraphe 1 du présent article.

3. Avant que l'une ou l'autre ne prenne des mesures pour cesser la coopération au titre du présent Accord, en tout ou partie, ou pour dénoncer le présent Accord, les Parties se consultent aux fins de prendre des mesures correctives et, le cas échéant, examinent attentivement les aspects ci-après, en tenant compte de la nécessité éventuelle de conclure d'autres accords appropriés :

a) Les effets de ces mesures; et

b) La question de savoir si les faits justifiant que l'on envisage ces mesures résultent d'un acte délibéré.

4. Le droit conféré par le présent article d'exiger la restitution des matières nucléaires, des matières ou des équipements transférés en application du présent Accord est exercé conformément aux conditions et procédures mutuellement acceptables pour les Parties.

5. À la suite des consultations visées au paragraphe 3 du présent article, les droits conférés par le présent article sont exercés par une Partie :

a) Dans le cas visé au paragraphe 1 du présent article, uniquement si l'autre Partie ne prend pas de mesures correctives dans un délai approprié; et

b) Dans le cas visé au paragraphe 2 du présent article, si elle constate qu'aucune mesure corrective n'a été prise.

Article 14

1. À la demande de l'une d'elles, les Parties se consultent sur les modifications à apporter au présent Accord. Le présent Accord peut être modifié par accord écrit des Parties. Les modifications entrent en vigueur suivant la procédure énoncée au paragraphe 1 de l'article 15.

2. Les annexes du présent Accord en font partie intégrante. Elles peuvent être modifiées au moyen d'un accord écrit entre les Parties sans modification du présent Accord. Les modifications des annexes entrent en vigueur à la date de réception par le Gouvernement du Japon de la notification écrite du Gouvernement de la République turque de l'accomplissement de ses procédures internes requises.

Article 15

1. Chaque Partie notifie à l'autre Partie, par la voie diplomatique, l'accomplissement des procédures internes requises pour l'entrée en vigueur du présent Accord. Le présent Accord entre en vigueur le trentième jour suivant la date de la réception de la dernière notification.

2. Le présent Accord reste en vigueur pour une période de 15 ans et est ensuite prorogé automatiquement pour des périodes de cinq ans chacune, à moins que l'une des Parties n'informe l'autre par écrit et par la voie diplomatique de son intention de le dénoncer, au plus tard six mois avant la date d'expiration.

3. Nonobstant la dénonciation du présent Accord, l'article premier, l'article 3, les paragraphes 2 et 3 de l'article 4, les articles 5 à 8, le paragraphe 2 de l'article 9 et les articles 10 à 13 continuent de déployer leurs effets.

EN FOI DE QUOI, les soussignés, à ce dûment autorisés par leurs Gouvernements respectifs, ont signé le présent Accord.

FAIT en double exemplaire, en langues anglaise, japonaise et turque, tous les textes faisant également foi, et signé à Ankara le 3 mai 2013 et à Tokyo, le 26 avril 2013. En cas de divergence d'interprétation, le texte anglais prévaut.

Pour le Gouvernement de la République turque :

TANER YILDIZ
Ministre de l'énergie et des ressources naturelles

Pour le Gouvernement du Japon :

FUMIO KISHIDA
Ministre des affaires étrangères

ANNEXE A

PARTIE A

1. Deutérium et eau lourde :

Deutérium, eau lourde (oxyde de deutérium) et tout composé de deutérium dans lequel le rapport atomique deutérium/hydrogène dépasse 1/5 000, destinés à être utilisés dans un réacteur nucléaire tel que défini au paragraphe 1 de la partie B ci-dessous, en quantités dépassant 200 kg d'atomes de deutérium pendant une période de 12 mois.

2. Graphite de pureté nucléaire :

Graphite d'une pureté supérieure à cinq parties par million d'équivalent en bore et d'une densité de plus de 1,50 g/cm^3, destiné à être utilisé dans un réacteur nucléaire tel que défini au paragraphe 1 de la partie B ci-dessous, en quantités dépassant 30 tonnes pendant une période de 12 mois.

PARTIE B

1. Réacteurs nucléaires complets :

Réacteurs nucléaires pouvant fonctionner de manière à maintenir une réaction de fission en chaîne auto-entretrenue contrôlée, exception faite des réacteurs de puissance nulle dont la production maximale prévue de plutonium ne dépasse pas 100 grammes par an.

2. Cuves de réacteur nucléaire :

Cuves métalliques ou principaux éléments de cuve fabriqués en atelier, spécialement conçus ou préparés pour contenir le cœur d'un réacteur nucléaire tel que défini au paragraphe 1 ci-dessus, ainsi que les éléments internes propres à un réacteur nucléaire définis au paragraphe 8 ci-dessous.

3. Machines pour le chargement et le déchargement du combustible nucléaire :

Matériel de manutention spécialement conçu ou préparé pour introduire ou extraire le combustible d'un réacteur nucléaire tel que défini au paragraphe 1 ci-dessus.

4. Équipement et barres de commande de réacteur nucléaire :

Barres spécialement conçues ou préparées, ainsi que leurs structures de soutien ou de suspension, leurs mécanismes d'entraînement ou leurs tubes de guidage, pour la commande du processus de fission au sein d'un réacteur nucléaire tel que défini au paragraphe 1 ci-dessus.

5. Tubes de pression de réacteur nucléaire :

Tubes spécialement conçus ou préparés pour contenir les éléments combustibles et le réfrigérant primaire d'un réacteur nucléaire tel que défini au paragraphe 1 ci-dessus, à une pression de service supérieure à 50 atmosphères.

6. Tubes de zirconium :

Zirconium métallique et alliages sous forme de tubes ou d'assemblages de tubes, en quantités supérieures à 500 kg par période de 12 mois, spécialement conçus ou préparés pour être utilisés dans un réacteur nucléaire tel que défini au paragraphe 1 ci-dessus, et dans lesquels le rapport entre hafnium et zirconium est inférieur à 1/500 parties en poids.

7.   Pompes du circuit primaire :

Pompes spécialement conçues ou préparées pour la circulation du réfrigérant primaire des réacteurs nucléaires tels que définis au paragraphe 1 ci-dessus.

8.   Internes de réacteur nucléaire :

Équipements internes de réacteur nucléaire spécialement conçus ou préparés pour être utilisés dans un réacteur nucléaire tel que défini au paragraphe 1 ci-dessus, notamment les colonnes entretoises, les canaux de combustible, les écrans thermiques, les déflecteurs, les plaques à grille du cœur et les plaques de diffuseur.

9.   Échangeurs thermiques :

Échangeurs thermiques (générateurs de vapeur) spécialement conçus ou préparés pour être utilisés dans le circuit de réfrigération primaire d'un réacteur nucléaire tel que défini au paragraphe 1 ci-dessus.

10. Instruments de détection et de mesure neutroniques :

Instruments de détection et de mesure neutroniques spécialement conçus ou préparés pour déterminer les flux de neutrons dans le cœur d'un réacteur nucléaire tel que défini au paragraphe 1 ci-dessus.

11. Usines de fabrication d'éléments combustibles de réacteur nucléaire, et matériel spécialement conçu ou préparé à cette fin.

12. Usines de conversion de l'uranium en vue de la fabrication d'éléments combustibles, et de séparation des isotopes de l'uranium, et matériel spécialement conçu ou préparé à cette fin.

PARTIE C

1.   Usines de conversion du plutonium en vue de la fabrication d'éléments combustibles, et de séparation des isotopes de l'uranium, et matériel spécialement conçu ou préparé à cette fin.

2.   Usines de retraitement des éléments combustibles irradiés, et matériel spécialement conçu ou préparé à cette fin.

3.   Usines de séparation des isotopes de l'uranium naturel, de l'uranium appauvri et des matières fissiles spéciales, et matériel, autre que les instruments d'analyse, spécialement conçu ou préparé à cette fin.

4.   Usines de production ou de concentration d'eau lourde, de deutérium et de composés de deutérium, et matériel spécialement conçu ou préparé à cette fin.

ANNEXE B
NIVEAUX DE PROTECTION PHYSIQUE

CATÉGORIE III

(telle que définie dans le tableau ci-joint)

Utilisation et entreposage dans une zone dont l'accès est contrôlé.

Transport assorti de précautions particulières comprenant notamment des arrangements préalables entre l'expéditeur, le destinataire et le transporteur, ainsi qu'un accord préalable entre les entités soumises à la juridiction et à la réglementation des États expéditeur et destinataire, respectivement, en cas de transport international, qui précisent l'heure, le lieu et les procédures de transfert de la responsabilité du transport.

CATÉGORIE II

(telle que définie dans le tableau ci-joint)

Utilisation et entreposage dans une zone protégée dont l'accès est contrôlé, c'est-à-dire dans une zone sous surveillance constante par des gardiens ou des dispositifs électroniques, entourée d'une barrière physique et comportant un nombre restreint de points d'entrée sous contrôle approprié, ou toute zone faisant l'objet d'un niveau de protection physique équivalent.

Transport assorti de précautions particulières comprenant notamment des arrangements préalables entre l'expéditeur, le destinataire et le transporteur, ainsi qu'un accord préalable entre les entités soumises à la juridiction et à la réglementation des États expéditeur et destinataire, respectivement, en cas de transport international, qui précisent l'heure, le lieu et les procédures de transfert de la responsabilité du transport.

CATÉGORIE I

(telle que définie dans le tableau ci-joint)

Les matières nucléaires relevant de cette catégorie doivent être protégées par des systèmes de haute fiabilité contre une utilisation non autorisée, comme suit :

Utilisation et entreposage dans une zone hautement protégée, c'est-à-dire une zone protégée telle que définie à la catégorie II ci-dessus, dont l'accès est en outre limité à des personnes dont la fiabilité a été contrôlée, et qui se trouve sous la surveillance de gardiens en communication étroite avec les autorités d'intervention appropriées. Les mesures particulières prises dans ce contexte doivent avoir pour objectif la détection et la prévention de toute attaque, de tout accès non autorisé ou de tout retrait non autorisé des matières nucléaires en cause.

Transport assorti de précautions particulières comme indiqué pour le transport concernant les catégories II et III, et en outre sous la surveillance constante d'escortes et dans des conditions de communication étroite avec les autorités d'intervention appropriées.

TABLEAU : CATÉGORIES DE MATIÈRES NUCLÉAIRES

Matières nucléaires	Forme	Catégorie I	Catégorie II	Catégorie III [c]
1. Plutonium [a]	Non irradiée [b]	2 kg ou plus	Moins de 2 kg, mais plus de 500 g	500 g ou moins, mais plus de 15 g
2. Uranium 235	Non irradiée [b]			
	- uranium enrichi à 20 % ou plus en ~~235U~~	5 kg ou plus	Moins de 5 kg, mais plus d'un kg	1 kg ou moins, mais plus de 15 g
	- uranium enrichi de 10 % à moins de 20 % en 235U		10 kg ou plus	Moins de 10 kg, mais plus d'un kg
	- uranium enrichi par rapport à l'état naturel, mais à moins de 10 % en 235U			10 kg ou plus
3. Uranium 233	Non irradiée [b]	2 kg ou plus	Moins de 2 kg, mais plus de 500 g	500 g ou moins, mais plus de 15 g
4. Combustible irradié			Uranium naturel ou appauvri, thorium ou combustible faiblement enrichi (moins de 10% de contenu fissile) [d/ e]	

a) À l'exclusion du plutonium contenant plus de 80 % de l'isotope 238.

b) Matières nucléaires non irradiées dans un réacteur ou matières nucléaires irradiées dans un réacteur, mais avec un niveau de rayonnement égal ou inférieur à 1 Gy/h (100 rad/h) à un mètre sans écran.

c) Les quantités ne relevant pas de la catégorie III et l'uranium naturel, l'uranium appauvri et le thorium doivent être protégés au moins conformément aux principes d'une gestion prudente.

d) Bien que ce niveau de protection soit recommandé, les Parties sont libres, après évaluation des circonstances particulières, d'assigner une catégorie différente de protection physique.

e) D'autres combustibles classés dans les catégories I ou II en vertu de leur teneur initiale en matière fissile avant irradiation peuvent être rétrogradés d'une catégorie lorsque le niveau de rayonnement dépasse 1 Gy/h (100 rad/h) à un mètre sans écran.

No. 52085

Turkey
and
China

Memorandum of Understanding on cooperation in the energy sector between the Ministry of Energy and Natural Resources of the Republic of Turkey and the National Energy Administration of the People's Republic of China. Beijing, 25 June 2009

Entry into force: *4 May 2014 by notification, in accordance with article VI*

Authentic texts: *Chinese, English and Turkish*

Registration with the Secretariat of the United Nations: *Turkey, 14 August 2014*

Turquie
et
Chine

Mémorandum d'accord relatif à la coopération dans le domaine de l'énergie entre le Ministère de l'énergie et des ressources naturelles de la République turque et l'Administration nationale de l'énergie de la République populaire de Chine. Beijing, 25 juin 2009

Entrée en vigueur : *4 mai 2014 par notification, conformément à l'article VI*

Textes authentiques : *chinois, anglais et turc*

Enregistrement auprès du Secrétariat de l'Organisation des Nations Unies : *Turquie, 14 août 2014*

[CHINESE TEXT – TEXTE CHINOIS]

土耳其共和国能源和自然资源部
与
中国国家能源局
关于在能源领域合作的谅解备忘录

序言

鉴于土耳其共和国能源和自然资源部与中国国家能源局（以下称为"双方"）均表示愿意发展和加强两国在能源领域的双边合作关系，经过友好磋商，达成以下共识：

第一条

土耳其共和国能源和自然资源部与中国国家能源局关于能源领域合作的谅解备忘录的宗旨是：在双方之间建立平等、互利的长期合作关系。

第二条

双方愿意在能源领域加强磋商，交换能源政策、战略、技术和项目信息，为两国能源企业在土耳其、中国和第三国开展务实合作创造条件。

第三条

合作包括，但不限于，以下主要领域：

•可再生能源（水电、风电、太阳能、地热能等）

•火电（煤、油、气为燃料）

•节能

- 联合维护变电站和水电站
- 制造旨在利用可再生能源（如风能、太阳能、小水电等）的发电系统
- 油气勘探开发
- 采矿技术
- 核电
- 太阳能利用设备制造
- 抽水蓄能电站
- 硼技术

第四条

执行合作的具体部门分别是：

（一）土方：土耳其共和国能源和自然资源部

中方：中国国家能源局

（二）双方相关企业及科研机构等

第五条

双方同意鼓励企业在遵守两国法律规章的基础上，探讨在能源领域进行双边互利合作的可能性。

第六条

本谅解备忘录在双方最终以书面形式相互通知已完成必要的内部法律程序后生效，有效期为五年。除非任何一方在届满六个月以前以书面形式发布失效声明，则本谅解备忘录自动延期五年。本谅解备忘录自一方收到另一方书面形式的请求或者失效声明起六个月终止。

本谅解备忘录一式三份，于 2009 年六月二十五日签署，用土耳其文、中文和英文分别书写，三种版本具有相同效力。如对文本解释出现争议，以英文文本为准。

土耳其共和国

能源和自然资源部

中华人民共和国

国家能源局

[ENGLISH TEXT – TEXTE ANGLAIS]

**Memorandum of Understanding on Cooperation in the Energy Sector
Between
the Ministry of Energy and Natural Resources of the Republic of Turkey
And
the National Energy Administration of the People's Republic of China**

Preamble

The Ministry of Energy and Natural Resources of the Republic of Turkey and the National Energy Administration of the People's Republic of China (hereinafter referred to as "the Parties") have expressed their willingness to develop and enhance bilateral cooperation in the energy sector, and through friendly consultation agreed the following:

Article I

The Memorandum of Understanding on Cooperation in the Energy Sector between the Ministry of Energy and Natural Resources of the Republic of Turkey and the National Energy Administration of the People's Republic of China is based on the principle of equality, mutual benefit, and long term cooperation.

Article II

The Parties are willing to enhance consultations in the energy sector, exchange information on energy policies, strategies, technologies and projects, and create opportunities and accommodate concrete cooperation between energy enterprises of the two countries in Turkey, China and third countries.

Article III

The cooperation shall comprise, but not be limited to, the following main areas:

- Renewable energy (hydro power, wind power, solar power, geothermal energy etc.)
- Thermal power (coal, oil and natural gas as fuel)
- Energy conservation
- Rehabilitation of transformer substations and hydroelectric power plants jointly
- Manufacturing electricity generation systems for the utilization of renewable energy sources such as wind, solar, small water sources etc
- Hydrocarbon exploration and production
- Mining Technologies
- Nuclear power
- Production of solar energy equipment
- Pumped storage hydroelectric power plants
- Boron technologies

Article IV

Specific organizations to implement the cooperation include:

1- Turkey : The Ministry of Energy and Natural Resources of the Republic of Turkey
   China : The National Energy Administration of the People's Republic of China

2- Related enterprises and research instutions from the Parties.

Article V

The Parties agree to encourage their enterprises to discuss possibilities for bilateral and mutually beneficial cooperation in the energy sector in line with applicable laws and regulations of both countries.

Article VI

This MoU will enter into force on the date of last written notification by which the Parties inform each other of the completion of the necessary internal legal procedures and shall remain in force for a period of five years. This MoU shall be automatically renewed for an additonal period of five years, unless either Party denounces it in writing six months prior to the expiration date. This MoU shall terminate six months after one Party receives the other Party's request or denouncement in written.

Signed in Beijing on June 25, 2009, in three originals in Turkish, Chinese and English, all texts being equally authentic. In case any dispute concerning the interpretation of the texts arise, the English text shall prevail.

For the Ministry of Energy and Natural
Resources of the Republic of Turkey

For the National Energy Administration of
the People's Republic of China

[TURKISH TEXT – TEXTE TURC]

Türkiye Cumhuriyeti Enerji ve Tabii Kaynaklar Bakanlığı
Ve
Çin Halk Cumhuriyeti Ulusal Enerji İdaresi
Arasında
Enerji Alanında İşbirliğine İlişkin Mutabakat Zaptı

Önsöz

Türkiye Cumhuriyeti Enerji ve Tabii Kaynaklar Bakanlığı ve Çin Halk Cumhuriyeti Ulusal Enerji İdaresi (bundan böyle "Taraflar" diye anılacaktır), enerji alanındaki karşılıklı işbirliğini geliştirme ve artırma niyetlerini beyan etmiş ve dostane müzakereler sonucu aşağıdaki konularda anlaşmışlardır:

Madde I

Türkiye Cumhuriyeti Enerji ve Tabii Kaynaklar Bakanlığı ve Çin Halk Cumhuriyeti Ulusal Enerji İdaresi arasındaki Enerji Alanında İşbirliğine İlişkin bu Mutabakat Zaptı, eşitlik, karşılıklı fayda ve uzun vadeli işbirliği esasına dayanmaktadır.

Madde II

Taraflar, Türkiye, Çin ve üçüncü ülkelerde iki ülkenin enerji girişimcileri arasında sağlam işbirliğini temin etme ve fırsatlar yaratma ve enerji politikaları, stratejiler, teknolojiler ve projeler hakkında bilgi değişimi ve enerji alanındaki diyaloğu artırma arzusundadırlar.

Madde III

İşbirliği, bunlarla sınırlı olmamak üzere, aşağıdaki alanları kapsamaktadır:

- Yenilenebilir Enerji (Hidro enerji, rüzgar enerjisi, güneş enerjisi, jeotermal enerji v.s.)
- Termal Enerji (kömür, petrol ve yakıt olarak doğal gaz)
- Enerji Tasarrufu
- Trafoların ve hidroelektrik santrallerinin beraberce rehabilitasyonu
- Rüzgar, güneş, küçük su kaynakları v.s. gibi yenilenebilir enerji kaynaklarının kullanımına ilişkin elektrik üretim sistemlerinin imalatı
- Hidrokarbonların aranması ve üretimi
- Maden Teknolojileri
- Nükleer Enerji
- Güneş enerjisi teçhizatı üretimi
- Pompalamalı depolu hidroelektrik santralleri
- Bor teknolojileri

Madde IV

İşbirliğini gerçekleştirecek organizasyonlar şunlardır:

1- Türkiye : Türkiye Cumhuriyeti Enerji ve Tabii Kaynaklar Bakanlığı
   Çin : Çin Halk Cumhuriyeti Ulusal Enerji İdaresi

2- Tarafların ilgili şirketleri ve araştırma kurumları

Madde V

Taraflar, her iki ülkede uygulanan kanunlar ve yönetmelikler doğrultusunda, Müteşebbislerini, enerji alanında karşılıklı ve ortak yararlar hususunda işbirliği olasılıklarını görüşmeye özendirme konusunda anlaşmaya varmışlardır.

Madde VI

Bu Mutabakat Zaptı, tarafların birbirlerine gerekli dahili kanuni prosedürleri tamamladıklarını bildiren son yazılı tebligat tarihinde yürürlüğe girecek ve beş yıl geçerli olacaktır. Bu Mutabakat Zaptı, taraflardan biri sona erme tarihinden altı ay önce yazılı olarak bildirmediği sürece ilave beş yıllık dönem için otomatik olarak yenilenecektir. Bu Mutabakat Zaptı, taraflardan biri diğer tarafın yazılı talebini veya ihbarını aldıktan altı ay sonra fesh olacaktır.

25 Haziran 2009 tarihinde Pekin'de Türkçe, Çince ve İngilizce lisanlarında üç orijinal nüsha olarak imzalanmış olup, her bir lisanda düzenlenmiş metinler eşit derecede geçerlidir. Anlaşma metninin yorumu ile ilgili herhangi bir anlaşmazlık halinde İngilizce anlaşma metni geçerli olacaktır.

Türkiye Cumhuriyeti
Enerji ve Tabii Kaynaklar Bakanlığı
Adına

Çin Halk Cumhuriyeti
Ulusal Enerji İdaresi
Adına

[TRANSLATION – TRADUCTION]

MÉMORANDUM D'ACCORD RELATIF À LA COOPÉRATION DANS LE DOMAINE DE L'ÉNERGIE ENTRE LE MINISTÈRE DE L'ÉNERGIE ET DES RESSOURCES NATURELLES DE LA RÉPUBLIQUE TURQUE ET L'ADMINISTRATION NATIONALE DE L'ÉNERGIE DE LA RÉPUBLIQUE POPULAIRE DE CHINE

Préambule

Le Ministère de l'énergie et des ressources naturelles de la République turque et l'Administration nationale de l'énergie de la République populaire de Chine (ci-après dénommés « les Parties ») ont exprimé leur volonté de développer et de renforcer la coopération bilatérale dans le secteur de l'énergie et, par la voie de consultations amicales, sont convenus de ce qui suit :

Article premier

Le Mémorandum d'accord relatif à la coopération dans le domaine de l'énergie entre le Ministère de l'énergie et des ressources naturelles de la République turque et l'Administration nationale de l'énergie de la République populaire de Chine repose sur les principes de l'égalité, de l'intérêt mutuel et de la coopération à long terme.

Article 2

Les Parties souhaitent intensifier les consultations dans le secteur de l'énergie, échanger des informations sur les politiques, stratégies, technologies et projets énergétiques et créer des débouchés et faciliter la coopération concrète entre les entreprises énergétiques des deux pays en Turquie, en Chine et dans des pays tiers.

Article 3

La coopération porte sur les domaines suivants, sans toutefois s'y limiter :

- Les sources d'énergie renouvelables (hydroélectricité, énergie éolienne, énergie solaire, énergie géothermique, etc.);

- L'énergie thermique (charbon, pétrole et gaz naturel comme combustible);

- La conservation de l'énergie;

- La réhabilitation conjointe de postes de transformation et de centrales hydroélectriques;

- Les systèmes de production d'électricité pour l'industrie manufacturière qui utilisent des sources d'énergie renouvelables telles que l'énergie éolienne, l'énergie solaire, les petites sources d'eau, etc.;

- La prospection et l'extraction d'hydrocarbures;

- Les techniques d'extraction;

- L'énergie nucléaire;
- La production d'équipements utilisant l'énergie solaire;
- Les centrales hydroélectriques de pompage-turbinage;
- Les technologies exploitant le bore.

Article 4

La coopération est mise en œuvre notamment par les organismes suivants :

1. En Turquie : le Ministère de l'énergie et des ressources naturelles de la République turque;
    En Chine : l'Administration nationale de l'énergie de la République populaire de Chine.
2. Les entreprises et établissements de recherche connexes des Parties.

Article 5

Les Parties s'engagent à encourager leurs entreprises à étudier les perspectives de coopération bilatérale et mutuellement avantageuse dans le secteur de l'énergie, conformément aux lois et règlements des deux pays.

Article 6

Le présent Mémorandum d'accord entrera en vigueur pour une période de cinq ans à la date de la dernière des notifications écrites par lesquelles les Parties s'informent mutuellement de l'accomplissement des procédures juridiques internes requises. Le présent Mémorandum d'accord est reconduit automatiquement pour une durée supplémentaire de cinq ans, sauf si l'une des Parties le dénonce par écrit six mois avant la date d'expiration. Le présent Mémorandum d'accord prend fin six mois après la réception par l'une des Parties de la demande ou de la dénonciation écrite de l'autre Partie.

FAIT à Beijing, le 25 juin 2009, en trois exemplaires originaux en langues chinoise, anglaise et turque, tous les textes faisant également foi. En cas de divergence d'interprétation, le texte anglais prévaut.

Pour le Ministère de l'énergie et des ressources naturelles
de la République turque :

[SIGNÉ]

Pour l'Administration nationale de l'énergie
de la République populaire de Chine :

[SIGNÉ]

No. 52086

―――

International Development Association
and
India

Financing Agreement (Accelerating Universal Access to early and effective tuberculosis care project) between India and the International Development Association (with schedules, appendix and International Development Association General Conditions for Credits and Grants, dated 31 July 2010). New Delhi, 30 May 2014

Entry into force: *26 June 2014 by notification*

Authentic text: *English*

Registration with the Secretariat of the United Nations: *International Development Association, 26 August 2014*

Not published in print, in accordance with article 12(2) of the General Assembly regulations to give effect to Article 102 of the Charter of the United Nations, as amended.

―――――

Association internationale de développement
et
Inde

Accord de financement (Projet d'accélération vers l'accès universel aux soins précoces et efficaces contre la tuberculose) entre l'Inde et l'Association internationale de développement (avec annexes, appendice et Conditions générales applicables aux crédits et aux dons de l'Association internationale de développement, en date du 31 juillet 2010). New Delhi, 30 mai 2014

Entrée en vigueur : *26 juin 2014 par notification*

Texte authentique : *anglais*

Enregistrement auprès du Secrétariat de l'Organisation des Nations Unies : *Association internationale de développement, 26 août 2014*

Non disponible en version imprimée, conformément au paragraphe 2 de l'article 12 du règlement de l'Assemblée générale destiné à mettre en application l'Article 102 de la Charte des Nations Unies, tel qu'amendé.

No. 52087

Belgium
and
Malta

Agreement between the Government of the Kingdom of Belgium and the Government of Malta on police cooperation. Brussels, 1 December 2005

Entry into force: *22 September 2012, in accordance with article 18*

Authentic texts: *Dutch, English and French*

Registration with the Secretariat of the United Nations: *Belgium, 12 August 2014*

Belgique
et
Malte

Convention entre le Gouvernement du Royaume de Belgique et le Gouvernement de Malte relative à la coopération policière. Bruxelles, 1ᵉʳ décembre 2005

Entrée en vigueur : *22 septembre 2012, conformément à l'article 18*

Textes authentiques : *néerlandais, anglais et français*

Enregistrement auprès du Secrétariat de l'Organisation des Nations Unies : *Belgique, 12 août 2014*

[DUTCH TEXT – TEXTE NÉERLANDAIS]

**VERDRAG
TUSSEN
DE REGERING VAN HET KONINKRIJK BELGIE
EN
DE REGERING VAN MALTA
BETREFFENDE
DE POLITIESAMENWERKING**

DE REGERING VAN HET KONINKRIJK BELGIË

en

DE REGERING VAN MALTA

Hierna genoemd de Verdragsluitende Partijen,

BEZORGD om de bevordering van de vriendschapsbanden en de samenwerking tussen de twee Staten en in het bijzonder de politiesamenwerking ;

DE WENS UITENDE de politiesamenwerking te versterken in het kader van de internationale overeenkomsten die ondertekend zijn door de twee Staten inzake het respect voor de fundamentele rechten en vrijheden, namelijk het Europees Verdrag van de Rechten van de Mens en de Fundamentele Vrijheden, alsook het Verdrag nr. 108 van de Raad van Europa van 28 januari 1981 inzake de bescherming van personen op het vlak van de geautomatiseerde verwerking van persoonsgegevens ;

OVERWEGENDE dat de internationaal georganiseerde criminaliteit een bedreiging vormt voor de sociaal-economische ontwikkeling van de Verdragsluitende Staten, dat de recente ontwikkelingen binnen de internationaal georganiseerde misdaad het functionneren van de respectievelijke Staten in gevaar brengen ;

OVERWEGENDE dat de strijd tegen de mensenhandel, de bestrijding van het illegaal reizen naar en vanuit het nationaal grondgebied en de illegale migratie, alsook de eliminatie van de georganiseerde netwerken deel uitmaken van de taken van de respectievelijke Regeringen en Parlementen van de Verdragsluitende Staten ;

OVERWEGENDE dat de productie van en de illegale handel in verdovende middelen en psychotrope stoffen een bedreiging betekenen voor de gezondheid en de veiligheid van onze medeburgers ;

OVERWEGENDE dat het eenvoudig overeenstemmen van de betreffende wetgevingen onvoldoende blijkt om het fenomeen van de illegale immigratie voldoende efficiënt te bestrijden ;

OVERWEGENDE dat het noodzakelijk is om een efficiënte, internationale politiesamenwerking uit te bouwen op het vlak van georganiseerde criminaliteit en illegale migratie door middel van uitwisseling en verwerking van gegevens, dit ter bestrijding en preventie van deze criminele activiteiten ;

OVERWEGENDE dat dit gegeven een reeks maatregelen noodzaken en een nauwe samenwerking vereisen tussen de verdragsluitende partijen ;

HEBBEN besloten onderhavig Verdrag te sluiten :

DEFINITIES

Artikel 1

Naar de zin van het huidig Verdrag verstaat men onder :

Internationale mensenhandel :

Elk opzettelijk gedrag, zoals hier beschreven :

a) het betreden van het grondgebied van de Verdragsluitende Staat vereenvoudigen, de doorreis, verblijf op of het verlaten van dit grondgebied indien er gebruik gemaakt is van dwang, meer bepaald geweld of bedreiging, of wanneer er gebruik gemaakt wordt van bedrog, misbruik van gezag of andere vormen van onder druk zetten, in die mate dat de persoon geen andere reële of aanvaardbare keuze heeft dan zich te onderwerpen aan die druk ;

b) het uitbuiten op eender welke wijze van een persoon, wetende dat die het grondgebied van de Verdragsluitende Staat is binnengekomen, er doorreist of er verblijft (in omstandigheden vermeld onder punt a).

Sexuele uitbuiting van kinderen :

Inbreuken die opgenomen zijn in artikel 34 van het Verdrag van de Verenigde Naties over de Rechten van het Kind van 20 november 1989, zijnde productie, verkoop, verdeling of andere vormen van handel in pornografisch materiaal waarbij kinderen betrokken zijn, en het bezitten van dat materiaal ten persoonlijken titel.

Technische ondersteuning :

De hulp, onder de vorm van logistieke steun, die gegeven wordt aan politie- en immigratiediensten.

Criminaliteit in verband met nucleair en radioactief materiaal :

Inbreuken, opgesomd in artikel 7§1 van het Verdrag inzake de fysieke bescherming van nucleair materiaal, ondertekend te Wenen en New York op 3 maart 1980.

Witwassen van geld :

Inbreuken, opgesomd in artikel 6§1 tot 3, van het Verdrag van de Europese Raad inzake witwassen, opsporen, inbeslagnemen en confisceren van de voorwerpen die voortkomen uit de misdaad, ondertekend in Straatsburg op 8 november 1990.

Georganiseerde criminaliteit :

Alle inbreuken, gepleegd door een « criminele organisatie » waaronder wordt verstaan een gestructureerde vereniging, bestaande uit minstens twee personen die samenwerken voor een welbepaalde tijd, met het oog op het plegen van strafbare feiten, die vrijheidsberoving, een gevangenisstraf van ten minste vier jaar of een zwaardere straf tot gevolg hebben. De inbreuken vormen een doel op zich of zijn een middel om materiële voordelen te verkrijgen en om desnoods de werking van de overheid overdreven te beïnvloeden.

Persoonsgegevens :

Alle informatie betreffende een geïdentificeerde of te identificeren fysieke persoon (betrokken persoon) ; te identificeren betekent dat de persoon direct of indirect te identificeren is, meer bepaald met als referentie een identificatienummer of één of meerdere specifieke kenmerken die eigen zijn aan diens fysische, fysiologische, psychische, economische, culturele of sociale identiteit.

Verwerking van persoonsgegevens :

Elke verwerking of reeks van verwerkingen die uitgevoerd wordt, al dan niet met behulp van geautomatiseerde procédés, zoals het verzamelen, opslaan, organiseren, behouden, aanpassen en wijzigen, verwijderen, consulteren, gebruiken, communiceren door transmissie, verdelen of andere vormen van het terbeschikkingstellen, bijeenbrengen, verbinden, alsook het beschermen, het uitwissen of vernietigen.

Verdovende middelen :

Omvat elke substantie, zowel plantaardige als synthetische, die voorkomen in Tabel I of Tabel II van het Enkelvoudig Verdrag inzake verdovende middelen dat op 30 maart 1961 in New York werd ondertekend.

Psychotrope substantie :

Omvat elke substantie, plantaardig of synthetisch, of elk natuurlijk product, vermeld in Tabel I, II, III, of IV van het Verdrag van 21 februari 1971 inzake psychotrope stoffen.

Illegale handel in verdovende middelen of psychotrope stoffen :

De teelt, de vervaardiging en/of handel in verdovende middelen of psychotrope stoffen, die strijdig zijn met de doelstellingen van het Verdrag van 30 maart 1961 inzake verdovende middelen, het Verdrag van 21 februari 1971 inzake psychotrope stoffen of het Verdrag van de Verenigde Naties van 19 december 1988 tegen de sluikhandel in verdovende middelen en psychotrope stoffen.

Dringend verzoek :

Een verzoek is dringend indien, met inachtneming van de formele administratieve procedure bij de centrale organen, de preventie- of opsporingsactie dreigt gehinderd of geschaad te worden.

DOMEINEN VAN SAMENWERKING

Artikel 2

1. De Verdragsluitende Partijen verbinden er zich toe de meest volledige samenwerking te bieden op het vlak van politiesamenwerking, met inachtneming van de regels en voorwaarden, vastgelegd in dit Verdrag.

2. De Verdragsluitende Partijen zullen samenwerken op het vlak van preventie, repressie en vervolging van misdrijven die onder de noemer georganiseerde criminaliteit vallen, met name :

    -   misdrijven tegen het leven, de gezondheid en de fysieke integriteit van personen ;
    -   misdrijven in verband met productie en illegale handel van drugs, psychotrope stoffen en precursoren ;
    -   illegale immigratie ;
    -   proxenetisme, mensenhandel en seksueel misbruik van kinderen ;
    -   afpersing ;
    -   diefstal, trafiek en illegale handel in wapens, munitie, explosieven, radioactieve substanties, nucleaire stoffen en andere gevaarlijke stoffen ;
    -   vervalsingen (vervaardiging, namaak, verandering en verdeling) van betaalmiddelen, cheques en waardepapieren ;
    -   criminaliteit op het vlak van handels- en financieel verkeer ;
    -   misdrijven tegen goederen, onder meer diefstal, trafiek in kunstwerken en historische voorwerpen ;
    -   diefstal, illegale handel en trafiek in motorvoertuigen en vervalsing en gebruik van vervalste documenten voor voertuigen ;
    -   witwassen van geld.

3. De zware misdrijven in het kader van de georganiseerde criminaliteit die niet worden bepaald in artikel 1, worden door de bevoegde nationale overheden beoordeeld volgens de nationale wetgeving van de Staten waartoe zij behoren.

Artikel 3

De Samenwerking tussen de Partijen zal eveneens betrekking hebben op :

-   de opsporing van verdwenen personen en hulp bij identificatie van niet-geïdentificeerde lijken ;
-   de opsporing op het grondgebied van een Partij van gestolen, verdwenen, verduisterde of verloren voorwerpen op het grondgebied van de andere Partij.

Artikel 4

De Partijen zullen samenwerken op de onder artikelen 2 en 3 vermelde domeinen via :

- uitwisseling van informatie over materies die onder de bevoegdheid vallen van de politie- en immigratiediensten ;
- uitwisseling van materiaal ;
- technische en wetenschappelijke ondersteuning, expertises en levering van gespecialiseerd technisch materiaal ;
- uitwisseling van ervaringen ;
- samenwerking op het vlak van de beroepsopleiding ;
- hulp bij de voorbereiding ter uitvoering van verzoeken tot rechtshulp in strafzaken ;

volgens de hieronder vermelde bepalingen.

INFORMATIEUITWISSELING

Artikel 5

De Verdragsluitende Partijen bieden elkaar bijstand en staan in voor een nauwe en permanente samenwerking. Zij zullen onder meer alle pertinente en belangrijke gegevens uitwisselen. Deze samenwerking kan de vorm aannemen van een permanent contact via de te benoemen verbindingsofficieren.

Artikel 6

1. De Verdragsluitende Partijen verbinden zich tot het verlenen van bijstand tussen hun politiediensten met inachtneming van het nationaal recht en binnen de grenzen van hun bevoegdheden, met het oog op de preventie en opsporing van strafbare feiten, op voorwaarde dat het nationaal recht van de aangezochte Verdragsluitende Partij het verzoek of de uitvoering ervan niet voorbehoudt aan de gerechtelijke overheden.

2. In specifieke gevallen heeft iedere Verdragsluitende Partij het recht om op eigen initiatief en overeenkomstig de nationale wetgeving informatie te verstrekken aan de betrokken Verdragsluitende Partij die belangrijk kan zijn met het oog op het verlenen van bijstand voor de preventie en repressie van inbreuken of om bedreigingen van de openbare orde en veiligheid te voorkomen.

Artikel 7

Elke informatie die door de aangezochte Verdragsluitende Partij wordt verstrekt, kan door de verzoekende Verdragsluitende Partij slechts als bewijsmiddel voor de ten laste gelegde feiten worden gebruikt, na een verzoek om rechtshulp krachtens het toepasbare internationale recht.

Artikel 8

1. Vragen om bijstand en antwoorden op die vragen moeten worden uitgewisseld tussen de centrale organen die door iedere Verdragsluitende Partij worden belast met de internationale politiesamenwerking en immigratie.

    Indien het onmogelijk is om de vraag via de voornoemde weg tijdig te stellen, kan, bij uitzondering en hoogdringendheid, de bevoegde overheid van de verzoekende Partij de vraag rechtstreeks aan de bevoegde overheid van de aangezochte Partij stellen, deze laatste kan dan onmiddellijk antwoorden. In die uitzonderlijke gevallen dient de verzoekende Partij zo vlug mogelijk het centraal orgaan belast met de internationale samenwerking in de aangezochte Verdragsluitende Partij op de hoogte te brengen van de rechtstreekse vraag waarbij het dringend karakter moet worden gemotiveerd.

2. De aanstelling van de centrale organen die met de internationale samenwerking zijn belast en de modaliteiten van de wederzijdse bijstand worden geregeld tussen de bevoegde ministers van de Verdragsluitende Partijen.

Artikel 9

De verzoekende bevoegde overheid moet de graad van vertrouwelijkheid waarborgen die de aangezochte bevoegde overheid van de andere Partij aan de informatie heeft toegekend. De graad van veiligheid die gewaarborgd wordt is deze van Interpol.

Artikel 10

1. De Verdragsluitende Partijen kunnen verbindingsofficieren van de ene Verdragsluitende Partij voor bepaalde of onbepaalde tijd bij de andere Verdragsluitende Partij detacheren.

2. De detachering van verbindingsofficieren voor bepaalde of onbepaalde tijd is erop gericht de samenwerking tussen de Verdragsluitende Partijen te bevorderen en te versnellen. In het bijzonder dienen er afspraken gemaakt te worden omtrent de ondersteuning

    a. in de vorm van informatieuitwisseling met het oog op preventieve en repressieve bestrijding van de criminaliteit ;

    b. op het vlak van de uitvoering van verzoeken om rechtshulp in strafzaken ;

    c. bij de opdrachten van de overheden die belast zijn met het toezicht op de buitengrenzen en de immigratie ;

    d. bij de opdrachten van de overheden die belast zijn met de preventie van de inbreuken op de openbare orde.

3. De taak van de verbindingsofficieren bestaat erin advies en ondersteuning te verlenen. Zij zijn niet bevoegd om politiemaatregelen autonoom uit te voeren. Ze verstrekken informatie en voeren hun taken uit binnen het geheel van instructies die hun werden gegeven door de Verdragsluitende Partij waarvan ze afkomstig zijn en door de Verdragsluitende Partij waarbij ze gedetacheerd zijn. Ze brengen regelmatig verslag uit bij het centraal orgaan dat belast is met de politiesamenwerking van de Verdragsluitende Partij waarbij ze gedetacheerd zijn.

4. De bevoegde ministers van de Verdragsluitende Partijen kunnen overeenkomen dat de verbindingsofficieren van de ene Verdragsluitende Partij die gedetacheerd zijn bij derde landen, eveneens de belangen van de andere Verdragsluitende Partij vertegenwoordigen.

BESCHERMING VAN PERSOONSGEGEVENS

Artikel 11

1. De verwerking van persoonsgegevens is onderworpen aan de respectieve nationale wetgevingen van elke Verdragsluitende Partij.

2. Wat de overbrenging van persoonsgegevens betreft, verbinden de Verdragsluitende Partijen er zich toe de persoonsgegevens te beschermen volgens de beginselen van het Verdrag van de Raad van Europa van 28 januari 1981 ter bescherming van persoonsgegevens en van de Aanbeveling A (87) 15 van 17 september 1987 van het Comité van Ministers van de Raad van Europa die het gebruik van persoonsgegevens voor politiedoeleinden regelt.

3. Wat de verwerking van de overgebrachte persoonsgegevens in toepassing van dit Verdrag betreft, zijn de volgende bepalingen van toepassing :

   a. de Verdragsluitende Partij waarvoor de persoonsgegevens bestemd zijn, mag de gegevens alleen gebruiken voor de doeleinden waarvoor dit Verdrag de overbrenging van dergelijke gegevens voorziet ;

   b. de gegevens mogen alleen gebruikt worden door gerechtelijke overheden, diensten en instanties die een taak of functie uitvoeren binnen het geheel van de doeleinden die zijn voorzien in dit Verdrag, meer bepaald in artikel 2 en 3. De Partijen moeten de lijst van de gebruikers uitwisselen ;

   c. de Verdragsluitende Partij die de gegevens overbrengt, dient erop toe te zien dat ze juist en volledig zijn en dat ze niet langer bewaard worden dan nodig is ; indien zij op eigen initiatief of als gevolg van een vraag van de betrokken persoon vaststelt dat de verstrekte gegevens onjuist zijn of niet overgebracht dienden te worden, moet de Verdragsluitende Partij waarvoor de gegevens bestemd zijn, daarvan onmiddellijk op de hoogte gebracht worden ; die Verdragsluitende Partij moet de gegevens corrigeren of vernietigen ;

   d. een Verdragsluitende Partij mag zich niet beroepen op het feit dat een andere Verdragsluitende Partij onjuiste gegevens zou hebben overgebracht om zich te ontdoen van haar in haar nationale wetgeving vastgestelde verantwoordelijkheid ten aanzien van een benadeeld persoon ;

   e. de overbrenging en ontvangst van persoonsgegevens dienen geregistreerd te worden. De Verdragsluitende Partijen dienen de lijst uit te wisselen waarin de overheden of diensten opgenomen zijn die de toestemming hebben om de registraties te raadplegen ;

   f. de toegang tot de gegevens wordt geregeld door de nationale wetgeving van de Verdragsluitende Partij waaraan de betrokken persoon zijn vraag richt. De gegevens worden slechts verstrekt na toestemming van de Verdragsluitende Partij waarvan de gegevens afkomstig zijn ;

g. de Verdragsluitende Partij waarvoor de gegevens bestemd zijn, mag ze alleen gebruiken voor de doeleinden die werden bepaald door de Verdragsluitende Partij die de gegevens verstrekt en met inachtneming van de voorwaarden die die Verdragsluitende Partij oplegt.

4. Wat de overbrenging van persoonsgegevens betreft, zijn de volgende bepalingen van toepassing :

a. de gegevens mogen alleen overgebracht worden aan politie- en immigratiediensten ; de gegevens mogen slechts aan andere diensten worden meegedeeld na voorafgaande toestemming van de Verdragsluitende Partij die de persoonsgegevens verstrekt ;

b. de Verdragsluitende Partij waarvoor de gegevens bestemd zijn, deelt desgewenst mee aan de Verdragsluitende Partij die de gegevens overbrengt waarvoor de gegevens werden gebruikt en welke resultaten de overgebrachte gegevens opleverden.

5. Elke Verdragsluitende Partij duidt een controle-autoriteit aan die, in navolging van het nationaal recht, belast is met de uitoefening, op haar grondgebied, van een onafhankelijke controle op de verwerking van persoonsgegevens, die wordt uitgevoerd op basis van onderhavig Verdrag. Ze moet nagaan of de bovengenoemde verwerking de rechten van de betrokken persoon al dan niet schendt. De controle-autoriteiten zijn eveneens bevoegd om de problemen te analyseren omtrent de toepassing en interpretatie van onderhavig Verdrag in verband met de verwerking van persoonsgegevens. Deze controle-autoriteiten kunnen overeenkomen samen te werken in het kader van de opdrachten die hen door onderhavig Verdrag worden toegekend.

Artikel 12

Wanneer persoonsgegevens worden overgebracht via een verbindingsofficier, zoals voorzien in artikel 10, worden de bepalingen van onderhavig Verdrag eveneens toegepast.

UITZONDERING

Artikel 13

Elk van de Partijen weigert bijstand wanneer het gaat om politieke of militaire misdrijven of wanneer die bijstand strijdig blijkt te zijn met de wettelijke bepalingen die van kracht zijn op haar grondgebied.

Elk van de Partijen kan bijstand weigeren of hem aan voorwaarden onderwerpen wanneer het gaat om misdrijven die in verband staan met de politieke of militaire misdrijven of wanneer de bijstandsverlening de soevereiniteit, de veiligheid, de openbare orde of andere essentiële belangen van de Staat zou kunnen bedreigen.

De Partij die de bijstand weigert, moet de andere Partij daarvan binnen de 30 dagen op de hoogte brengen en de redenen van die weigering toelichten.

ANDERE VORMEN VAN SAMENWERKING

Artikel 14

1. De Verdragsluitende Partijen maken afspraken om elkaar wederzijds bijstand te verlenen op het vlak van beroepsopleiding en technische bijstand aangaande de problemen betreffende de werking van de politie.

2. De Verdragsluitende Partijen maken afspraken om hun praktische ervaringen uit te wisselen omtrent alle bovenbedoelde gebieden van onderhavig Verdrag.

3. De modaliteiten van wederzijdse bijstand worden vastgelegd in overeenkomsten, die worden gesloten tussen de bevoegde ministers van de Verdragsluitende Partijen.

UITVOERING VAN HET VERDRAG

Artikel 15

1. De bevoegde ministers van de Verdragsluitende Partijen kunnen permanente of tijdelijke werkgroepen oprichten die belast zijn met het onderzoek van de gemeenschappelijke problemen omtrent repressie en preventie van de criminaliteit zoals voorzien in artikel 2 en de samenwerking zoals voorzien in artikel 3 en, eventueel, met de uitwerking van voorstellen om, indien nodig, de praktische en technische aspecten van de samenwerking tussen de Verdragsluitende Partijen te verbeteren.

2. De onkosten die worden gemaakt in het kader van de samenwerking, zullen respectievelijk door elke Partij worden gedragen, behalve wanneer de gerechtigde vertegenwoordigers van de Partijen daar anders over beslissen.

3. De bevoegde ministers van de Verdragsluitende Partijen richten een evaluatiegroep op die om de drie jaar een rapport zal voorleggen aan de ministers.

GESCHILLENREGELING

Artikel 16

Alle geschillen betreffende de interpretatie of de toepassing van onderhavig Verdrag zullen worden beslecht door een gemengde adviescommissie.

Er wordt een gemengde adviescommissie opgericht, samengesteld uit vertegenwoordigers van Buitenlandse Zaken, Binnenlandse Zaken en Justitie, die periodiek zal samenkomen op verzoek van de ene of de andere Staat, om de regeling van de problemen, die zullen opduiken bij de interpretatie of de toepassing van onderhavig Verdrag, te vergemakkelijken.

SLOTBEPALINGEN

Artikel 17

De bepalingen van onderhavig Verdrag kunnen enkel worden toegepast wanneer ze verenigbaar zijn met het nationaal recht.

Het toezicht op de uitvoering van onderhavig Verdrag wordt gerealiseerd overeenkomstig het nationaal recht van elke Verdragsluitende Partij.

Artikel 18

De Verdragsluitende Partijen informeren elkaar schriftelijk en langs diplomatieke weg over de afhandeling van de grondwettelijke formaliteiten, vereist voor de inwerkingtreding van onderhavig Verdrag.

Het Verdrag zal in werking treden 60 dagen na de datum waarop de laatste bekendmaking wordt ontvangen.

Onderhavig Verdrag wordt gesloten voor onbeperkte tijd. Elke Partij kan het Verdrag opzeggen door de andere Partij langs diplomatieke weg aan te schrijven. Het Verdrag wordt verbroken na zes maanden volgend op de datum van het aanschrijven.

Artikel 19

Elke Partij kan aan de andere Partij voorstellen doen toekomen die een wijziging van onderhavig Verdrag beogen. De wijzigingen aan onderhavig Verdrag worden door de Partijen in onderlinge overeenstemming besloten.

Ter staving hebben de ondergetekenden, die hieromtrent bevoegd zijn, hun handtekening onder onderhavig Verdrag geplaatst.

OPGESTELD te Brussel, op 1 december 2005, in twee originele exemplaren, in de Engelse, Franse en Nederlandse taal. De drie teksten zijn in gelijke mate rechtsgeldig.

<table>
<tr><td>**VOOR DE REGERING
VAN HET KONINKRIJK BELGIË :**</td><td>**VOOR DE REGERING
VAN MALTA :**</td></tr>
<tr><td>Laurette ONKELINX,
Minister van Justitie</td><td>Hon. Dr Tonio BORG,
Vice-Eerste Minister</td></tr>
<tr><td>Patrick DEWAEL,
Minister van Binnenlandse Zaken</td><td></td></tr>
</table>

[ENGLISH TEXT – TEXTE ANGLAIS]

**AGREEMENT
BETWEEN
THE GOVERNMENT OF THE KINGDOM OF BELGIUM
AND
THE GOVERNMENT OF MALTA
ON
POLICE COOPERATION**

THE GOVERNMENT OF THE KINGDOM OF BELGIUM

and

THE GOVERNMENT OF MALTA

Hereinafter referred to as the Contracting Parties,

DESIRING to tighten the bonds of friendship and to promote the cooperation between the two States, and in particular taking into consideration the common desire to strengthen the police cooperation between them ;

AIMING at enhancing this police cooperation within the framework of the international commitments adhered to by these two States pertaining to the respect of the fundamental rights and freedoms, such as the Convention on the Protection of Human Rights and Fundamental Freedoms of 4 November 1950 as well as the Convention n°108 of the Council of Europe of 28 January 1981 for the Protection of Individuals with regard to Automatic Processing of Personal Data ;

CONSIDERING that international organized crime constitutes a serious threat to the socio-economic development of the Contracting States, and that the recent evolution of international organized crime jeopardizes their institutional functioning ;

CONSIDERING that the fight against illegal trafficking in human beings, the suppression of illegal entries and departures into and from the territory of the States, illegal immigration, as well as the suppression of organized networks that take part in these illegal actions, are a subject of concern for the Governments and Parliaments of the Contracting States ;

CONSIDERING that the illicit production and distribution of narcotic drugs and psychotropic substances jeopardize the health and safety of the citizens ;

CONSIDERING that merely harmonizing the pertinent legislations is not sufficient to effectively fight the phenomenon of clandestine migrations ;

CONSIDERING that an efficient international police cooperation in the sphere of organized crime and illegal migrations, in particular through the exchange and processing information, is crucial to combat and prevent such criminal activities ;

AWARE that this necessity calls for a number of appropriate measures as well as a close cooperation between the Contracting Parties ;

HAVE agreed as follows :

DEFINITIONS

Article 1

For the purposes of this agreement, the following terms shall mean :

International trafficking in human beings :

All intention to :

a) facilitate the entry, transit, residence or departure from the territory of a Contracting Party, resorting to this end to compelling actions, in particular the use of violence or threats, or by resorting to deceit, abuse of authority or other forms of pressure in such a way that the concerned person has no other option but to submit to those pressures ;

b) exploit, in whichever way, an individual while being fully aware of the conditions under which this individual entered, transited or resided on the territory of the State that is a Party to this agreement (cf. point a).

Sexual exploitation of children :

The criminal offences described in Article 34 of the UN Convention on the Rights of the Child, on 20 November 1989, including the production, sale and distribution or other forms of traffic in child pornography and the possession of such material for personal purposes.

Technical support :

Technical support is the logistic support offered to law enforcement and immigration authorities.

Crime connected with nuclear and radioactive substances :

The criminal offences listed in Article 7(1) of the Convention on Physical Protection of Nuclear Material, signed in Vienna and New-York on 3 March 1980.

Money laundering :

The criminal offences listed in Article 6 (1) to (3) of the Convention of the Council of Europe on Laundering, Search, Seizure and Confiscation of the proceeds from Crime, signed at Strasbourg on 8 November 1990.

Organized Crime :

All offences committed by a "criminal organization", defined as a structured association, established over a period of time, of more than two persons, acting in concert with a view to committing offences which are punishable by deprivation of liberty or a detention order of a maximum of at least four years or more serious penalty, whether such offences are an end in themselves or a means of obtaining material benefits and, where appropriate, of improperly influencing the operation of public authorities.

Personal data :

Any information relating to an identified or identifiable natural person (data subject) ; an identifiable person is one who can be identified, directly or indirectly, in particular by reference to an identification number or to one or more factors specific to his physical, physiological, mental, economic, cultural or social identity.

Processing of personal data :

Any operation or set of operations which is performed upon personal data, whether or not by automatic means such as collection, recording, organization, storage, adaptation or alteration, retrieval, consulting, use, disclosure by transmission, dissemination or otherwise making available, alignment or combination, blocking erasure or destruction.

Narcotic drug :

Refers to any of the substances, natural or synthetic, in Schedules I and II of the Single Convention on Narcotic Drugs, signed at New-York on 30 March 1961.

Psychotropic substance :

Refers to any substance, natural or synthetic, or any natural material in Schedules I, II, III and IV of the Convention on Psychotropic substances, on 21 February 1971.

Illicit traffic in narcotic drugs or psychotropic substances :

The production and manufacture of and the traffic in narcotic drugs or psychotropic substances contrary to the provisions of the Convention on Narcotic Drugs signed on 30 March 1961, of the Convention on Psychotropic Substances signed on 21 February 1971 or of the UN Convention against Illicit Traffic in Narcotic Drugs and Psychotropic Substances signed on 19 December 1988.

Urgent queries :

A request is considered urgent whenever the formal administration proceedings with the central authorities may hamper or compromise the prevention or investigation.

FIELDS OF COOPERATION

Article 2

1. The Contracting Parties undertake to afford each other, in accordance with the provisions and conditions of this Agreement, the widest cooperation in the matter of police cooperation.

2. The Contracting Parties shall provide cooperation in all matters pertaining to the prevention, suppression and prosecution of offences derived from organized crime, and in particular :

   - Crimes against life and physical integrity of a person and against the health of a person ;
   - Crimes connected with the production of and the illicit traffic in narcotic drugs, psychotropic substances and precursors ;
   - Illegal immigrations ;
   - Procuring, traffic in human beings and sexual exploitation of children ;
   - Extortion ;
   - Theft, traffic and illegal trade of firearms, ammunitions, explosives, radioactive substances, nuclear material and other hazardous substances ;
   - Forgeries (manufacturing, counterfeiting, transformation and distribution) of means of payment, cheques and securities ;
   - Crimes with respect to commercial and financial exchanges ;
   - Crimes against properties, i. e. theft, traffic in works of arts and historic objects ;
   - Crimes against the environment ;
   - Theft, illegal trade and traffic in motor vehicles, forgery and use of forgeries related to vehicles ;
   - Money laundering.

3. The serious crimes which stem from organized crime and which are not defined in article 1 shall be evaluated by the competent national services in accordance with the national legislations of the States to which they belong.

Article 3

The Parties shall also collaborate with respect to :

   - the searches for missing persons and the identification of unidentified corpses ;
   - the searches on the territory of one Party for stolen, missing, embezzled or lost objects on the territory of the other Party.

Article 4

The Parties shall cooperate in the fields referred to in articles 2 and 3 by :

   - exchanging information pertaining to the fields within the competence of the law enforcement and immigration authorities ;
   - the exchanging equipment ;
   - providing technical and scientific assistance, know-how as well as specialized technical equipment ;
   - exchanging experiences ;
   - providing assistance in professional training ;

- assisting in the preparation of the execution of requests for legal assistance in penal matters ;

in accordance with the conditions set hereafter.

INFORMATION EXCHANGE

Article 5

The Contracting Parties shall provide assistance and shall guarantee a close and permanent cooperation. They shall proceed to an exchange of all the pertinent and substantial data. This cooperation may be provided by means of permanent contact through the intermediary of Liaison officers to be appointed.

Article 6

1. The Contracting Parties commit themselves to have their police units provide assistance, conform with the requirements of their national legislation and within the limits of their competencies, with a view to preventing and investigating punishable acts, assuming that the national legislation of the requested Contracting Party does not reserve the request or its execution to the judicial authorities.

2. In specific cases, each Contracting Party may, in compliance with the national legislation and on proper initiative, communicate information to the Contracting Party concerned which is deemed necessary for the latter in order to assist in the prevention and repression of offences such as referred to in the section 2 of this Agreement or in the prevention of threats to the public order and safety.

Article 7

Any information provided by the requested Contracting Party may only be used by the requesting Contracting Party as evidence for the indictment, subject to a request for legal assistance in conformity with prevailing international regulations.

Article 8

1. Requests for assistance and replies to these requests must be exchanged through the Central Authorities declared, by each Contracting Party, competent for international police cooperation and immigration.

In the event that the request cannot be executed within an appropriate time scale through the aforementioned channel, it may exceptionally and in cases of urgency only, be forwarded by the competent authorities of the requesting Contracting Party directly to the competent authorities of the requested Party, which may immediately respond. In these exceptional cases, the requesting authority must inform, as quickly as possible, the Central Authority that has been granted jurisdiction by the requested Contracting Party in matters of international cooperation, of the direct request motivating the urgency.

2. The competent Ministers of the Contracting Parties shall assign the Central Authorities that will be competent for international cooperation and shall, define the modalities of mutual assistance.

Article 9

The requesting competent authority has to ensure the degree of confidentiality with which the requested competent authority of the other Party has marked the information. The degrees of security are those used by INTERPOL.

Article 10

1. The Contracting Parties may assign, for a limited or unlimited period of time, liaison officers from one Contracting Party to the other Contracting Party.

2. Assigning liaison officers for a limited or unlimited period of time aims at promoting and accelerating the cooperation between the Contracting Parties, in particular by agreeing to lend assistance :

    a.   by exchanging information to combat crime in a preventive and repressive way ;

    b.   in the execution of requests for mutual assistance in criminal matters ;

    c.   for the purposes of executing assignments of authorities in charge of surveillance at external borders and immigration ;

    d.   for the purposes of executing assignments of authorities in charge of preventing threats to the public order.

3. Liaison officers give advice and assistance. They have no jurisdiction to independently carry out police actions. They provide information and carry out their assignments within the scope of directions that are given by their home country and by the Contracting Party to which they have been assigned. They regularly report to the Central Authority in charge of police cooperation of the Contracting Party to which they have been assigned.

4. The competent Ministers of the Contracting Parties may agree that the liaison officers of one Contracting Party assigned to a third country also represent the interests of the other Contracting Party.

PROTECTION OF PERSONAL DATA

Article 11

1. In application of this Agreement, the processing of personal data is subject to the respective national laws of each Contracting Party.

2. As regards the processing of personal data in application of this Agreement, the Contracting Parties shall ensure a degree of protection of these personal data in accordance with the provisions of the Convention for the Protection of Individuals with regard to Automatic Processing of Personal Data of the Council of Europe of 28 January 1981 and the Recommendation R (87) 15 of 17 September 1987 of the Committee of Ministers of the Council of Europe Regulating the Use of Personal Data in the Police Sector.

3. As regards the processing of personal data transmitted in application of this Agreement, the following provisions shall apply :

   a. the requesting Contracting Party shall not use these data beyond the scope for which this Agreement provides for the transmission of such data ;

   b. the data may only be used by the judicial authorities, services and instances that fulfil a task or function in the framework of the purposes set out in this Agreement and in particular in accordance with articles 2 and 3. The Parties shall communicate the list of users ;

   c. the Contracting Party that transmits data shall see to the correctness and completeness of the data and shall ensure that these data are only stored for the time deemed necessary. If it is established, either of own initiative or following a request of the person in question, that incorrect data or data which should not have been transmitted, have been furnished, the requesting Contracting Party or Parties must be promptly informed and they must proceed to the correction or destruction of the data ;

   d. one Contracting Party may not put forward that another Contracting Party transmitted incorrect data so as to pass off its responsibility in conformity with domestic law, with regard to a prejudiced individual ;

   e. the transmission and reception of personal data must be registered. The Contracting Parties shall communicate the list of the authorities or services that have jurisdiction to consult the registration ;

   f. the access to the data is subject to the national legislation of the Contracting Party to which the person in question addresses his request. The data may only be communicated to this person after prior authorization of the Contracting Party at the origin of the data ;

   g. The Contracting Party to which the data are destined shall not use the data for purposes other than those specified by the requested Contracting Party and shall comply with the conditions set out by this Contracting Party ;

4. As regards the transmission, the following provisions shall apply :

   a. the communication of data should only be permissible to police and immigration bodies ; the communication of data to other bodies with the same objectives should only be permissible after prior authorization of the Contracting Party that furnishes the data ;

b.   on request, the Contracting Party to which the data are destined shall inform the Contracting Party that transmits the data about their use and the results obtained based on the transmitted data.

5.   Each Contracting Party designates a supervising authority that is put in charge, in accordance with domestic law, of carrying out an independent control on the personal data pursuant to this Agreement and of verifying whether the processing of information does not cause prejudice to the rights of the person in question. These supervising authorities also have jurisdiction to analyze difficulties related to the application or interpretation of this Agreement concerning the processing of personal data. The supervising authorities may agree to cooperate within the scope of the tasks set out in this Agreement.

Article 12

The provisions of this Agreement shall also apply in the event that the personal data are communicated through the intermediary of a liaison officer referred to in article 10.

EXCEPTION

Article 13

Each Party may deny assistance if the request relates to political offences or offences under military criminal law or if this assistance would prejudice the prevailing legal provisions on its territory.

Each Contracting Party may deny assistance or may subject it to certain conditions if it concerns offences related to offences regarded as being of a political or military nature or if the execution of the assistance would prejudice the sovereignty, security, public order or other essential interests of the State.

Party that denies assistance must inform the other Party within 30 days explaining the reasons of denial.

OTHER KINDS OF COOPERATION

Article 14

1.   The Contracting Parties undertake to afford each other a mutual assistance in the field of professional training and technical assistance with regard to issues of police functioning.

2.   The Contracting Parties shall agree to exchange their practical experiences in all fields referred to in this Agreement.

3.   The modalities for mutual assistance shall be defined by means of agreements between the competent ministers of the Contracting Parties.

IMPLEMENTATION OF THE AGREEMENT

Article 15

1. The competent ministers of the Contracting Parties can set up permanent or occasional work groups to study mutual problems regarding the repression and prevention of crime referred to in article 2 and the scope of cooperation referred to in article 3 and to put forward, if deemed necessary, propositions in order to improve, if needed, the practical and technical aspects of the cooperation between the Contracting Parties.

2. The cost entailed by the cooperation shall be borne by each Party, unless otherwise determined between the representatives of the Parties, duly authorized.

3. The competent ministers of the Contracting Parties set up an evaluation committee that will report three years to the Ministers.

SETTLEMENT OF DISPUTES

Article 16

Each controversy that arises following the interpretation or the application of this Agreement shall be settled by a mixed advisory commission.

A mixed advisory commission is created, which consists of delegates of the Ministries of Foreign Affairs, the Interior and Justice. They shall meet periodically at the request of one or others State, in order to facilitate the settlement of problems that arise from the interpretation or application of this Agreement.

FINAL PROVISIONS

Article 17

The provisions of this Agreement are only applied if they are compatible with the national legislation.

The execution of this Agreement will be supervised in conformity with the national legislation of each Contracting Party.

Article 18

The Contracting Parties shall inform each other, in writing and through diplomatic channels, of the completion of constitutional formalities required for the entry into force of the present Agreement.

This Agreement shall enter into force 60 days after the date of receipt of the last notification.

This Agreement is concluded for an unlimited duration. Either Contracting Party may terminate this Agreement by giving written notice to the other Party to be forwarded through diplomatic channels. Termination shall become effective six months after transmission of such notice.

Article 19

Any Party may forward to the other Party all suggestions to amend this Agreement. The Parties confirm the changes made to this Agreement by Mutual consent.

IN WITNESS WHEREOF, the undersigned, duly authorized thereto, have signed this Agreement.

DONE at Brussels, on the 1st day of December 2005, in duplicate, in the English, French and Dutch languages, the three texts being equally authentic.

FOR THE GOVERNMENT OF THE KINGDOM OF BELGIUM :	FOR THE GOVERNMENT OF MALTA :
Laurette ONKELINX, Minister of Justice	Hon. Dr Tonio BORG, Deputy Prime Minister
Patrick DEWAEL, Minister of the Interior	

[FRENCH TEXT – TEXTE FRANÇAIS]

CONVENTION
ENTRE
LE GOUVERNEMENT DU ROYAUME DE BELGIQUE
ET
LE GOUVERNEMENT DE MALTE
RELATIVE
A LA COOPERATION POLICIERE

LE GOUVERNEMENT DU ROYAUME DE BELGIQUE

et

LE GOUVERNEMENT DE MALTE

Ci-après dénommés les Parties Contractantes,

SOUCIEUX de promouvoir les rapports d'amitié et la coopération entre les deux Etats, et en particulier renforcer la coopération policière entre eux ;

DÉSIREUX de renforcer cette coopération policière dans le cadre des engagements internationaux souscrits par les deux Etats en matière de respect des droits et libertés fondamentales, notamment la Convention européenne des Droits de l'Homme et des Libertés fondamentales du 4 novembre 1950 ainsi que la Convention du Conseil de l'Europe n° 108 du 28 janvier 1981 pour la protection des personnes à l'égard du traitement automatisé des données à caractère personnel ;

CONSIDÉRANT que la criminalité organisée internationale représente une menace grave pour le développement socio-économique des Etats contractants et que les développements récents de la criminalité organisée internationale mettent en péril leur fonctionnement institutionnel ;

CONSIDÉRANT que la lutte contre la traite des êtres humains et la répression des entrées et sorties illégales du territoire des Etats et des migrations illégales, ainsi que l'élimination des filières organisées, font partie des préoccupations des Gouvernements et des Parlements respectifs des Etats contractants ;

CONSIDÉRANT que la production et le commerce illégal de stupéfiants et de substances psychotropes constituent un danger pour la santé et la sécurité de nos concitoyens ;

CONSIDÉRANT que la seule harmonisation des législations pertinentes ne suffit pas pour combattre le phénomène de l'immigration clandestine avec suffisamment d'efficacité ;

CONSIDÉRANT que la nécessité d'une coopération policière internationale efficace dans le domaine de la criminalité organisée et des migrations illégales, notamment par l'échange et le traitement des informations, est indispensable pour combattre et prévenir ces activités criminelles ;

CONSIDÉRANT que l'accomplissement de cette nécessité appelle une série de mesures appropriées et une étroite coopération entre les Parties Contractantes ;

ONT résolu de conclure la présente Convention :

DÉFINITIONS

Article 1

Au sens de la présente Convention, on entend par :

Traite internationale des êtres humains :

Tout comportement intentionnel suivant :

a)   faciliter l'entrée sur le territoire de la Partie Contractante, le transit, le séjour ou la sortie sur ce territoire s'il est fait usage, à cette fin, de la contrainte, notamment de violences ou de menaces, ou s'il y a recours à la tromperie, à l'abus d'autorité ou à d'autres formes de pression de manière telle que la personne n'a d'autre choix véritable que de se soumettre à ces pressions ;

b)   exploiter de quelque manière que ce soit une personne en connaissance de cause que cette personne est entrée, transite ou réside sur le territoire de l'Etat parti à la présente Convention (dans les conditions indiquées au point a).

Exploitation sexuelle des enfants :

Les infractions visées par l'article 34 de la Convention des Nations Unies relative aux droits de l'enfant du 20 novembre 1989, en ce compris la production, la vente, la distribution ou d'autres formes de trafic de matériel à caractère pornographique impliquant des enfants et la détention à des fins personnelles de ce type de matériel.

Assistance technique :

Par assistance technique, il faut entendre l'aide apportée en matière de soutien logistique aux services de police et d'immigration.

Criminalité liée aux matières nucléaires et radioactives :

Les infractions telles qu'énumérées à l'article 7§1 de la Convention sur la protection physique des matières nucléaires, signée à Vienne et à New York le 3 mars 1980.

Blanchiment d'argent :

Les infractions telles qu'énumérées à l'article 6§1 à 3 de la Convention du Conseil de l'Europe, relative au blanchiment, au dépistage, à la saisie et à la confiscation des produits du crime, signée à Strasbourg le 8 novembre 1990.

Criminalité organisée :

Toute infraction commise par une "organisation criminelle", définie comme une association structurée, de plus de deux personnes, établie dans le temps et agissant de façon concertée en vue de commettre des infractions punissables d'une peine privative de liberté ou d'une mesure de sûreté privative de liberté d'un minimum de quatre ans ou d'une peine plus grave, ces infractions constituant une fin en soi ou un moyen pour obtenir des avantages patrimoniaux, et, le cas échéant, influencer indûment le fonctionnement d'autorités publiques.

Données à caractère personnel :

Toute information concernant une personne physique identifiée ou identifiable (personne concernée) ; est réputée identifiable une personne qui peut être identifiée, directement ou indirectement, notamment par référence à un numéro d'identification ou à un ou plusieurs éléments spécifiques, propres à son identité physique, physiologique, psychique, économique, culturelle ou sociale.

Traitement des données à caractère personnel :

Toute opération ou ensemble d'opérations effectuées ou non à l'aide de procédés automatisés, telles que la collecte, l'enregistrement, l'organisation, la conservation, l'adaptation ou la modification, l'extraction, la consultation, l'utilisation, la communication par transmission, diffusion ou toute autre forme de mise à disposition, le rapprochement ou l'interconnexion, ainsi que le verrouillage, l'effacement ou la destruction.

Stupéfiant :

Désigne toute substance, qu'elle soit d'origine naturelle ou synthétique, figurant aux Tableaux I et II de la Convention unique sur les stupéfiants signée à New-York le 30 mars 1961.

Substance psychotrope :

Désigne toute substance, qu'elle soit d'origine naturelle ou synthétique, ou tout produit naturel du tableau I, II, III ou IV de la Convention sur les substances psychotropes du 21 février 1971.

Trafic illicite de stupéfiants ou de substances psychotropes :

La culture, la fabrication ou le trafic de stupéfiants ou de substances psychotropes contraires aux buts de la Convention du 30 mars 1961 sur les stupéfiants, de la Convention du 21 février 1971 sur les substances psychotropes ou de la Convention des Nations Unies du 19 décembre 1988 sur le trafic illicite de stupéfiants et de substances psychotropes.

Demande urgente :

Une demande est qualifiée d'urgente dans les cas où le passage par la procédure administrative formelle auprès des organes centraux risque d'entraver ou de compromettre l'action de prévention ou de recherche.

DOMAINES DE COOPÉRATION

Article 2

1. Les Parties Contractantes s'engagent à s'accorder mutuellement, selon les règles et sous les conditions déterminées par la présente Convention, la coopération la plus large en ce qui concerne la coopération policière.

2. Les Parties Contractantes coopéreront à la prévention, la répression et la poursuite d'infractions relevant de la criminalité organisée, et en particulier :

    -   les infractions contre la vie, l'intégrité physique et la santé des personnes ;
    -   les infractions liées à la production et au trafic illicite de stupéfiants, substances psychotropes et précurseurs ;
    -   l'immigration clandestine ;
    -   le proxénétisme, la traite des êtres humains et l'exploitation sexuelle des enfants ;
    -   l'extorsion ;
    -   le vol, le trafic et le commerce illégal d'armes, munitions, explosifs, substances radioactives, matières nucléaires et autres substances dangereuses ;
    -   les falsifications (fabrication, contrefaçon, transformation et distribution) des moyens de paiements, chèques et titres ;
    -   la criminalité dans le domaine des échanges commerciaux et financiers ;
    -   les délits contre les biens, entre autres le vol, le trafic d'œuvres d'arts et d'objets historiques ;
    -   le vol, le commerce illégal et le trafic de véhicules à moteurs et la falsification et l'usage des documents falsifiés de véhicules ;
    -   le blanchiment d'argent.

3. Les infractions graves relevant de la criminalité organisée qui ne sont pas définies à l'article premier sont appréciées par les autorités nationales compétentes selon la législation nationale des Etats auxquels elles appartiennent.

Article 3

La collaboration entre les Parties portera également sur :

-   la recherche des personnes disparues et l'aide à l'identification de cadavres non identifiés ;
-   la recherche sur le territoire d'une Partie d'objets volés, disparus, détournés ou égarés sur le territoire de l'autre.

Article 4

Les Parties coopéreront dans les domaines spécifiés dans les articles 2 et 3 par :

-   les échanges d'informations concernant les domaines ressortissant à la compétence des services de police et de l'immigration ;
-   les échanges de matériel ;
-   l'assistance technique et scientifique, les expertises et les fournitures de matériel technique spécialisé ;
-   un échange d'expériences ;

- la coopération dans le domaine de la formation professionnelle ;
- l'aide à la préparation de l'exécution des demandes d'entraide judiciaire en matière pénale ;

selon les dispositions ci-après.

LES ÉCHANGES D'INFORMATIONS

Article 5

Les Parties Contractantes se prêteront assistance et assureront une coopération étroite et permanente. Elles procèderont notamment à un échange de toutes les informations pertinentes et importantes. Cette coopération peut prendre la forme d'un contact permanent par l'intermédiaire d'officiers de liaison à désigner.

Article 6

1. Les Parties Contractantes s'engagent à ce que leurs services de police s'accordent, dans le respect du droit national et dans les limites de leurs compétences, l'assistance aux fins de la prévention et de la recherche de faits punissables, pour autant que le droit national de la Partie Contractante requise ne réserve pas la demande ou son exécution aux autorités judiciaires.

2. Dans des cas particuliers, chaque Partie Contractante peut, dans le respect de son droit national et sans y être invitée, communiquer à la Partie Contractante concernée des informations qui peuvent être importantes pour celle-ci aux fins de l'assistance pour la prévention et la répression d'infractions ou pour la prévention de menaces pour l'ordre et la sécurité publics.

Article 7

Toute information fournie par la Partie Contractante requise ne peut être utilisée par la Partie Contractante Requérante aux fins d'apporter la preuve des faits incriminés qu'après une demande d'entraide judiciaire, conformément aux dispositions du droit international applicable.

Article 8

1. Les demandes d'assistance et les réponses à ces demandes doivent être échangées entre les organes centraux chargés, par chaque Partie Contractante, de la coopération policière internationale et de l'immigration.

    Lorsque la demande ne peut être faite en temps utile par la voie susvisée, elle peut, exceptionnellement et en cas d'urgence uniquement, être adressée par les autorités compétentes de la Partie Contractante requérante directement aux autorités compétentes de la Partie requise et celles-ci peuvent y répondre directement. Dans ces cas exceptionnels, l'autorité requérante doit aviser dans les meilleurs délais l'organe central chargé, dans la Partie Contractante requise, de la coopération internationale, de sa demande directe et en motiver l'urgence.

2. La désignation des organes centraux chargés de la coopération internationale ainsi que les modalités de l'assistance mutuelle sont réglées par des arrangements entre les Ministres compétents des Parties Contractantes.

Article 9

L'autorité compétente requérante doit garantir le degré de confidentialité que l'autorité compétente requise de l'autre Partie a attribué à l'information. Les degrés de sécurité sont ceux utilisés par INTERPOL.

Article 10

1. Les Parties Contractantes peuvent détacher, pour une durée déterminée ou indéterminée, des officiers de liaison d'une Partie Contractante auprès de l'autre Partie Contractante.

2. Le détachement d'officiers de liaison pour une durée déterminée ou indéterminée a pour but de promouvoir et d'accélérer la coopération entre les Parties Contractantes, notamment en convenant de l'assistance :

   a. sous la forme d'échange d'informations aux fins de la lutte tant préventive que répressive contre la criminalité ;

   b. dans l'exécution de demandes d'entraide en matière pénale ;

   c. pour les besoins de l'exercice des missions des autorités chargées de la surveillance des frontières extérieures et de l'immigration ;

   d. pour les besoins de l'exercice des missions des autorités chargées de la prévention des menaces pour l'ordre public.

3. Les officiers de liaison ont une mission d'avis et d'assistance. Ils ne sont pas compétents pour l'exécution autonóme de mesures de police. Ils fournissent des informations et exécutent leurs missions dans le cadre des instructions qui leur sont données par la Partie Contractante d'origine et par la Partie Contractante auprès de laquelle ils sont détachés. Ils font régulièrement rapport à l'organe central chargé de la coopération policière de la Partie Contractante auprès de laquelle ils sont détachés.

4. Les Ministres compétents des Parties Contractantes peuvent convenir que les officiers de liaison d'une Partie Contractante détachés auprès d'Etats tiers représentent également les intérêts de l'autre Partie Contractante.

PROTECTION DES DONNÉES À CARACTÈRE PERSONNEL

Article 11

1. Le traitement des données à caractère personnel, en application de la présente Convention, est soumis au droit national respectif de chaque Partie Contractante.

2. En ce qui concerne le traitement de données à caractère personnel en application de la présente Convention, les Parties Contractantes s'engagent à réaliser un niveau de protection des données à caractère personnel qui respecte les principes de la Convention du Conseil de l'Europe du 28 janvier 1981 pour la protection des données à caractère personnel et de la Recommandation R (87) 15 du 17 septembre 1987 du Comité des Ministres du Conseil de l'Europe visant à réglementer l'utilisation des données à caractère personnel dans le secteur de la police.

3. En ce qui concerne le traitement des données à caractère personnel transmises en application de la présente Convention, les dispositions ci-après s'appliquent :

   a. les données ne peuvent être utilisées par la Partie Contractante destinataire qu'aux seules fins pour lesquelles la présente Convention prévoit la transmission de telles données ;

   b. les données ne peuvent être utilisées que par les autorités judiciaires, les services et instances qui assurent une tâche ou remplissent une fonction dans le cadre des fins visées dans la présente Convention et plus particulièrement les articles 2 et 3. Les parties communiqueront la liste des utilisateurs ;

   c. la Partie Contractante qui transmet les données est tenue de veiller à l'exactitude et au caractère complet de celles-ci; elle est également tenue de veiller à ce que ces données ne soient pas conservées plus longtemps que nécessaire. Si elle constate, soit de sa propre initiative, soit suite à une demande de la personne concernée, que des données incorrectes ou qui n'auraient pas dû être transmises ont été fournies, la Partie Contractante destinataire doit en être informée sans délai ; cette dernière est tenue de procéder à la correction ou à la destruction des données ;

   d. une Partie Contractante ne peut invoquer le fait qu'une autre Partie Contractante ait transmis des données incorrectes pour se décharger de la responsabilité qui lui incombe conformément à son droit national, à l'égard d'une personne lésée ;

   e. la transmission et la réception de données à caractère personnel doivent être enregistrées. Les Parties Contractantes se communiquent la liste des autorités et services autorisés à consulter l'enregistrement ;

   f. l'accès aux données est régi par le droit national de la Partie Contractante à laquelle la personne concernée présente sa demande. La communication des données au demandeur n'est possible qu'après accord préalable de la Partie Contractante qui est à l'origine des données ;

   g. les données ne peuvent être utilisées par la Partie Contractante destinataire qu'aux seules fins indiquées par la Partie Contractante qui les fournit et dans le respect des conditions imposées par cette Partie Contractante.

4. En ce qui concerne la transmission, les dispositions ci-après s'appliquent :

   a. les données ne peuvent être transmises qu'aux seuls services et autorités de police et de l'immigration; la communication des données à d'autres services ne pourra avoir lieu qu'après autorisation préalable de la Partie Contractante qui les fournit ;

   b. sur demande, la Partie Contractante destinataire informe la Partie Contractante qui transmet les données de l'usage qui en a été fait et des résultats obtenus sur la base des données transmises.

5.   Chaque Partie Contractante désigne une autorité de contrôle chargée, dans le respect du droit national, d'exercer sur son territoire un contrôle indépendant des traitements de données à caractère personnel effectués sur la base de la présente Convention et de vérifier si lesdits traitements ne sont pas attentatoires aux droits de la personne concernée. Ces autorités de contrôle sont également compétentes pour analyser les difficultés d'application ou d'interprétation de la présente Convention portant sur le traitement des données à caractère personnel. Ces autorités de contrôle peuvent s'entendre pour collaborer dans le cadre des missions qui leur sont reconnues par la présente Convention.

Article 12

Si des données à caractère personnel sont transmises par l'intermédiaire d'un officier de liaison visé à l'article 10, les dispositions de la Présente Convention sont également d'application.

EXCEPTION

Article 13

Chacune des Parties Contractantes refuse l'assistance lorsqu'il s'agit d'infractions politiques ou militaires ou lorsque cette assistance s'avère contraire aux dispositions légales en vigueur sur son territoire.

Chacune des Parties Contractantes peut refuser l'assistance ou la soumettre à des conditions lorsqu'il s'agit d'infractions connexes aux infractions politiques ou militaires ou lorsque la réalisation de l'assistance pourrait menacer la souveraineté, la sécurité, l'ordre public ou d'autres intérêts essentiels de l'Etat.

La Partie qui refuse l'assistance doit en informer l'autre Partie dans les 30 jours, en expliquant les raisons de ce refus.

AUTRES FORMES DE COOPÉRATION

Article 14

1.   Les Parties Contractantes s'entendent pour s'accorder une assistance mutuelle dans le domaine de la formation professionnelle et de l'assistance technique pour les problèmes relatifs au fonctionnement de la police.

2.   Les Parties Contractantes s'entendent pour échanger leurs expériences pratiques dans tous les domaines susvisés par la présente Convention.

3.   Les modalités de l'assistance mutuelle sont réglées par des arrangements entre les Ministres compétents des Parties Contractantes.

MISE EN ŒUVRE DE LA CONVENTION

Article 15

1. Les Ministres compétents des Parties Contractantes peuvent créer des groupes de travail permanents ou occasionnels chargés d'examiner des problèmes communs concernant la répression et la prévention des domaines de la criminalité visés à l'article 2 et les domaines de coopération visés à l'article 3 et d'élaborer, le cas échéant, des propositions aux fins d'améliorer, si besoin est, les aspects pratiques et techniques de la coopération entre les Parties Contractantes.

2. Les frais liés à la réalisation de la coopération seront respectivement à charge de chaque Partie, sauf disposition contraire entre les représentants des Parties, dûment habilités.

3. Les Ministres compétents des Parties Contractantes créent un groupe d'évaluation qui fera un rapport aux Ministres tous les trois ans.

RÈGLEMENT DES DIFFÉRENDS

Article 16

Tout différend occasionné par l'interprétation ou l'application de la présente Convention sera résolu par une commission mixte consultative.

Il est créé une commission mixte consultative, composée de représentants des ministères des Affaires étrangères, de l'Intérieur et de la Justice, qui se réunira périodiquement à la demande de l'un ou de l'autre Etat, afin de faciliter le règlement des problèmes qui surgiront de l'interprétation ou de l'application de la présente Convention.

DISPOSITIONS FINALES

Article 17

Les dispositions de la présente Convention ne sont applicables que dans la mesure où elles sont compatibles avec le droit national.

La surveillance de l'exécution de la présente Convention s'effectuera conformément au droit national de chacune des Parties Contractantes.

Article 18

Les Parties Contractantes se notifieront mutuellement, par écrit et par la voie diplomatique, l'accomplissement des formalités constitutionnelles requises pour l'entrée en vigueur de la présente Convention.

La Convention entrera en vigueur 60 jours après la date de réception de la dernière notification.

La présente Convention est conclue pour une durée illimitée. Toute Partie peut la dénoncer au moyen d'une notification écrite adressée par voie diplomatique à l'autre Partie. La dénonciation prendra effet six mois après la date de son envoi.

Article 19

Toute Partie peut faire parvenir à l'autre Partie toutes propositions tendant à modifier la présente Convention. Les Parties arrêtent d'un commun accord les modifications à la présente Convention.

EN FOI DE QUOI, les soussignés, dûment autorisés à cet effet, ont apposé leur signature au bas de la présente Convention.

FAIT à Bruxelles, le 1ᵉʳ décembre 2005, en deux exemplaires, dans les langues anglaise, française et néerlandaise, les trois textes faisant également foi.

POUR LE GOUVERNEMENT   POUR LE GOUVERNEMENT
DU ROYAUME DE BELGIQUE :   DE MALTE :

Laurette ONKELINX,   Hon. Dr Tonio BORG,
Ministre de la Justice   Vice-Premier Ministre

Patrick DEWAEL,
Ministre de l'Intérieur

No. 52088

—

Belgium
and
St. Lucia

Agreement between the Kingdom of Belgium and Saint Lucia for the exchange of information relating to tax matters. Brussels, 7 December 2009

Entry into force: *20 February 2014, in accordance with article 13*

Authentic text: *English*

Registration with the Secretariat of the United Nations: *Belgium, 26 August 2014*

Belgique
et
Sainte-Lucie

Accord entre le Royaume de Belgique et Sainte-Lucie relatif à l'échange de renseignements en matière fiscale. Bruxelles, 7 décembre 2009

Entrée en vigueur : *20 février 2014, conformément à l'article 13*

Texte authentique : *anglais*

Enregistrement auprès du Secrétariat de l'Organisation des Nations Unies : *Belgique, 26 août 2014*

[ENGLISH TEXT – TEXTE ANGLAIS]

AGREEMENT

BETWEEN

THE KINGDOM OF BELGIUM

AND

SAINT LUCIA

FOR

THE EXCHANGE OF INFORMATION RELATING TO TAX MATTERS

THE GOVERNMENT OF THE KINGDOM OF BELGIUM

AND

THE GOVERNMENT OF SAINT LUCIA,

DESIRING to facilitate the exchange of information with respect to taxes,

HAVE AGREED as follows:

Article 1

Object and Scope of the Agreement

The competent authorities of the Contracting Parties shall provide assistance through exchange of information that is foreseeably relevant to the administration and enforcement of the domestic laws of the Contracting Parties concerning taxes covered by this Agreement. Such information shall include information that is foreseeably relevant to the determination, assessment and collection of such taxes, the recovery and enforcement of tax claims, or the investigation or prosecution of tax matters. Information shall be exchanged in accordance with the provisions of this Agreement and shall be treated as confidential in the manner provided in Article 8. The rights and safeguards secured to persons by the laws or administrative practice of the requested Party remain applicable to the extent that they do not unduly prevent or delay effective exchange of information.

Article 2

Jurisdiction

A Requested Party is not obligated to provide information which is neither held by its authorities nor in the possession or control of persons who are within its territorial jurisdiction.

Article 3

Taxes Covered

1. The taxes which are the subject of this Agreement are all taxes imposed or administered by either Contracting Party including any identical or substantially similar taxes imposed after the date of signature of the Agreement.

2. This agreement shall also apply to taxes imposed in Belgium by its political subdivisions or local authorities from the date on which Belgium shall notify the other Contracting Party through diplomatic channels that Belgium agrees on such application.

Article 4

Definitions

1. For the purposes of this Agreement, unless otherwise defined:

    a) the term "Contracting Party" means Saint Lucia or Belgium as the context requires;

    b) the term "Saint Lucia" means the country of Saint Lucia;

c)   the term "Belgium" means the Kingdom of Belgium; used in a geographical sense, it means the territory of the Kingdom of Belgium, including the territorial sea and any other area in the sea and in the air within which the Kingdom of Belgium, in accordance with international law, exercises sovereign rights or its jurisdiction;

d)   the term "competent authority" means

    i)   in the case of Saint Lucia, the Minister of Finance or the Minister's authorised representative;
    ii) in the case of Belgium, the Minister of Finance or his authorised representative;

e)   the term "person" includes an individual, a company and any other body of persons;

f)   the term "company" means any body corporate or any entity that is treated as a body corporate for tax purposes;

g)   the term "publicly traded company" means any company whose principal class of shares is listed on a recognised stock exchange provided its listed shares can be readily purchased or sold by the public. Shares can be purchased or sold "by the public" if the purchase or sale of shares is not implicitly or explicitly restricted to a limited group of investors;

h)   the term "principal class of shares" means the class or classes of shares representing a majority of the voting power and value of the company;

i)   the term "recognised stock exchange" means any stock exchange agreed upon by the competent authorities of the Contracting Parties;

j)   the term "collective investment fund or scheme" means any pooled investment vehicle, irrespective of legal form. The term "public collective investment fund or scheme" means any collective investment fund or scheme provided the units, shares or other interests in the fund or scheme can be readily purchased, sold or redeemed by the public. Units, shares or other interests in the fund or scheme can be readily purchased, sold or redeemed "by the public" if the purchase, sale or redemption is not implicitly or explicitly restricted to a limited group of investors;

k)   the term "tax" means any tax to which the Agreement applies;

l)   the term "applicant Party" means the Contracting Party requesting information;

m)   the term "requested Party" means the Contracting Party requested to provide information;

n)   the term "information gathering measures" means laws and administrative or judicial procedures that enable a Contracting Party to obtain and provide the requested information;

o)   the term "information" means any fact, statement or record in any form whatever;

p)   the term "criminal tax matters" means tax matters involving intentional conduct which is liable to prosecution under the criminal laws of the applicant Party;

q)   the term " criminal laws" means all criminal laws designated as such under domestic law irrespective of whether contained in the tax laws, the criminal code or other statutes.

2. The term "Anstalten" for the purposes of the Agreement shall be interpreted in accordance with paragraphs 52 and 53 of the Commentary to the OECD Model Agreement on Exchange of Information on Tax Matters.

3. As regards the application of this Agreement at any time by a Contracting Party, any term not defined therein shall, unless the context otherwise requires, have the meaning that it has at that time under the law of that Party, any meaning under the applicable tax laws of that Party prevailing over a meaning given to the term under other laws of that Party.

Article 5

Exchange of Information Upon Request

1. The competent authority of the requested Party shall provide upon request information for the purposes referred to in Article 1. Such information shall be exchanged without regard to whether the conduct being investigated would constitute a crime under the laws of the requested Party if such conduct occurred in the territorial jurisdiction of the requested Party.

2. If the information in the possession of the competent authority of the requested Party is not sufficient to enable it to comply with the request for information, that Party shall use all relevant information gathering measures to provide the applicant Party with the information requested, notwithstanding that the requested Party may not need such information for its own tax purposes.

3. If specifically requested by the competent authority of an applicant Party, the competent authority of the requested Party shall provide information under this Article, to the extent allowable under its domestic laws, in the form of depositions of witnesses and authenticated copies of original records.

4. Each Contracting Party shall ensure that its competent authorities for the purposes specified in Article 1 of the Agreement, have the authority to obtain and provide upon request:

    a) information held by banks, other financial institutions, and any person acting in an agency or fiduciary capacity including nominees and trustees;

    b) information regarding the ownership of companies, partnerships, trusts, foundations, "Anstalten" and other persons, including, within the constraints of Article 2, ownership information on all such persons in an ownership chain; in the case of trusts, information on settlors, trustees and beneficiaries; and in the case of foundations, information on founders, members of the foundation council and beneficiaries. Further, this Agreement does not create an obligation on the Contracting Parties to obtain or provide ownership information with respect to publicly traded companies or public collective investment funds or schemes unless such information can be obtained without giving rise to disproportionate difficulties.

5. The competent authority of the applicant Party shall provide the following information to the competent authority of the requested Party when making a request for information under the Agreement to demonstrate the foreseeable relevance of the information to the request:

    a) the identity of the person under examination or investigation;

b) a statement of the information sought including its nature and the form in which the applicant Party wishes to receive the information from the requested Party;

c) the tax purpose for which the information is sought;

d) grounds for believing that the information requested is held in the requested Party or is in the possession or control of a person within the jurisdiction of the requested Party;

e) to the extent known, the name and address of any person believed to be in possession of the requested information;

f) a statement that the request is in conformity with the law and administrative practices of the applicant Party, that if the requested information was within the jurisdiction of the applicant Party then the competent authority of the applicant Party would be able to obtain the information under the laws of the applicant Party or in the normal course of administrative practice and that it is in conformity with this Agreement;

g) a statement that the applicant Party has pursued all means available in its own territory to obtain the information, except those that would give rise to disproportionate difficulties.

6. The competent authority of the requested Party shall forward the requested information as promptly as possible to the applicant Party. To ensure a prompt response, the competent authority of the requested Party shall:

a) Confirm receipt of a request in writing to the competent authority of the applicant Party and shall notify the competent authority of the applicant Party of deficiencies in the request, if any, within 60 days of the receipt of the request.

b) If the competent authority of the requested Party has been unable to obtain and provide the information within 90 days of receipt of the request, including if it encounters obstacles in furnishing the information or it refuses to furnish the information, it shall immediately inform the applicant Party, explaining the reason for its inability, the nature of the obstacles or the reasons for its refusal.

Article 6

Tax Examinations Abroad

1. A Contracting Party may allow representatives of the competent authority of the other Contracting Party to enter the territory of the first-mentioned Party to interview individuals and examine records with the written consent of the persons concerned. The competent authority of the second-mentioned Party shall notify the competent authority of the first-mentioned Party of the time and place of the meeting with the individuals concerned.

2. At the request of the competent authority of one Contracting Party, the competent authority of the other Contracting Party may allow representatives of the competent authority of the first-mentioned Party to be present at the appropriate part of a tax examination in the second-mentioned Party.

3. If the request referred to in paragraph 2 is acceded to, the competent authority of the Contracting Party conducting the examination shall, as soon as possible, notify the competent authority of the other Party about the time and place of the examination, the authority or official designated to carry out the examination and the procedures and conditions required by the first-mentioned Party for the conduct of the examination. All decisions with respect to the conduct of the tax examination shall be made by the Party conducting the examination.

Article 7

Possibility of Declining a Request

1. The requested Party shall not be required to obtain or provide information that the applicant Party would not be able to obtain under its own laws for purposes of the administration or enforcement of its own tax laws. The competent authority of the requested Party may decline to assist where the request is not made in conformity with this Agreement.

2. The provisions of this Agreement shall not impose on a Contracting Party the obligation to supply information which would disclose any trade, business, industrial, commercial or professional secret or trade process. Notwithstanding the foregoing, information of the type referred to in Article 5, paragraph 4, shall not be treated as such a secret or trade process merely because it meets the criteria in that paragraph.

3. The provisions of this Agreement shall not impose on a Contracting Party the obligation to obtain or provide information, which would reveal confidential communications between a client and an attorney, solicitor or other admitted legal representative where such communications are:

   a) produced for the purposes of seeking or providing legal advice or

   b) produced for the purposes of use in existing or contemplated legal proceedings.

4. The requested Party may decline a request for information if the disclosure of the information would be contrary to public policy (ordre public).

5. A request for information shall not be refused on the ground that the tax claim giving rise to the request is disputed.

6. The requested Party may decline a request for information if the information is requested by the applicant Party to administer or enforce a provision of the tax law of the applicant Party, or any requirement connected therewith, which discriminates against a national of the requested Party as compared with a national of the applicant Party in the same circumstances.

Article 8

Confidentiality

1. Any information received by a Contracting Party under this Agreement shall be treated as confidential and may be disclosed only to persons or authorities (including courts and administrative bodies) in the jurisdiction of the Contracting Party concerned with the assessment or collection of, the enforcement or prosecution in respect of, or the determination of appeals in relation to, the taxes covered by this Agreement. Such persons or authorities shall use such information only for such purposes. They may disclose the information in public court proceedings or in judicial decisions. The information may not be disclosed to any other person or entity or authority or any other jurisdiction without the express written consent of the competent authority of the requested Party.

2. In case of exchange of information in respect of an identified or identifiable individual, the provisions of Chapter 6, in particular the Article 199, of the Economic Partnership Agreement between the Cariforum States and the European Community and its Member States of 15 Ocotber 2008 shall be applied accordingly.

Article 9

Costs

Incidence of costs incurred in providing assistance shall be agreed by the Contracting Parties.

Article 10

Implementation Legislation

The Contracting Parties shall take all necessary legislative steps to comply with, and give effect to, the terms of the Agreement.

Article 11

Other international agreements or arrangements

The possibilities of assistance provided by this Agreement do not limit, nor are they limited by, those contained in existing international agreements or other arrangements between the Contracting Parties which relate to co-operation in tax matters.

Article 12

Mutual Agreement Procedure

1. Where difficulties or doubts arise between the Contracting Parties regarding the implementation or interpretation of the Agreement, the competent authorities shall endeavour to resolve the matter by mutual agreement.

2. In addition to the agreements referred to in paragraph 1, the competent authorities of the Contracting Parties may mutually agree on the procedures to be used under Articles 5 and 6.

3. The competent authorities of the Contracting Parties may communicate with each other directly for purposes of reaching agreement under this Article.

4. The Contracting Parties may also agree on other forms of dispute resolution.

Article 13

Entry into Force

1. This Agreement shall enter into force when each Party has notified the other of the completion of its necessary internal procedures for entry into force. Upon entry into force, it shall have effect:

   a) for criminal tax matters on that date; and

   b) for all other matters covered in Article 1 on that date, but only in respect of taxable periods beginning on or after that date, or where there is no taxable period, all charges to tax arising on or after that date.

2. Notwithstanding paragraph 1 of this Article, paragraph 5, f) of Article 5 and the first sentence of paragraph 1 of Article 7 shall only have effect for both parties from the date on which Belgium shall notify Saint Lucia through diplomatic channels that Belgium has implemented legislation providing for the exchange of banking information for purposes of its own tax laws.

Article 14

Termination

1. Either Contracting Party may terminate the Agreement by serving a notice of termination either through diplomatic channels or by letter to the competent authority of the other Contracting Party.

2. Such termination shall become effective on the first day of the month following the expiration of a period of six months after the date of receipt of notice of termination by the other Contracting Party.

3. Following termination of the Agreement the Contracting Parties shall remain bound by the provisions of Article 8 with respect to any information obtained under the Agreement.

IN WITNESS WHEREOF, the undersigned, being duly authorised thereto, have signed the Agreement.

DONE at Brussels, on the ...7.ᵗᵉ... day of .... December .... 2009.

FOR THE GOVERNMENT
OF THE KINGDOM OF BELGIUM:

FOR THE GOVERNMENT
OF SAINT LUCIA:

[TRANSLATION – TRADUCTION]

ACCORD ENTRE LE ROYAUME DE BELGIQUE ET SAINTE-LUCIE RELATIF À L'ÉCHANGE DE RENSEIGNEMENTS EN MATIÈRE FISCALE

Le Gouvernement du Royaume de Belgique et le Gouvernement de Sainte-Lucie,

Désireux de faciliter l'échange de renseignements en matière fiscale,

Sont convenus de ce qui suit :

Article premier. Objet et champ d'application de l'Accord

Les autorités compétentes des Parties contractantes s'accordent une assistance par l'échange de renseignements vraisemblablement pertinents pour l'administration et l'application de la législation interne des Parties contractantes relative aux impôts visés par le présent Accord. Ces renseignements sont ceux vraisemblablement pertinents pour la détermination, l'établissement et la perception de ces impôts, pour le recouvrement et l'exécution des créances fiscales ou pour les enquêtes ou les poursuites en matière fiscale. Les renseignements sont échangés conformément aux dispositions du présent Accord et tenus confidentiels selon les modalités prévues à l'article 8. Les droits et protections dont bénéficient les personnes en vertu des dispositions législatives ou réglementaires ou des pratiques administratives de la Partie requise restent applicables dans la mesure où ils n'entravent ou ne retardent pas indûment un échange effectif de renseignements.

Article 2. Compétence

La Partie requise n'est pas tenue de fournir des renseignements qui ne sont ni détenus par ses autorités ni en la possession ou sous le contrôle de personnes relevant de sa compétence territoriale.

Article 3. Impôts visés

1.   Les impôts visés par le présent Accord sont tous les impôts établis ou administrés par l'une ou l'autre Partie contractante, y compris les impôts identiques ou analogues qui seraient établis après la date de signature de l'Accord.

2.   Le présent Accord s'applique aussi aux impôts perçus en Belgique par ses subdivisions politiques ou collectivités locales, à compter de la date à laquelle la Belgique notifie par la voie diplomatique à l'autre Partie contractante qu'elle consent à cette application.

Article 4. Définitions

1.   Aux fins du présent Accord, sauf définition contraire :

a) L'expression « Partie contractante » désigne Sainte-Lucie ou la Belgique, selon le contexte;

b) Le terme « Sainte-Lucie » désigne le pays du même nom;

c) Le terme « Belgique » désigne le Royaume de Belgique; employé dans un sens géographique, il désigne le territoire du Royaume de Belgique, y compris la mer territoriale ainsi que les zones maritimes et les espaces aériens sur lesquels, en conformité avec le droit international, le Royaume de Belgique exerce des droits souverains ou sa compétence;

d) L'expression « autorité compétente » désigne :

   i) En ce qui concerne Sainte-Lucie, le Ministre des finances ou son représentant autorisé;

   ii) En ce qui concerne la Belgique, le Ministre des finances ou son représentant autorisé;

e) Le terme « personne » inclut une personne physique, une société et tout autre groupement de personnes;

f) Le terme « société » désigne toute personne morale ou toute entité considérée fiscalement comme une personne morale;

g) L'expression « société cotée » désigne toute société dont la catégorie principale d'actions est cotée sur une bourse reconnue, les actions cotées de la société devant pouvoir être achetées ou vendues facilement par le public. Les actions peuvent être achetées ou vendues « par le public » si l'achat ou la vente des actions n'est pas implicitement ou explicitement restreint à un groupe limité d'investisseurs;

h) L'expression « catégorie principale d'actions » désigne la ou les catégories d'actions représentant la majorité des droits de vote et de la valeur de la société;

i) L'expression « bourse reconnue » désigne toute bourse déterminée d'un commun accord par les autorités compétentes des Parties contractantes;

j) L'expression « fonds ou dispositif de placement collectif » désigne tout instrument de placement groupé, quelle que soit sa forme juridique. Le terme « fonds ou dispositif de placement collectif public » désigne tout fonds ou dispositif de placement collectif dont les parts, actions ou autres participations peuvent être facilement achetées, vendues ou rachetées par le public. Les parts, actions ou autres participations au fonds ou dispositif peuvent être facilement achetées, vendues ou rachetées « par le public » si l'achat, la vente ou le rachat n'est pas implicitement ou explicitement restreint à un groupe limité d'investisseurs;

k) Le terme « impôt » désigne tout impôt auquel s'applique l'Accord;

l) L'expression « Partie requérante » désigne la Partie contractante qui demande les renseignements;

m) L'expression « Partie requise » désigne la Partie contractante à laquelle les renseignements sont demandés;

n) L'expression « mesures de collecte de renseignements » désigne les dispositions législatives et réglementaires ainsi que les procédures administratives ou judiciaires qui permettent à une Partie contractante d'obtenir et de fournir les renseignements demandés;

o) Le terme « renseignement » désigne tout fait, énoncé ou document, quelle que soit sa forme;

p) L'expression « en matière fiscale pénale » désigne toute affaire fiscale faisant intervenir un acte intentionnel passible de poursuites en vertu du droit pénal de la Partie requérante;

q) L'expression « droit pénal » désigne toute disposition pénale qualifiée comme telle en vertu de la législation nationale, qu'elle fasse partie de la législation fiscale, du code pénal ou d'autres lois.

2. Aux fins de l'Accord, le terme « Anstalten » doit être interprété conformément aux paragraphes 52 et 53 du commentaire relatif au Modèle d'accord de l'OCDE sur l'échange de renseignements en matière fiscale.

3. Aux fins de l'application du présent Accord à tout moment par une Partie contractante, tout terme qui n'y est pas défini a, sauf si le contexte exige une interprétation différente, le sens que lui attribue la législation de cette Partie au moment considéré, le sens attribué à ce terme par la législation fiscale applicable de cette Partie prévalant sur le sens que lui attribuent d'autres lois de cette Partie.

Article 5. *Échange de renseignements sur demande*

1. L'autorité compétente de la Partie requise fournit les renseignements sur demande aux fins visées à l'article premier. Ces renseignements doivent être échangés, que l'acte faisant l'objet de l'enquête constitue ou non une infraction pénale, au regard de la législation de la Partie requise, s'il s'était produit sur le territoire de cette Partie.

2. Si les renseignements en la possession de l'autorité compétente de la Partie requise ne sont pas suffisants pour lui permettre de donner suite à la demande de renseignements, cette Partie prend toutes les mesures adéquates de collecte de renseignements nécessaires pour fournir à la Partie requérante les renseignements demandés, même si la Partie requise n'a pas besoin de ces renseignements à ses propres fins fiscales.

3. Sur demande spécifique de l'autorité compétente d'une Partie requérante, l'autorité compétente de la Partie requise fournit les renseignements visés au présent article, dans la mesure où sa législation interne le lui permet, sous la forme de dépositions de témoins et de copies certifiées conformes aux documents originaux.

4. Chaque Partie contractante fait en sorte que ses autorités compétentes aient le droit, aux fins visées à l'article premier de l'Accord, d'obtenir et de fournir, sur demande :

a) Les renseignements détenus par les banques, les autres institutions financières et toute personne agissant en qualité de mandataire ou de fiduciaire;

b) Les renseignements concernant la propriété des sociétés, des sociétés de personnes, des fiducies, des fondations, des « Anstalten » et d'autres personnes, y compris, dans les limites de l'article 2, les renseignements en matière de propriété concernant toutes ces personnes lorsqu'elles font partie d'une chaîne de propriété; dans le cas d'une fiducie, les renseignements sur les constituants, les fiduciaires et les bénéficiaires et, dans le cas d'une fondation, les renseignements sur les fondateurs, les membres du conseil de la fondation et les bénéficiaires. En outre, le présent Accord n'oblige pas les Parties contractantes à obtenir ou fournir les renseignements en matière de propriété concernant des sociétés cotées ou des fonds ou dispositifs de placement collectif publics, sauf si ces renseignements peuvent être obtenus sans susciter des difficultés disproportionnées.

5. L'autorité compétente de la Partie requérante fournit les informations ci-après à l'autorité compétente de la Partie requise lorsqu'elle soumet une demande de renseignements en vertu de l'Accord, afin de démontrer la pertinence vraisemblable des renseignements demandés :

a) L'identité de la personne faisant l'objet d'un contrôle ou d'une enquête;

b) Une déclaration concernant les renseignements recherchés, notamment leur nature et la forme sous laquelle la Partie requérante souhaite les recevoir de la Partie requise;

c) Le but fiscal dans lequel les renseignements sont demandés;

d) Les raisons qui donnent à penser que les renseignements demandés sont détenus dans la Partie requise ou sont en la possession ou sous le contrôle d'une personne relevant de la compétence de la Partie requise;

e) Dans la mesure où ils sont connus, les nom et adresse de toute personne dont il y a lieu de penser qu'elle est en possession des renseignements demandés;

f) Une déclaration attestant que la demande est conforme à la législation et aux pratiques administratives de la Partie requérante, que, si les renseignements demandés relevaient de la compétence de la Partie requérante, l'autorité compétente de cette Partie pourrait obtenir les renseignements en vertu de son droit ou dans le cadre normal de ses pratiques administratives et que la demande est conforme au présent Accord;

g) Une déclaration attestant que la Partie requérante a utilisé, pour obtenir les renseignements, tous les moyens disponibles sur son propre territoire, hormis ceux qui susciteraient des difficultés disproportionnées.

6. L'autorité compétente de la Partie requise transmet aussi rapidement que possible à la Partie requérante les renseignements demandés. Pour assurer une réponde rapide, l'autorité compétente de la Partie requise :

a) Accuse réception de la demande par écrit à l'autorité compétente de la Partie requérante et, dans les 60 jours à compter de la réception de la demande, l'avise des éventuelles lacunes de la demande;

b) Si l'autorité compétente de la Partie requise n'a pu obtenir et fournir les renseignements dans les 90 jours à compter de la réception de la demande, y compris dans le cas où elle rencontre des obstacles pour fournir les renseignements ou refuse de fournir les renseignements, elle en informe immédiatement la Partie requérante, en indiquant les raisons de l'incapacité dans laquelle elle se trouve de fournir les renseignements, la nature des obstacles rencontrés ou les motifs de son refus.

Article 6. Contrôles fiscaux à l'étranger

1. Une Partie contractante peut autoriser des représentants de l'autorité compétente de l'autre Partie contractante à se rendre sur son territoire pour interroger des personnes physiques et examiner des documents, avec le consentement écrit des personnes concernées. L'autorité compétente de la deuxième Partie fait connaître à l'autorité compétente de la première Partie la date et le lieu de la réunion avec les personnes physiques concernées.

2. À la demande de l'autorité compétente d'une Partie contractante, l'autorité compétente de l'autre Partie contractante peut autoriser des représentants de l'autorité compétente de la première Partie à assister à la phase appropriée d'un contrôle fiscal dans la deuxième Partie.

3. Si la demande visée au paragraphe 2 est acceptée, l'autorité compétente de la Partie contractante qui conduit le contrôle fait connaître aussitôt que possible à l'autorité compétente de l'autre Partie la date et le lieu du contrôle, le nom de l'autorité ou du fonctionnaire chargé de conduire le contrôle, ainsi que les procédures et conditions exigées par la première Partie pour la

conduite du contrôle. Toute décision relative à la conduite du contrôle fiscal est prise par la Partie qui conduit le contrôle.

Article 7. Possibilité de décliner une demande

1.   La Partie requise n'est pas tenue d'obtenir ou de fournir des renseignements que la Partie requérante ne pourrait pas obtenir en vertu de son propre droit pour l'exécution ou l'application de sa propre législation fiscale. L'autorité compétente de la Partie requise peut refuser l'assistance lorsque la demande n'est pas soumise en conformité avec le présent Accord.

2.   Les dispositions du présent Accord n'obligent pas une Partie contractante à fournir des renseignements qui révéleraient un secret commercial, industriel ou professionnel ou un procédé commercial. Nonobstant ce qui précède, les renseignements du type visé au paragraphe 4 de l'article 5, ne sont pas traités comme un tel secret ou procédé commercial du simple fait qu'ils remplissent les critères prévus à ce paragraphe.

3.   Les dispositions du présent Accord n'obligent pas une Partie contractante à obtenir ou à fournir des renseignements qui divulgueraient des communications confidentielles entre un client et un avocat ou un autre représentant juridique agréé lorsque ces communications :

a)   Ont pour but de demander ou fournir un avis juridique; ou

b)   Sont destinées à être utilisées dans une action en justice en cours ou envisagée.

4.   La Partie requise peut rejeter une demande de renseignements si la divulgation des renseignements est contraire à son ordre public.

5.   Une demande de renseignements ne peut être rejetée au motif que la créance fiscale faisant l'objet de la demande est contestée.

6.   La Partie requise peut rejeter une demande de renseignements si les renseignements sont demandés par la Partie requérante pour appliquer ou exécuter une disposition de la législation fiscale de la Partie requérante, ou toute obligation s'y rattachant, qui est discriminatoire à l'encontre d'un ressortissant de la Partie requise par rapport à un ressortissant de la Partie requérante se trouvant dans les mêmes circonstances.

Article 8. Confidentialité

1.   Tout renseignement reçu par une Partie contractante en vertu du présent Accord est tenu confidentiel et est porté à la seule connaissance des personnes ou autorités (y compris les tribunaux et les organes administratifs) relevant de la compétence de cette Partie contractante qui sont concernées par l'établissement, la perception, le recouvrement ou l'exécution des impôts visés par le présent Accord, ou par les poursuites ou les décisions en matière de recours se rapportant à ces impôts. Ces personnes ou autorités ne peuvent utiliser ces renseignements qu'à ces fins. Elles peuvent en faire état lors d'audiences publiques de tribunaux ou dans des décisions judiciaires. Les renseignements ne peuvent être communiqués à aucune autre personne, entité ou autorité, ni à aucune autre juridiction sans l'autorisation écrite expresse de l'autorité compétente de la Partie requise.

2.   Lorsque l'échange de renseignements concerne une personne physique identifiée ou identifiable, les dispositions du chapitre 6, en particulier l'article 199, de l'Accord de partenariat économique du 15 octobre 2008 entre les États du Cariforum et la Communauté européenne et ses États membres sont appliquées en conséquence.

Article 9. Frais

La répartition des frais encourus pour fournir l'assistance est convenue par les Parties contractantes.

Article 10. Dispositions d'application

Les Parties contractantes prennent toutes les mesures législatives nécessaires pour se conformer au présent Accord et lui donner effet.

Article 11. Autres accords et arrangements internationaux

Les possibilités d'assistance découlant de tous accords ou autres arrangements internationaux en vigueur entre les Parties contractantes qui se rapportent à la coopération en matière fiscale ne limitent pas celles que prévoit le Présent accord et ne sont pas limitées par celles-ci.

Article 12. Procédure amiable

1.   En cas de difficultés ou de doutes entre les Parties contractantes au sujet de l'application ou de l'interprétation de l'Accord, les autorités compétentes s'efforcent de régler la question par voie d'accord amiable.

2.   Outre les accords visés au paragraphe 1, les autorités compétentes des Parties contractantes peuvent déterminer d'un commun accord les procédures à suivre en application des articles 5 et 6.

3.   Les autorités compétentes des Parties contractantes peuvent communiquer entre elles directement lorsqu'elles recherchent un accord en application du présent article.

4.   Les Parties contractantes peuvent également convenir d'autres formes de règlement des différends.

Article 13. Entrée en vigueur

1.   Le présent Accord entre en vigueur lorsque chacune des Parties a notifié à l'autre l'accomplissement de ses procédures internes nécessaires pour l'entrée en vigueur. Dès l'entrée en vigueur, il prend effet :

a) En matière fiscale pénale, à cette date; et

b) Pour toutes les autres questions visées à l'article premier, à cette date, mais seulement en ce qui concerne les périodes imposables commençant à cette date ou pour la suite ou, à défaut de période imposable, toutes les impositions prenant naissance à cette date ou pour la suite.

2.   Nonobstant le paragraphe 1 du présent article, l'alinéa f) du paragraphe 5 de l'article 5 et la première phrase du paragraphe 1 de l'article 7 ne sont applicables pour les deux Parties qu'à partir de la date à laquelle la Belgique notifie par la voie diplomatique à Sainte-Lucie que la Belgique a mis en œuvre une législation prévoyant l'échange de renseignements bancaires aux fins de l'application de sa propre législation fiscale.

Article 14. Dénonciation

1.   Chacune des Parties contractantes peut dénoncer l'Accord en notifiant cette dénonciation par la voie diplomatique ou par lettre à l'autorité compétente de l'autre Partie contractante.

2.   Cette dénonciation prend effet le premier jour du mois suivant l'expiration d'un délai de six mois à compter de la date de réception de la notification de dénonciation par l'autre Partie contractante.

3.   Après la dénonciation de l'Accord, les Parties contractantes restent liées par les dispositions de l'article 8 pour tous renseignements obtenus en application de l'Accord.

EN FOI DE QUOI, les soussignés, à ce dûment autorisés, ont signé l'Accord.

FAIT à Bruxelles, le 7 décembre 2009.

Pour le Gouvernement du Royaume de Belgique :

[SIGNÉ]

Pour le Gouvernement de Sainte-Lucie :

[SIGNÉ]

No. 52089

———

Belgium, Luxembourg, Netherlands
and
South Africa

Agreement between the Governments of the Benelux States and the Government of the Republic of South Africa on the exemption of visa requirements for holders of diplomatic, official and/or service passports. Pretoria, 22 February 2013

Entry into force: *1 August 2014, in accordance with article 12*

Authentic texts: *Dutch, English and French*

Registration with the Secretariat of the United Nations: *Belgium, 12 August 2014*

———

Belgique, Luxembourg, Pays-Bas
et
Afrique du Sud

Accord entre les Gouvernements des États du Benelux et le Gouvernement de la République d'Afrique du Sud relatif à l'exemption de l'obligation de visa pour les titulaires de passeports diplomatiques, officiels et/ou de service. Pretoria, 22 février 2013

Entrée en vigueur : *1er août 2014, conformément à l'article 12*

Textes authentiques : *néerlandais, anglais et français*

Enregistrement auprès du Secrétariat de l'Organisation des Nations Unies : *Belgique, 12 août 2014*

Participant	Notification	
Belgium	3 Jun 2014	n
Luxembourg	11 Apr 2013	n
Netherlands	22 Nov 2013	n
South Africa	21 Feb 2014	n

Participant	Notification	
Afrique du Sud	21 févr 2014	n
Belgique	3 juin 2014	n
Luxembourg	11 avr 2013	n
Pays-Bas	22 nov 2013	n

[DUTCH TEXT – TEXTE NÉERLANDAIS]

PREAMBULE

**OVEREENKOMST
TUSSEN
DE REGERINGEN VAN DE BENELUX-STATEN
EN
DE REGERING VAN DE REPUBLIEK ZUID-AFRIKA
INZAKE
DE AFSCHAFFING VAN DE VISUMPLICHT
VOOR HOUDERS VAN DIPLOMATIEKE, OFFICIËLE EN/OF DIENSTPASPOORTEN**

DE REGERINGEN VAN DE BENELUX-STATEN

EN

DE REGERING VAN DE REPUBLIEK ZUID-AFRIKA

(die hierna gezamenlijk worden aangeduid als de "Partijen" en afzonderlijk als een "Partij");

IN HET BESEF dat de Regeringen van de Benelux-Staten gezamenlijk optreden op basis van de Overeenkomst tussen het Koninkrijk België, het Groothertogdom Luxemburg en het Koninkrijk der Nederlanden inzake de verlegging van de personencontrole naar de buitengrenzen van het Benelux-gebied, die op 11 april 1960 in Brussel werd ondertekend;

VERLANGENDE de onderdanen van de Republiek Zuid-Afrika en de onderdanen van de Benelux-Staten die houders zijn van geldige nationale diplomatieke, officiële en/of dienstpaspoorten makkelijker toegang te geven tot hun onderscheiden landen;

BEREID om een Overeenkomst aan te gaan inzake de afschaffing van de visumplicht voor houders van geldige nationale diplomatieke, officiële en/of dienstpaspoorten;

KOMEN HIERBIJ het volgende **OVEREEN**:

ARTIKEL 1
BEGRIPSOMSCHRIJVINGEN

Tenzij anders vermeld, wordt in deze Overeenkomst verstaan onder:

- "Benelux-Staten": het Koninkrijk België, het Groothertogdom Luxemburg en het Koninkrijk der Nederlanden;

- "Benelux-gebied": het gezamenlijke grondgebied in Europa van het Koninkrijk België, het Groothertogdom Luxemburg en het Koninkrijk der Nederlanden.

ARTIKEL 2
BEVOEGDE AUTORITEITEN

De bevoegde autoriteiten die verantwoordelijk zijn voor de uitvoering van deze Overeenkomst zijn:

(a) Voor de Regering van de Republiek Zuid-Afrika: het "Department of Home Affairs"; en

(b) Voor de Regeringen van de Benelux-Staten: voor het Koninkrijk België: de Federale Overheidsdienst Buitenlandse Zaken, Buitenlandse Handel en Ontwikkelingssamen-werking; voor het Groothertogdom Luxemburg: het Ministerie van Buitenlandse Zaken en Immigratie en voor het Koninkrijk der Nederlanden: het Ministerie van Buitenlandse Zaken.

ARTIKEL 3
AFSCHAFFING VAN DE VISUMPLICHT

(1) Onderdanen van de Republiek Zuid-Afrika die houders zijn van geldige nationale diplomatieke, officiële en/of dienstpaspoorten kunnen voor een verblijf van ten hoogste drie (3) maanden het Benelux-gebied zonder visum binnenkomen.

(2) Onderdanen van de Benelux-Staten die houders zijn van geldige nationale diplomatieke, officiële en/of dienstpaspoorten kunnen voor een verblijf van ten hoogste drie (3) maanden de Republiek Zuid-Afrika zonder visum binnenkomen.

ARTIKEL 4
GEACCREDITEERDE VERTEGENWOORDIGERS

(1) Onderdanen van de Staat van de ene Partij die zijn aangesteld bij diplomatieke of consulaire zendingen of bij zendingen bij internationale organisaties die gelegen zijn in de Staat van de andere Partij en die houders zijn van geldige nationale diplomatieke, officiële en/of dienstpaspoorten alsmede hun echtgeno(o)t(e) of wettelijke partner en minderjarige kinderen die houders zijn van geldige nationale diplomatieke, officiële en/of dienstpaspoorten kunnen het grondgebied van de Ontvangende Partij zonder visum binnenkomen, verlaten en er verblijven zolang de accreditatie loopt.

276

(2) De Partijen stellen elkaar in kennis van de aankomst van voornoemde ambtenaren en de ambtenaren nemen de accreditatieregeling van de andere Partij in acht.

ARTIKEL 5
WEIGERING VAN TOEGANG

Onverminderd de artikelen 3 en 4, behoudt elke Regering zich het recht voor de toegang tot haar grondgebied te weigeren aan personen die als ongewenst zijn gesignaleerd of wier aanwezigheid in het land wordt beschouwd als een gevaar voor de openbare orde of voor de nationale veiligheid.

ARTIKEL 6
TOEPASSING VAN DE WETTEN

Tenzij hierin is voorzien, doet deze Overeenkomst geen afbreuk aan de wetten en voorschriften die in de Benelux-Staten en de Republiek Zuid-Afrika van toepassing zijn met betrekking tot de toegang tot het grondgebied, het verblijf, de vestiging en de verwijdering van vreemdelingen, alsmede met betrekking tot het verrichten van enigerlei arbeid.

ARTIKEL 7
OVERNAME

Elke Partij verbindt zich ertoe te allen tijde en zonder formaliteiten de personen over te nemen, die zijn binnengekomen op vertoon van een geldig nationaal diplomatiek, officieel en/of dienstpaspoort dat is uitgereikt door de autoriteiten van het Koninkrijk België, het Groothertogdom Luxemburg, het Koninkrijk der Nederlanden of van de Republiek Zuid-Afrika.

ARTIKEL 8
DOCUMENTATIE

De Partijen doen elkaar langs diplomatieke weg de specimens van hun nieuwe of gewijzigde nationale diplomatieke, officiële en/of dienstpaspoorten toekomen, alsmede de gegevens betreffende het gebruik van deze paspoorten, zulks voor zover mogelijk zestig (60 dagen) vóór deze in omloop worden gebracht.

ARTIKEL 9
REGELING VAN GESCHILLEN

Geschillen tussen de Partijen inzake de toepassing of uitlegging van deze Overeenkomst worden in der minne geregeld via overleg of onderhandelingen tussen de Partijen.

ARTIKEL 10
WIJZIGING

Deze Overeenkomst kan in onderlinge overeenstemming van de Partijen te allen tijde worden gewijzigd via een uitwisseling van nota's tussen de Partijen langs diplomatieke weg.

ARTIKEL 11
DEPOSITARIS

De Federale Overheidsdienst Buitenlandse Zaken, Buitenlandse Handel en Ontwikkelingssamen-werking van het Koninkrijk België ('De Belgische Regering") is depositaris van deze Overeenkomst. De depositaris voorziet elke Partij van een gewaarmerkt afschrift van het origineel.

ARTIKEL 12
INWERKINGTREDING, LOOPTIJD EN BEËINDIGING

(1)   Deze Overeenkomst treedt voor de duur van één (1) jaar in werking op de eerste dag van de tweede maand volgend op de dag van de laatste kennisgeving waaruit blijkt dat aan alle grondwettelijke en wettelijke formaliteiten voor de inwerkingtreding ervan is voldaan. Indien de Overeenkomst dertig (30) dagen voor het verstrijken van die periode niet is opgezegd, wordt zij geacht voor onbepaalde tijd te zijn verlengd.

(2)   Na het verstrijken van de eerste periode van een jaar kan elke Partij de Overeenkomst opzeggen door dertig (30) dagen van tevoren de Belgische Regering daarvan mededeling te doen.

(3)   De opzegging van de Overeenkomst door een van de Partijen heeft de beëindiging ervan tot gevolg.

(4)   De Belgische Regering stelt de andere Partijen in kennis van de ontvangst van de in dit artikel bedoelde kennisgevingen alsmede van de in dit artikel bedoelde mededeling.

ARTIKEL 13
OPSCHORTING

Deze Overeenkomst kan door elk der Partijen worden opgeschort. Van deze opschorting dient onverwijld langs diplomatieke weg kennis te worden gegeven aan de Belgische Regering. Deze zal de overige Partijen van de ontvangst van deze kennisgeving op de hoogte stellen. Hetzelfde geldt voor het ongedaan maken van de opschorting.

ARTIKEL 14
TOEPASSING OP HET KONINKRIJK DER NEDERLANDEN

Wat het Koninkrijk der Nederlanden betreft, kan de toepassing van deze Overeenkomst worden uitgebreid tot Aruba, Curaçao, Sint Maarten en tot het Caribische deel van Nederland (Bonaire, Sint Eustatius en Saba).

TEN BLIJKE WAARVAN, de ondertekenende Partijen, die daartoe naar behoren zijn gemachtigd door hun onderscheiden Regeringen, deze in de Engelse, de Franse en de Nederlandse taal gestelde Overeenkomst hebben ondertekend. In geval van verschil in uitlegging is de Engelse tekst doorslaggevend.

GEDAAN te Pretoria op .... 22 februari 2013 ....

VOOR DE REGERING VAN HET KONINKRIJK BELGIË:

VOOR DE REGERING VAN HET GROOTHERTOGDOM LUXEMBURG:

VOOR DE REGERING VAN HET KONINKRIJK DER NEDERLANDEN:

VOOR DE REGERING VAN DE REPUBLIEK ZUID-AFRIKA:

[ENGLISH TEXT – TEXTE ANGLAIS]

PREAMBLE

**AGREEMENT
BETWEEN
THE GOVERNMENTS OF THE BENELUX STATES
AND
THE GOVERNMENT OF THE REPUBLIC OF SOUTH AFRICA
ON
THE EXEMPTION OF VISA REQUIREMENTS
FOR HOLDERS OF DIPLOMATIC, OFFICIAL AND/OR SERVICE PASSPORTS**

THE GOVERNMENTS OF THE BENELUX STATES

AND

THE GOVERNMENT OF THE REPUBLIC OF SOUTH AFRICA

(hereinafter jointly referred to as the "Parties" and separately as a "Party");

RECOGNISING that the Governments of the Benelux States are acting jointly under the Agreement between the Kingdom of Belgium, the Grand Duchy of Luxembourg and the Kingdom of the Netherlands signed at Brussels on 11 April 1960 concerning the transfer of immigration control to the outer frontiers of Benelux;

DESIRING to facilitate the entry of citizens of the Republic of South Africa and citizens of the Benelux States who are holders of valid national diplomatic, official and/or service passports into their respective countries;

PREPARED to conclude an Agreement on the exemption of visa requirements for holders of valid national diplomatic, official and/or service passports;

HEREBY AGREE as follows:

ARTICLE 1
DEFINITIONS

In this Agreement, unless the context indicates otherwise:

- "Benelux States" shall mean the Kingdom of Belgium, the Grand Duchy of Luxembourg and the Kingdom of the Netherlands;

- "Benelux territory" shall mean the joint territories in Europe of the Kingdom of Belgium, the Grand Duchy of Luxembourg and the Kingdom of the Netherlands.

ARTICLE 2
COMPETENT AUTHORITIES

The Competent Authorities responsible for the implementation of this Agreement shall be:

(a) for the Government of the Republic of South Africa, the Department of Home Affairs; and

(b) for the Governments of the Benelux States: for the Kingdom of Belgium, the Federal Public Service Foreign Affairs, Foreign Trade and Development Cooperation, for the Grand Duchy of Luxembourg, the Ministry of Foreign Affairs and Immigration and for the Kingdom of the Netherlands, the Ministry of Foreign Affairs.

ARTICLE 3
EXEMPTION FROM VISA REQUIREMENTS

(1) Nationals of the Republic of South Africa who are holders of valid national diplomatic, official and/or service passports may enter the Benelux States' territory without a visa and stay in the territory for a period not exceeding three (3) months.

(2) Nationals of the Benelux States who are holders of valid national diplomatic, official and/or service passports may enter the territory of the Republic of South Africa without a visa and stay for a period not exceeding three (3) months.

ARTICLE 4
ACCREDITED REPRESENTATIVES

(1) Nationals of the State of one Party assigned to Diplomatic or Consular missions or missions to international organizations located in the State of the other Party bearing valid national diplomatic, official and/or service passports and their spouse or legal partner and under aged children bearing national valid diplomatic, official and/or service passports may enter, depart and stay in the territory of the receiving Party without visas for the duration of their accreditation.

(2)   The Parties shall notify each other of the arrival of the said officials and the officials shall comply with the accreditation regulations of the other Party.

ARTICLE 5
REFUSAL OF ADMISSION

Notwithstanding Articles 3 and 4 each Government reserves the right to refuse to admit to its territory any person regarded as being undesirable or whose presence in the country is regarded as prejudicial to law and order or national security.

ARTICLE 6
APPLICATION OF LAWS

Except as herein provided this Agreement shall not affect the laws and regulations in force in the Benelux States and the Republic of South Africa governing entry, length of stay, residence and expulsion and any form of occupation of foreigners.

ARTICLE 7
READMISSION

Each Party undertakes to readmit to its territory, at any time and without formalities, persons who entered the said territory under a valid national diplomatic, official and/or service passport issued by the Authorities of the Kingdom of Belgium, the Grand Duchy of Luxembourg, the Kingdom of the Netherlands or the Republic of South Africa.

ARTICLE 8
DOCUMENTATION

The Parties shall transmit through diplomatic channels specimens of their new or modified national diplomatic, official and/or service passports, and also the particulars concerning the use of these passports, as far as possible, sixty (60) days before their date of introduction.

ARTICLE 9
SETTLEMENT OF DISPUTES

Any dispute between the Parties arising from the application or interpretation of this Agreement shall be settled amicably through consultation or negotiations between the Parties.

ARTICLE 10
AMENDMENT

This Agreement may be amended at any time by mutual consent of the Parties through an Exchange of Notes between the Parties through the diplomatic channel.

ARTICLE 11
DEPOSITARY

The Federal Public Service Foreign Affairs, Foreign Trade and Development Cooperation of the Kingdom of Belgium ("The Belgian Government") shall act as depositary to this Agreement. The depositary shall issue each Party with a certified copy of the original.

ARTICLE 12
ENTRY INTO FORCE, DURATION AND TERMINATION

(1)   This Agreement shall enter into force for one (1) year on the first day of the second month from the date of the last notification confirming that all constitutional and legal requirements for its entry into force have been fulfilled. This Agreement shall be considered as extended for an unlimited period, unless it is denounced by any Party thirty (30) days prior to the expiry of this period.

(2)   On the expiry of the first period of one year any Party may denounce this Agreement subject to thirty (30) days' previous notice to the Belgian Government.

(3)   The denunciation by any Party shall cause this Agreement to terminate.

(4)   The Belgian Government shall inform the other Parties of the receipt of any notification referred to in this Article, as well as of receipt of the communication referred to in this Article.

ARTICLE 13
SUSPENSION

The application of this Agreement may be suspended by any Party. Suspension shall be notified immediately to the Belgian Government through the diplomatic channel. The Belgian Government shall inform the other Parties of the receipt of such notification. The same procedure shall be adopted when the suspension is lifted.

ARTICLE 14
APPLICATION TO THE KINGDOM OF THE NETHERLANDS

As regards the Kingdom of the Netherlands the application of this Agreement may be extended to Aruba, Curaçao, Sint Maarten and the Caribbean part of the Netherlands (the islands of Bonaire, Sint Eustatius and Saba).

IN WITNESS WHEREOF, the undersigned, having been duly authorized thereto by their respective Governments, have signed this Agreement in the English, French and Dutch languages. In case of divergence in the interpretation the English text shall prevail.

DONE at Pretoria on this ..... 22nd .. day of .... February, 2013 ....

FOR THE GOVERNMENT OF THE KINGDOM OF BELGIUM:

FOR THE GOVERNMENT OF THE GRAND DUCHY OF LUXEMBOURG:

FOR THE GOVERNMENT OF THE KINGDOM OF THE NETHERLANDS:

FOR THE GOVERNMENT OF THE REPUBLIC OF SOUTH AFRICA:

G.N.M. Pandor

[FRENCH TEXT – TEXTE FRANÇAIS]

PREAMBULE

ACCORD
ENTRE
LES GOUVERNEMENTS DES ETATS DU BENELUX
ET
LE GOUVERNEMENT DE LA REPUBLIQUE D'AFRIQUE DU SUD
RELATIF
A L'EXEMPTION DE L'OBLIGATION DE VISA
POUR LES TITULAIRES DE PASSEPORTS DIPLOMATIQUES,
OFFICIELS ET/OU DE SERVICE

LES GOUVERNEMENTS DES ETATS DU BENELUX

AINSI QUE

LE GOUVERNEMENT DE LA REPUBLIQUE D'AFRIQUE DU SUD

(ci-après dénommés ensemble «les Parties» et séparément «Partie»);

RECONNAISSANT que les Gouvernements des États du Benelux agissent de concert en vertu de la Convention entre le Royaume de Belgique, le Grand-Duché de Luxembourg et le Royaume des Pays-Bas concernant le transfert du contrôle des personnes vers les frontières extérieures du territoire du Benelux, signée à Bruxelles, le 11 avril 1960;

SOUHAITANT faciliter l'entrée, dans leur pays respectif, des citoyens de la République d'Afrique du Sud et des citoyens des États du Benelux qui sont titulaires de passeports diplomatiques, officiels et/ou de service nationaux valables;

DISPOSES à conclure un Accord relatif à l'exemption de l'obligation de visa pour les titulaires de passeports diplomatiques, officiels et/ou de service nationaux valables;

SONT CONVENUS des dispositions suivantes:

ARTICLE 1er
DEFINITIONS

Aux termes du présent Accord, à moins que le contexte ne requière une autre interprétation, il faut entendre:

- par «des États du Benelux» : le Royaume de Belgique, le Grand-Duché de Luxembourg et le Royaume des Pays-Bas;

- par le «territoire du Benelux» : l'ensemble des territoires, en Europe, du Royaume de Belgique, du Grand-Duché de Luxembourg et du Royaume des Pays-Bas.

ARTICLE 2
AUTORITES COMPETENTES

Les autorités compétentes responsables de la mise en œuvre du présent Accord seront:

(a) pour le Gouvernement de la République d'Afrique du Sud, le Département de l'Intérieur; et

(b) pour les Gouvernements des États du Benelux: pour le Royaume de Belgique, le Service Public Fédéral Affaires étrangères, Commerce extérieur et Coopération au Développement, pour le Grand-Duché de Luxembourg, le Ministère des Affaires étrangères et de l'Immigration et pour le Royaume des Pays-Bas, le Ministère des Affaires étrangères.

ARTICLE 3
EXEMPTION DE L'OBLIGATION DE VISA

(1) Les ressortissants de la République d'Afrique du Sud qui sont titulaires de passeports diplomatiques, officiels et/ou de service nationaux valables peuvent entrer sans visa sur le territoire des États du Benelux en vue d'un séjour d'une durée de trois (3) mois au maximum.

(2) Les ressortissants des États du Benelux qui sont titulaires de passeports diplomatiques, officiels et/ou de service nationaux valables peuvent entrer sans visa sur le territoire de la République d'Afrique du Sud en vue d'un séjour d'une durée de trois (3) mois au maximum.

ARTICLE 4
REPRESENTANTS ACCREDITES

(1) Les ressortissants de l'État de l'une des Parties affectés à des missions diplomatiques ou consulaires ou des missions auprès d'organisations internationales situées sur le territoire de l'État de l'autre Partie, et porteurs de passeports diplomatiques, officiels et/ou de service nationaux valables ainsi que leur conjoint(e) ou partenaire légal(e) et leurs enfants mineurs porteurs de passeports diplomatiques, officiels et/ou de service nationaux valables peuvent entrer sur le territoire de la Partie d'accueil, le quitter ou y séjourner sans visa pour la durée de leur accréditation.

(2)   Les Parties se notifient par écrit l'arrivée desdits fonctionnaires et les fonctionnaires respectent les réglementations en matière d'accréditation de l'autre Partie.

ARTICLE 5
REFUS D'ADMISSION

Nonobstant les articles 3 et 4, chaque Gouvernement se réserve le droit de refuser l'accès de son territoire aux personnes considérées comme indésirables ou comme pouvant compromettre par leur présence l'ordre public ou la sécurité nationale.

ARTICLE 6
APPLICATION DES LOIS

Sauf en ce qui concerne les dispositions y afférentes, le présent Accord ne porte pas atteinte aux lois et règlements en vigueur dans les États du Benelux et dans la République d'Afrique du Sud concernant l'accès au territoire, la durée du séjour, l'établissement et l'éloignement des étrangers, ainsi que toute forme d'activité professionnelle des étrangers.

ARTICLE 7
READMISSION

Chaque Partie s'engage à réadmettre sur son territoire à tout moment et sans formalité, les personnes qui sont entrées sur ce territoire sous le couvert d'un passeport diplomatique, officiel et/ou de service national valable, délivré par les Autorités du Royaume de Belgique, du Grand-Duché de Luxembourg, du Royaume des Pays-Bas ou de la République d'Afrique du Sud.

ARTICLE 8
DOCUMENTATION

Les Parties se transmettent par la voie diplomatique les spécimens de leurs passeports diplomatiques, officiels et/ou de service nationaux, nouveaux ou modifiés, ainsi que les données concernant l'emploi de ces passeports et ce, dans la mesure du possible, soixante (60) jours avant leur mise en circulation.

ARTICLE 9
REGLEMENT DES DIFFERENDS

Tout différend né de l'application ou de l'interprétation du présent Accord sera réglé à l'amiable par voie de consultation ou de négociations entre les Parties.

ARTICLE 10
AMENDEMENT

Le présent Accord peut, à tout moment, faire l'objet d'amendements par consentement mutuel entre les Parties au moyen d'un échange de notes entre les Parties par la voie diplomatique.

ARTICLE 11
DEPOSITAIRE

Le Service Public Fédéral Affaires étrangères, Commerce extérieur et Coopération au Développement du Royaume de Belgique («de Gouvernement belge») agira en qualité de dépositaire du présent Accord. Le dépositaire délivrera à chaque Partie une copie conforme de l'original.

ARTICLE 12
ENTREE EN VIGUEUR, DUREE ET DENONCIATION

(1) Le présent Accord entrera en vigueur le premier jour du deuxième mois suivant la date de la dernière notification attestant de l'accomplissement de toutes les formalités constitutionnelles et légales pour son entrée en vigueur, pour une durée d'une (1) année. S'il n'a pas été dénoncé trente (30) jours avant la fin de cette période, l'Accord sera considéré comme prolongé pour une durée indéterminée.

(2) A l'expiration de la première période d'un an, chacune des Parties pourra le dénoncer moyennant un préavis de trente (30) jours adressé au Gouvernement belge.

(3) La dénonciation par une des Parties entraînera l'abrogation du présent Accord.

(4) Le Gouvernement belge avisera les autres Parties de la réception de toute notification visée dans le présent Article, ainsi que de la réception de la communication visée dans cet Article.

ARTICLE 13
SUSPENSION

L'application du présent Accord peut être suspendue par l'une ou l'autre des Parties. La suspension devra être notifiée immédiatement au Gouvernement belge par la voie diplomatique. Le Gouvernement belge avisera les autres Parties de la réception de cette notification. La même procédure sera suivie lorsque la suspension sera levée.

ARTICLE 14
APPLICATION AU ROYAUME DES PAYS-BAS

En ce qui concerne le Royaume des Pays-Bas, l'application du présent Accord peut être étendue à Aruba, Curaçao, Sint Maarten et à la partie caraïbe des Pays-Bas (Bonaire, Sint Eustatius et Saba).

EN FOI DE QUOI les signataires, dûment mandatés à cet effet par leurs Gouvernements respectifs, ont signé le présent Accord en langue française, néerlandaise et anglaise. En cas de divergence d'interprétation, le texte anglais prévaudra.

FAIT à Pretoria le ...... 22 Février 2013 ......

POUR LE GOUVERNEMENT DU ROYAUME DE BELGIQUE:

POUR LE GOUVERNEMENT DU GRAND-DUCHE DE LUXEMBOURG:

POUR LE GOUVERNEMENT DU ROYAUME DES PAYS-BAS:

POUR LE GOUVERNEMENT DE LA REPUBLIQUE D'AFRIQUE DU SUD:

No. 52090

———

International Bank for Reconstruction and Development
and
Croatia

Loan Agreement (Second Economic Recovery Development Policy Loan) between the Republic of Croatia and the International Bank for Reconstruction and Development (with schedules, appendix and International Bank for Reconstruction and Development General Conditions for Loans, dated 12 March 2012). Zagreb, 30 April 2014

Entry into force: *11 July 2014 by notification*

Authentic text: *English*

Registration with the Secretariat of the United Nations: *International Bank for Reconstruction and Development, 26 August 2014*

Not published in print, in accordance with article 12(2) of the General Assembly regulations to give effect to Article 102 of the Charter of the United Nations, as amended.

———

Banque internationale pour la reconstruction et le développement
et
Croatie

Accord de prêt (Deuxième Prêt relatif à la politique de développement pour la relance économique) entre la République de Croatie et la Banque internationale pour la reconstruction et le développement (avec annexes, appendice et Conditions générales applicables aux prêts de la Banque internationale pour la reconstruction et le développement, en date du 12 mars 2012). Zagreb, 30 avril 2014

Entrée en vigueur : *11 juillet 2014 par notification*

Texte authentique : *anglais*

Enregistrement auprès du Secrétariat de l'Organisation des Nations Unies : *Banque internationale pour la reconstruction et le développement, 26 août 2014*

Non disponible en version imprimée, conformément au paragraphe 2 de l'article 12 du règlement de l'Assemblée générale destiné à mettre en application l'Article 102 de la Charte des Nations Unies, tel qu'amendé.

No. 52091

———

International Bank for Reconstruction and Development
and
Morocco

Loan Agreement (First Capital Market Development and small and medium-sized enterprise finance development policy loan) between the Kingdom of Morocco and the International Bank for Reconstruction and Development (with schedules, appendix and International Bank for Reconstruction and Development General Conditions for Loans, dated 12 March 2012). Rabat, 27 May 2014

Entry into force: *30 July 2014 by notification*

Authentic text: *English*

Registration with the Secretariat of the United Nations: *International Bank for Reconstruction and Development, 26 August 2014*

Not published in print, in accordance with article 12(2) of the General Assembly regulations to give effect to Article 102 of the Charter of the United Nations, as amended.

———

Banque internationale pour la reconstruction et le développement
et
Maroc

Accord de prêt (Premier prêt d'appui à une politique de développement visant l'approfondissement du marché des capitaux et le financement de petites et moyennes entreprises) entre le Royaume du Maroc et la Banque internationale pour la reconstruction et le développement (avec annexes, appendice et Conditions générales applicables aux prêts de la Banque internationale pour la reconstruction et le développement, en date du 12 mars 2012). Rabat, 27 mai 2014

Entrée en vigueur : *30 juillet 2014 par notification*

Texte authentique : *anglais*

Enregistrement auprès du Secrétariat de l'Organisation des Nations Unies : *Banque internationale pour la reconstruction et le développement, 26 août 2014*

Non disponible en version imprimée, conformément au paragraphe 2 de l'article 12 du règlement de l'Assemblée générale destiné à mettre en application l'Article 102 de la Charte des Nations Unies, tel qu'amendé.

No. 52092

United Nations
and
Fiji

Exchange of letters constituting an Agreement between the United Nations and the Government of the Republic of Fiji regarding the hosting of the "Regional Workshop on gender statistics and human rights reporting statistics" to be held in Nadi, Fiji, from 4 to 8 August 2014. New York, 28 July 2014 and 31 July 2014

Entry into force: *31 July 2014 by the exchange of the said letters*

Authentic text: *English*

Registration with the Secretariat of the United Nations: *ex officio, 1 August 2014*

Not published in print, in accordance with article 12(2) of the General Assembly regulations to give effect to Article 102 of the Charter of the United Nations, as amended.

Organisation des Nations Unies
et
Fidji

Échange de lettres constituant un accord entre l'Organisation des Nations Unies et le Gouvernement de la République des Fidji relatif à l'organisation de « l'Atelier régional sur les statistiques en matière de genre et de rapports sur les droits de l'homme » qui se tiendra à Nadi, Fidji, du 4 au 8 août 2014. New York, 28 juillet 2014 et 31 juillet 2014

Entrée en vigueur : *31 juillet 2014 par l'échange desdites lettres*

Texte authentique : *anglais*

Enregistrement auprès du Secrétariat de l'Organisation des Nations Unies : *d'office, 1er août 2014*

Non disponible en version imprimée, conformément au paragraphe 2 de l'article 12 du règlement de l'Assemblée générale destiné à mettre en application l'Article 102 de la Charte des Nations Unies, tel qu'amendé.

No. 52093

Poland
and
India

Agreement between the Government of the Polish People's Republic and the Government of the Republic of India for the avoidance of double taxation and the prevention of fiscal evasion with respect to taxes on income. Warsaw, 21 June 1989

Entry into force: *26 October 1989 by notification, in accordance with article 30*

Authentic texts: *English, Hindi and Polish*

Registration with the Secretariat of the United Nations: *Poland, 5 August 2014*

Pologne
et
Inde

Accord entre le Gouvernement de la République populaire de Pologne et le Gouvernement de la République de l'Inde tendant à éviter la double imposition et à prévenir l'évasion fiscale en matière d'impôts sur le revenu. Varsovie, 21 juin 1989

Entrée en vigueur : *26 octobre 1989 par notification, conformément à l'article 30*

Textes authentiques : *anglais, hindi et polonais*

Enregistrement auprès du Secrétariat de l'Organisation des Nations Unies : *Pologne, 5 août 2014*

[ENGLISH TEXT – TEXTE ANGLAIS]

A G R E E M E N T

between

the Government of the Polish People's Republic

and

the Government of the Republic of India

for

the Avoidance of Double Taxation and the Prevention
of Fiscal Evasion with Respect to Taxes on Income

The Government of the Polish People's Republic and the Government of the Republic of India desiring to further develop and
facilitate the economic relationship between the two countries,
and having decided to conclude an Agreement for the avoidance
of double taxation and the prevention of fiscal evasion with
respect to taxes on income,

Have agreed as follows:

Article 1

Personal Scope

This Agreement shall apply to persons who are residents of
one or both of the Contracting States.

Article 2

Taxes Covered

1. The taxes to which this Agreement shall apply are:
   a) in Poland:
      i) the income tax (podatek dochodowy);
      ii) the tax on wages and salaries (podatek of
          wynagrodzeń);
      iii) the equalisation tax (podatek wyrównawczy); and
      iv) the agriculture tax (podatek rolny);
          (hereinafter referred to as "Polish tax").

b) in India:
  i) the income-tax including any surcharge thereon im-
     posed under the Income-tax Act, 1961;
  ii) the surtax imposed under the Companies (Profits)
      Surtax Act, 1964;
      (hereinafter referred to as "Indian tax").

2. The Agreement shall also apply to any identical or substantially similar taxes which are imposed by either Contracting State after the date of signature of the present
   Agreement in addition to, or in place of, the taxes referred to in paragraph 1. The competent authorities of the
   Contracting States shall notify each other of any substantial changes which are made in their respective taxation
   laws, which are the subject of this Agreement.

Article 3

General Definitions

1. In this Agreement, unless the context otherwise requires:
   a) the term "Poland" means the Polish People's Republic
      and when used in a geographical sense means the ter-
      ritory of the Polish People's Republic and any maritime
      area adjacent to the territorial waters of the Polish
      People's Republic within which, under the laws of the
      Polish People's Republic and in accordance with inter-
      national law, the Polish People's Republic has sover-
      eignty or sovereign and exclusive rights.
   b) the term "India" means the Republic of India and when
      used in a geographical sense means the territory of the
      Republic of India and any maritime area adjacent to the
      territorial waters of the Republic of India within
      which, under the laws of India and in accordance with
      international law, India has sovereignty or sovereign
      and exclusive rights.

c) the terms "a Contracting State" and "the other Contracting State" mean Poland or India, as the context
requires;

d) the term "tax" means Polish tax or Indian tax as the
context requires, but shall not include any amount
which is payable in respect of any default or omission
in relation to the taxes to which this Agreement applies or which represents a penalty imposed relating
to those taxes;

e) the term "person" includes an individual, a company and
any other entity which is treated as a taxable unit
under the taxation laws in force in the respective Contracting States;

f) the term "company" means any body corporate or any entity which is treated as a company or body corporate
under the taxation laws in force in the respective Contracting States;

g) the terms "enterprise of a Contracting State" and "enterprise of the other Contracting State" mean respectively an enterprise carried on by a resident of a Contracting State and an enterprise carried on by a resident of the other Contracting State;

h) the term "competent authority" means in the case of
Poland, the Minister of Finance or his authorised re-
presentative; and in the case of India, the Central
Government in the Ministry of Finance (Department of
Revenue) or their authorised representative;

i) the term "national" means any individual possessing
the nationality of a Contracting State and any legal
person, partnership or association deriving the status
from the laws in force in the Contracting State;

j) the term "international traffic" means any transport
by a ship or aircraft operated by an enterprise of a

Contracting State, except when the ship or aircraft is operated solely between places in the other Contracting State.

2. As regards the application of the Agreement by a Contracting State, any term not defined therein shall, unless the context otherwise requires, have the meaning which it has under the law of that State concerning the taxes to which the Agreement applies.

Article 4

Fiscal Residence

1. For the purposes of this Agreement, the term "resident of a Contracting State" means any person who, under the laws of that State, is liable to tax therein by reason of his domicile, residence, place of management or any other criterion of a similar nature.

2. Where by reason of the provisions of paragraph 1, an individual is a resident of both Contracting States, then his status shall be determined as follows:

   a) he shall be deemed to be a resident of the State in which he has a permanent home available to him; if he has a permanent home available to him in both States, he shall be deemed to be a resident of the State with which his personal and economic relations are closer (centre of vital interests);

   b) if the State in which he has his centre of vital interests cannot be determined, or if he has not a permanent home available to him in either State, he shall be deemed to be a resident of the State in which he has an habitual abode;

c) if he has an habitual abode in both States or in neither of them, he shall be deemed to be a resident of the State of which he is a national;

d) if the question of residence cannot be determined according to the provisions of sub-paragraphs (a) to (c), the competent authorities of the Contracting States shall settle the question by mutual agreement.

3. Where by reason of the provisions of paragraph 1, a person other than an individual is a resident of both Contracting States, then it shall be deemed to be a resident of the State in which its place of effective management is situated.

Article 5

Permanent Establishment

1. For the purposes of this Agreement, the term "permanent establishment" means a fixed place of business through which the business of the enterprise is wholly or partly carried on.

2. The term "permanent establishment" includes especially:
   a) a place of management;
   b) a branch;
   c) an office;
   d) a factory;
   e) a workshop;
   f) a mine, an oil or gas well, a quarry or any other place of extraction of natural resources;
   g) a warehouse in relation to a person providing storage facilities for others;
   h) a farm, plantation or other place where agriculture, forestry, plantation or related activities are carried on;

i) a premises used as a sales outlet or for receiving or soliciting orders;

j) an installation or structure used for the exploration of natural resources;

k) a building site or construction, installation or assembly project or supervisory activities in connection therewith, where such site, project or activities continue for a period of more than six months.

3. Notwithstanding the preceding provisions of this Article, the term "permanent establishment" shall be deemed not to include:

a) the use of facilities solely for the purpose of storage or display of goods or merchandise belonging to the enterprise:

b) the maintenance of a stock of goods or merchandise belonging to the enterprise solely for the purpose of storage or display;

c) the maintenance of a stock of goods or merchandise belonging to the enterprise solely for the purpose of processing by another enterprise;

d) the maintenance of a fixed place of business solely for the purpose of purchasing goods or merchandise, or of collecting information, for the enterprise;

e) the maintenance of a fixed place of business solely for the purpose of advertising, for the supply of information, for scientific research, or for similar activities which have a preparatory or auxiliary character, for the enterprise.

However, the provisions of sub-paragraph (a) to (e) shall not be applicable where the enterprise maintains any other fixed place of business in the other Contracting State for any purposes other than the purposes specified in the said sub-paragraphs.

4. Notwithstanding the provisions of paragraphs 1 and 2 where a person – other than an agent of an independent status to whom paragraph 5 applies is acting in a Contracting State on behalf of an enterprise of the other Contracting State, that enterprise shall be deemed to have a permanent establishment in the first-mentioned State, if

a) he has and habitually exercises in that State an authority to conclude contracts on behalf of the enterprise, unless his activities are limited to the purchase of goods or merchandise for the enterprise; or

b) he has no such authority, but habitually maintains in the first-mentioned State a stock of goods or merchandise from which he regularly delivers goods or merchandise on behalf of the enterprise.

5. An enterprise of a Contracting State shall not be deemed to have a permanent establishment in the other Contracting State merely because it carries on business in that other State through a broker, general commission agent or any other agent of an independent status provided that such persons are acting in the ordinary course of their business. However, when the activities of such an agent are devoted wholly or almost wholly on behalf of that enterprise itself or on behalf of that enterprise and other enterprises controlling, controlled by, or subject to the same common control, as that enterprise, he will not be considered an agent of an independent status within the meaning of this paragraph.

6. The fact that a company which is a resident of a Contracting State controls or is controlled by a company which is a resident of the other Contracting State, or which carries on business in that other Contracting State (whether

through a permanent establishment or otherwise), shall not of itself constitute either company a permanent establishment of the other.

Article 6

Income from Immovable Property

1. Income derived by a resident of a Contracting State from immovable property (including income from agriculture or forestry) situated in the other Contracting State may be taxed in that other State.

2. The term "immovable property" shall have the meaning which it has under the law of the Contracting State in which the property in question is situated. The term shall in any case include property accessory to immovable property, livestock and equipment used in agriculture and forestry, rights to which the provisions of general law respecting landed property apply, usufruct of immovable property and rights to variable or fixed payments as consideration for the working of, or the right to work, mineral deposits, sources and other natural resources. Ships, boats and aircraft shall not be regarded as immovable property.

3. The provisions of paragraph 1 shall also apply to income derived from the direct use, letting, or use in any other form of immovable property.

4. The provisions of paragraphs 1 and 3 shall also apply to the income from immovable property of an enterprise and to income from immovable property used for the performance of independent personal services.

Article 7

Business Profits

1. The profits of an enterprise of a Contracting State shall
   be taxable only in that State unless the enterprise carries on business in the other Contracting State through a
   permanent establishment situated therein. If the enterprise
   carries on business as aforesaid, the profits of the enterprise may be taxed in the other State but only so much of
   them as is attributable to (a) that permanent establishment; (b) sales in that other State of goods or merchandise of the same or similar kind as those sold through
   that permanent establishment; or (c) other business activities carried on in that other State of the same or similar
   kind as those effected through that permanent establishment.

2. Subject to the provisions of paragraph 3, where an enterprise of a Contracting State carries on business in the
   other Contracting State through a permanent establishment
   situated therein, there shall in each Contracting State be
   attributed to that permanent establishment the profits
   which it might be expected to make if it were a distinct
   and separate enterprise engaged in the same or similar activities under the same or similar conditions and dealing
   wholly independently with the enterprise of which it is a
   permanent establishment. In any case where the correct
   amount of profits attributable to a permanent establishment
   is incapable of determination or the determination there
   of presents exceptional difficulties, the profits attributable to the permanent establishment may be estimated on a
   reasonable basis.

3. In the determination of the profits of a permanent establishment, there shall be allowed as deduction expenses

which are incurred for the purposes of the business of the
permanent establishment including executive and general
administrative expenses so incurred, whether in the State
in which the permanent establishment is situated or else-
where, in accordance with the provisions of an subject to
the limitations of the taxation laws of that State. However,
no such deduction shall be allowed in respect of amounts, if
any, paid (otherwise than towards reimbursement of actual
expenses) by the permanent establishment to the head office
of the enterprises or any of its other offices, by way of
royalties, fees or other similar payments in return for the
use of patents, know-how or other rights, or by way of commission or other charges, for specific services performed
or for management, or, except in the case of a banking enterprise, by way of interest on moneys lent to the permanent
establishment. Likewise, no account shall be taken, in the
determination of the profits of a permanent establishment,
for amounts charged (otherwise than towards reimbursement of
actual expenses) by the permanent establishment to the head
office of the enterprise or any of its other offices, by way
of royalties, fees or other similar payments in return for
the use of patents, know-how or other rights, or by way of
commission or other charges for specific services performed
or for management, or, except in the case of a banking enterprise, by way of interest on moneys lent to the head office of the enterprise or any of its other offices.

4. No profits shall be attributed to a permanent establishment
by reasons of the mere purchase by that permanent establishment of goods or merchandise for the enterprise.

5. For the purposes of the preceding paragraphs, the profits
to be attributed to the permanent establishment shall be

determined by the same method year by year unless there
is good and sufficient reason to the contrary.

6. Where profits include items of income which are dealt with
separately in other articles of this Agreement, then the
provisions of those articles shall not be affected by the
provisions of this article.

Article 8

Air Transport

1. Profits derived by an enterprise of a Contracting State
from the operation of aircraft in international traffic
shall be taxable only in that State.

2. The provisions of paragraph 1 shall also apply to profits
from the participation in a pool, a joint business or an
international operating agency.

3. For the purposes of this article, interest on funds connected with the operation of aircraft in international
traffic shall be regarded as profits derived from the
operation of such aircraft, and the provisions of article
12 shall not apply in relation to such interest.

4. The term "operation of aircraft" shall mean business of
transportation by air of passengers, mail, livestock or
goods carried on by the owners or lessees or charterers
of aircraft, including the sale of tickets for such transportation on behalf of other enterprises, the incidental
lease of aircraft and any other activity directly connected
with such transportation.

Article 9

Shipping

1. Profits from the operation of ships in international traffic shall be taxable only in the Contracting State in which the place of effective management of the enterprise is situated.

2. If the place of effective management of an enterprise carrying on shipping in international traffic is aboard a ship, then it shall be deemed to be situated in the Contracting State in which the home harbour of the ship is situated, or, if there is no such home harbour, in the Contracting State of which the operator of the ship is a resident.

3. The provisions of paragraph 1 shall also apply to profits derived from the participation in a pool, a joint business or in an international operating agency.

4. Notwithstanding anything contained in paragraph 1 and Article VIII of the Agreement dated 27 June, 1960 between the Government of the Polish People's Republic and the Government of India regarding shipping co-operation, income derived by an enterprise of a Contracting State from the operation of ships from the ports of the other Contracting State to the ports of third countries and from the ports of third countries to the ports of the other Contracting State may be taxed in the other Contracting State, but the tax imposed in that other Contracting State shall be reduced by an amount equal to 50 per cent thereof.

Article 10

Associated Enterprises

Where:

a) an enterprise of a Contracting State participates directly or indirectly in the management, control or capital of an enterprise of the other Contracting State, or

b) the same persons participate directly or indirectly in the management, control or capital of an enterprise of a Contracting State and an enterprise of the other Contracting State,

and in either case conditions are made or imposed between the two enterprises in their commercial or financial relations which differ from those which would be made between independent enterprises, then any profits which would, but for those conditions, have accrued to one of the enterprises, but, by reason of those conditions, have not so accrued, may be included in the profits of that enterprise and taxed accordingly.

Article 11

Dividends

1. Dividends paid by a company which is resident of a Contracting State to a resident of the other Contracting State may be taxed in that other State.

2. However, such dividends may also be taxed in the Contracting State of which the company paying the dividends is a resident and according to the laws of that State, but if the recipient is the beneficial owner of the dividends, the tax so charged shall not exceed 15 per cent of the gross amount of the dividends where such dividends relate to contributions made after the entry into force of this Agreement.

This paragraph shall not affect the taxation of the company in respect of the profits out of which the dividends are paid.

3. The term "dividends" as used in this article means income from shares or other rights, not being debt-claims, participating in profits, as well as income from other corporate rights which is subjected to the same taxation treatment as income from shares by the laws of the State of which the company making the distribution is resident.

4. The provisions of paragraphs 1 and 2 shall not apply if the beneficial owner of the dividends, being a resident of a Contracting State, carries on business in the other Contracting State of which the company paying the dividends is a resident, through a permanent establishment situated therein or performs in that other State independent personal services from a fixed base situated therein, and the holding in respect of which the dividends are paid is effectively connected with such permanent establishment or fixed base. In such case, the provisions of article 7, or article 15, as the case may be, shall apply.

5. Where a company which is a resident of a Contracting State derives profits or income from the other Contracting State, that other State may not impose any tax on the dividends paid by the company except in so far as such dividends are paid to a resident of that other State or so far as the holding in respect of which the dividends are paid is effectively connected with a permanent establishment or a fixed base situated in that other State, nor subject the company's undistributed profits to a tax on the company's undistributed profits, even if the dividends paid or the undistributed profits consist wholly or partly of profits or income arising in such other State.

Article 12

Interest

1. Interest arising in a Contracting State and paid to a resident of the other Contracting State may be taxed in that
other State.

2. However, such interest may also be taxed in the Contracting
State in which it arises and according to the laws of that
State, but if the recipient is the beneficial owner of the
interest the tax so charged shall not exceed 15 per cent of
the gross amount of the interest.

3. Notwithstanding the provisions of paragraph 2, -
a) interest arising in a Contracting State shall be exempt
from tax in that State provided it is derived and beneficially owned by:
    i) the Government, a political sub-division or a local
    authority of the other Contracting State;
    or
    ii) the Central Bank of the other Contracting State;
b) interest arising in a Contracting State shall be exempt
from tax in that State if it is beneficially owned by a
resident of the other Contracting State and is derived
in connection with a loan or credit extended or endorsed
by:
    i) in the case of Poland, Bank Handlowy w Warszawie SA,
    to the extent such interest is attributable to fin-
    ancing of exports and imports only;
    ii) in the case of India, the Export-Import Bank of
    India (Exim Bank) to the extent such interest is at-
    tributable to financing of exports and imports only;
    iii) any institution of a Contracting State in charge of
    public financing of external trade;

iv) any other person provided that the loan or credit
is approved by the Government of the first-mentioned Contracting State.

4. The term "interest" as used in this article means income
from debt-claims of every kind, whether or not secured by
mortgage and whether or not carrying a right to participate
in the debtor's profits, and in particular, income from
government securities and income from bonds or debentures,
including premiums and prizes attaching to such securities,
bonds or debentures. Penalty charges for late payment shall
not be regarded as interest for the purpose of this article.

5. The provisions of paragraphs 1 and 2 shall not apply if
the beneficial owner of the interest, being a resident of
a Contracting State, carries on business in the other Contracting State in which the interest arises, through a permanent establishment situated therein, or performs in that
other State independent personal services from a fixed base
situated therein, and the debt-claim in respect of which
the interest is paid is effectively connected with such
permanent establishment or fixed base. In such case, the
provisions of article 7 or article 15, as the case may be,
shall apply.

6. Interest shall be deemed to arise in a Contracting State
when the payer is that Contracting State itself, a political sub-division, a local authority or a resident of that
State. Where, however, the person paying the interest,
whether he is a resident of a Contracting State or not,
has in a Contracting State a permanent establishment or a
fixed base in connection with which the indebtedness on
which the interest is paid was incurred, and such interest
is borne by such permanent establishment or fixed base,

then such interest shall be deemed to arise in the Contracting State in which the permanent establishment or fixed base is situated.

7. Where, by reason of a special relationship between the payer and the beneficial owner or between both of them and some other person, the amount of the interest, having regard to the debt-claim for which it is paid, exceeds the amount which would have been agreed upon by the payer and the beneficial owner in the absence of such relationship, the provisions of this article shall apply to the last mentioned amount. In such case, the excess part of the payments shall remain taxable according to the laws of each Contracting State, due regard being had to the other provisions of this Agreement.

Article 13

Royalties and Fees for Technical Services

1. Royalties and fees for technical services arising in a Contracting State and paid to a resident of the other Contracting State may be taxed in that other State.

2. However, such royalties and fees for technical services may also be taxed in the Contracting State in which they arise and according to the laws of that State, but if the recipient is the beneficial owner of the royalties, or fees for technical services, the tax so charged shall not exceed 22.5 per cent of the gross amount of the royalties or fees for technical services.

3. The term "royalties" as used in this article means payments of any kind received as a consideration for the use of, or the right to use, any copyright of literary, artistic or scientific work, including cinematograph films or

tapes used for radio or television broadcasting, any patent, trade mark, design or model, plan, secret formula or process, or for the use of, or the right to use, industrial, commercial or scientific equipment, or for information concerning industrial, commercial or scientific experience.

4. The term "fees for technical services" as used in this article means payments of any amount to any person other than payments to an employee of a person making payments, in consideration for the services of a managerial, technical or consultancy natury, including the provision of services of technical or other personnel.

5. The provisions of paragraphs 1 and 2 shall not apply if the beneficial owner of the royalties or fees for technical services, being a resident of a Contracting State, carries on business in the other Contracting State in which the royalties or fees for technical services arise, through a permanent establishment situated therein, or performs in that other State independent personal services from a fixed base situated therein, and the right, property or contract in respect of which the royalties or fees for technical services are paid is effectively connected with such permanent establishment or fixed base. In such case, the provisions of article 7 or article 15, as the case may be, shall apply.

6. Royalties and fees for technical services shall be deemed to arise in a Contracting State when the payer is that State itself, a political sub-division, a local authority or a resident of that State. Where, however, the person paying the royalties or fees for technical services, whether he is a resident of a Contracting State or not, has in a Contracting State a permanent establishment or a

fixed base in connection with which the liability to pay
the royalties or fees for technical services was incurred,
and such royalties or fees for technical services are borne
by such permanent establishment or fixed base, then such
royalties or fees for technical services shall be deemed
to arise in the State in which the permanent establishment
or fixed base is situated.

7. Where, by reason of special relationship between the payer
and the beneficial owner or between both of them and some
other person, the amount of royalties or fees for technical services paid exceeds the amount which would have been
paid in the absence of such relationship, the provisions
of this article shall apply only to the last-mentioned
amount. In such case, the excess part of the payments shall
remain taxable according to the laws of each Contracting
State, due regard being had to the other provisions of
this Agreement.

Article 14

Capital Gains

1. Gains derived by a resident of a Contracting State from
the alienation of immovable property, referred to in
article 6, and situated in the other Contracting State may
be taxed in that other State.

2. Gains from the alienation of movable property forming part
of the business property of a permanent establishment
which an enterprise of a Contracting State has in the
other Contracting State or of movable property pertaining
to a fixed base available to a resident of a Contracting
State in the other Contracting State for the purpose of
performing independent personal services, including such

gains from the alienation of such a permanent establishment (alone or together with the whole enterprise) or of
such fixed base, may be taxed in that other State.

3. Gains from the alienation of ships or aircraft operated
   in international traffic or movable property pertaining
   to the operation of such ships or aircraft shall be taxable only in the Contracting State of which the alienator
   is a resident.

4. Gains from the alienation of shares of the capital stock
   of a company the property of which consists directly or
   indirectly principally of immovable property situated in
   a Contracting State may be taxed in that State.

5. Gains from the alienation of shares other than those mentioned in paragraph 4 in a compamy which is a resident of
   a Contracting State may be taxed in that State.

6. Gains from the alienation of any property other than that
   mentioned in paragraphs 1, 2, 3, 4 and 5 shall be taxable
   only in the Contracting State of which the alienator is
   a resident.

Article 15

Independent Personal Services

1. Income derived by an individual who is a resident of a
   Contracting State from the performance of professional
   services or other independent activities of a similar
   character shall be taxable only in that State except in
   the following circumstances when such income may also be
   taxed in the other Contracting State:
   a) if he has a fixed base regularly available to him in
      the other Contracting State for the purpose of perform-
      ing his activities; in that case, only so much of the

income as is attributable to that fixed base may be taxed in that other State; or

b) if his stay in the other Contracting State is for a period or periods amounting to or exceeding in the aggregate 183 days in the relevant "previous year" of "year of income", as the case may be; in that case, only so much of the income as is derived from his activities performed in that other State may be taxed in that other State.

2. The term "professional services" includes independent scientific, literary, artistic, educational or teaching activities, as well as the independent activities of physicians, surgeons, lawyers, engineers, architects, dentists and accountants.

Article 16

Dependent Personal Services

1. Subject to the provisions of articles 17, 18, 19, 20, 21 and 22, salaries, wages and other similar remuneration derived by a resident of a Contracting State in respect of an employment shall be taxable only in that State unless the employment is exercised in the other Contracting State. If the employment is so exercised, such remuneration as is derived therefrom may be taxed in that other State.

2. Notwithstanding the provisions of paragraph 1, remuneration derived by a resident of a Contracting State in respect of an employment exercised in the other Contracting State shall be taxable only in the first-mentioned State if:

a) the recipient is present in the other State for a period or periods not exceeding in the aggregate 183 days in the relevant "previous year" or "year of income", as the case may be; and

b) the remuneration is paid by, or on behalf of, an employer
   who is not a resident of the other State; and

c) the remuneration is not borne by a permanent establishment
   or a fixed base which the employer has in the other State.

3. Notwithstanding the preceding provisions of this article,
   remuneration derived in respect of an employment exercised
   aboard a ship or aircraft operated in international traffic,
   by an enterprise of a Contracting State may be taxed in that
   State.

Article 17

Directors' Fees Remuneration of Top Level
Managerial Officials

1. Directors' fees and similar payments derived by a resident of
   a Contracting State in his capacity as a member of the Board
   of Directors of a company which is a resident of the other
   Contracting State may be taxed in that other State.

2. Salaries, wages and other similar remuneration derived by a
   resident of a Contracting State in his capacity as an offical
   in a top-level managerial position of a company which is a resident of the other Contracting State may be taxed in that
   other State.

Article 18

Income Earned by Entertainers and Athletes

1. Notwithstanding the provisions of articles 15 and 16, income
   derived by a resident of a Contracting State as an entertainer
   such as a theatre, motion picture, radio or television artists
   or a musician or as an athlete, from his personal activities as
   such exercised in the other Contracting State may be taxed in
   that other State.

2. Where income in respect of personal activities exercised by an entertainer or athlete in his capacity as such accrues not to the entertainer or athlete himself but to another person, that income may, notwithstanding the provisions of articles 7, 15 and 16, be taxed in the Contracting State in which the activities of the entertainer or athlete are exercised.

3. Notwithstanding the provisions of paragraph 1, income derived by an entertainer or an athlete who is a resident of a Constructing State from his personal activities as such exercised in the other Contracting State, shall be taxable only in the first-mentioned Contracting State, if the activities in the other Contracting State are within the framework of cultural or sports exchange programme agreed to by both Contracting States and are supported wholly or substantially from the public funds of the first-mentioned Contracting State, including any of its political subdivisions or local authorities.

4. Notwithstanding the provisions of paragraph 2 and articles 7, 15 and 16, where income in respect of personal activities exercised by an entertainer or an athlete in his capacity as such in a Contracting State accrues not to the entertainer or athlete himself but to another person, that income shall be taxable only in the other Contracting State, if the activities of that other person are within the framework of cultural or sports exchange programme agreed to by both Contracting States and are supported wholly or substantially from the public funds of that other State, including any of its political subdivisions or local authorities.

Article 19

Remuneration and Pensions in Respect of Government Service

1. a) Remuneration other than a pension, paid by a Contracting State or a political sub-division or a local authority thereof to an individual in respect of services rendered to that Contracting State or a political sub-division or local authority thereof in the discharge of function of a governmental nature, shall be taxable only in that Contracting State.

   b) However, such remuneration shall be taxable only in the other Contracting State if the services are rendered in that other State and the individual is a resident of that State who:

      i) is a national of that State; or

      ii) did not become a resident of that State solely for the purpose of rendering the services.

2. a) Any pension paid by, or out of funds created by a Contracting State or a political sub-division or a local authority thereof to an individual in respect of services rendered to that State or sub-division or authority shall be taxable only in that State.

   b) However, such pension shall be taxable only in the other Contracting State if the individual is a resident of, and a national of that other State.

3. The provisions of articles 16, 17 and 18 shall apply to remuneration and pensions in respect of services rendered in connection with a business carried on by a Contracting State or a political sub-division or local authority thereof.

Article 20

Non-Government Pensions and Annuities

1. Any pension, other than a pension referred to in article 19, or any annuity derived by a resident of a Contracting State from sources within the other Contracting State may be taxed only in the first-mentioned Contracting State.

2. The term "pension" means a periodic payment made in consideration of past services or by way of compensation for injuries received in the course of performance of services.

3. The term "annuity" means a stated sum payable periodically at stated times during life or during a specified or ascertainable period of time, under an obligation to make the payments in return for adequate and full consideration in money or money's worth.

Article 21

Payments Received by Students and Apprentices

1. Payments with a student or business apprentice who is or was immediately before visiting a Contracting State a resident of the other Contracting State and who is present in the first-mentioned State solely for the purpose of his education or training receives for the purpose of his maintenance, education or training shall not be taxed in that State, provided that such payments arise from sources outside that State.

2. Income derived by a student or business apprentice in respect of activities exercised in a Contracting State in which he is present solely for the purpose of his education or training, shall not be taxable in that State, unless it exceeds the amount necessary for his maintenance, education or training.

3. The benefits of this article shall extend only for such period of time as may be reasonable or customarily required to complete the education or training undertaken, but in no event shall any individual have the benefits of this article, for more than five consecutive years from the date of his first arrival in that other Contracting State.

4. For the purposes of this article and article 22, an individual shall be deemed to be a resident of a Contracting State if he is resident in that Contracting State in the "previous year" or the "year of income", as the case may be, in which he visits the other Contracting State or in the immediately preceding "previous year" or the "year of income".

Article 22

Payments Received by Professors, Teachers and Research Scholars

1. A professor or teacher who is or was a resident of one of the Contracting State immediately before visiting the other Contracting State for the purpose of teaching or engaging in research, or both, at a university, college, school or other approved institution in that other Contracting State shall be exempt from tax in that other State or any remuneration for such teaching or research for a period not exceeding two years from the date of his arrival in that other State.

2. This article shall not apply to income from research if such research is not in public interest but is undertaken primarily for the private benefit of a specific person or persons.

3. For the purposes of paragraph 1, "approved institution"
means an institution which has been approved in this
regard by the competent authority of the concerned Contracting State.

Article 23

Other Income

1. Subject to the provisions of paragraph 2, items of income
of a resident of a Contracting State, wherever arising,
which are not expressly dealt with in the foregoing articles of this Agreement, shall be taxable only in that Contracting State.

2. The provisions of paragraph 1 shall not apply to income,
other than income from immovable property as defined in
paragraph 2 of article 6, if the recipient of such income,
being a resident of a Contracting State, carries on business
in the other Contracting State through a permanent establishment situated therein, or performs in that other State
independent personal services from a fixed base situated
therein, and the right or property in respect of which the
income is paid is effectively connected with such permanent
establishment or fixed base. In such case, the provisions
of article 7 or article 15, as the case may be, shall apply.

3. Notwithstanding the provisions of paragraphs 1 and 2, items
of income of a resident of a Contracting State not dealt
with in the foregoing articles of this Agreement, and arising in the other Contracting State may be taxed in that
other State.

4. The competent authorities of the Contracting States may
communicate with each other directly for the purpose of

reaching an agreement in the sense of the preceding paragraphs. The competent authorities shall through consultations develop appropriate bilateral procedures, conditions, methods and techniques for the implementation of
the mutual agreement procedure provided for in this article.

Article 24

Elimination of Double Taxation

1. The laws in force in either of the Contracting States will
continue to govern the taxation of income in the respective
Contracting States except where provisions to the contrary
are made in this Agreement.

2. In both the Contracting States, double taxation will be
avoided in the following manner:

   a) Where a resident of a Contracting State derives income
   which, in accordance with the provisions of this Agreement, may be taxed in the other Contracting State, the
   first-mentioned State shall, subject to the provisions
   of sub-paragraph b) of this paragraph, exempt such
   income from tax but may, in calculating tax on the remaining income of that person, apply the rate of tax
   which would have been applicable if the exempted income
   had not been so exempted.

   b) Either of the Contracting States when imposing taxes on
   its residents may include in the tax base upon which
   such taxes are imposed the items of income which according to the provisions of articles 11, 12 and 13 of this
   Agreement may also be taxed in the other State but shall
   allow as a deduction from the amount of tax computed on
   such a base an amount equal to the tax paid in the other
   Contracting State. Such deducation shall not, however,

exceed that part of tax leviable by the first-mentioned State, as computed before the deduction is given, which is appropriate to the income which, in accordance with the provisions of articles 11, 12 and 13 of this Agreement may be taxed in the other State.

3. For the purposes of sub-paragraph (b) of paragraph 2 the term "tax paid in the other Contracting State" shall be deemed to include any amount which would have been payable as tax but for any relief by way of a deduction allowed in computing the taxable income or an exemption or a reduction of tax or otherwise under the laws relating to taxation of income in force in that other Contracting State.

Article 25

Non-Discrimination

1. The nationals of a Contracting State shall not be subjected in the other Contracting State to any taxation or any requirement connected therewith which is other or more burdensome than the taxation, and connected requirements to which nationals of that other State in the same circumstances and under the same conditions are or may be subjected.

2. The taxation on a permanent establishment which an enterprise of a Contracting State has in the other Contracting State shall not be less favourably levied in that other State than the taxation levied on enterprises of that other State carrying on the same activities in the same circumstances or under the same conditions.

3. Nothing contained in this article shall be construed as obliging a Contracting State to grant to persons not

resident in that State any personal allowances, reliefs, reductions and deductions for taxation purposes which are by law available only to persons who are so resident.

4. Enterprises of a Contracting State, the capital of which is wholly or partly owned or controlled, directly or indirectly, by one or more residents of the other Contracting State, shall not be subjected in the first-mentioned Contracting State to any taxation or any requirement connected therewith which is other or more burdensome than the taxation and connected requirements to which other similar enterprises of that first-mentioned State are or may be subjected in the same circumstances and under the same conditions.

5. In this article, the term "taxation" means taxes which are the subject of this Agreement.

6. Except where the provisions of article 11, paragraph 7 of Article 12, or paragraph 7 of article 13 of this Agreement apply, interest, royalties and other disbursements paid by an enterprise of a Contracting State to a resident of the other Contracting State shall, for the purpose of determining the taxable profits of such enterprise, be deductible under the same conditions as if they had been paid to a resident of the first-mentioned State. Similarly, any debts of an enterprise of a Contracting State to a resident of the other Contracting State shall, for the purpose of determining the taxable capital of such enterprise, be deductible under the same conditions as if they had been contracted to a resident of the first-mentioned State.

7. The exemptions, reliefs, reductions, deductions and allowances for taxation purpose available under the domestic

laws of the two Contracting States shall not be adversely affected by any provision of this Agreement.

Article 26

Mutual Agreement Procedure

1. Where a resident of a Contracting State considers that the actions of one or both of the Contracting States result or will result for him in taxation not in accordance with this Agreement, he may, notwithstanding the remedies provided by the national laws of those States, present his case to the competent authority of the Contracting State of which he is a resident. This case must be presented within three years of the date of receipt of notice of the action which gives rise to taxation not in accordance with the Agreement.

2. The competent authority shall endeavour, if the objection appears to it to be justified and if it is not itself able to arrive at an appropriate solution, to resolve the case by mutual agreement with the competent authority of the other Contracting State, with a view to avoidance of taxation not in accordance with the Agreement. Any agreement reached shall be implemented notwithstanding any time limits in the national laws of the Contracting States.

3. The competent authorities of the Contracting States shall endeavour to resolve by mutual agreement any difficulties or doubts arising as to the interpretation or application of the Agreement. They may also consult together for the elimination of double taxation in cases not provided for in the Agreement.

4. The competent authorities of the Contracting States may communicate with each other directly for the purpose of

reaching an agreement in the sense of the preceding paragraphs. When it seems advisable in order to reach agreement to have an oral exchange of opinions, such exchange may take place through a Commission consisting of representatives of the competent authorities of the Contracting States.

Article 27

Exchange of Information

1. The competent authorities of the Contracting States shall exchange such information (including documents) as is necessary for carrying out the provisions of the Agreement or of the domestic laws of the Contracting States concerning taxes covered by the Agreement, in so far as the taxation thereunder is not contrary to the Agreement, in particular for the prevention of fraud or evasion of such taxes. Any information received by a Contracting State shall be treated as secret in the same manner as information obtained under the domestic laws of that State. However, if the information is originally regarded as secret in the transmitting State, it shall be disclosed only to persons or authorities (including courts and administrative bodies) involved in the assessment or collection of, the enforcement or prosecution in respect of, or the determination of appeals in relation to, the taxes which are the subject of the Agreement. Such persons or authorities shall use the information only for such purposes but may disclose the information in public court proceedings or in judicial decisions. The competent authorities shall, through consultation, develop appropriate conditions, methods and techniques concerning the matters in respect of which such exchange of information

shall be made, including, where appropriate, exchange of information regarding tax avoidance.

2. The exchange of information or documents shall be either on a routine basis or on request with reference to particular cases or both. The competent authorities of the Contracting States shall agree from time to time on the list of the information or documents which shall be furnished on a routine basis.

3. In no case shall the provisions of paragraph 1 be construed so as to impose on a Contracting State the obligation:

   a) to carry out administrative measures at variance with the laws or administrative practice of that or of the other Contracting State;

   b) to supply information or documents which are not obtainable under the laws or in the normal course of the administration of that or of the other Contracting State;

   c) to supply information or documents which would disclose any trade, business, industrial, commercial or professional secret or trade process or information the disclosure of which would be contrary to public policy.

Article 28
Assistance in Collection

1. The Contracting States undertake to lend assistance and support to each other, in the collection of the taxes to which this Agreement relates, in the cases where the taxes are definitely due according to the laws of the States making the request.

2. In the case of a request for enforcement of collection, tax claims of either of the Contracting States which have been finally determined will be accepted for enforcement by the other Contracting State to which the request is made and collected in that State in accordance with the laws applicable to the enforcement and collection of its taxes.

3. In the case of Poland tax, the request will be sent by the Minister of Finance, Poland or his authorised representative to the Central Board of Direct Taxes, Department of Revenue, Ministry of Finance, India and will be accompanied by such certificate as is required by the laws of Poland to establish that the taxes have been finally determined and are due from the taxpayer.

4. In the case of Indian tax, the request will be sent by the Central Board of Direct Taxes, Department of Revenue, Ministry of Finance, India to Minister of Finance, Poland or his authorised representative and will be accompanied by such certificate as is required by the laws of India to establish that the taxes have been finally determined and are due from the taxpayer.

5. Where the tax claim has not become final by reason of its being subject to appeal or any other preceeding, a Contracting State may, in order to protect its revenues, request the other Contracting State to take such interim measures in this behalf as are lawful under the laws of that other Contracting State.

6. A request for assistance in collection of taxes due from a taxpayer shall be made only if adequate assets of that taxpayer are not available for recovering the taxes from him in the Contracting State making the request.

7. The Contracting State in which tax is recovered in pursuance of paragraphs 1, 2 and 5 of this article shall immediately thereafter remit the amount so recovered to the Contracting State which made the request.

Article 29

Diplomatic and Consular Activities

Nothing in this Agreement shall affect the fiscal privileges of diplomatic or consular officials under the general rules of international law or under the provisions of special agreements.

Article 30

Entry into Force

Each of the Contracting States shall notify to the other the completion of the procedures required by its law for the bringing into force of this Agreement. This Agreement shall enter into force on the date of the later of these notifications and shall thereupon have effect:

a) in Poland, in respect of income arising in any year of income beginning on or after the first day of January next following the calendar year in which the later on the notifications is given;

b) In India, in respect of income arising in any previous year beginning on or after the first day of April next following the calendar year in which the later of the notifications is given.

Article 31

Termination

This Agreement shall remain in force indefinitely but either of the Contracting States may, on or before the thirtieth day

of June in any calendar year beginning after the expiration
of a period of five years from the date of its entry into
force, give the other Contracting State through diplomatic
channels, written notice of termination and, in such event,
this Agreement shall cease to have effect:

a) in Poland, in respect of income arising in any year of
income beginning on or after the 1st day of January
next following the calendar year in which the notice
of termination is given.

b) in India, in respect of income arising in any previous
year beginning on or after the 1st day of April next
following the calendar year in which the notice is
given,

In witness whereof the undersigned, being duly authorised
thereto, have signed the present Agreement.

Done in duplicate at Warsaw
this   2/1 st.   day of   June   one thousand
nine hundred and eighty nine   in the Polish,
Hindi and English languages, all the texts being equally
authentic. In case of divergence between the Polish and Hindi
texts, the English text shall prevail.

For the Government
of the Polish People's
Republic

For the Government
of the Republic
of India

[HINDI TEXT – TEXTE HINDI]

आय पर करों के सम्बन्ध में दोहरे कराधान के परिहार

और राजस्व अपवंचन की रोकथाम के लिए

पोलैंड लोक गणराज्य की सरकार

और

भारत गणराज्य की सरकार

के बीच करार

पोलैंड लोक गणराज्य की सरकार और भारत गणराज्य
की सरकार ने दोनों देशों के बीच आर्थिक संबंधों को और मजबूत
करने तथा उन्हें और आगे बढ़ाने की इच्छा से, और आय पर
करों के सम्बन्ध में दोहरे कराधान के परिहार और राजस्व-
अपवंचन की रोकथाम के लिए एक करार सम्पन्न करने का निर्णय
लेकर नीचे लिखे अनुसार सहमत हुई हैं :

अनुच्छेद - I

वैयक्तिक क्षेत्र

यह करार उन व्यक्तियों पर लागू होगा जो संविदाकारी
राज्यों में से किसी एक अथवा दोनों के निवासी हैं ।

अनुच्छेद- II

करार के अन्तर्गत आने वाले कर
----

1. जिन करों पर यह करार लागू होगा, वे इस प्रकार हैं :-

    {क} भारत में :

    I}   आयकर अधिनियम, 1961 के अंतर्गत आयकर
            और उस पर लगाया जाने वाला कोई अधिभार ;

    II}   कम्पनी {लाभ} अतिरिक्त कर अधिनियम, 1964
            के अंतर्गत लगाया जाने वाला अतिकर
            {जिन्हें इसमें इसके बाद " भारतीय कर " कहा
            जाएगा } ।

    {ख} पोलैंड में :

    I}   आयकर (पोडटेक डचोडोकी) ;

    II}   मजदूरी और वेतन पर कर { पोडटेक ओड
            वाइनग्रोज्जेन } ;

    III }   समता-कर { पोडटेक वाइरड्वनाव्जी } ; और

    IV }   कृषि कर { पोडटेक रोलनी } ;
            {जिन्हें इसमें इसके बाद " पोलिश कर " कहा
            जाएगा } ।

2. यह करार किसी भी समरूप अथवा सारत: इसी तरह के करों
पर भी लागू होगा जो वर्तमान करार पर हस्ताक्षर होने की तारीख के

पश्चात् पैराग्राफ-। में उल्लिखित करों के अतिरिक्त अथवा उनके स्थान पर दोनों संविदाकारी राज्यों में से किसी एक संविदाकारी राज्य द्वारा लगाए जाएँगी । संविदाकारी राज्यों के सक्षम प्राधिकारी उन महत्वपूर्ण परिवर्तनों के सम्बन्ध में एक-दूसरे को सूचित करेंगे जो उनके अपने-अपने ऐसे कराधान कानूनों में किए गए हों, जो इस करार के विषय हैं ।

अनुच्छेद - 3

सामान्य परिभाषाएँ

।॰   इस करार में, जबतक विषयगत पाठ में अन्यथा अपेक्षित नहीं हो :-

{क} "भारत " राज्य से अभिप्राय है भारत गणराज्य और जब इसका प्रयोग भौगोलिक विचार से किया जाए तो इससे अभिप्राय है भारत गणराज्य का राज्य क्षेत्र और भारत गणराज्य के समुद्रवर्ती राज्य क्षेत्र का निकटवर्ती कोई समुद्रीय क्षेत्र जिसमें भारतीय कानून और अन्तरराष्ट्रीय कानूनों के अनुसार भारत की प्रभुसत्ता हो अथवा प्रभुसत्ता संबंधी तथा सम्पूर्ण अधिकार हों । "

{ख} "पोलैंड " शब्द से अभिप्राय है पोलैंड लोक गणराज्य और जब इसका प्रयोग भौगोलिक विचार से किया जाए तो उससे अभि-प्राय है पोलैंड लोक गणराज्य और पोलैंड लोक गणराज्य के समुद्रवर्ती राज्य क्षेत्र का निकटवर्ती कोई समुद्रीय क्षेत्र जिसमें पोलैंड लोक गणराज्य के कानूनों और अन्तरराष्ट्रीय कानूनों के अनुसार पोलैंड लोक गणराज्य की प्रभुसत्ता या प्रभुसत्ता संबंधी तथा सम्पूर्ण अधिकार हों । "

{ग} " एक संविदाकारी राज्य " और "दूसरा संविदाकारी राज्य " पदों का आशय विषयगत पाठ जो अपेक्षा के अनुसार "भारत "

338

या " पोलैंड " से है ;

[ब] "कर" शब्द का आशय, विषयगत पाठ की अपेक्षा के अनुसार, भारतीय कर अथवा पोलिश कर से है परन्तु इनमें ऐसी कोई रकम शामिल नहीं होगी जो उन करों के संबंध में किसी चूक अथवा भूल के संदर्भ में देय हो जिन पर यह करार लागू होता हो अथवा उन करों के संबंध में लगाया गया कोई अर्थदण्ड हो ;

[उ॰] "व्यक्ति" शब्द में व्यष्टि, कंपनी और ऐसी कोई भी अन्य सत्ता शामिल है जो संबंधित संविदाकारी राज्यों में प्रवृत्त कराधान कानूनों के अंतर्गत कर लगने योग्य इकाई मानी जाती हो ;

[च] "कंपनी" शब्द का आशय किसी भी ऐसे निगमित निकाय अथवा किसी भी ऐसी सत्ता से है, जो संबंधित संविदाकारी राज्यों में प्रवृत्त कराधान कानूनों के अंतर्गत कोई कंपनी अथवा निगमित निकाय के रूप में मानी जाती हो ;

[छ] " एक संविदाकारी राज्य का उद्यम " और " दूसरे संविदाकारी राज्य का उद्यम " पदों का आशय क्रमशः एक संविदाकारी राज्य के किसी निवासी द्वारा संचालित किसी उद्यम और दूसरे संविदाकारी राज्य के किसी निवासी द्वारा संचालित किसी उद्यम से है ;

[ज] "सक्षम प्राधिकारी " शब्दों का आशय भारत के मामले में केन्द्रीय सरकार के वित्त मंत्रालय [राजस्व विभाग] अथवा उनके प्राधिकृत प्रतिनिधि से है ; और पोलैंड के मामले में वित्त मंत्री या उसके प्राधिकृत प्रतिनिधि से है ;

[झ] "राष्ट्रिक" शब्द का आशय किसी संविदाकारी राज्य की राष्ट्रीयता धारण करने वाले किसी व्यष्टि और किसी भी ऐसे विधिक व्यक्ति, भागीदारी अथवा संस्था से है जिसे अपनी हैसियत किसी संविदाकारी राज्य में प्रवृत्त कानूनों से प्राप्त होती हो ;

{3जे} "अन्तरराष्ट्रीय यातायात" पद का आशय किसी संविदाकारी राज्य के किसी उद्यम द्वारा संचालित किसी जलयान अथवा वायुयान द्वारा की गई किसी ढुलाई से है, सिवाय उस स्थिति के जब जलयान अथवा वायुयान केवल दूसरे संविदाकारी राज्य के स्थानों के बीच ही चलाया जाता हो ।

2. जहाँ तक किसी संविदाकारी राज्य द्वारा इस करार को लागू किए जाने का सम्बन्ध है, किसी शब्दावली का, जो उसमें परि- भाषित नहीं हुआ हो, जब तक विषयगत पाठ में अन्यथा अपेक्षित नहीं हो, तब तक वही अर्थ होगा जो उस राज्य के उन करों से संबंधित कानूनों के अंतर्गत होता है जिन पर यह करार लागू होता है ।

अनुच्छेद – 4

राजस्व प्रयोजन संबंधी निवासस्थान
----

1. इस करार के प्रयोजनों के लिए, किसी "संविदाकारी राज्य का निवासी " पद का आशय किसी भी ऐसे व्यक्ति से है जिस पर, उस राज्य के कानून के अंतर्गत, उसके अधिवास, निवास, प्रबंध स्थान अथवा उस प्रकार के किसी अन्य मानदण्ड के आधार पर, वहाँ पर कर लगाया जा सकता है ।

2. जहाँ पैराग्राफ-1 के उपबंधों के कारण व्यष्टि दोनों संविदा- कारी राज्यों का निवासी हो तो वहाँ उसकी हैसियत निम्नानुसार तय की जाएगी :

{क} उसे उस राज्य का निवासी माना जाएगा जहाँ उसे एक स्थायी निवास-गृह उपलब्ध हो ; यदि उसे दोनों संविदाकारी राज्यों में स्थायी निवास-गृह उपलब्ध हो, तो वह उस संविदाकारी राज्य का निवासी माना जाएगा, जिसके साथ उसके व्यक्तिगत और आर्थिक सम्बन्ध घनिष्ठतर हों {महत्वपूर्ण हितों का केन्द्र};

{घ} यदि उस संविदाकारी राज्य का, जिसमें उसके महत्वपूर्ण
हित निहित हैं, निश्चय नहीं किया जा सकता हो, अथवा
यदि उसे दोनों संविदाकारी राज्यों में कोई स्थायी निवास
उपलब्ध नहीं हो, तो वह उस राज्य का निवासी माना
जाएगा जिसमें वह व्यावहारिक रूप से रहता हो ;

{ङ} यदि उसका दोनों ही राज्यों में ऐसा आवास हो जिसमें
वह सामान्यत: रहता हो अथवा उनमें से किसी भी राज्य में
ऐसा आवास नहीं हो, तो वह उस राज्य का निवासी माना
जाएगा, जिसका वह राष्ट्रिक है ;

{च} यदि उप-पेराग्राफ {क} से {ग} के उपबंधों के अनुसार निवास-
स्थान का प्रश्न सुनिश्चित नहीं किया जा सकता हो, तो
संविदाकारी राज्यों के सक्षम प्राधिकारी पारस्परिक सहमति
द्वारा इस प्रश्न का समाधान करेंगे ।

3. जहां किसी व्यष्टि से भिन्न कोई व्यक्ति, पेराग्राफ-1 के
उपबंधों के कारण, दोनों संविदाकारी राज्यों का निवासी
हो तो वह उस संविदाकारी राज्य का निवासी माना
जाएगा जिसमें उसका वास्तविक प्रबंध का स्थान स्थित है ।

अनुच्छेद - 5

स्थायी संस्थापन
----

1. इस करार के प्रयोजनों के लिए " स्थायी संस्थापन " पद का
आशय कारोबार के उस निश्चित स्थान से है जहां से उद्यम का कारोबार
पूर्णत: अथवा अंशत: किया जाता है ।

2. "स्थायी संस्थापन " पद में विशेषतया निम्नलिखित शामिल
होंगे :

{क} प्रबंध-व्यवस्था का कोई स्थान ;

{ख} कोई शाखा ;

{ग} कोई कार्यालय ;

{घ} कोई कारखाना ;

{ड॰} कोई कार्यशाला ;

{च} कोई खान, तेल अथवा गैस कूप, खदान अथवा प्राकृतिक संसाधनों के निष्कर्षण का कोई अन्य स्थान ;

{छ} कोई माल-गोदाम जिसमें कोई व्यक्ति दूसरों के लिए भण्डारण सुविधाएं मुहैया करता हो ;

{ज} कोई फार्म, बागान अथवा अन्य स्थान जहां कृषि, वनपालन, बागबानी अथवा तत्सम्बन्धी कार्य किए जाते हों ;

{झ} कोई परिसर जिसका प्रयोग विक्रय स्थल अथवा आदेश प्राप्त करने अथवा मंगवाने के लिए किया जाता हो ;

{ञ} कोई प्रतिष्ठान अथवा संरचना जिसका प्रयोग प्राकृतिक संसाधनों की खोज के लिए किया जाता है ;

{ट} कोई भवन स्थल अथवा कोई निर्माण-कार्य, प्रतिष्ठान अथवा संयोजन परियोजना {एसेम्बली प्राजेक्ट} अथवा उससे संबंधित पर्यवेक्षी कार्यकलाप, जहां ऐसा स्थल, परियोजना अथवा कार्यकलाप छ: माह से अधिक चालु रहते हों ।

3. इस अनुच्छेद के पूर्ववर्ती उपबंधों के होते हुए भी, " स्थायी संस्थापन " पद में निम्नलिखित को शामिल नहीं माना जाएगा :-

{क} उद्यम के माल अथवा पण्य वस्तुओं के केवल भण्डारण अथवा प्रदर्शन के प्रयोजनार्थ सुविधाओं का प्रयोग ;

{ख} केवल भण्डारण अथवा प्रदर्शन के प्रयोजनार्थ उद्यम के माल अथवा पण्य वस्तुओं का स्टाक रखना ;

〔ग〕 किसी अन्य उद्यम द्वारा केवल संसाधित किए जाने के
प्रयोजनार्थ उद्यम के माल अथवा पण्य वस्तुओं का स्टॉक
रखना :

〔घ〕 किसी उद्यम के लिए माल अथवा पण्य वस्तुओं का
केवल क्रय करने अथवा सूचना एकत्र करने के प्रयोजनार्थ
कारोबार का कोई निश्चित स्थान रखना :

〔ङ•〕 उद्यम के लिए, केवल विज्ञापन देने, सूचना प्रदान करने,
वैज्ञानिक अनुसंधान अथवा ऐसे समान कार्यकलापों के
संबंध में जो प्रारम्भिक अथवा सहायक स्वरूप के हों :
कारोबार का कोई निश्चित स्थान रखना :

तथापि, उप-पैराग्राफ 〔क〕 से 〔ङ•〕 तक के उपबंध वहाँ लागू नहीं होंगे
जहाँ उक्त उप-पैराग्राफों में विनिर्दिष्ट प्रयोजनों से भिन्न किन्हीं प्रयोजनों
के लिए दूसरे संविदाकारी राज्य में किसी उद्यम द्वारा कारोबार का कोई
अन्य निश्चित स्थान रखा जाता हो ।

4॰ पैराग्राफ । और 2 के उपबंधों के होते हुए भी, जहाँ किसी
स्वतन्त्र हैसियत के अभिकर्ता, जिसपर पैराग्राफ 5 लागू होता हो, से
भिन्न कोई व्यक्ति एक संविदाकारी राज्य में दूसरे संविदाकारी राज्य के
किसी उद्यम की ओर से कार्य कर रहा है तो उस उद्यम का प्रथमोल्लिखित
राज्य में उस स्थिति में एक स्थायी संस्थापन होना माना जाएगा, यदि –

〔क〕 उसे उस राज्य में उद्यम की ओर से संविदाएं सम्पन्न
करने का प्राधिकार प्राप्त हो और वह व्यावहारिक
रूप से उस प्राधिकार का प्रयोग करता हो, जब तक
कि उसके कार्यकलाप उस उद्यम के लिए माल अथवा पण्य
वस्तुएं खरीदने तक ही सीमित नहीं हों ।

〔ख〕 उसके पास ऐसा कोई प्राधिकार न हो, परन्तु वह
प्रथमोक्त राज्य में व्यावहारिक रूप से माल अथवा पण्य
वस्तुओं का स्टॉक रखता हो जिसमें से वह उस उद्यम

की ओर से माल और पण्य वस्तुओं की नियमित
रूप से डिलीवरी करता हो ;

5. एक संविदाकारी राज्य के उद्यम का दूसरे संविदाकारी राज्य
में मात्र इस कारण कोई स्थायी संस्थापन होना नहीं माना जाएगा कि
वह उस दूसरे राज्य में किसी दलाल, सामान्य कमीशन एजेन्ट अथवा स्वतन्त्र
हैसियत वाले किसी अन्य एजेन्ट के माध्यम से कारोबार करता है, बशर्ते
ऐसे व्यक्ति अपने कारोबार का काम सामान्य रूप से कर रहे हों । लेकिन,
जब किसी ऐसे एजेन्ट के कार्यकलाप पूर्णतः अथवा प्रायःपूर्णतः स्वयं उस
उद्यम की ओर से अथवा उस उद्यम और अन्य उद्यमों की ओर से किए जाते
हों जो उस उद्यम को नियंत्रित करते हों, उस उद्यम द्वारा नियंत्रित हों
अथवा उसी तरह के सामान्य नियंत्रण के अधीन हों, तो उसे उस स्थिति में
इस पैराग्राफ के अभिप्राय के अन्तर्गत एक स्वतन्त्र हैसियत का एजेन्ट नहीं
समझा जाएगा ।

6. यदि कोई कम्पनी, जो एक संविदाकारी राज्य की निवासी
है, किसी ऐसी कम्पनी को नियंत्रित करती है अथवा किसी ऐसी कम्पनी
द्वारा नियंत्रित होती है, जो दूसरे संविदाकारी राज्य की निवासी है,
अथवा जो उस दूसरे संविदाकारी राज्य में ‖ चाहे किसी स्थायी संस्थापन
के माध्यम से अथवा अन्यथा ‖ कारोबार करती है तो मात्र इस तथ्य से ही
उन दोनों कम्पनियों में से किसी भी कम्पनी को दूसरे का स्थायी संस्थापन
नहीं माना जाएगा ।

अनुच्छेद - 6
अचल सम्पत्ति से आय

1. एक संविदाकारी राज्य के किसी निवासी द्वारा दूसरे संविदा-
कारी राज्य में स्थित अचल सम्पत्ति ‖कृषि अथवा वानिकी सहित ‖ से
प्राप्त आय पर उस दूसरे राज्य में कर लगाया जा सकेगा ।

2. "अचल सम्पत्ति" पद का अर्थ वही होगा जो उस संविदाकारी

राज्य के कानून के अंतर्गत उसका अर्थ है जिसमें सम्बन्धित सम्पत्ति स्थित है । इस पद में किसी भी हालत में ये शामिल होंगे - अचल सम्पत्ति के अवसाधन के रूप में सम्पत्ति, कृषि और वानिकी में प्रयुक्त पशुधन और उपस्कर, ऐसे अधिकार जिनपर भू-सम्पत्ति सम्बन्धी सामान्य कानून के उपबंध लागू होते हों, अचल सम्पत्ति के भोगने के अधिकार और खनिज भण्डार, स्रोत तथा अन्य प्राकृतिक संसाधनों के संचालन के लिए अथवा कार्य करने के अधिकार से प्रतिफल के रूप में परिवर्तनीय अथवा नियत अदायगियों के अधिकार । जलयान, नौकाएं तथा वायुयान अचल सम्पत्ति नहीं माने जाएंगे ।

3. पैराग्राफ 1 के उपबंध , अचल सम्पत्ति के प्रत्यक्ष उपभोग, उसे किराए पर देने अथवा किसी अन्य प्रकार के प्रयोग से होने वाली आय पर भी लागू होंगे ।

4. पैराग्राफ 1 तथा 3 के उपबंध, किसी उद्यम की अचल सम्पत्ति से अर्जित आय पर तथा स्वतंत्र व्यक्तिगत सेवाओं के निष्पादन के लिए प्रयुक्त अचल सम्पत्ति से अर्जित आय पर भी लागू होंगे ।

अनुच्छेद - 7

कारोबार के लाभ

1. किसी संविदाकारी राज्य के किसी उद्यम के लाभ पर केवल उसी राज्य में कर लगाया जाएगा जब तक वह उद्यम दूसरे संविदाकारी राज्य में स्थित किसी स्थायी संस्थापन के माध्यम से उस राज्य में कारो- बार नहीं करता हो । यदि वह उद्यम उपर्युक्त तरीके से कारोबार करता हो तो उस उद्यम के लाभों पर दूसरे राज्य में कर लगाया जा सकता है, किन्तु उसके केवल उतने अंश पर ही कर लगेगा जो निम्नलिखित के कारण उत्पन्न हुआ माना जा सकता है -(क) उस स्थायी संस्थापन ;(ख) उस दूसरे राज्य में एक-समान अथवा उससे मिलते-जुलते माल अथवा पण्य वस्तुओं की बिक्री जो उस स्थायी संस्थापन के माध्यम से की जाती है ; अथवा

{ग} उस दूसरे राज्य में कारोबार सम्बन्धी किए जाने वाले एक-समान अन्य कार्यकलाप अथवा उससे मिलते-जुलते कार्यकलाप, जो उस स्थायी संस्थापन के माध्यम से किए जाते हों ।

2. पैराग्राफ 3 के उपबंधों के अधीन रहते हुए, जहां एक संविदाकारी राज्य का कोई उद्यम दूसरे संविदाकारी राज्य में स्थित किसी स्थायी संस्थापन के जरिए कारोबार करता हो, वहां प्रत्येक संविदाकारी राज्य में होने वाले लाभ को उस स्थायी संस्थापन का लाभ समझा जाएगा जो उसको प्राप्त होने की तब अपेक्षा रहती जब वह एक-समान या उससे मिलती-जुलती परिस्थितियों में एक-समान या उससे मिलते-जुलते कार्यकलापों में लगा हुआ कोई निश्चित और भिन्न उद्यम होता और उस उद्यम के साथ पूर्णत: स्वतन्त्र रूप से कारोबार करता, जिसका यह एक स्थायी संस्थापन है । किसी भी हालत में जहां किसी स्थायी संस्थापन के कारण लाभों की सही राशि का निर्धारण करना संभव नहीं है अथवा उसके निर्धारण में असाधारण कठिनाइयां आती हैं तो स्थायी संस्थापन के कारण उत्पन्न होने वाले लाभों की गणना किसी उचित आधार पर की जाएं ।

3. किसी स्थायी संस्थापन के लाभों के निर्धारण में, वे व्यय की कटौतियों के रूप में स्वीकार किये जाएंगे, जो स्थायी संस्थापन के कारोबार के प्रयोजनार्थ किए गए हों, जिनमें इस प्रकार किए गए कार्यकारी अथवा तथा प्रशासनिक व्यय भी शामिल होंगे जो उस राज्य के कराधान कानूनों के उपबंधों के अनुसार हों, और उनकी परिधि के अन्दर आते हों, फिर चाहे वे उस राज्य में किए गए हों जहां स्थायी संस्थापन स्थित है अथवा अन्यत्र किए गए हों । किन्तु, स्थायी संस्थापन द्वारा उद्यम के प्रधान-कार्यालय को अथवा उसके अन्य कार्यालयों में से किसी कार्यालय { वास्तविक व्यय की प्रतिपूर्ति से भिन्न रूप में } को पेटेंटों, जानकारी अथवा अन्य अधिकारों के उपयोग के बदले रायल्टियों, फीसों अथवा ऐसी ही अन्य अदायगियों के तौर पर अथवा की गई विशिष्ट सेवाओं अथवा प्रबन्ध-व्यवस्था के लिए कमीशन अथवा अन्य प्रभारों के तौर पर, अथवा किसी बैंक उद्यम के मामले को छोड़कर, स्थायी संस्थापन को उधार दिए गए धन

पर ब्याज के रूप में यदि कोई रकमें अदा की गई हों तो उनके संबंध में ऐसी किसी कटौती की स्वीकृति नहीं दी जाएगी । इसी प्रकार किसी स्थायी संस्थापन के लाभों का निर्धारण करने में, उन रकमों को हिसाब में नहीं लिया जाएगा, जो स्थायी संस्थापन द्वारा उद्यम के प्रधान कार्यालय को या उसके अन्य कार्यालयों में से किसी कार्यालय के स्थायी संस्थापन द्वारा पेटेंटों, जानकारी अथवा अन्य अधिकारों के उपयोग के बदले रायॅल्टियों, फीसों अथवा ऐसी ही अन्य अदायगियों के रूप में की गई विशिष्ट सेवाओं अथवा प्रबंध-व्यवस्था के लिए कमीशन अथवा अन्य प्रभारों के रूप में, अथवा किसी बैंक उद्यमों के मामलों को छोड़कर उद्यम के प्रधान कार्यालय को अथवा उसके अन्य कार्यालयों में से किसी कार्यालय को उधार दिए गए ऋन पर ब्याज के रूप में उद्यम के प्रधान कार्यालय या उसके अन्य कार्यालयों में से किसी कार्यालय § वास्तविक व्यय की प्रतिपूर्ति से भिन्न रूप में § को प्रभारित की गई हो

4. कोई लाभ केवल इस कारण से किसी स्थायी संस्थापन को प्राप्त हुआ नहीं माना जाएगा कि उस स्थायी संस्थापन द्वारा उद्यम के लिए माल या पण्य वस्तुएं खरीदी गई हैं ।

5. पूर्ववर्ती पैराग्राफों के प्रयोजनार्थ स्थायी संस्थापन के कारण उत्पन्न हुए समझे जाने वाले लाभों को तब तक वर्षानुवर्ष उसी पद्धति से निर्धारित किया जाता रहेगा, जब तक कि उसके विपरीत कोई ठीक तथा पर्याप्त कारण नहीं हों ।

6. जहां लाभों में आय की वे मदें शामिल हैं जिनका इस करार के के अन्य अनुच्छेदों में विवेचन किया गया है, वहां उन अनुच्छेदों के उपबंध इस अनुच्छेद के उपबंधों से प्रभावित नहीं होंगे ।

अनुच्छेद - 8

विमान परिवहन
----

1. किसी संविदाकारी राज्य के किसी उद्यम द्वारा अन्तरराष्ट्रीय यातायात में वायुयान परिचालन से प्राप्त लाभों पर केवल उसी राज्य में कर लगाया जाएगा ।

2. पैराग्राफ । के उपबंध किसी पूल, किसी संयुक्त कारोबार अथवा किसी अन्तरराष्ट्रीय परिचालन एजेंसी में भागीदारी से प्राप्त लाभों पर भी लागू होंगे ।

3. इस अनुच्छेद के प्रयोजनों के लिए , अन्तरराष्ट्रीय यातायात में वायुयान परिचालन से सम्बन्धित निधियों पर ब्याज को ऐसे वायुयान के परिचालन से प्राप्त लाभ माना जाएगा, तथा अनुच्छेद 12 के उपबंध ऐसे ब्याज के मामले में लागू नहीं होंगे ।

4. " वायुयान-परिचालन " पद से तात्पर्य होगा-वायुयान के मालिकों या पट्टेदारों अथवा अव्रक्रेताओं द्वारा यात्रियों, डाक, पशुधन अथवा माल का वायुयान द्वारा परिवहन करने का कारोबार जिसमें अन्य उद्यमों की ओर से ऐसे परिवहन के लिए टिकटों की बिक्री, वायुयान का आनुषंगिक पट्टा तथा ऐसे परिवहन से प्रत्यक्षत: संबंधित कोई अन्य कार्यकलाप शामिल हैं ।

अनुच्छेद - 9

जहाजरानी
----

1. अन्तरराष्ट्रीय यातायात में जलयान के प्रचालन से अर्जित लाभों पर केवल उसी संविदाकारी राज्य में ही कर लगाया जाएगा जिसमें उद्यम के वास्तविक प्रबंध का स्थान स्थित है ।

2. यदि अन्तरराष्ट्रीय यातायात में नौ-परिवहन का कार्य कर रहे किसी जहाजरानी उद्यम की वास्तविक प्रबंध-व्यवस्था का स्थान किसी जलयान में ही हो तो उसे उस संविदाकारी राज्य में स्थित माना जाएगा जिसमें उस जलयान का अपना बंदरगाह स्थित है, अथवा यदि उस जलयान का अपना ऐसा कोई बंदरगाह नहीं है तो उसे उस संविदा- कारी राज्य में स्थित माना जाएगा जिसमें उस जलयान का संचालक निवासी है ।

3. किसी पूल, किसी संयुक्त कारोबार अथवा किसी अन्तर्राष्ट्रीय परिचालन अभिकरण में भागीदारी से प्राप्त लाभों पर पैरा । के उपबंध

भी लागू होंगि ।

4. पैराग्राफ । और जहाजरानी के क्षेत्र में सहयोग के बारे में भारत सरकार और पोलैंड लोक गणराज्य की सरकार के बीच हुए दिनांक 27 जून, 1960 के करार के अनुच्छेद IZIII में शामिल बातों के होते हुए भी, किसी संविदाकारी राज्य के किसी उद्यम द्वारा अन्य संविदाकारी राज्य की बंदरगाह से तीसरे देशों की बंदरगाहों के बीच जलयानों के संचालन से प्राप्त आय पर उक्त दूसरे राज्य में कर लगेगा लेकिन उक्त दूसरे राज्य में लगाए गए कर को उसके 50 प्रतिशत तक की राशि के बराबर कम कर दिया जाएगा ।

अनुच्छेद- 10

सहयोगी उद्यम

जहाँ :

{क} एक संविदाकारी राज्य का कोई उद्यम दूसरे संविदाकारी राज्य के किसी उद्यम की प्रबंध-व्यवस्था, नियंत्रण अथवा पूँजी में प्रत्यक्षतः या अप्रत्यक्षतः भाग लेता है ; अथवा

{ख} वे ही व्यक्ति एक संविदाकारी राज्य के किसी उद्यम और दूसरे संविदाकारी राज्य के किसी उद्यम की प्रबंध-व्यवस्था नियंत्रण या पूँजी में प्रत्यक्षतः अथवा अप्रत्यक्षतः भाग लेते हैं ;

और दोनों में से किसी भी अवस्था में, दोनों उद्यमों के बीच उनके वाणिज्यिक अथवा वित्तीय सम्बन्धों में ऐसी शर्तें रखी अथवा लगाई जाती हैं, जो उन शर्तों से भिन्न हैं, जोकि स्वतंत्र उद्यमों के बीच रखी जाती हैं, वहाँ ऐसा कोई भी लाभ, जो उन शर्तों के नहीं होने की स्थिति में उन उद्यमों में से एक उद्यम को प्राप्त हुआ होता, किन्तु उन शर्तों के कारण उस प्रकार प्राप्त नहीं हुआ, तो वे लाभ उस उद्यम के लाभों में शामिल किए जा सकेंगे और उन पर तदनुसार कर लगाया जा सकेगा

अनुच्छेद – ।।

लाभांश

।. एक संविदाकारी राज्य की निवासी किसी कम्पनी द्वारा दूसरे संविदाकारी राज्य के किसी निवासी को अदा किए गए लाभांश पर कर उस दूसरे राज्य में लगाया जा सकता है ।

2. तथापि, ऐसे लाभांशों पर उस संविदाकारी राज्य में भी कर लग सकता है जिस राज्य की लाभांश अदा करने वाली कम्पनी निवासी है और यह कर उस राज्य के कानूनों के अनुसार लगेगा, लेकिन यदि प्राप्तकर्ता लाभांशों का हितभोगी स्वामी है तो इस प्रकार लगाया गया कर लाभांशों की सकल रकम के 15 प्रतिशत से अधिक नहीं होगा जहां ऐसे लाभांश इस करार के प्रवृत्त होने के बाद किए गए अदायगों से सम्बन्धित होते हैं ।
यह पैराग्राफ ऐसे लाभांशों के संबंध में कम्पनी के कराधान को प्रभावित नहीं करेगा, जिसमें से लाभांश अदा किए जाते हैं ।

3. इस अनुच्छेद में यथाप्रयुक्त "लाभांश" पद का अर्थ है शेयरों से अथवा अन्य अधिकारों से प्राप्त आय, जो ऋण-दावे नहीं हों, लाभों में सम्मिलित हों, तथा अन्य नियमित अधिकारों से प्राप्त आय जिस पर उसी प्रकार की कराधान व्यवस्था लागू होती है, जो उस राज्य के कानूनों द्वारा शेयर से प्राप्त आय पर लागू होती है, जिस राज्य की वितरण करने वाली कम्पनी निवासी है ।

4. पैराग्राफ । और 2 के उपबंध उस स्थिति में लागू नहीं होंगे , यदि लाभांशों का हितभोगी स्वामी, संविदाकारी राज्य का निवासी होने के कारण, दूसरे संविदाकारी राज्य में, जिसकी लाभांश अदा करने वाली कम्पनी निवासी हो, स्थित किसी स्थायी संस्थापन के माध्यम से कारोबार करता हो अथवा उस दूसरे राज्य में स्थित किसी निश्चित

स्थान में उसमें स्वतन्त्र व्यक्तिगत सेवाएँ प्रदान करता हो और वह सम्पत्ति, जिसके सम्बन्ध में लाभांश अदा किए जाते हैं, वह इस प्रकार के स्थायी संस्थापन अथवा निश्चित स्थान से प्रभावी रूप से सम्बन्धित हो । ऐसे मामले में अनुच्छेद 7 अथवा 15 के उपबंध यथास्थिति लागू होंगे ।

5. जहाँ कोई कम्पनी जो एक संविदाकारी राज्य की निवासी है और वह दूसरे संविदाकारी राज्य से लाभ अथवा आय प्राप्त करती है, वहाँ वह दूसरा राज्य, कम्पनी द्वारा अदा किए गए लाभांशों पर किसी प्रकार का कर नहीं लगाएगा जहाँ तक कि उस दूसरे राज्य के किसी निवासी को इस प्रकार के लाभांश अदा नहीं किए जाते अथवा जहाँ तक कि वह सम्पत्ति जिसके संबंध में लाभांश अदा किए जाते हैं, उस दूसरे राज्य में स्थित किसी स्थायी संस्थापन से अथवा किसी निश्चित स्थान से प्रभावी रूप से सम्बद्ध नहीं है अथवा कम्पनी के अवितरित लाभों पर लगाया जा सकने वाला कर नहीं लगाया जाएगा चाहे अदा किए गए लाभांश अथवा अवितरित लाभ पूर्ण रूप से अथवा आंशिक रूप से उस दूसरे राज्य में उत्पन्न होने वाले लाभ अथवा आय के रूप में ही हों ।

अनुच्छेद - 12

ब्याज

1. एक संविदाकारी राज्य में उत्पन्न होने वाले तथा दूसरे संविदाकारी राज्य के निवासी को अदा किए जाने वाले ब्याज पर उस दूसरे राज्य में कर लगाया जा सकेगा ।

2. किन्तु, इस प्रकार के ब्याज पर उस संविदाकारी राज्य में भी और उस राज्य के कानून के अनुसार कर लगाया जा सकेगा जिस राज्य में वह अर्जित होता है, किन्तु यदि प्राप्तकर्ता ब्याज का हितभोगी

स्वामी है तो इस प्रकार प्रभारित कर, ब्याज की सकल रकम के 15 प्रतिशत से अधिक नहीं होगा ।

3. पैराग्राफ 2 के उपबंधों के होते हुए भी –

{क} एक संविदाकारी राज्य में अर्जित होने वाले ब्याज पर उस राज्य में कर से छूट दी जाएगी क्शर्तें कि वह निम्नलिखित द्वारा प्राप्त किया गया हो या उनका उस पर हितभोगी स्वामित्व हो:

{i} दूसरे संविदाकारी राज्य की सरकार, राजनैतिक उप-प्रभाग अथवा स्थानीय प्राधिकरण ; अथवा

{ii} दूसरे संविदाकारी राज्य का सेंट्रल बैंक ।

{ख} एक संविदाकारी राज्य में अर्जित होने वाले ब्याज को उस राज्य में कर से छूट दी जाएगी यदि उस पर दूसरे संविदाकारी राज्य के निवासी का हितभोगी स्वामित्व हो और वह निम्नलिखित द्वारा दिए गए अथवा समर्थित ऋण अथवा उधार के संबंध में प्राप्त किया जाता हो :

{i} पोलैंड के मामले में, बैंक हैंडलोवी डब्ल्यू वारशाजांवी एस0 ए0 जिस सीमा तक ऐसा ब्याज केवल आयातों-निर्यातों की वित्त-व्यवस्था करने के कारण होता है ;

{ii} भारत के मामले में, भारतीय आयात-निर्यात बैंक { एग्ज़िम बैंक }; जिस सीमा तक ऐसा ब्याज केवल आयातों-निर्यातों की वित्त-व्यवस्था करने के कारण होता है;

{iii} किसी संविदाकारी राज्य के विदेश व्यापार की सार्वजनिक वित्त व्यवस्था करने वाला कोई भी संस्थान ;

(iv) कोई अन्य व्यक्ति बशर्ते कि ऋण अथवा
उधार प्रथमोल्लिखित संविदाकारी राज्य
की सरकार द्वारा अनुमोदित हो ।

4. इस अनुच्छेद में व्याप्रयुक्त "ब्याज" शब्द का आशय प्रत्येक
प्रकार के ऋण संबंधी दावों से प्राप्त आय से है चाहे वह बंधक द्वारा
प्रतिभूत हो अथवा नहीं और चाहे ऋणदाता के लाभों में भागीदारी
का अधिकार प्राप्त हो अथवा नहीं, और खास तौर पर सरकारी
प्रतिभूतियों से प्राप्त आय और बंध-पत्रों अथवा ऋण-पत्रों, जिनमें ऐसी
प्रतिभूतियों, बंध-पत्रों अथवा ऋण-पत्रों के संबंध में प्रदान किए जाने वाले
प्रीमियम और पुरस्कार शामिल हैं, से प्राप्त आय । विलम्बित अदायगी
के लिए अर्थदण्ड सम्बन्धी प्रभारों को इस अनुच्छेद के प्रयोजन के लिए
ब्याज नहीं समझा जाएगा ।

5. पैराग्राफ । और 2 के उपबंध उस स्थिति में लागू नहीं होंगे
यदि ब्याज का हितभोगी स्वामी, एक संविदाकारी राज्य का निवासी
होने के नाते, दूसरे संविदाकारी राज्य में जिसमें ब्याज अर्जित हुआ हो,
स्थित किसी स्थायी संस्थापन के माध्यम से व्यापार करता है, अथवा
उस दूसरे राज्य में स्थित एक निश्चित स्थान से वहां स्वतंत्र वैयक्तिक
सेवाएं प्रदान करता है और जिस ऋण-दावे के बारे में ब्याज अदा किया
जाता है वह इस प्रकार के स्थायी संस्थापन अथवा निश्चित स्थान से
प्रभावी रूप से सम्बन्धित है । इस प्रकार के मामले में, अनुच्छेद 7 अथवा
अनुच्छेद 15 के उपबंध, जैसा भी मामला हो, लागू होंगे ।

6. किसी संविदाकारी राज्य में ब्याज, उत्पन्न हुआ माना
जाएगा, यदि ब्याज अदा करने वाला स्वयं वह संविदाकारी राज्य,
कोई राजनैतिक उप-प्रभाग, कोई स्थानीय प्राधिकरण अथवा उस राज्य
का कोई निवासी हो । किन्तु, जहां ब्याज अदा करने वाले व्यक्ति
का, चाहे वह संविदाकारी राज्य का निवासी हो, अथवा नहीं,
संविदाकारी राज्य में कोई स्थायी संस्थापन अथवा निश्चित स्थान
हो, जिसके संबंध में वह ऋण लिया गया था जिस पर ब्याज की अदायगी

की गयी है, और इस प्रकार का ब्याज उस स्थायी संस्थापन अथवा निश्चित स्थान द्वारा वहन किया जाता है, तब वह ब्याज उस संविदाकारी राज्य में उत्पन्न हुआ माना जाएगा जिसमें वह स्थायी संस्थापन अथवा निश्चित स्थान स्थित है ।

7. जहां, ब्याज अदा करने वाले और हितभोगी स्वामी के बीच अथवा उन दोनों के बीच तथा किसी अन्य व्यक्ति के बीच विशेष सम्बन्ध होने के कारण, अदा की गयी ब्याज की रकम, उस ऋण-दावे को ध्यान में रखते हुए जिसके लिए ब्याज की रकम अदा की गयी है, उस रकम से बढ़ जाती है, जिसके संबंध में, इस प्रकार के संबंध नहीं होने की स्थिति में, अदा करने वाले और हितभोगी स्वामी के बीच सहमति हो गयी होती, वहां इस अनुच्छेद के उपबंध अन्तिम वर्णित रकम पर लागू होंगे । ऐसे मामले में, अदायगी के अतिरिक्त भाग पर, इस करार के अन्य उपबंधों का सम्यक् अनुपालन करते हुए, प्रत्येक संविदाकारी राज्य के कानूनों के अनुसार कर लगाया जाएगा ।

अनुच्छेद - 13

रायल्टियां और तकनीकी सेवाओं के लिए शुल्क

1. एक संविदाकारी राज्य में उत्पन्न होने वाली और दूसरे संविदाकारी राज्य के किसी निवासी को अदा की गयी रायल्टियों तथा तकनीकी सेवाओं के लिए फीस पर उस दूसरे राज्य में कर लगाया जा सकेगा ।

2. लेकिन, इस प्रकार की रायल्टियों और तकनीकी सेवाओं के लिए फीस पर उस संविदाकारी राज्य में तथा उस राज्य के कानूनों के अनुसार भी कर लगाया जा सकेगा जिसमें ये उत्पन्न हुये हों । परन्तु यदि प्राप्तकर्ता रायल्टियों अथवा तकनीकी सेवाओं के लिए फीस का

354

हितभोगी स्वामी हो तो इस प्रकार प्रभारित कर, रायल्टियों अथवा तकनीकी सेवाओं के लिए फीस की स्कल रकम के 22•5 प्रतिशत से अधिक नहीं होगा ।

3. इस अनुच्छेद में यथा-प्रयुक्त "रायल्टियों " शब्द का आशय किसी साहित्यिक, कलात्मक तथा वैज्ञानिक कृतियों, जिसमें चलचित्र फिल्मों अथवा रेडियो अथवा दूरदर्शन प्रसारण के लिए टेपों के प्रतिलिप्याधिकार, कोई पेटेन्ट, ट्रेड मार्क, डिजाइन अथवा माडल, प्लान, गुप्त फार्मूला अथवा प्रक्रिया के प्रयोग के लिए, अथवा प्रयोगाधिकार के लिए, अथवा औद्योगिक, वाणिज्यक अथवा वैज्ञानिक उपस्कर, अथवा औद्योगिक, वाणिज्यक अथवा वैज्ञानिक अनुभव से संबंधित जानकारी के प्रयोग अथवा प्रयोगाधिकार के प्रतिफल के रूप में प्राप्त किसी भी प्रकार की अदायगी ।

4. इस अनुच्छेद में यथा-प्रयुक्त " तकनीकी सेवाओं के लिए फीस " पद का आशय प्रबंधकीय, तकनीकी अथवा परामर्शदात्री स्वरूप की सेवाओं, जिनमें तकनीकी अथवा अन्य कार्मिकों की सेवाओं की व्यवस्था भी शामिल है, के प्रतिफल में, अदायगियां करने वाले व्यक्ति के कर्मचारी को की गई अदायगियों से भिन्न, किसी भी व्यक्ति को की गयी किसी भी रकम की अदायगियां ।

5. पैराग्राफ । तथा 2 के उपबंध उस स्थिति में लागू नहीं होंगे यदि रायल्टियों अथवा तकनीकी सेवाओं के लिए फीस का हितभोगी स्वामी जो एक संविदाकारी राज्य का निवासी है, दूसरे संविदाकारी राज्य में, जिसमें रायल्टियां अथवा तकनीकी सेवाओं के लिए फीस उद्भूत होती है, उसमें स्थित किसी स्थायी संस्थापन के माध्यम से कारोबार करता है अथवा उस दूसरे राज्य में स्थित किसी निश्चित स्थान से स्वतंत्र व्यक्तिगत सेवाएं निष्पादित करता है तथा वह अधिकार, सम्पत्ति अथवा संविदा , जिसके संबंध में रायल्टियां अथवा तकनीकी सेवाओं के लिए फीस अदा की जाती है, ऐसे स्थायी संस्थापन अथवा निश्चित स्थान से प्रभावी रूप से संबंधित है । ऐसे

मामले में, अनुच्छेद 7 अथवा अनुच्छेद 15 के उपबंध , जैसा भी मामला हो, लागू होंगे ।

6. किसी संविदाकारी राज्य में रायल्टियों तथा तकनीकी सेवाओं के लिए फीस उस स्थिति में उद्भूत हुई मानी जाएगी यदि अदा करने वाला स्वयं वह राज्य, उसका कोई राजनीतिक उप-प्रभाग, कोई स्थानीय प्राधिकरण अथवा उस राज्य का कोई निवासी हो । परन्तु, जहां रायल्टियों अथवा तकनीकी सेवाओं के लिए फीस अदा करने वाले व्यक्ति का, चाहे वह किसी संविदाकारी राज्य का निवासी है अथवा नहीं, किसी संविदाकारी राज्य में कोई स्थायी संस्थापन अथवा निश्चित स्थान हो जिसके संबंध में रायल्टियों अथवा तकनीकी सेवाओं के लिए फीस अदा करने की देनदारी उत्पन्न हुई हो, तथा ऐसी रायल्टियों अथवा तकनीकी सेवाओं के लिए फीस ऐसे स्थायी संस्थापन अथवा निश्चित स्थान द्वारा वहन की जाती है तब ऐसी रायल्टियों अथवा तकनीकी सेवाओं के लिए फीस उस राज्य में उद्भूत हुई मानी जाएगी जिसमें उक्त स्थायी संस्थापन अथवा निश्चित स्थान स्थित है ।

7. जहां अदा करने वाले तथा हितभोगी स्वामी के बीच अथवा उन दोनों और कुछ अन्य व्यक्तियों के बीच विशिष्ट संबंध होने के कारण रायल्टियों अथवा तकनीकी सेवाओं के लिए अदा की गई फीस की रकम उस रकम से बढ़ जाती है जो ऐसे संबंधों के नहीं होने की स्थिति में अदा की गई होती, तो वहां इस अनुच्छेद के उपबंध केवल अन्तिम-वर्णित रकम पर लागू होंगे । ऐसे मामले में, अदायगियों की रकम का अतिरिक्त भाग इस करार के अन्य उपबंधों को सम्यक रूप से ध्यान में रखते हुए प्रत्येक संविदाकारी राज्य के कानूनों के अनुसार कर लगाए जाने योग्य रहेगा ।

अनुच्छेद – 14

पूंजी अभिलाभ
----

1. एक संविदाकारी राज्य के किसी निवासी द्वारा अनुच्छेद 6

में उल्लिखित और दूसरे संविदाकारी राज्य में स्थित अचल सम्पत्ति के अंतरण से प्राप्त होने वाले अभिलाभों पर उस दूसरे राज्य में कर लगाया जा सकेगा ।

2. चल सम्पत्ति के अंतरण से प्राप्त हुए अभिलाभों पर, जो एक संविदाकारी राज्य के किसी उद्यम के स्थायी संस्थापन की व्यापारिक सम्पत्ति का भाग है तथा दूसरे संविदाकारी राज्य में स्थित है अथवा जो एक संविदाकारी राज्य के किसी निवासी को स्वतंत्र व्यक्तिगत सेवाओं के निष्पादन के प्रयोजनार्थ दूसरे संविदाकारी राज्य में उपलब्ध निश्चित स्थान से संबंधित चल सम्पत्ति हों, जिनमें ऐसे स्थायी संस्थापन [अकेले अथवा सम्पूर्ण उद्यम के साथ] अथवा ऐसे निश्चित स्थान के अन्तरण से होने वाले ऐसे अभिलाभ भी शामिल हैं, उन पर दूसरे राज्य में कर लगाया जा सकेगा ।

3. अन्तरराष्ट्रीय यातायात में चलाए जाने वाले जलयानों अथवा वायुयानों अथवा इस प्रकार के जलयानों अथवा वायुयानों के संचालन से संबंधित चल सम्पत्ति, के अंतरण से प्राप्त अभिलाभों पर केवल उस संविदाकारी राज्य में कर लगाया जा सकेगा जिसका कि अन्तरणकर्ता निवासी है ।

4. किसी ऐसी कम्पनी के पूंजीगत स्टॉक के शेयरों के अन्तरण से प्राप्त अभिलाभों पर, जिसकी सम्पत्ति प्रत्यक्ष: अथवा अप्रत्यक्ष: प्रधानतः किसी संविदाकारी राज्य में स्थित अचल सम्पत्ति हो, उसी राज्य में कर लगाया जा सकेगा ।

5. किसी ऐसी कम्पनी में पैराग्राफ 4 में उल्लिखित शेयरों से भिन्न शेयरों के अन्तरण से प्राप्त अभिलाभों पर, जो किसी संविदा- कारी राज्य की निवासी हो, उस राज्य में ही कर लगाया जा सकेगा ।

6. पैराग्राफ 1, 2, 3, 4, और 5 में उल्लिखित सम्पत्ति से भिन्न किसी भी सम्पत्ति के अन्तरण से प्राप्त अभिलाभों पर उसी संविदाकारी राज्य में कर लगाया जा सकेगा जिसका अन्तरणकर्त्ता निवासी है ।

अनुच्छेद - 15

स्वतन्त्र व्यक्तिगत सेवाएं

1. किसी व्यष्टि द्वारा जो एक संविदाकारी राज्य का निवासी है, व्यावसायिक सेवाओं अथवा उसी स्वरूप के अन्य स्वतंत्र कार्यकलापों के निष्पादन से प्राप्त आय, निम्नलिखित परिस्थितियों को छोड़कर, जब ऐसी आय पर दूसरे संविदाकारी राज्य में भी कर लगाया जा सकेगा, केवल उसी राज्य में कराधेय होगी :-

   {क} यदि उसे अपने कार्यकलापों के निष्पादन के प्रयोजनार्थ दूसरे संविदाकारी राज्य में एक निश्चित स्थान नियमित रूप से उपलब्ध है तो उस मामले में उस दूसरे राज्य में उतनी रकम पर कर लगाया जा सकेगा जो उस निश्चित स्थान के कारण उद्भूत हुई मानी जा सकती है ; अथवा

   {ख} यदि दूसरे संविदाकारी राज्य में ठहरने की उसकी अवधि अथवा अवधियां उस दूसरे राज्य के संगत "पूर्ववर्ती वर्ष " अथवा " आय वर्ष " में जैसा भी मामला हो, कुल मिलाकर 183 दिन अथवा उससे अधिक हो, तो उस मामले में, उक्त आय के केवल उतने ही भाग पर उस दूसरे राज्य में कर लगाया जा सकेगा जो उस दूसरे राज्य में निष्पादित उसके कार्यकलापों से प्राप्त होती हो ।

2. " व्यावसायिक सेवाएं " पद में स्वतंत्र वैज्ञानिक, साहित्यिक, कलात्मक, शैक्षिक अथवा अध्यापन संबंधी कार्यकलाप तथा चिकित्सकों,

शल्य-चिकित्सकों, वकीलों, इंजीनियरों, वास्तुविदों, दन्त-चिकित्सकों तथा लेखापालों के स्वतंत्र कार्यकलाप शामिल हैं ।

अनुच्छेद - 16

पराश्रित व्यक्तिगत सेवाएं

1. अनुच्छेद 17, 18, 19, 20, 21 तथा 22 के उपबंधों के अधीन रहते हुए, एक संविदाकारी राज्य के किसी निवासी द्वारा किसी नियोजन के संबंध में प्राप्त वेतन, मजदूरी तथा इसी प्रकार के अन्य पारिश्रमिक पर केवल उसी राज्य में कर लगाया जा सकेगा जब तक कि उसका नियोजन दूसरे संविदाकारी राज्य में नहीं हो । यदि इस प्रकार नियोजन किया जाता है तो ऐसे पारिश्रमिक पर, जो वहां से प्राप्त होता है, उस दूसरे राज्य में कर लगाया जा सकेगा ।

2. पैराग्राफ 1 के उपबंधों के होते हुए भी, एक संविदाकारी राज्य के किसी निवासी द्वारा दूसरे संविदाकारी राज्य में किए गए किसी नियोजन के संबंध में प्राप्त पारिश्रमिक पर केवल प्रथमोल्लिखित राज्य में ही कर लगाया जा सकेगा, यदि :

{क} प्राप्तकर्ता संगत "पूर्ववर्ती वर्ष" अथवा "आय वर्ष" में कुल मिलाकर 183 दिन से अनधिक की अवधि अथवा अवधियों के लिए उस दूसरे राज्य में मौजूद रहा हो ;

{ख} पारिश्रमिक किसी ऐसे नियोजक द्वारा अथवा उसकी ओर से अदा किया जाता है जो उस दूसरे राज्य का निवासी नहीं है ; और

{ग} पारिश्रमिक नियोजक के किसी ऐसे स्थायी संस्थापन अथवा निश्चित स्थान द्वारा वहन नहीं किया गया हो, जो दूसरे राज्य में स्थित है ।

3. इस अनुच्छेद के पूर्ववर्ती उपबंधों के होते हुए भी, एक संविदा-

कारी राज्य के किसी उद्यम द्वारा अन्तरराष्ट्रीय यातायात में जलयान अथवा वायुयान के परिचालन में किए गए किसी नियोजन के संबंध में प्राप्त पारिश्रमिक पर उसी राज्य में कर लगाया जा सकेगा ।

अनुच्छेद - 17

निदेशकों की फीस तथा उच्च स्तरीय प्रबंधकीय
अधिकारियों का पारिश्रमिक

1. एक संविदाकारी राज्य के किसी निवासी द्वारा किसी ऐसी कम्पनी के निदेशक-मण्डल के एक सदस्य की हैसियत से, जो दूसरे संविदाकारी राज्य की निवासी है, प्राप्त निदेशक की फीस तथा उससे मिलती-जुलती अदायगियों पर कर उस दूसरे राज्य में लगाया जा सकेगा ।

2. एक संविदाकारी राज्य के किसी निवासी द्वारा, किसी ऐसी कम्पनी के, जो दूसरे राज्य की निवासी है, उच्च स्तरीय प्रबंधकीय पद पर नियुक्त कर्मचारी की हैसियत से प्राप्त वेतन, मजदूरी तथा उससे मिलते-जुलते पारिश्रमिक पर उस दूसरे राज्य में कर लगाया जा सकेगा ।

अनुच्छेद - 18

मनोरंजनकर्ताओं तथा खिलाड़ियों द्वारा अर्जित आय

1. अनुच्छेद 15 तथा 16 के उपबंधों के होते हुए भी, किसी संविदाकारी राज्य के किसी निवासी द्वारा मनोरंजनकर्ता के रूप में, जैसे कि एक थियेटर, चलचित्र, रेडियो अथवा दूरदर्शन कलाकार अथवा एक संगीतकार अथवा एक खिलाड़ी के रूप में अपने व्यक्तिगत कार्य-कलापों से, जिन्हें वह दूसरे संविदाकारी राज्य में सम्पन्न करता है, प्राप्त आय पर कर उस दूसरे राज्य में लग सकेगा ।

2. जहाँ किसी मनोरंजनकर्त्ता अथवा खिलाड़ी द्वारा इस प्रकार की अपनी हैसियत में सम्पन्न किए गए व्यक्तिगत कार्यकलापों के संबंध में उद्भूत होने वाली आय स्वयं मनोरंजनकर्त्ता अथवा खिलाड़ी को प्राप्त नहीं होती है अपितु किसी अन्य व्यक्ति को प्राप्त होती है, वहाँ अनुच्छेद 7, 15 और 16 के उपबंधों के होते हुए भी उस आय पर कर उस संविदाकारी राज्य में लग सकेगा जिसमें उक्त मनोरंजनकर्त्ता अथवा खिलाड़ी द्वारा ऐसे कार्यकलाप किए गए हों ।

3. पैराग्राफ। के उपबंधों के होते हुए भी किसी मनोरंजनकर्त्ता अथवा किसी खिलाड़ी द्वारा, जो एक संविदाकारी राज्य का निवासी है, दूसरे संविदाकारी राज्य में उसी हैसियत से किए गए अपने व्यक्तिगत कार्यकलापों से अर्जित आय प्रथमोल्लिखित संविदाकारी राज्य में ही कर-योग्य होगी, यदि दूसरे संविदाकारी राज्य में कार्यकलाप दोनों संविदाकारी राज्यों द्वारा स्वीकृत सांस्कृतिक अथवा खेल-कूद कार्यक्रम के आदान-प्रदान के दायरे में आते हैं और जिसमें उसके राजनैतिक उप-प्रभाग अथवा स्थानीय प्राधिकरण भी शामिल हैं, प्रथमोल्लिखित संविदाकारी राज्य की सार्वजनिक निधियों से पूर्णत: अथवा पर्याप्तत: समर्थित होते हैं ।

4. पैराग्राफ 2 तथा अनुच्छेद 7, 15 और 16 के उपबंधों के होते हुए भी, जहाँ किसी मनोरंजनकर्त्ता अथवा किसी खिलाड़ी द्वारा उसी हैसियत में एक संविदाकारी राज्य में किए गए व्यक्तिगत कार्य-कलापों के संबंध में प्राप्त आय, मनोरंजनकर्त्ता अथवा खिलाड़ी को स्वयं प्राप्त नहीं होती है परन्तु किसी अन्य व्यक्ति को प्राप्त होती है तो वह आय केवल दूसरे संविदाकारी राज्य में ही कर-योग्य होगी, यदि उस दूसरे व्यक्ति के कार्यकलाप दोनों संविदाकारी राज्यों द्वारा स्वीकृत सांस्कृतिक अथवा खेल-कूद कार्यक्रमों के आदान-प्रदान के दायरे में आते हैं, उस दूसरे राज्य की सार्वजनिक निधियों से पूर्णत: अथवा पर्याप्तत: समर्पित किया गया हो जिसमें उसके राजनैतिक उप-प्रभाग अथवा स्थानीय प्राधिकरण भी शामिल हैं ।

अनुच्छेद – 19

सरकारी सेवा के संबंध में पारिश्रमिक तथा पेंशनें
----

1. {क} एक संविदाकारी राज्य अथवा उसके किसी राजनैतिक उप-प्रभाग अथवा उसके किसी स्थानीय प्राधिकरण द्वारा किसी व्यष्टि को उस राज्य अथवा उसके किसी उप-प्रभाग अथवा उसके किसी स्थानीय प्राधिकरण के लिए किसी सरकारी स्वरूप की स्वीकृतियों के निर्वहण में की गई सेवाओं के संबंध में प्रदत्त पेंशन से भिन्न पारिश्रमिक पर कर केवल उस संविदाकारी राज्य में ही लग सकेगा ।

{ख} लेकिन, ऐसे पारिश्रमिक पर कर दूसरे संविदाकारी राज्य में केवल तब लग सकेगा यदि सेवाएं उस दूसरे राज्य में प्रदान की जाती हैं तथा वह व्यष्टि उस राज्य का निवासी है जो :

{i} उस राज्य का राष्ट्रिक है ; अथवा

{ii} मात्र सेवाएं देने के प्रयोजनार्थ उस राज्य का निवासी नहीं बना था ।

2. {क} किसी संविदाकारी राज्य द्वारा अथवा उसके किसी राजनैतिक उप-प्रभाग अथवा किसी स्थानीय प्राधिकरण द्वारा अथवा सृजित किए गए कोष में से किसी व्यष्टि को उसके द्वारा उस राज्य अथवा उप-प्रभाग अथवा प्राधिकरण के निमित्त की गई सेवाओं के लिए प्रदत्त किसी पेंशन पर कर केवल उसी राज्य में लग सकेगा ।

{ख} तथापि, ऐसी पेंशन केवल दूसरे संविदाकारी राज्य में कर-योग्य हो सकेगी यदि व्यष्टि उस दूसरे राज्य का कोई निवासी है तथा उसका एक राष्ट्रिक है ।

3. अनुच्छेद 16, 17 और 18 के उपबंध किसी संविदाकारी राज्य अथवा उसके किसी राजनैतिक उप-प्रभाग अथवा स्थानीय प्राधिकरण द्वारा किए गए कारोबार के सिलसिले में की गई सेवाओं के संबंध में प्राप्त पारिश्रमिक तथा पेंशनों पर लागू होंगे ।

अनुच्छेद - 20

गैर-सरकारी पेंशन तथा वार्षिकी

उल्लिखित पेंशन से भिन्न किसी अन्य पेंशन पर, जो दूसरे संविदाकारी राज्य में आन्तरिक स्रोतों से प्राप्त हुई हो, केवल प्रथमोल्लिखित राज्य में ही कर लगेगा ।

2. "पेंशन " शब्द का अर्थ है पिछली सेवाओं को ध्यान में रखते हुए अथवा सेवाओं के निष्पादन के दौरान चोटग्रस्त होने के लिए प्रतिपूर्ति के रूप में की गई कोई आवधिक अदायगी ।

3. "वार्षिकी " शब्द का अर्थ उस नियत राशि से है जो धन अथवा धन के मूल्य में पर्याप्त तथा पूरे प्रतिफल के लिए अदायगियाँ करने के किसी दायित्व के अधीन जीवन-पर्यन्त अथवा किसी विनिर्दिष्ट या निश्चित समयावधि के दौरान नियत अवधि पर समय-समय पर देय हो ।

अनुच्छेद - 21

विद्यार्थियों और प्रशिक्षुओं द्वारा प्राप्त अदायगियाँ

1. ऐसी अदायगियों पर, जिन पर कोई विद्यार्थी अथवा व्यावसायिक प्रशिक्षु, जो किसी संविदाकारी राज्य का दौरा करने के तुरन्त पहले किसी संविदाकारी राज्य का कोई निवासी है अथवा था और जो मात्र अपनी जीविका, शिक्षा अथवा प्रशिक्षण के प्रयोजनार्थ अपनी शिक्षा अथवा प्रशिक्षण प्राप्त करने हेतु प्रथम-उल्लिखित राज्य में उपस्थित है, उस राज्य में कर नहीं लगाया जा सकेगा बशर्ते कि ऐसी अदायगियाँ उस राज्य के बाहर के स्रोत से उद्भूत होती हों ।

2. किसी विद्यार्थी अथवा व्यावसायिक प्रशिक्षु द्वारा किसी ऐसे संविदाकारी राज्य में, जिसमें वह मात्र अपनी शिक्षा अथवा प्रशिक्षण के प्रयोजनार्थ उपस्थित हैं, किए गए कार्यकलापों के संबंध में प्राप्त आय उस राज्य में कर-योग्य नहीं होगी जब तक कि यह राशि उसके भरण-पोषण, शिक्षा अथवा प्रशिक्षण के लिए आवश्यक राशि से अधिक न हो ।

3. उस अनुच्छेद का लाभ केवल ऐसी अवधि तक के लिए बढ़ाया जाएगा जो शिक्षा अथवा शुरू किए गए प्रशिक्षण को पूरा करने के लिए उचित अथवा साधारणतया अपेक्षित हो परन्तु इस अनुच्छेद का लाभ किसी व्यष्टि को किसीभी हालत में उस दूसरे संविदाकारी राज्य में उसके प्रथमत: पहुंचने की तारीख से लगातार पांच वर्षों से अधिक अवधि के लिए प्राप्त नहीं होगा ।

4. इस अनुच्छेद तथा अनुच्छेद 22 के प्रयोजनार्थ, किसी व्यष्टि को एक संविदाकारी राज्य का निवासी माना जाएगा यदि वह उस संविदाकारी राज्य का उस " पूर्ववर्ती वर्ष " अथवा "आय वर्ष"में, जैसी भी स्थिति हो, जिसमें वह दूसरे संविदाकारी राज्य का दौरा करता है अथवा तत्काल पूर्ववर्ती "पिछले वर्ष " अथवा "आय वर्ष " में निवासी रहा हो ।

अनुच्छेद -22

प्राध्यापकों, अध्यापकों तथा शोध-छात्रों द्वारा

प्राप्त अदायगियां
----

1. किसी प्राध्यापक अथवा अध्यापक को, जो दूसरे संविदा-कारी राज्य के किसी विश्वविद्यालय, महाविद्यालय, विद्यालय अथवा दूसरी मान्यताप्राप्त संस्था में अध्यापन कार्य अथवा शोध कार्य करने अथवा दोनों के प्रयोजनार्थ दूसरे संविदाकारी राज्य का दौरा करने से तत्काल पूर्व संविदाकारी राज्यों में से एक राज्य का निवासी है अथवा था, ऐसे अध्यापन अथवा शोध कार्य के लिए किसी भी पारिश्रमिक पर उस दूसरे राज्य में उसके पहुंचने की तारीख से अधिक से अधिक 2 वर्ष की अवधि के लिए कर से छूट प्राप्त होगी ।

2. यह अनुच्छेद शोध कार्य से प्राप्त आय पर लागू नहीं होगा यदि ऐसा शोध कार्य जन-हित में नहीं है बल्कि मुख्यत: किसी विशिष्ट व्यक्ति अथवा व्यक्तियों के निजी लाभ के लिये है ।

3. पैराग्राफ । के प्रयोजनार्थ, " मान्यता प्राप्त संस्था " का अर्थ ऐसी संस्था से है जिसे संबंधित संविदाकारी राज्य के सक्षम प्राधिकारी द्वारा इस संबंध में अनुमोदित किया गया हो ।

अनुच्छेद - 23

अन्य आय
----

1. पैराग्राफ 2 के उपबंधों के अधीन रहते हुए भी एक संविदा- कारी राज्य के किसी निवासी की आय की वे मदें, जहां-कहीं उद्भूत होती हों, जिन पर इस करार के पूर्वोक्त अनुच्छेदों में विशेष रूप से विचार नहीं किया गया है, केवल उस संविदाकारी राज्य में कर लगने योग्य होंगी ।

2. पैराग्राफ । के उपबंध, अनुच्छेद 6 के पैराग्राफ 2 में यथा- परिभाषित अचल सम्पत्ति से प्राप्त होने वाली आय से भिन्न आय पर लागू नहीं होंगी, यदि ऐसी आय का प्राप्तकर्त्ता, एक संविदाकारी राज्य का निवासी होने के कारण, दूसरे संविदाकारी राज्य में स्थित किसी स्थायी संस्थापन के माध्यम से उसमें कारबार करता है अथवा उस दूसरे संविदाकारी राज्य में स्थित निश्चित स्थान से स्वतंत्र व्यक्तिगत सेवाएं निष्पादित करता है और जिस अधिकार अथवा सम्पत्ति के संबंध में आय अदा की जाती है वह ऐसे स्थायी संस्थापन अथवा निश्चित स्थान से प्रभावी रूप से संबद्ध है । ऐसे मामले में, अनुच्छेद 7 अथवा अनुच्छेद 15 के उपबंध, जैसी भी स्थिति हो, लागू होंगे ।

3. पैराग्राफ । तथा 2 के उपबंधों के होते हुए भी, एक संविदाकारी राज्य के किसी निवासी की आय की उन मदों पर, जिनका इस करार के पूर्ववर्ती अनुच्छेदों में विचार नहीं किया गया है और जो दूसरे संविदाकारी राज्य में उद्भूत होती है, कर उस दूसरे राज्य में लगाया जा सकेगा ।

4. संविदाकारी राज्यों के सक्षम प्राधिकारी पूर्ववर्ती पैराग्राफों के अनुसार किसी करार के होने के प्रयोजन के लिए प्रत्यक्ष रूप से एक-दूसरे के साथ सम्पर्क स्थापित कर सकते हैं । सक्षम प्राधिकारी विचार-विमर्श के द्वारा इस अनुच्छेद में दिए गए पारस्परिक करार प्रक्रिया के कार्यान्वयन हेतु, समुचित द्विपक्षीय प्रक्रियाओं, शर्तों, पद्धतियों और कार्य-पद्धतियों का विकास करेंगे ।

अनुच्छेद - 24

दोहरे कराधान की समाप्ति

1. दोनों ही संविदाकारी राज्यों में लागू कानून अपने-अपने संविदाकारी राज्यों में आय के कराधान को शासित करते रहेंगे सिवाय उसके कि जहां इस करार में उनके प्रतिकूल कोई उपबंध बनाए जाते हैं ।

2. दोनों संविदाकारी राज्यों में दोहरे कराधान का परिहार निम्नलिखित तरीके से किया जाएगा :

    {क} जहां एक संविदाकारी राज्य का कोई निवासी ऐसी आय प्राप्त करता है जिस पर, इस करार के उपबंधों के अनुसार, दूसरे संविदाकारी राज्य में कर लगाया जा सकेगा, वहां प्रथमोल्लिखित राज्य, इस पैराग्राफ के उप-पैरा {ख} के उपबंधों

के अधीन रहते हुए, ऐसी आय को कर से छूट दे सकता है परन्तु उस व्यक्ति की शेष आय पर कर की संगणना करने में कर की वह दर लागू कर सकता है जो उस स्थिति में लागू होती यदि छूट-प्राप्त आय पर इस प्रकार की छूट नहीं दी गई होती ।

(ख) दोनों ही संविदाकारी राज्य अपने निवासियों पर कर लगाते समय, कर के उस आधार में जिस पर इस प्रकार के कर लगाए जाते हैं, आय की उन मदों को शामिल कर सकेंगे जिन पर इस करार के अनुच्छेद 11, 12 और 13 के उपबंधों के अनुसार दूसरे राज्य में भी कर लगाया जा सकता है लेकिन ऐसे आधार पर संगणित कर की राशि में से दूसरे संविदाकारी राज्य में अदा की गई कर की राशि के बराबर की कटौती देंगे । तथापि, ऐसी कटौती प्रथमोल्लिखित राज्य द्वारा लगाए जाने योग्य कर के उस भाग से अधिक नहीं होगी, जैसाकि कटौती मंजूर करने से पहले संगणित किया गया हो, जो उस आय के अनुकूल हो जिस पर इस करार के अनुच्छेद 11, 12, और 13 के उपबंधों के अनुसार दूसरे राज्य में कर लगाया जा सकेगा ।

3. पैराग्राफ 2 के उप-पैराग्राफ (ख) के प्रयोजनार्थ "दूसरे संविदा- कारी राज्य में अदा किया गया कर " पदावली में ऐसी कोई भी रकम शामिल की गई मानी जाएगी जो दूसरे संविदाकारी राज्य में प्रवृत्त आय के कराधान से संबंधित कानूनों के अंतर्गत कर लगने योग्य आय की संगणना करने में अनुमत कटौती अथवा छूट अथवा कर की कटौती अथवा अन्यथा रूप में किसी राहत के नहीं होने की स्थिति में देय होगी ।

अनुच्छेद- 25

सम-व्यवहार
----

1.   एक संविदाकारी राज्य के राष्ट्रिकों पर दूसरे संविदा-
कारी राज्य में ऐसे किसी कराधान अथवा तत्संबंधी ऐसी कोई
अपेक्षा लागू नहीं की जाएगी जो उस कराधान से और उन संबंधित
अपेक्षाओं से भिन्न अथवा अधिक भारपूर्ण हो, जो उस दूसरे राज्य
के राष्ट्रिकों पर वैसी ही परिस्थितियों में अथवा वैसी ही शर्तों
के अधीन लागू होती है अथवा हो सकती है ।

2.   एक संविदाकारी राज्य के किसी उद्यम के दूसरे संविदा-
कारी राज्य में स्थित किसी स्थायी संस्थापन पर उस दूसरे
राज्य में ऐसा कोई कर नहीं लगाया जाएगा जो उस दूसरे राज्य
में उन्हीं परिस्थितियों में तथा वैसी ही शर्तों के अधीन उसी
तरह के कार्यकलाप करने वाले उद्यमों पर लगाये जाने वाले कराधान
से अपेक्षाकृत कम अनुकूल हो ।

3.   इस अनुच्छेद में निहित किसी भी बात का यह अर्थ नहीं
लगाया जाएगा कि वह एक संविदाकारी राज्य को, कराधान
के प्रयोजनों के लिए, उस राज्य के अनिवासी व्यष्टियों को कोई
ऐसी वैयक्तिक छूटें, राहतें, घटौतियां तथा कटौतियां प्रदान करने
के लिए बाध्य करता है जो कानून द्वारा उस राज्य के निवासी
व्यष्टियों को ही उपलब्ध हैं ।

4.   एक संविदाकारी राज्य के उद्यमों पर, जिनकी पूंजी पूर्णतः
अथवा अंशतः दूसरे संविदाकारी राज्य के एक अथवा एक से अधिक
निवासियों के, प्रत्यक्षतः अथवा अप्रत्यक्षतः स्वामित्व अथवा नियंत्रण
में है, प्रथमोल्लिखित संविदाकारी राज्य में कोई ऐसा कराधान
अथवा तत्संबंधी कोई ऐसी अपेक्षा लागू नहीं की जाएगी जो उस
कराधान और तत्संबंधी अपेक्षाओं से भिन्न अथवा अधिक भारपूर्ण
हो, जो उस प्रथमोल्लिखित राज्य के अन्य वैसे ही उद्यमों पर

उन्हीं परिस्थितियों तथा वैसी ही शर्तों पर लागू होती है अथवा हो सकती है ।

5. इस अनुच्छेद में, " कराधान " पद का आशय उन करों से है जो इस करार के विषय हैं ।

6. उन मामलों को छोड़कर जिनमें इस करार के अनुच्छेद-11, अनुच्छेद-12 के पैराग्राफ 7 अथवा अनुच्छेद 13 के पैराग्राफ 7 के उपबंध लागू होते हैं एक संविदाकारी राज्य के किसी उद्यम द्वारा दूसरे संविदाकारी राज्य के किसी निवासी को अदा किया गया ब्याज, रायल्टियां और अन्य भुगतान, ऐसे उद्यम के कर लगने योग्य लाभों का निर्धारण करने के प्रयोजनार्थ उन्हीं समान शर्तों के अधीन कटौती पाने योग्य होंगे, जैसे कि वे प्रथमोल्लिखित राज्य के किसी निवासी को अदा किए गए थे । इसी प्रकार, एक संविदाकारी राज्य के किसी उद्यम द्वारा दूसरे संविदाकारी राज्य के किसी निवासी को दिए गए कोई ऋण, ऐसे उद्यम की कर लगने योग्य पूंजी के निर्धारण के प्रयोजनार्थ उन्हीं समान शर्तों के अधीन कटौती पाने योग्य होंगे जैसे कि वे प्रथमोल्लिखित राज्य के किसी निवासी को अनुबंधित किए गए थे ।

7. दोनों संविदाकारी राज्यों के स्वदेशी कानूनों के अंतर्गत कराधान प्रयोजनों के लिए उपलब्ध छूटों, राहतों, कटौतियों, घटौतियों और मोक पर इस करार के किसी उपबंध से प्रतिकूल प्रभाव नहीं पड़ेगा ।

अनुच्छेद - 26

पारस्परिक करार कार्यविधि

1. जहां एक संविदाकारी राज्य का कोई निवासी यह समझता है कि एक अथवा दोनों संविदाकारी राज्यों के कार्यों के कारण उस पर जो कर लगाया जाता है अथवा लगाया जाएगा

वह इस करार के अनुरूप नहीं है, तो वह इन राज्यों के राष्ट्रीय कानूनों द्वारा उपबंधित उपचारों के होते हुए भी अपना मामला उस संविदाकारी राज्य के सक्षम प्राधिकारी को प्रस्तुत कर सकता है जिसका कि वह निवासी है । यह मामला, उस कार्यवाही के नोटिस की प्राप्ति की तारीख से तीन वर्ष के भीतर अक्षय प्रस्तुत किया जाना चाहिए जिसके कारण ऐसा कर लगाया गया हो जो इस करार के अनुरूप नहीं हो ;

2. यदि सक्षम प्राधिकारी को आपत्ति उचित लगे और यदि वह स्वयं किसी उपयुक्त हल पर पहुंचने में असमर्थ हो तो वह ऐसे कराधान के परिहार की दृष्टि से, जो इस करार के अनुरूप नहीं है, दूसरे संविदाकारी राज्य के सक्षम प्राधिकारी की परस्पर सहमति द्वारा उस मामले को हल करने का प्रयास करेगा । जो भी करार हो गया हो, उसे संविदाकारी राज्यों के कानूनों में निहित किसी भी समय-सीमा के होने के बावजूद भी कार्यान्वित किया जाएगा ।

3. इस करार की व्याख्या करने अथवा इसे लागू करने में यदि कोई कठिनाइयां अथवा शंकाएं उत्पन्न हों तो संविदाकारी राज्यों के सक्षम प्राधिकारी उन्हें पारस्परिक सहमति से हल करने का प्रयास करेंगे । वे ऐसे मामलों में दोहरे कराधान को दूर करने के लिए परस्पर परामर्श कर सकेंगे जिनकी इस करार में व्यवस्था नहीं की गई है ।

4. पूर्वोक्त पैराग्राफों के अभिप्राय के अन्तर्गत सहमति के प्रयोजनार्थ संविदाकारी राज्यों के सक्षम प्राधिकारी एक-दूसरे के साथ सीधे पत्र-व्यवहार कर सकते हैं । जब किसी समझौते पर पहुंचने के लिए विचारों का मौखिक आदान-प्रदान करना उपयुक्त प्रतीत होता हो, वहां ऐसा आदान-प्रदान एक आयोग के जरिए किया जा सकता है जिसमें संविदाकारी राज्य के सक्षम प्राधिकारियों के प्रतिनिधि हों ।

अनुच्छेद - 27

सूचना का आदान-प्रदान

।• संविदाकारी राज्यों के सक्षम प्राधिकारी ऐसी सूचना का
§ जिसमें दस्तावेज भी शामिल हैं § आदान-प्रदान करेंगे जो इस करार
के उपबंधों के अथवा संविदाकारी राज्यों के उन करों से संबंधित
आन्तरिक कानूनों के उपबंधों को कार्यान्वित करने के लिए आवश्यक
हैं, जो इस करार के अंतर्गत आते हैं, जहाँ तक कि उनके अधीन
विद्यमान कराधान-व्यवस्था विशेष रूप से ऐसे करों की जालसाज़ी
अथवा अपवंचन को रोकने के लिए करार के प्रतिकूल नहीं हो । किसी
संविदाकारी राज्य द्वारा प्राप्त की गई कोई भी सूचना उसी प्रकार
गुप्त मानी जाएगी जिस प्रकार उस राज्य के आन्तरिक कानूनों के
अन्तर्गत प्राप्त की गई सूचना मानी जाती है । लेकिन, यदि उक्त
सूचना को, सूचना भेजने वाले राज्य में मूल रूप से गुप्त समझा जाता
है तो उसे केवल ऐसे व्यक्तियों अथवा प्राधिकारियों § जिनमें न्यायालय
और प्रशासनिक निकाय भी शामिल हैं § को प्रकट किया जाएगा, जो
उन करों के निर्धारण अथवा उनकी वसूली, उनके प्रवर्तन अथवा अभि-
योजन के संबंध में अथवा उनसे संबंधित अपीलों के निर्धारण में अन्तर्ग्रस्त
हों, जो इस करार के विषय हैं । ऐसे व्यक्ति अथवा प्राधिकारी
उक्त सूचना का उपयोग केवल ऐसे ही प्रयोजनों के लिए करेंगे परन्तु वे
उक्त सूचना को सार्वजनिक तौर पर न्यायालय की कार्यवाही अथवा
न्यायिक निर्णयों में प्रकट कर सकेंगे । सक्षम प्राधिकारी, विचार-विमर्श
के माध्यम से उन मामलों से संबंधित समुचित शर्तों, पद्धतियों और
तकनीकों को विकसित करेंगे, जिनके बारे में सूचना का ऐसा आदान-
प्रदान किया जाएगा, जिसमें, जहाँ-कहीं उपयुक्त हो, कर के परिहार
के संबंध में सूचना का आदान-प्रदान भी शामिल है ।

2. सूचना अथवा दस्तावेजों का आदान-प्रदान या तो नेमी आधार पर अथवा किन्हीं विशिष्ट मामलों में अनुरोध मिलने पर अथवा दोनों तरह से किया जाएगा । संविदाकारी राज्यों के सक्षम प्राधिकारी समय-समय पर परस्पर यह तय करेंगे कि किस-किस सूचना का या किन-किन दस्तावेजों का नेमी आधार पर आदान-प्रदान किया जाएगा ।

3. किसी भी स्थिति में, पैराग्राफ । के उपबंधों का यह अर्थ नहीं लगाया जाएगा कि वे एक संविदाकारी राज्यको निम्नलिखित कार्य करने के लिए बाध्य करते हैं :-

{क} उस संविदाकारी राज्य अथवा दूसरे संविदाकारी राज्य के कानूनों अथवा प्रशासनिक परिपाटी से हट कर कोई प्रशासनिक उपाय करना ;

{ख} ऐसी सूचना अथवा दस्तावेज सप्लाई करना जो उस राज्य अथवा दूसरे संविदाकारी राज्य के कानूनों के अन्तर्गत अथवा सामान्य प्रशासनिक प्रक्रिया के दौरान प्राप्त नहीं हो सकते ;

{ग} कोई ऐसी सूचना अथवा दस्तावेज सप्लाई करना जिससे कोई व्यापारिक, व्यावसायिक, औद्योगिक,वाणिज्यिक अथवा वृत्तिक भेद खुल जाएगा अथवा कोई व्यापारिक प्रक्रिया अथवा सूचना, जिसको प्रकट करना सार्वजनिक नीति के विपरीत होगा ।

अनुच्छेद - 28

कर-वसूली में सहयोग

1. संविदाकारी राज्य इस करार से संबंधित करों की वसूली में उन मामलों में एक-दूसरे राज्य की मदद करने और समर्थन देने का जिम्मा लेते हैं, जहां अनुरोधकर्ता राज्य के कानूनों के अनुसार, कर

निश्चित रूप से देय हैं ।

2. वसूली के प्रवर्तन के किसी अनुरोध के मामले में किसी भी संविदाकारी राज्य के कर संबंधी दावों को, जिनका अन्तिम रूप से पता लगाया जा चुका है, उस दूसरे संविदाकारी राज्य द्वारा प्रवर्तन के लिए स्वीकार किया जाएगा जिससे अनुरोध किया गया है, और उनकी वसूली उस राज्य के करों के प्रवर्तन और उनकी वसूली हेतु लागू कानूनों के अनुसार की जाएगी ।

3. भारतीय कर के मामले में अनुरोधपत्र को केन्द्रीय प्रत्यक्ष कर बोर्ड, राजस्व विभाग, वित्त मंत्रालय ,भारत द्वारा वित्त मंत्री पोलैंड अथवा उनके प्राधिकृत प्रतिनिधि के पास भेजा जाएगा और उसके साथ ऐसा प्रमाणपत्र संलग्न होगा जैसा कि भारत के कानूनों में यह स्थापित करने के लिए अपेक्षित है कि करों का अन्तिम रूप से निर्धारण कर लिया गया है और वे करदाता द्वारा देय हैं ।

4. पोलैंड कर के मामले में, अनुरोधपत्र वित्त मंत्री, पोलैंड अथवा उनके प्राधिकृत प्रतिनिधि द्वारा केन्द्रीय प्रत्यक्ष कर बोर्ड, राजस्व विभाग, वित्त मंत्रालय, भारत के पास भेजा जाएगा और उसके साथ ऐसा प्रमाणपत्र संलग्न होगा कि पोलैंड के कानूनों में यह स्थापित करने के लिए अपेक्षित है कि करों का अन्तिम रूप से निर्धारण कर लिया गया है और वे करदाता द्वारा देय हैं ।

5. जहां कर संबंधी दावा इस संबंध में आपत्ति किए जाने अथवा किसी अन्य कार्यवाही के कारण निर्णय नहीं बना हो, वहां एक संविदाकारी राज्य अपने राजस्व को बचाने के लिए दूसरे संविदा- कारी राज्य से उसके बारे में ऐसे अंतरिम उपाय करने का अनुरोध कर सकता है जो उस दूसरे संविदाकारी राज्य के कानूनों के अंतर्गत इस तरह देय हैं ।

6. किसी करदाता से प्राप्तव्य करों की वसूली में सहायता के लिए अनुरोध तभी किया जाएगा जब अनुरोध करने वाले संविदाकारी राज्य में उस करदाता से कर वसूल करने के लिए उसकी पर्याप्त परिसम्पत्तियाँ उपलब्ध न हों ।

7. जिस संविदाकारी राज्य में इस अनुच्छेद के पैराग्राफ 1, 2 और 5 के अनुसरण में कर वसूल किया जाता है, वह राज्य इस प्रकार वसूल की गई रकम को तत्पश्चात तुरन्त दूसरे संविदाकारी राज्य को भेजेगा, जिसमे अनुरोध किया था ।

अनुच्छेद - 29

राजनयिक तथा कौंसुली कार्यकलाप

इस करार में निहित किसी व्यवस्था का, अन्तरराष्ट्रीय विधि के सामान्य नियमों के अंतर्गत अथवा विशेष करारों के उपबंधों के अंतर्गत राजनयिक अथवा कौंसुली अधिकारियों के वित्तीय विशेषा-धिकारों पर कोई प्रभाव नहीं पड़ेगा ।

अनुच्छेद - 30

प्रवर्त्तन

प्रत्येक संविदाकारी राज्य दूसरे संविदाकारी राज्य को इस करार को प्रवर्त्तित करने के लिए उसके कानून के अधीन अपेक्षित कार्यविधियों के पूरा हो जाने के बारे में अधिसूचित करेगा । यह करार, इन अधिसूचनाओं में से बाद वाली अधिसूचना की तारीख को लागू होगा और उसके बाद :

    {क} भारत में, उस केलेण्डर वर्ष के जिसमें बाद वाली अधिसूचना दी गई है, अगले अनुवर्ती वर्ष के, अप्रेल माह के प्रथम दिन को अथवा उसके पश्चात आरम्भ

होने वाले किसी पूर्ववर्ती वर्ष में उद्भूत होने वाली आय के संबंध में ;

{ख} पोलैंड में, उस केलेण्डर वर्ष के, जिसमें बाद वाली अधिसूचना दी गई है, अगले अनुवर्ती वर्ष के जनवरी माह के प्रथम दिन को अथवा उसके पश्चात् आरम्भ होने वाले किसी वर्ष में उद्भूत हुई आय के सम्बंध में ।

अनुच्छेद - 31

समाप्ति

यह करार अनिश्चित समय तक लागू रहेगा परन्तु दोनों में से कोई भी संविदाकारी राज्य इस करार के लागू होने की तारीख से पाँच वर्ष की अवधि पूरी हो जाने के पश्चात् आरम्भ होने वाले किसी भी केलेण्डर वर्ष के 30 जून को अथवा उसके पूर्व, राजनयिक माध्यमों से, दूसरे संविदाकारी राज्य को समाप्ति का लिखित नोटिस दे सकता है और ऐसी स्थिति में यह करार :

{क} भारत में, जिस केलेण्डर वर्ष में नोटिस दिया जाता है उसके अगले परवर्ती वर्ष के अप्रेल के प्रथम दिन को अथवा उसके पश्चात् आरम्भ होने वाले किसी पूर्ववर्ती वर्ष में उद्भूत होने वाली आय के संबंध में ;

{ख} पोलैंड में, जिस केलेण्डर वर्ष में समाप्ति का नोटिस दिया जाता है उसके अगले परवर्ती वर्ष के जनवरी के प्रथम दिन को अथवा उसके पश्चात् आरम्भ होने वाले किसी आय वर्ष में उद्भूत होने वाली आय के संबंध में, निष्प्रभावी हो जाएगा ।

जिसके साक्ष्य में, इसके लिए विधिवत प्राधिकृत अधोहस्ताक्षरियों ने इस करार पर हस्ताक्षर किए हैं ।

.........वारसी.............में वर्ष .... एक हजार नौ सो ....नवासी...... के ....जून........माह के ....अकोरसवॅ........दिन को पोलिश, हिन्दी और अंग्रेजी भाषाओं में दो-दो प्रतियों में सम्पन्न किया गया, जिसके सभी पाठ समान्तः प्रामाणिक हैं । पोलिश और हिन्दी पाठों में भिन्नता होने की स्थिति में अंग्रेजी पाठ मान्य होगा ।

पोलैण्ड लोक गणराज्य
की सरकार की ओर से

भारत गणराज्य की
सरकार की ओर से

[POLISH TEXT – TEXTE POLONAIS]

UMOWA

między Rządem Polskiej Rzeczypospolitej Ludowej

a

Rządem Republiki Indii

w sprawie

unikania podwójnego opodatkowania i zapobiegania uchylaniu się od opodatkowania w zakresie podatków od dochodu

Rząd Polskiej Rzeczypospolitej Ludowej i Rząd Republiki Indii, powodowane chęcią dalszego rozwijania i ułatwiania wzajemnych stosunków gospodarczych pomiędzy dwoma państwami i postanawiając zawrzeć Umowę w sprawie unikania podwójnego opodatkowania i zapobiegania uchylaniu się od opodatkowania w zakresie podatków od dochodu, uzgodniły co następuje:

Artykuł 1

Zakres podmiotowy

Niniejsza Umowa dotyczy osób, które mają miejsce zamieszkania lub siedzibę w jednym lub w obu Umawiających się Państwach.

Artykuł 2

Podatki, których dotyczy Umowa

1. Do podatków, których dotyczy Umowa należą:

a/ w Polsce:

i/ podatek dochodowy

ii/ podatek od wynagrodzeń

iii/ podatek wyrównawczy

iv/ podatek rolny

/zwane dalej "podatkami polskimi"/

b/ w Indiach:

  i/ podatek dochodowy włączając wszelkie dopłaty do nie-
     go nakładane na podstawie ustawy o podatku dochodo-
     wym, 1961,

  ii/ dopłata nakładana na podstawie ustawy o dodatkowym
      podatku od spółek, 1964,

  /zwane dalej "podatkami indyjskimi"/.

2. Niniejsza Umowa będzie także stosowana do wszystkich podatków takiego samego lub zasadniczo podobnego rodzaju, które
   będą wprowadzane przez którekolwiek z Umawiających się
   Państw obok lub w miejsce podatków, o których mowa w ustępie 1, po podpisaniu niniejszej Umowy.
   Właściwe władze Umawiających się Państw będą informowały
   się wzajemnie, o każdych zasadniczych zmianach, jakie za-
   szły w ich odpowiednich przepisach podatkowych, będących
   przedmiotem niniejszej Umowy.

Artykuł 3

Ogólne definicje

1. W rozumieniu niniejszej Umowy, jeżeli z jej treści nie wynika
   inaczej:

  a/ określenie "Polska" oznacza Polską Rzeczypospolitą Ludową
     i użyte w znaczeniu geograficznym oznacza terytorium Pol-
     skiej Rzeczypospolitej Ludowej i każdy obszar morski przy-
     legły do wód terytorialnych Polskiej Rzeczypospolitej Ludo-
     wej nad którym na podstawie prawa Polskiej Rzeczypospoli-
     tej Ludowej i zgodnie z prawem międzynarodowym Polska
     Rzeczpospolita Ludowa posiada suwerenność lub suweren-
     ne i wyłączne prawa;

b/ określenie "Indie" oznacza Republikę Indii i użyte w
znaczeniu geograficznym oznacza terytorium Republiki
Indii i każdy obszar morski przyległy do wód terytorial-
nych Republiki Indii nad którym na podstawie prawa Republiki Indii i zgodnie z prawem międzynarodowym Republi-
ka Indii posiada suwerenność lub suwerenne i wyłączne
prawa;

c/ określenia "Umawiające się Państwo" i "drugie Umawiające się Państwo" oznaczają odpowiednio Polskę lub
Indie;

d/ określenie "podatek" oznacza odpowiednio podatek polski
lub indyjski, lecz nie obejmuje żadnej kwoty, która jest
płatna w związku z bankructwem lub zaniedbaniem związanym z podatkami, których dotyczy niniejsza Umowa lub
która stanowi opłatę karną nałożoną w związku z tymi podatkami;

e/ określenie "osoba" obejmuje osobę fizyczną, spółkę i każdą jednostkę, która podlega opodatkowaniu zgodnie z prawem podatkowym obowiązującym w Umawiających się
Państwach;

f/ określenie "spółka" oznacza osobę prawną lub jakąkolwiek
jednostkę, którą traktuje się jak spółkę lub osobę prawną
zgodnie z prawem podatkowym obowiązującym w Umawiających się Państwach;

g/ określenia "przedsiębiorstwo Umawiającego się Państwa"
i "przedsiębiorstwo drugiego Umawiającego się Państwa"
oznaczają odpowiednio przedsiębiorstwo, prowadzone
przez osobę mającą miejsce zamieszkania lub siedzibę
w jednym Umawiającym się Państwie i przedsiębiorstwo
prowadzone przez osobę mającą miejsce zamieszkania
lub siedzibę w drugim Umawiającym się Państwie;

h/ określenie "właściwa władza" oznacza w przypadku Polski Ministra Finansów lub jego upoważnionego przedstawiciela; i w przypadku Indii Rząd Centralny - Ministerstwo Finansów /Departament Dochodów Państwa/ lub ich upoważnionego przedstawiciela;

i/ określenie "obywatel" oznacza wszelkie osoby fizyczne posiadające obywatelstwo Umawiającego się Państwa oraz wszelkie osoby prawne, spółki jawne lub stowarzyszenia utworzone na podstawie prawa obowiązującego w Umawiającym się Państwie;

j/ określenie "komunikacja międzynarodowa" oznacza wszelki transport wykonywany przez statek lub samolot będący w użytkowaniu przedsiębiorstwa Umawiającego się Państwa, z wyjątkiem przypadków gdy statek lub samolot jest użytkowany tylko w ruchu między miejscami położonymi w drugim Umawiającym się Państwie.

2. Przy stosowaniu niniejszej Umowy przez Umawiające się Państwo, jeżeli z treści przepisu nie wynika inaczej, jakiekolwiek określenie, niezdefiniowane w niej odmiennie, będzie miało takie znaczenie, jakie ma według prawa tego Państwa w zakresie podatków, których dotyczy Umowa.

Artykuł 4

Miejsce zamieszkania dla celów podatkowych

1. W rozumieniu niniejszej Umowy określenie "osoba mająca miejsce zamieszkania lub siedzibę w Umawiającym się Państwie" oznacza każdą osobę, która zgodnie z prawem tego Państwa podlega tam opodatkowaniu z uwagi na jej miejsce zamieszkania, miejsce stałego pobytu, siedzibę zarządu, albo gdy stosuje się wobec niej inne kryteria o podobnym charakterze.

2. Jeżeli stosownie do postanowień ustępu 1 osoba fizyczna ma
   miejsce zamieszkania w obu Umawiających się Państwach,
   to jej status będzie określony według następujących zasad:

   a/ osobę uważa się za mającą miejsce zamieszkania w tym
      Państwie, w którym ma ona stałe miejsce zamieszkania.
      Jeżeli ma ona stałe miejsce zamieszkania w obu Umawiają-
      cych się Państwach, wówczas uważa się ją za mającą miej-
      sce zamieszkania w tym Państwie, z którym ma ona ściślej-
      sze powiązania osobiste i gospodarcze /ośrodek interesów
      życiowych/;

   b/ jeżeli nie można ustalić, w którym Państwie osoba ma ośro-
      dek interesów życiowych, albo jeżeli nie posiada ona stałe-
      go miejsca zamieszkania w żadnym z Umawiających się
      Państw, to uważa się ją za mającą miejsce zamieszkania
      w tym Państwie, w którym zazwyczaj przebywa;

   c/ jeżeli przebywa ona zazwyczaj w obydwu Państwach lub nie
      przebywa zazwyczaj w żadnym z nich, to będzie ona uważa-
      na za mającą miejsce zamieszkania w tym Państwie, któ-
      rego jest obywatelem;

   d/ jeżeli miejsca zamieszkania tej osoby nie można ustalić
      zgodnie z postanowieniami liter a, b lub c, właściwe władze
      Umawiających się Państw rozstrzygną tę sprawę w drodze
      wzajemnego porozumienia.

3. Jeżeli stosownie do postanowień ustępu 1, osoba nie będąca osobą fizyczną ma siedzibę w obu Umawiających się Państwach,
   uważa się ją za mającą siedzibę w tym Państwie, w którym
   znajduje się miejsce jej rzeczywistego zarządu.

Artykuł 5

Zakład

1. W rozumieniu niniejszej Umowy określenie "zakład" oznacza stałą placówkę, poprzez którą całkowicie lub częściowo prowadzona jest działalność przedsiębiorstwa.

2. Określenie "zakład" obejmuje w szczególności:

a/ miejsce zarządu;

b/ filię;

c/ biuro;

d/ zakład fabryczny;

e/ warsztat;

f/ kopalnię lub źródło ropy naftowej lub gazu, kamieniołom, albo inne miejsce wydobywania bogactw naturalnych;

g/ magazyn, w stosunku do osoby zajmującej się dostarczaniem innym usług magazynowych;

h/ gospodarstwo rolne, plantację lub inne miejsce na którym prowadzona jest działalność rolna, leśna, ogrodnicza lub inna z nią związana;

i/ lokale wykorzystywane jako punkty sprzedaży, używane dla otrzymywania lub uzyskiwania zamówień;

j/ urządzenie lub budowlę wykorzystywane do poszukiwań bogactw naturalnych;

k/ plac budowy lub budowę, urządzenie lub przedsięwzięcie montażowe albo działalność nadzorczą związaną z nimi, jeżeli okres ich prowadzenia przekracza 6 miesięcy.

3. Bez względu na postanowienia niniejszego artykułu określenie "zakład" nie obejmuje:

a/ użytkowania urządzeń wyłącznie w celu składowania lub wystawiania dóbr albo towarów należących do przedsiębiorstwa;

b/ utrzymywania zapasów dóbr albo towarów, należących do przedsiębiorstwa, wyłącznie w celu składowania lub wystawiania;

c/ utrzymywania zapasów dóbr albo towarów, należących do przedsiębiorstwa, wyłącznie w celu przerobu przez inne przedsiębiorstwo;

d/ utrzymywania stałej placówki wyłącznie w celu zakupu dóbr lub towarów albo w celu uzyskiwania informacji dla przedsiębiorstwa;

e/ utrzymywania stałej placówki, wyłącznie w celu reklamowym, dostarczania informacji, prowadzenia badań naukowych lub wykonywania podobnych działalności o charakterze przygotowawczym albo pomocniczym dla przedsiębiorstwa.

Jednakże, postanowienia liter a - e, nie będą miały zastosowania, jeżeli przedsiębiorstwo utrzymuje jakąkolwiek inną stałą placówkę w drugim Umawiającym się Państwie dla jakichkolwiek celów innych niż cele wymienione w postanowieniach zawartych w powyższych literach.

4. Bez względu na postanowienia ustępów 1 i 2, jeżeli osoba - inna aniżeli niezależny przedstawiciel, do którego mają zastosowanie postanowienia ustępu 5 - działa w Umawiającym się Państwie w imieniu przedsiębiorstwa drugiego Umawiającego się Państwa, to wówczas przedsiębiorstwo będzie uważane za posiadające zakład w pierwszym wymienionym Państwie jeżeli:

a/ posiada ona i zwyczajowo wykonuje w tym Państwie uprawnienie do zawierania kontraktów w imieniu tego przedsiębiorstwa, chyba, że jego działalność jest ograniczona do zakupu dóbr lub towarów dla przedsiębiorstwa; lub

b/ nie posiada ona takiego uprawnienia ale zwyczajowo prowadzi w pierwszym wymienionym Państwie skład dóbr lub towarów z którego regularnie dostarcza dobra lub towary w imieniu tego przedsiębiorstwa.

5. Nie będzie uważać się, że przedsiębiorstwo Umawiającego
   się Państwa posiada zakład w drugim Umawiającym się Państwie tylko z tego powodu, że wykonuje ono w tym drugim
   Państwie czynności przez maklera, komisanta albo każdego
   innego niezależnego przedstawiciela, jeżeli te osoby działają
   w ramach swojej zwykłej działalności. Jednakże, jeżeli działalność takiego niezależnego przedstawiciela jest prowadzona
   w całości lub prawie w całości w imieniu tego samego przedsiębiorstwa lub w imieniu tego przedsiębiorstwa i innych
   przedsiębiorstw kontrolujących, kontrolowanych przez lub
   znajdujących się pod tą samą kontrolą jak to przedsiębiorstwo,
   nie będzie on traktowany jako niezależny przedstawiciel w rozumieniu tego ustępu.

6. Fakt, że spółka mająca siedzibę w Umawiającym się Państwie
   kontroluje lub jest kontrolowana przez spółkę, która ma siedzibę w drugim Umawiającym się Państwie, albo która prowadzi działalność w tym drugim Państwie /przez posiadany tam
   zakład albo w inny sposób/, nie wystarcza, aby którąkolwiek
   z tych spółek uważać za zakład drugiej spółki.

Artykuł 6

Dochód z nieruchomości

1. Dochód uzyskiwany przez osobę mającą miejsce zamieszkania
   lub siedzibę w Umawiającym się Państwie z majątku nieruchomego /włączając dochody z eksploatacji gospodarstw rolnych i leśnych/, położonego w drugim Umawiającym się Państwie, może być opodatkowany w tym drugim Państwie.

2. Określenie "majątek nieruchomy" ma znaczenie zgodne z prawem Umawiającego się Państwa, w którym majątek ten jest
   położony. Określenie to obejmuje w każdym przypadku majątek przynależny do majątku nieruchomego, żywy i martwy
   inwentarz gospodarstw rolnych i leśnych, prawa, do których
   mają zastosowanie ogólne przepisy, dotyczące majątku nieru-

chomego, użytkowanie nieruchomości i prawa do zmiennych lub stałych świadczeń z tytułu eksploatacji albo prawa do eksploatacji zasobów mineralnych, źródeł i innych bogactw naturalnych.

Statki i samoloty nie stanowią majątku nieruchomego.

3. Postanowienia ustępu 1 stosuje się do dochodów uzyskiwanych z bezpośredniego użytkowania, najmu, jak również każdego innego rodzaju użytkowania majątku nieruchomego.

4. Postanowienia ustępów 1 i 3 stosuje się również do dochodu z majątku nieruchomego przedsiębiorstwa oraz do dochodu z majątku nieruchomego, który służy do wykonywania wolnego zawodu.

Artykuł 7

Zyski przedsiębiorstw

1. Zyski przedsiębiorstwa Umawiającego się Państwa będą podlegać opodatkowaniu tylko w tym Państwie, chyba że przedsiębiorstwo prowadzi działalność w drugim Umawiającym się Państwie przez położony tam zakład. Jeżeli przedsiębiorstwo wykonuje działalność w ten sposób, zyski przedsiębiorstwa mogą być opodatkowane w drugim Państwie, jednak tylko do takiej wysokości, w jakiej mogą być przypisane:

a/ temu zakładowi;

b/ wpływom ze sprzedaży w tym drugim Państwie dóbr i towarów tego samego lub podobnego rodzaju jak sprzedawane przez ten zakład; lub

c/ innej działalności gospodarczej prowadzonej w tym drugim Państwie tego samego lub podobnego rodzaju jak działalność wykonywana przez ten zakład.

2. Z zastrzeżeniem postanowień ustępu 3, jeżeli przedsiębiorstwo Umawiającego się Państwa wykonuje działalność w drugim Umawiającym się Państwie przez położony tam zakład, to w każdym Umawiającym się Państwie należy przypisać temu zakładowi takie zyski, które mógłby on osiągnąć, gdyby wykonywał taką samą lub podobną działalność, w takich samych lub podobnych warunkach jako samodzielne przedsiębiorstwo i był całkowicie niezależny w stosunkach z przedsiębiorstwem, którego jest zakładem. W każdym przypadku, w którym przypisanie zakładowi właściwej wysokości zysku jest niemożliwe do określenia lub określenie takie jest wyjątkowo trudne, zyski przypisane zakładowi mogą być oszacowane na rozsądnej bazie.

3. Przy ustalaniu zysków zakładu dopuszcza się odliczenie nakładów ponoszonych w związku z działalnością tego zakładu, włącznie z kosztami zarządzania i ogólnymi kosztami administracyjnymi, niezależnie od tego, czy powstały w tym Państwie, w którym zakład jest położony, czy gdzie indziej, zgodnie z postanowieniami przepisów podatkowych obowiązujących w tym Państwie. Jednakże, żadne takie odliczenie nie będzie dopuszczone w odniesieniu do nakładów, jeżeli miałyby miejsce /w sposób inny aniżeli zwrot faktycznych nakładów/ przez zakład na rzecz zarządu przedsiębiorstwa lub jakichkolwiek jego oddziałów w formie należności licencyjnych, opłat lub innych podobnych płatności w zamian za wykorzystanie patentów, know - how lub innych praw albo w formie prowizji, lub innych opłat za świadczone usługi szczególnego rodzaju, lub za zarządzanie, za wyjątkiem, gdy dotyczy to banku, w formie odsetek od pieniędzy pożyczonych zakładowi.

Podobnie, żaden rachunek nie będzie uwzględniany przy określaniu zysków zakładu dla ustalania kwot obciążeń /inaczej niż poprzez zwrot faktycznych wydatków/ ponoszonych przez zakład na rzecz zarządu przedsiębiorstwa lub jakikolwiek jego oddział w formie należności licencyjnych, opłat lub innych podobnych płatności w zamian za wykorzystanie patentów know - how, innych praw albo w formie prowizji lub innych opłat za świadczone usługi szczególnego rodzaju lub za zarządzanie albo za wyjątkiem, gdy dotyczy to banku w formie odsetek od pieniędzy pożyczonych zarządowi przedsiębiorstwa lub jakiemukolwiek z jego oddziałów.

4. Nie można przypisać zakładowi zysku tylko z tytułu samego zakupu dóbr lub towarów przez ten zakład dla przedsiębiorstwa.

5. Przy stosowaniu poprzednich ustępów ustalanie zysków zakładu powinno być dokonywane każdego roku w ten sam sposób, chyba, że istnieją uzasadnione powody aby postąpić inaczej.

6. Jeżeli w zyskach mieszczą się dochody, do których stosuje się odrębne uregulowania w innych artykułach niniejszej Umowy, postanowienia tych artykułów nie będą naruszane przez postanowienia niniejszego artykułu.

Artykuł 8

Transport lotniczy

1. Zyski przedsiębiorstwa Umawiającego się Państwa, pochodzące z eksploatacji samolotów w komunikacji międzynarodowej będą podlegać opodatkowaniu tylko w tym Państwie.

2. Postanowienia ustępu 1 będą miały zastosowanie również do zysków z uczestnictwa w umowie poolowej, we wspólnym przedsiębiorstwie lub w międzynarodowym związku eksploatacyjnym.

3. Przy zastosowaniu niniejszego artykułu, odsetki od funduszy związanych z eksploatacją samolotów w komunikacji międzynarodowej będą traktowane jak zyski pochodzące z eksploatacji samolotów i postanowienia artykułu 12 nie będą miały zastosowania do takich odsetek.

4. Ckreślenie "eksploatacja samolotów" oznacza działalność
w zakresie przewozu powietrznego prowadzoną przez właści-
cieli samolotów, dzierżawców lub czarterujących, włącznie
ze sprzedażą biletów na takie przewozy w imieniu innych
przedsiębiorstw, jednostkowe wynajmowanie samolotu i każdą
inną działalność bezpośrednio związaną z takimi przewozami.

Artykuł 9

Transport morski

1. Zyski pochodzące z eksploatacji statków w komunikacji międzynarodowej będą podlegać opodatkowaniu tylko w tym Umawiającym się Państwie, w którym znajduje się miejsce faktycznego zarządu przedsiębiorstwa.

2. Jeżeli miejsce faktycznego zarządu przedsiębiorstwa zajmują-
cego się transportem morskim w komunikacji międzynarodowej, znajduje się na pokładzie statku morskiego, uważa się,
że znajduje się ono w tym Umawiającym się Państwie, w którym leży port macierzysty statku, a jeżeli nie ma on portu
macierzystego, w tym Umawiającym się Państwie, w którym
osoba eksploatująca statek ma miejsce zamieszkania lub siedzibę.

3. Postanowienia ustępu 1 będą miały zastosowanie również do
zysków z uczestnictwa w umowie poolowej, we wspólnym
przedsiębiorstwie lub w międzynarodowym związku eksploatacyjnym.

4. Bez względu na postanowienia ustępu 1 i Artykułu VIII Umowy
z dnia 27 czerwca 1960 r. pomiędzy Rządem Polskiej Rzeczypospolitej Ludowej i Rządem Republiki Indii, dotyczącej współ-
pracy żeglugowej, dochód uzyskany przez przedsiębiorstwo Umawiającego się Państwa z eksploatacji statków w komunikacji mor-
skiej prowadzonej z portów drugiego Umawiającego się
Państwa do portów trzecich krajów i z portów trzecich krajów

do portów drugiego Umawiającego się Państwa, może być opodatkowany w drugim Umawiającym się Państwie, lecz podatek nakładany w tym drugim Umawiającym się Państwie będzie zredukowany o kwotę równą 50 procentom tego podatku.

Artykuł 10

Przedsiębiorstwa powiązane

Jeżeli:

a/ przedsiębiorstwo Umawiającego się Państwa bierze udział bezpośrednio, bądź pośrednio w zarządzaniu, kontroli lub w majątku przedsiębiorstwa drugiego Umawiającego się Państwa albo

b/ te same osoby bezpośrednio, bądź pośrednio biorą udział w zarządzaniu, kontroli lub w majątku przedsiębiorstwa Umawiającego się Państwa i przedsiębiorstwa drugiego Umawiającego się Państwa,

i w jednym i drugim przypadku między dwoma przedsiębiorstwami w zakresie ich stosunków handlowych lub finansowych, zostaną umówione lub narzucone warunki, różniące się od warunków, które by ustaliły między sobą niezależne przedsiębiorstwa, wówczas zyski, które osiągałoby jedno z przedsiębiorstw bez tych warunków, ale których z powodu tych warunków nie osiągnęło, mogą być uznane za zyski tego przedsiębiorstwa i odpowiednio opodatkowane.

Artykuł 11

Dywidendy

1. Dywidendy, wypłacane przez spółkę mającą siedzibę w Umawiającym się Państwie osobie mającej miejsce zamieszkania lub siedzibę w drugim Umawiającym się Państwie, mogą być opodatkowane w tym drugim Państwie.

2. Jednakże, dywidendy te mogą być również opodatkowane w
tym Umawiającym się Państwie i według prawa tego Państwa,
w którym spółka wypłacająca dywidendy ma swoją siedzibę,
ale jeżeli odbiorca dywidend jest ich właścicielem, to podatek
wymierzony nie może przekroczyć 15 procent kwoty dywidendy
brutto - jeżeli ta dywidenda jest pochodną wkładów dokonanych
po wejściu w życie niniejszej Umowy.

Postanowienia niniejszego ustępu nie naruszają opodatkowania
spółki od zysków, z których są wypłacane dywidendy.

3. Użyte w niniejszym artykule określenie "dywidendy" oznacza
dochody z akcji lub innych praw związanych z udziałem w zyskach, z wyjątkiem wierzytelności, jak również dochody z innych udziałów w spółce, które są traktowane w ten sam sposób
dla celów opodatkowania jak wpływy z akcji, przez prawo podatkowe tego Państwa, w którym spółka wypłacająca dywidendy ma siedzibę.

4. Postanowień ustępów 1 i 2 nie stosuje się, jeżeli odbiorca
dywidend, mający miejsce zamieszkania lub siedzibę w Umawiającym się Państwie, wykonuje w drugim Umawiającym się
Państwie, w którym znajduje się siedziba spółki płacącej dywidendy, działalność zarobkową przez zakład położony w tym
Państwie, bądź wykonuje w tym drugim Państwie wolny zawód,
w oparciu o stałą placówkę, która jest w nim położona i gdy
udział, z tytułu którego wypłaca się dywidendy, rzeczywiście
wiąże się z działalnością takiego zakładu lub stałej placówki.
W takim przypadku postanowienia artykułu 7 lub artykułu 15,
w zależności od konkretnego przypadku, będą miały zastosowanie.

5. Jeżeli spółka, której siedziba znajduje się w Umawiającym się
Państwie, osiąga zyski albo dochody z drugiego Umawiającego
się Państwa, wówczas to drugie Państwo nie może ani obciążać podatkiem dywidend wypłacanych przez tę spółkę, z wy-

jątkiem przypadku, gdy takie dywidendy są wypłacane osobie mającej miejsce zamieszkania lub siedzibę w tym drugim Państwie lub w przypadku, gdy udział, z którego tytułu dywidendy są wypłacane, rzeczywiście wiąże się z działalnością zakładu lub stałej placówki położonej w tym drugim Państwie, ani też nie może obciążać nie wydzielonych zysków spółki podatkiem od nie wydzielonych zysków, nawet gdy wypłacane dywidendy lub niewydzielone zyski całkowicie lub częściowo pochodzą z zysków albo dochodów osiągniętych w drugim Państwie.

Artykuł 12

Odsetki

1. Odsetki, które powstają w Umawiającym się Państwie i wypłacane są osobie mającej miejsce zamieszkania lub siedzibę w drugim Umawiającym się Państwie, mogą być opodatkowane w tym drugim Państwie.

2. Jednakże odsetki takie mogą być także opodatkowane w Umawiającym się Państwie, w którym powstają i zgodnie z ustawodawstwem tego Państwa, lecz jeżeli ich odbiorca jest ich właścicielem, podatek ustalony w ten sposób nie może przekroczyć 15 procent kwoty brutto tych odsetek.

3. Bez względu na postanowienia ustępu 2:

   a/ odsetki, powstające w Umawiającym się Państwie będą zwolnione od opodatkowania w tym Państwie jeżeli pochodzą i są należne:

   i/ Rządowi, jednostce terytorialnej lub władzy lokalnej drugiego Umawiającego się Państwa; lub

   ii/ Centralnemu Bankowi drugiego Umawiającego się Państwa;

b/ odsetki, powstające w Umawiającym się Państwie będą
zwolnione od opodatkowania w tym Państwie, jeżeli są
należne osobie mającej miejsce zamieszkania lub siedzibę
w drugim Umawiającym się Państwie i powstały w związku
z pożyczką lub kredytem przyznanym lub gwarantowanym
przez:

 i/ w przypadku Polski, Bank Handlowy w Warszawie S.A.,
 w zakresie takim w jakim takie odsetki są związane jedynie z finansowaniem eksportu i importu,

 ii/ w przypadku Indii, the Export - Import Bank of India
 /Exim Bank/ w zakresie takim w jakim takie odsetki są
 związane jedynie z finansowaniem eksportu i importu,

 iii/ każdą inną instytucję Umawiającego się Państwa pro-
 wadzącą państwowe finansowanie handlu zagranicznego,

 iv/ każdą inną osobę, przy założeniu, że pożyczka lub kre-
 dyt jest aprobowana przez Rząd pierwszego wymienionego Umawiającego się Państwa.

4. Określenie "odsetki" użyte w niniejszym artykule oznacza dochód z wszelkiego rodzaju roszczeń zarówno zabezpieczonych
jak i nie zabezpieczonych prawem zastawu hipotecznego lub
prawem uczestniczenia w zyskach dłużnika i w szczególności
dochód od gwarancji rządowych, dochód z obligacji i listów
zastawnych włączając premie i nagrody związane z takimi
gwarancjami, obligacjami i listami zastawnymi. Obciążenia
karne z tytułu opóźnionych płatności nie będą uznawane jako
odsetki dla celów tego artykułu.

5. Postanowień ustępów 1 i 2 nie stosuje się, jeżeli odbiorca odsetek, będący ich właścicielem, mający miejsce zamieszkania
lub siedzibę w Umawiającym się Państwie, wykonuje w drugim Umawiającym się Państwie, w którym powstają odsetki,
działalność zarobkową poprzez położony tam zakład, bądź
wykonuje w tym drugim Państwie wolny zawód, korzystając

ze stałej placówki, która jest w nim położona i jeżeli wierzy-
telność, z tytułu której są płacone odsetki, rzeczywiście wiąże się z działalnością takiego zakładu lub stałej placówki.
W takim przypadku postanowienia artykułu 7 lub artykułu 15,
w zależności od konkretnego przypadku, będą miały zastosowanie.

6. Uważa się, że odsetki powstają w Umawiającym się Państwie,
gdy płatnikiem jest to Państwo, jego jednostka polityczna,
władza lokalna lub osoba mająca w tym Państwie miejsce zamieszkania lub siedzibę. Jeżeli osoba wypłacająca odsetki, niezależnie od tego, czy jest osobą mającą miejsce zamieszkania
lub siedzibę w Umawiającym się Państwie czy nie, posiada
jednak w Umawiającym się Państwie zakład lub stałą placówkę,
w związku z działalnością której powstało zadłużenie, z tytułu
którego są wypłacane odsetki i takie odsetki są wypłacane
przez ten zakład lub stałą placówkę, to odsetki te będą uważane za powstające w Umawiającym się Państwie, w którym zakład lub stała placówka są położone.

7. Jeżeli między dłużnikiem a wierzycielem lub między nimi
obydwoma a osobą trzecią istnieją szczególne stosunki i dlatego zapłacone odsetki, mające związek z roszczeniem wyni-
kającym z długu, przekraczają kwotę, którą dłużnik i wierzy-
ciel uzgodniliby bez tych stosunków, to postanowienia niniejszego artykułu stosuje się tylko do tej ostatniej wymienionej kwoty.
W tym przypadku nadwyżka ponad tę kwotę podlega opodatkowaniu zgodnie z prawem każdego Umawiającego się Państwa i z
uwzględnieniem innych postanowień niniejszej Umowy.

393

Artykuł 13
Należności licencyjne i opłaty za usługi techniczne

1. Należności licencyjne i opłaty za usługi techniczne, powstające
   w Umawiającym się Państwie, wypłacane osobie mającej miejsce
   zamieszkania lub siedzibę w drugim Umawiającym się Państwie,
   mogą być opodatkowane w tym drugim Państwie.

2. Jednakże należności i opłaty za usługi techniczne mogą być także opodatkowane w tym Umawiającym się Państwie, w którym
   powstają i zgodnie z prawem tego Państwa, lecz gdy odbiorca
   tych należności lub opłat jest ich właścicielem, podatek ustalony
   w ten sposób nie może przekroczyć 22, 5 procent kwoty brutto
   tych należności i opłat.

3. Określenie "należności licencyjne", użyte w niniejszym artykule,
   oznacza wszelkiego rodzaju należności uzyskiwane z tytułu użytkowania lub prawa do użytkowania każdego prawa autorskiego
   do dzieła literackiego, artystycznego lub naukowego, włącznie
   z filmami dla kin oraz filmami i taśmami dla telewizji lub radia,
   patentu, znaku towarowego, wzoru lub modelu, planu, tajemnicy
   technologii lub procesu produkcyjnego, jak również za użytkowanie lub prawo do użytkowania urządzenia przemysłowego, han-
   dlowego lub naukowego lub za informacje związane z doświad-
   czeniem zdobytym w dziedzinie przemysłowej, handlowej lub
   naukowej.

4. Określenie "opłaty za usługi techniczne", użyte w niniejszym
   artykule oznacza płatności jakiejkolwiek kwoty na rzecz jakiejkolwiek osoby inne niż płatności na rzecz zatrudnionego przez
   osobę dokonującą takiej płatności w powiązaniu z usługami no-
   szącymi charakter zarządzania, techniczny lub konsultacyjny
   włączając wynagrodzenia za usługi personelu technicznego lub
   innego.

5. Postanowień ustępu 1 i 2 nie stosuje się, jeżeli właściciel
   należności licencyjnych lub opłat za usługi techniczne mający
   miejsce zamieszkania lub siedzibę w Umawiającym się Państwie wykonuje w drugim Umawiającym się Państwie, z którego pochodzą należności licencyjne i opłaty za usługi techniczne,
   działalność zarobkową przez zakład w nim położony, bądź
   wolny zawód za pomocą tam położonej stałej placówki, a prawa lub majątek, z tytułu których wypłacane są należności licencyjne lub opłaty za usługi techniczne, rzeczywiście wiążą się
   z działalnością takiego zakładu lub stałej placówki. W takim
   przypadku postanowienia artykułu 7 lub artykułu 15, w zależności od konkretnego przypadku, będą miały zastosowanie.

6. Uważa się, że należności licencyjne i opłaty za usługi techniczne powstają w Umawiającym się Państwie, gdy płatnikiem jest
   to Państwo, jego jednostka administracyjna, władza lokalna
   albo osoba mająca w tym Państwie miejsce zamieszkania lub
   siedzibę. Jeżeli jednak osoba wypłacająca należności licencyjne lub opłaty za usługi techniczne, bez względu na to, czy ma
   ona w Umawiającym się Państwie miejsce zamieszkania lub
   siedzibę, posiada w Umawiającym się Państwie zakład lub
   stałą placówkę, w związku z działalnością których powstał
   obowiązek zapłaty tych należności licencyjnych i opłat za usługi techniczne i zakład lub stała placówka pokrywają te należności, to uważa się, że należności licencyjne i opłaty za te usługi
   techniczne powstają w Państwie, w którym położony jest ten
   zakład lub ta stała placówka.

7. Jeżeli między płatnikiem a właścicielem należności licencyjnych i opłat za usługi techniczne lub między nimi obydwoma
   a osobą trzecią istnieją szczególne stosunki i dlatego zapłacone opłaty licencyjne i za usługi techniczne mające związek
   z użytkowaniem, prawem lub informacją, za które są płacone
   przekraczają kwotę, którą płatnik i właściciel należności licencyjnych i opłat za usługi techniczne uzgodniliby bez tych

stosunków, to postanowienia niniejszego artykułu stosuje się
tylko do tej ostatnio wymienionej kwoty. W tym przypadku
nadwyżka ponad tę kwotę podlega opodatkowaniu zgodnie z prawem każdego Umawiającego się Państwa i z uwzględnieniem
innych postanowień niniejszej Umowy.

Artykuł 14

Zyski ze sprzedaży majątku

1. Zyski osiągane przez osobę mającą miejsce zamieszkania lub
   siedzibę w Umawiającym się Państwie, z przeniesienia tytułu
   własności majątku nieruchomego, o którym mowa w artykule 6,
   a położonego w drugim Umawiającym się Państwie, mogą być
   opodatkowane w tym drugim Państwie.

2. Zyski z przeniesienia tytułu własności majątku ruchomego sta-
   nowiącego część majątku zakładu, który przedsiębiorstwo Umawiającego się Państwa posiada w drugim Umawiającym się
   Państwie, lub z przeniesienia tytułu własności majątku ruchomego, należącego do stałej placówki, którą osoba zamieszkała
   lub mająca siedzibę w Umawiającym się Państwie dysponuje
   w drugim Umawiającym się Państwie w celu wykonywania
   wolnego zawodu, łącznie z zyskami, które zostaną osiągnięte
   z tytułu przeniesienia własności takiego zakładu /odrębnie
   albo razem z całym przedsiębiorstwem/ lub takiej stałej
   placówki, mogą być opodatkowane w tym drugim Państwie.

3. Zyski osiągnięte z przeniesienia tytułu własności statków lub
   samolotów eksploatowanych w komunikacji międzynarodowej,
   oraz z tytułu własności majątku ruchomego związanego z
   eksploatacją takich statków, samolotów będą opodatkowane
   tylko w tym Umawiającym się Państwie, w którym osoba
   przenosząca tytuł własności ma miejsce zamieszkania lub
   siedzibę.

4. Zyski z przeniesienia akcji w kapitale spółki, których posiadanie dotyczy bezpośrednio lub pośrednio nieruchomości znajdującej się w Umawiającym się Państwie mogą być opodatkowane w tym Państwie.

5. Zyski z przeniesienia akcji innych niż wymienione w ustępie 4, w kapitale spółki, która ma siedzibę w Umawiającym się Państwie, mogą być opodatkowane w tym Państwie.

6. Zyski z przeniesienia tytułu własności majątku nie wymienionego w ustępach 1, 2, 3, 4 i 5 podlegają opodatkowaniu tylko w tym Umawiającym się Państwie w którym osoba przenosząca tytuł własności ma miejsce zamieszkania lub siedzibę.

Artykuł 15

Wolne zawody

1. Dochód, który osoba mająca miejsce zamieszkania w Umawiającym się Państwie osiąga z tytułu wykonywania wolnego zawodu albo z innej samodzielnej działalności o podobnym charakterze, mogą być opodatkowane tylko w tym Państwie, za wyjątkiem następujących okoliczności kiedy taki dochód może być również opodatkowany w drugim Umawiającym się Państwie:

a/ jeżeli dla wykonywania swojej działalności w drugim Umawiającym się Państwie dysponuje ona zwykle stałą placówką; w takim przypadku dochód może być opodatkowany w tym drugim Umawiającym się Państwie, jednak tylko o tyle, o ile może być przypisany tej stałej placówce lub

b/ jeżeli przebywa ona w drugim Umawiającym się Państwie przez okres lub okresy wynoszące lub przekraczające łącznie 183 dni w odpowiednim "poprzednim roku" lub "roku dochodowym" w zależności od przypadku; wówczas dochód tej osoby może być opodatkowany w tym drugim Umawiającym się Państwie, jednak tylko w tej części w jakiej pochodzi z wykonywania działalności w tym drugim Państwie.

2. Określenie "wolny zawód" obejmuje samodzielnie wykonywaną działalność naukową, literacką, artystyczną, wychowawczą
lub oświatową, jak również samodzielnie wykonywaną działalność lekarzy, chirurgów, prawników, inżynierów, architektów,
dentystów oraz księgowych.

Artykuł 16

Praca najemna

1. Z zastrzeżeniem postanowień artykułów 17, 18, 19, 20, 21
i 22 pensje, płace i podobne wynagrodzenia, które osoba mająca miejsce zamieszkania w Umawiającym się Państwie osiąga
z pracy najemnej, mogą podlegać opodatkowaniu tylko w tym
Państwie, chyba że praca wykonywana jest w drugim Umawiającym się Państwie. Jeżeli praca jest tam wykonywana, to
osiągane za nią wynagrodzenie może być opodatkowane w tym
drugim Państwie.

2. Bez względu na postanowienia ustępu 1 wynagrodzenia, jakie
osoba mająca miejsce zamieszkania w Umawiającym się Państwie osiąga z pracy najemnej, wykonywanej w drugim Umawiającym się Państwie, będą podlegać opodatkowaniu tylko w pierwszym wymienionym Państwie jeżeli:

a/ odbiorca przebywa w drugim Państwie przez okres lub
okresy nie przekraczające łącznie 183 dni odpowiednio
"poprzedniego roku" lub "roku dochodowego"; i

b/ wynagrodzenia są wypłacane przez osobę lub w imieniu osoby, która nie ma w tym drugim Państwie miejsca zamieszkania lub siedziby, oraz

c/ wynagrodzenia nie są ponoszone przez zakład lub stałą placówkę, którą pracodawca posiada w drugim Państwie.

3. Bez względu na postanowienia niniejszego artykułu, wynagrodzenia z pracy najemnej, wykonywanej na pokładzie statku lub samolotu w komunikacji międzynarodowej, przez przedsiębiorstwo Umawiającego się Państwa, mogą być opodatkowane w tym Państwie.

Artykuł 17

Wynagrodzenia dyrektorów i wysokiej rangi urzędników zarządu

1. Wynagrodzenia dyrektorów i podobne należności, które osoba mająca miejsce zamieszkania w Umawiającym się Państwie osiąga z tytułu członkostwa w radzie nadzorczej albo zarządzie spółki, mającej siedzibę w drugim Umawiającym się Państwie, mogą być opodatkowane w tym drugim Państwie.

2. Wynagrodzenia, płace i inne podobne należności, które osoba mająca miejsce zamieszkania w Umawiającym się Państwie osiąga z tytułu zatrudnienia na stanowisku kierowniczym wyższego szczebla w spółce mającej siedzibę w drugim Umawiającym się Państwie, mogą być opodatkowane w tym drugim Państwie.

Artykuł 18

Dochody osiągane przez artystów i sportowców

1. Bez względu na postanowienia artykułów 15 i 16 dochód uzyskany przez osobę mającą miejsce zamieszkania w Umawiającym się Państwie, z tytułu działalności artystycznej na przykład artysty scenicznego, filmowego, radiowego lub telewizyjnego, jak też muzyka lub sportowca, z osobiście wykonywanej w tym charakterze działalności w drugim Umawiającym się Państwie, mogą być opodatkowane w tym drugim Państwie.

2. Jeżeli dochód osiągnięty z osobiście wykonywanej działalności artysty lub sportowca nie przypada na rzecz tego artysty lub

sportowca, lecz na rzecz innej osoby, dochód taki, bez względu na postanowienia artykułów 7, 15 i 16, może być opodatkowany w Umawiającym się Państwie, w którym działalność tego artysty lub sportowca jest wykonywana.

3. Bez względu na postanowienia ustępu 1 dochód uzyskany przez artystę lub sportowca, mającego miejsce zamieszkania w Umawiającym się Państwie z osobiście wykonywanej działalności w drugim Umawiającym się Państwie będzie opodatkowany tylko w tym pierwszym wymienionym Umawiającym się Państwie, jeżeli działalność taka jest wykonywana w drugim Umawiającym się Państwie w ramach programu wymiany kulturalnej lub sportowej przyjętego przez obydwa Umawiające się Państwa i jest finansowana w pełni lub częściowo z funduszy publicznych pierwszego wymienionego Umawiającego się Państwa włączając wszelkie jego jednostki polityczne oraz władze lokalne.

4. Bez względu na postanowienia ustępu 2 i artykułów 7, 15 i 16, jeżeli dochód uzyskany z osobiście wykonywanej działalności artysty lub sportowca mającego miejsce zamieszkania w Umawiającym się Państwie, nie jest należny temu artyście lub sportowcowi ale innej osobie, dochód taki będzie opodatkowany tylko w tym drugim Umawiającym się Państwie, jeżeli działalność tej innej osoby jest wykonywana w ramach programu wymiany kulturalnej lub sportowej, przyjętego przez obydwa Umawiające się Państwa i jest finansowana w całości lub częściowo z funduszy publicznych tego drugiego państwa włączając wszelkie jego jednostki polityczne oraz władze lokalne.

Artykuł 19

Wynagrodzenia i emerytury pracowników państwowych

1. a/ Wynagrodzenie, inne niż emerytura, wypłacane przez Umawiające się Państwo, lub jego jednostkę polityczną, bądź władzę lokalną każdej osobie fizycznej z tytułu usług świad-

czonych na rzecz tego Państwa, lub takiej jego jednostki
bądź władzy, po wypełnieniu przez tę osobę funkcji o charakterze państwowym, podlega opodatkowaniu tylko w tym
Umawiającym się Państwie.

b/ Jednakże takie wynagrodzenie będzie podlegać opodatkowaniu tylko w tym drugim Umawiającym się Państwie, jeżeli
usługi są świadczone w tym drugim Państwie, a osoba je
otrzymująca ma miejsce zamieszkania w tym drugim Państwie oraz osoba ta:

i/ jest obywatelem tego Państwa; lub

ii/ nie stała się osobą mającą miejsce zamieszkania w tym
Państwie wyłącznie w celu świadczenia tych usług.

2. a/ Każda emerytura wypłacana bezpośrednio bądź z funduszy
Umawiającego się Państwa lub jego jednostki politycznej,
bądź władzy lokalnej każdej osobie fizycznej z tytułu usług,
świadczonych na rzecz tego Państwa lub takiej jednostki
lub władzy, będzie podlegać opodatkowaniu wyłącznie w
tym Państwie.

b/ Jednakże, taka emerytura będzie opodatkowana tylko w drugim Umawiającym się Państwie, jeśli osoba ją otrzymująca posiada miejsce zamieszkania w tym Państwie i jest
obywatelem tego drugiego Państwa.

3. Postanowienia artykułów 16, 17 i 18 będą stosowane do wynagrodzeń oraz emerytur mających związek z działalnością gospodarczą prowadzoną przez Umawiające się Państwa, jego
jednostkę polityczną lub władzę lokalną.

Artykuł 20

Renty i emerytury pracowników niepaństwowych

1. Jakakolwiek emerytura, inna niż emerytura wymieniona w
artykule 19, lub jakakolwiek renta otrzymywana przez osobę

mającą miejsce zamieszkania w Umawiającym się Państwie,
ze źródeł w drugim Umawiającym się Państwie podlega opodatkowaniu tylko w tym pierwszym wymienionym Umawiającym
się Państwie.

2. Określenie "emerytura" oznacza określoną płatność dokonywa-
ną w zamian za uprzednią służbę lub w drodze odszkodowania
za szkody poniesione w trakcie wykonywania tej służby.

3. Określenie "renta" oznacza określoną sumę płatną okresowo
i w określonym czasie podczas życia lub w pewnym określonym
lub dającym się wymierzyć okresie czasu jako spełnienie zobo-
wiązania dokonania płatności w zamian za odpowiednio i w pełni dokonane zobowiązanie pieniężne lub w równoważniku da-
nej kwoty pieniężnej.

Artykuł 21

Należności otrzymywane przez studentów i praktykantów

1. Należności otrzymywane na utrzymanie, kształcenie się lub
odbywanie praktyki przez studenta lub praktykanta, który ma
albo bezpośrednio przed przybyciem do Umawiającego się Państwa miał miejsce zamieszkania w drugim Umawiającym się
Państwie i który przebywa w pierwszym wymienionym Państwie
wyłącznie w celu nauki lub szkolenia, nie będą podlegały opodatkowaniu w tym Państwie, jeżeli należności te pochodzą ze
źródeł spoza tego Państwa.

2. Dochody uzyskiwane przez studenta lub praktykanta w związku
z działalnością wykonywaną w Umawiającym się Państwie, w
którym przebywa wyłącznie w celu nauki lub szkolenia, nie
będą podlegały opodatkowaniu w tym Państwie, chyba że kwota
ich przekracza kwotę niezbędną na jego utrzymanie, naukę
lub praktykę.

3. Postanowienia niniejszego artykułu będą mogły być zastoso-
wane wyłącznie w okresie, który zazwyczaj przyjęty jest dla
ukończenia nauki lub praktyki, w żadnym przypadku postanowienia niniejszego artykułu nie będą miały zastosowania do
jakiejkolwiek osoby fizycznej po okresie dłuższym niż pięć
kolejnych lat, licząc od daty jej pierwszego przybycia do tego
drugiego Umawiającego się Państwa.

4. W rozumieniu niniejszego artykułu i artykułu 22, osoba fizyczna będzie uważana za mającą miejsce zamieszkania w Umawiającym się Państwie, jeżeli miała ona miejsce zamieszkania w
tym Umawiającym się Państwie odpowiednio "w poprzednim
roku" lub "roku podatkowym", w którym przybyła ona do drugiego Umawiającego się Państwa lub w bezpośrednio poprze-
dzającym "poprzednim roku" lub "roku podatkowym".

Artykuł 22

Należności otrzymywane przez profesorów, nauczycieli i wykładowców

1. Profesor lub nauczyciel, który ma lub miał miejsce zamieszkania w jednym z Umawiających się Państw bezpośrednio
przed przybyciem do drugiego Umawiającego się Państwa,
w celu nauczania lub prowadzenia prac badawczych, lub w obu
celach, na uniwersytecie, szkole wyższej, szkole bądź innej
uznanej placówce w tym drugim Umawiającym się Państwie,
będzie zwolniony od opodatkowania w tym drugim Państwie z
tytułu wynagrodzenia za takie nauczanie albo prowadzenie prac
badawczych, przez okres nie przekraczający 2 lat od daty jego
przybycia do tego drugiego Państwa.

2. Niniejszego artykułu nie stosuje się do dochodów z tytułu prac
badawczych, jeżeli takie prace badawcze nie są podejmowane
w interesie publicznym, ale głównie dla prywatnej korzyści
określonej osoby lub osób.

3. W rozumieniu ustępu 1 określenie "uznana placówka" oznacza placówkę, która została uznana za taką przez właściwe władze odpowiedniego Umawiającego się Państwa.

Artykuł 23

Inne dochody

1. Z zastrzeżeniem postanowień ustępu 2 części dochodu osoby mającej miejsce zamieszkania lub siedzibę w Umawiającym się Państwie bez względu na to gdzie powstają, które nie zostały wyraźnie wymienione w poprzednich artykułach niniejszej Umowy, będą opodatkowane tylko w tym Umawiającym się Państwie.

2. Postanowienia ustępu 1 nie będą stosowane do dochodu innego niż dochód z nieruchomości, o których mowa w artykule 6 ustęp 2, jeśli odbiorca takiego dochodu, mający miejsce zamieszkania lub siedzibę w Umawiającym się Państwie, prowadzi działalność gospodarczą w drugim Umawiającym się Państwie za pośrednictwem zakładu tam położonego bądź wykonuje w tym drugim Państwie wolny zawód, wykorzystując położoną tam stałą placówkę, a prawo, bądź majątek z tytułu którego wypłacany jest dochód są rzeczywiście powiązane z takim zakładem lub stałą placówką. W takim przypadku postanowienia artykułu 7 lub artykułu 15 będą stosowane w zależności od konkretnego przypadku.

3. Bez względu na postanowienia ustępów 1 i 2 części dochodu osoby mającej miejsce zamieszkania lub siedzibę w Umawiającym się Państwie, a o których nie było mowy w poprzednich artykułach niniejszej Umowy, powstające w drugim Umawiającym się Państwie mogą być opodatkowane w tym drugim Państwie.

4. Właściwe władze Umawiających się Państw mogą bezpośrednio komunikować się ze sobą w celu osiągnięcia porozumienia w rozumieniu powyższych ustępów.

Właściwe władze ustalą w drodze konsultacji odpowiednie dwustronne sposoby, warunki i techniki w celu realizacji procedury wzajemnego porozumienia przewidzianej w tym artykule.

Artykuł 24

Unikanie podwójnego opodatkowania

1. Prawa obowiązujące w każdym z Umawiających się Państw będą w dalszym ciągu miały zastosowanie do opodatkowania dochodu w odpowiednim Umawiającym się Państwie chyba, że co innego zostało przewidziane w niniejszej Umowie.

2. W obu Umawiających się Państwach będzie się unikać podwójnego opodatkowania w następujący sposób:

a/ Jeżeli osoba mająca miejsce zamieszkania lub siedzibę w Umawiającym się Państwie osiąga dochód, który zgodnie z postanowieniami niniejszej Umowy może być opodatkowany w drugim Umawiającym się Państwie, to pierwsze wymienione Państwo będzie, z zastrzeżeniem postanowień litery b niniejszego ustępu, zwalniać taki dochód od opodatkowania, jednakże może, przy obliczaniu podatku od pozostałego dochodu takiej osoby zastosować stawkę podatku, która byłaby zastosowana, gdyby zwolniony dochód nie uzyskał takiego zwolnienia.

b/ Każde z Umawiających się Państw przy nakładaniu podatków na osoby mające w nich miejsce zamieszkania lub siedzibę może włączyć do podstawy, od której te podatki są wymierzane te części dochodu, które zgodnie z postanowieniami artykułów 11, 12 i 13 niniejszej Umowy mogą być także opodatkowane w drugim Państwie, lecz zezwoli na potrącenie z kwoty podatku obliczonej na tej podstawie kwoty równej podatkowi zapłaconemu w drugim Umawiającym się Państwie.

Takie potrącenie nie może jednakże przekroczyć tej części podatku należnego w pierwszym wymienionym Państwie wyliczonego przed dokonaniem potrącenia i która
odnosi się do dochodu, który zgodnie z postanowieniami
artykułów 11, 12 i 13 niniejszej Umowy może być opodatkowany w tym drugim Państwie.

3. W rozumieniu postanowień ustępu 2 litera b określenie "podatek zapłacony w drugim Umawiającym się Państwie", obejmuje jakąkolwiek kwotę, która byłaby płatna z tytułu podatku,
z wyjątkiem jakiejkolwiek ulgi w drodze potrącenia dozwolone-
go przy obliczaniu dochodu, podlegającego opodatkowaniu lub
zwolnienia, obniżki podatku lub w inny sposób zgodnie z obowiązującym w drugim Umawiającym się Państwie prawem,
dotyczącym opodatkowania dochodów.

Artykuł 25

Równe traktowanie

1. Obywatele Umawiającego się Państwa nie będą poddani w drugim Umawiającym się Państwie ani opodatkowaniu i związanym z nim obowiązkiem, które są inne lub bardziej uciążliwe
od opodatkowania i związanym z nim obowiązkiem od tych, którym w tych samych okolicznościach i w tych samych warunkach
są lub mogą być poddani obywatele tego drugiego Państwa.

2. Opodatkowanie zakładu, który przedsiębiorstwo Umawiającego
się Państwa posiada w tym drugim Umawiającym się Państwie
nie będzie w tym drugim Państwie bardziej niekorzystne niż
opodatkowanie przedsiębiorstw tego drugiego Państwa w tych
samych okolicznościach i na tych samych warunkach.

3. Żadne z postanowień niniejszego artykułu nie będzie rozumia-
ne jako zobowiązujące Umawiające się Państwo do udzielenia
osobom, nie mającym miejsca zamieszkania lub siedziby w
tym Państwie żadnych osobistych ulg, obniżek i potrąceń w ce-

lach podatkowych, które zgodnie z prawem są dostępne wyłącznie dla osób mających w nim miejsce zamieszkania lub
siedzibę.

4. Przedsiębiorstwa Umawiającego się Państwa, których majątek
w całości lub w części, bezpośrednio albo pośrednio należy,
lub jest przez nie kontrolowany, do osoby lub osób mających
miejsce zamieszkania lub siedzibę w drugim Umawiającym się
Państwie, nie będą w pierwszym Umawiającym się Państwie
poddane opodatkowaniu, ani związanym z nim obowiązkom,
które są inne lub bardziej uciążliwe, aniżeli opodatkowanie
i związane z nim obowiązki, którym są lub mogą być poddane
podobne przedsiębiorstwa pierwszego Umawiającego się Państwa w tych samych okolicznościach i na tych samych warunkach.

5. Użyte w niniejszym artykule określenie "opodatkowanie" oznacza podatki, które są przedmiotem niniejszej Umowy.

6. Z wyjątkiem przypadków stosowania postanowień artykułu 11,
artykułu 12 ustęp 7, lub artykułu 13 ustęp 7 niniejszej Umowy,
odsetki, należności licencyjne i inne płatności dokonywane
przez przedsiębiorstwo Umawiającego się Państwa osobie mającej miejsce zamieszkania lub siedzibę w drugim Umawiającym
się Państwie są potrącane przy określaniu zysku takiego przedsiębiorstwa, podlegającego opodatkowaniu, na takich samych
warunkach jakby były wypłacane osobie mającej miejsce zamieszkania lub siedzibę w pierwszym wymienionym Państwie.

Podobnie jakiekolwiek zadłużenie przedsiębiorstwa Umawiającego się Państwa w stosunku do osoby mającej miejsce zamieszkania lub siedzibę w drugim Umawiającym się Państwie,
będzie potrącane przy określeniu, podlegającego opodatkowaniu majątku tego przedsiębiorstwa na tych samych warunkach,
jak gdyby ono powstało w stosunku do osoby mającej miejsce
zamieszkania lub siedzibę w pierwszym wymienionym Państwie.

7. Żadne z postanowień niniejszej Umowy nie narusza zwolnień, ulg, obniżek, potrąceń w celach podatkowych przewidzianych prawem wewnętrznym w obu Umawiających się Państwach.

Artykuł 26

Procedura wzajemnego porozumiewania się

1. Jeżeli osoba mająca miejsce zamieszkania lub siedzibę w Umawiającym się Państwie jest zdania, że czynności Państwa lub obu Umawiających się Państw wprowadziły lub wprowadzą dla niej opodatkowanie, które nie odpowiada niniejszej Umowie, wówczas może ona, niezależnie od środków odwoławczych, przewidzianych w prawie wewnętrznym tych Państw przedłożyć swoją sprawę właściwej władzy tego Umawiającego się Państwa, w którym ma ona miejsce zamieszkania lub siedzibę. Sprawa winna być przedłożona w ciągu 3 lat licząc od daty otrzymania powiadomienia o działaniu powodującym opodatkowanie sprzeczne z niniejszą Umową.

2. Właściwa władza podejmie starania jeżeli uzna zarzut za uzasadniony i jeżeli nie może sama spowodować zadowalającego rozwiązania, aby rozstrzygnąć sprawę w porozumieniu z właściwą władzą drugiego Umawiającego się Państwa, mając na celu uniknięcie opodatkowania niezgodnego z niniejszą Umową. Każde osiągnięte porozumienie zostanie wprowadzone w życie bez względu na terminy przewidziane przez ustawodawstwo wewnętrzne Umawiających się Państw.

3. Właściwe władze Umawiających się Państw będą czynić starania aby w drodze wzajemnego porozumienia usuwać jakiekolwiek trudności lub wątpliwości, które mogą powstawać przy interpretacji lub stosowaniu Umowy. Mogą one również porozumiewać się w celu uniknięcia podwójnego opodatkowania w przypadkach, które nie są uregulowane Umową.

4. Właściwe władze Umawiających się Państw w celu osiągnięcia porozumienia wskazanego w poprzednich ustępach mogą
kontaktować się ze sobą bezpośrednio. Jeżeli uzna się, że
aby osiągnąć porozumienie należy przeprowadzić ustną wymianę poglądów, wówczas taka wymiana poglądów może odbyć się
w ramach Komisji złożonej z przedstawicieli właściwych władz
Umawiających się Państw.

Artykuł 27

Wymiana informacji

1. Właściwe władze Umawiających się Państw będą wymieniały
informacje /włącznie z dokumentami/ konieczne do stosowania
postanowień niniejszej Umowy, a także informacje o ustawo-
dawstwie wewnętrznym Umawiających się Państw dotyczące podatków wymienionych w niniejszej Umowie w takim zakresie,
w jakim opodatkowanie, jakie ono przewiduje, nie jest sprzeczne z Umową, w szczególności w celu zapobiegania oszustwu
lub uchylaniu się od opodatkowania. Wszelkie informacje uzyskane przez Umawiające się Państwo będą stanowiły tajemnicę na
takiej samej zasadzie jak informacje uzyskane zgodnie z prawem wewnętrznym tego Państwa. Jednakże, jeżeli informacje
są pierwotnie uznane za tajemnicę w przekazującym Państwie,
będą one mogły być wyjawione jedynie osobom lub władzom
/w tym sądom i jednostkom administracyjnym/ zajmującym się
wymiarem i poborem, egzekucją i ściganiem lub rozpatrywa-
niem odwołań w zakresie podatków objętych niniejszą Umową.
Te osoby lub władze będą wykorzystywały takie informacje
wyłącznie w tych celach, ale mogą je wyjawić w postępowaniu
przed sądem powszechnym lub orzeczeniach sądowych. Właściwe władze ustalą w drodze konsultacji odpowiednie warunki,
metody, techniki w zakresie spraw w których będzie odbywała
się wymiana informacji, włączając, gdzie będzie to celowe
wymianę informacji dotyczących unikania opodatkowania.

2. Wymiana informacji lub dokumentów będzie się odbywała w
   sposób przyjęty zwyczajowo lub na prośbę ze wskazaniem
   konkretnego przypadku lub w obu tych sposobach. Właściwe
   władze Umawiających się Państw będą uzgadniały okresowo
   listę informacji lub dokumentów, które będą dostarczane w
   drodze zwyczajowej.

3. Postanowienia ustępu 1 nie mogą być w żadnym przypadku
   interpretowane tak, jak gdyby zobowiązywały jedno z Umawiających się Państw do:

   a/ stosowania środków administracyjnych, które nie są zgodne
      z ustawodawstwem lub praktyką administracyjną tego lub
      drugiego Państwa;

   b/ udzielania informacji lub dostarczania dokumentów, któ-
      rych uzyskanie nie byłoby możliwe zgodnie z prawem albo
      w ramach normalnej praktyki administracyjnej tego lub
      drugiego Umawiającego się Państwa;

   c/ udzielania informacji lub dostarczania dokumentów, które
      ujawniłyby jakąkolwiek tajemnicę handlową, gospodarczą,
      przemysłową, kupiecką lub zawodową albo tryb działalno-
      ści przedsiębiorstwa, lub informacji których udzielanie
      sprzeciwiałoby się porządkowi publicznemu.

Artykuł 28

Pomoc w zakresie poboru podatków

1. Umawiające się Państwa zobowiązują się do udzielania pomo-
   cy i wzajemnego wspomagania w poborze podatków do których
   ma zastosowanie niniejsza Umowa w przypadkach w których
   podatki są ostatecznie należne zgodnie z prawem Państw
   składających wniosek.

2. W przypadku wniosków o egzekucję poboru, roszczenia podatkowe jakiegokolwiek z Umawiających się Państw, które
zostały ostatecznie ustalone zostaną przyjęte do egzekucji
przez drugie Umawiające się Państwo, któremu wniosek jest
składany i pobrane w tym Państwie zgodnie z prawem mającym zastosowanie do egzekucji poboru jego podatków.

3. W przypadku podatków polskich wniosek będzie przesłany
przez Ministra Finansów w Polsce lub jego upoważnionego
przedstawiciela do Centralnego Zarządu Podatków Bezpoś rednich Departamentu Dochodów Ministerstwa Finansów Indii
wraz z takimi zaświadczeniami jakie są wymagane zgodnie
z prawem polskim do ustalenia, że podatki zostały ostatecznie określone i są należne od podatnika.

4. W przypadku podatków indyjskich, wniosek będzie przesłany
przez Centralny Zarząd Podatków Bezpoś rednich Departamentu
Dochodów Ministerstwa Finansów Indii do Ministra
Finansów w Polsce lub jego upoważnionego przedstawiciela
wraz z takimi zaświadczeniami jakie są wymagane zgodnie z
prawem indyjskim do ustalenia, że podatki zostały ostatecznie
określone i są należne od podatnika.

5. W przypadku, jeżeli roszczenie podatkowe nie uprawomocniło
się z tego powodu, że podlega zaskarżeniu lub jakiemukolwiek
innemu postępowaniu, Umawiające się Państwo może, w celu
ochrony swoich dochodów złożyć wniosek drugiemu Umawiającemu się Państwu do podjęcia takich środków zabezpieczających
w jego imieniu, które są zgodne z prawem tego drugiego
Umawiającego się Państwa.

6. Wniosek o pomoc w poborze podatków należnych od podatnika
będzie składany jedynie wtedy, jeżeli odpowiedni majątek tego
podatnika nie jest dostępny do ściągnięcia od niego podatków
w Umawiającym się Państwie składającym wniosek.

7. Umawiające się Państwo, w którym podatek został ściągnię-
ty zgodnie z postanowieniami ustępów 1, 2 i 5 niniejszego
artykułu, przekaże niezwłocznie ściągniętą kwotę Umawiającemu Państwu składającemu wniosek.

Artykuł 29

Pracownicy dyplomatyczni i konsularni

Przepisy niniejszej Umowy nie naruszają przywilejów podatkowych, przysługujących pracownikom dyplomatycznym i konsular-
nym na podstawie ogólnych zasad prawa międzynarodowego lub
postanowień umów szczególnych.

Artykuł 30

Wejście w życie

Każde z Umawiających się Państw notyfikuje drugie Państwo o
zakończeniu postępowania wymaganego przez jego prawo dla
wejścia niniejszej Umowy w życie. Umowa wejdzie w życie w
dniu otrzymania noty późniejszej i będzie miała zastosowanie:

a/ w Polsce w stosunku do dochodu, powstałego w jakimkolwiek
roku, zaczynającym się w dniu lub po dniu 1 stycznia następnego roku kalendarzowego, w którym późniejsza notyfikacja
została przekazana;

b/ w Indiach w stosunku do dochodu powstałego w jakimkolwiek
poprzednim roku, zaczynającym się w dniu lub po dniu 1 kwietnia następnego roku kalendarzowego, w którym późniejsza notyfikacja została przekazana.

Artykuł 31

Wypowiedzenie

Niniejsza Umowa została zawarta na czas nieokreślony, lecz
każde z Umawiających się Państw może w dniu lub przed dniem

30 czerwca każdego roku kalendarzowego, rozpoczynającego się po upływie pięcioletniego okresu od dnia jej wejścia w życie, przekazać drugiemu Umawiającemu się Państwu w drodze dyplomatycznej notyfikację wypowiedzenia i w tym przypadku niniejsza Umowa przestanie obowiązywać:

a/ w Polsce w stosunku do dochodu, powstałego w jakimkolwiek roku, zaczynającym się w dniu lub po dniu 1 stycznia następnego roku kalendarzowego, w którym notyfikacja została przekazana;

b/ w Indiach w stosunku do dochodu, powstałego w jakimkolwiek poprzednim roku rozpoczynającym się w dniu lub po dniu 1 kwietnia następnego roku kalendarzowego, w którym notyfikacja została przekazana.

Na dowód czego niżej podpisani, należycie do tego upoważnieni, podpisali niniejszą Umowę.

Sporządzono w 2 egzemplarzach w Warszawie dnia 21 czerwca   1989 r. każdy w językach polskim, hindi i angielskim, przy czym wszystkie teksty są jednakowo autentyczne. W przypadku rozbieżności pomiędzy tekstami w języku polskim i hindi, tekst angielski uważany będzie za rozstrzygający.

Z upoważnienia   Z upoważnienia

RZĄDU POLSKIEJ   RZĄDU REPUBLIKI INDII
RZECZYPOSPOLITEJ
LUDOWEJ

[TRANSLATION – TRADUCTION]

ACCORD ENTRE LE GOUVERNEMENT DE LA RÉPUBLIQUE POPULAIRE DE POLOGNE ET LE GOUVERNEMENT DE LA RÉPUBLIQUE DE L'INDE TENDANT À ÉVITER LA DOUBLE IMPOSITION ET À PRÉVENIR L'ÉVASION FISCALE EN MATIÈRE D'IMPÔTS SUR LE REVENU

Le Gouvernement de la République populaire de Pologne et le Gouvernement de la République de l'Inde, désireux d'élargir et de faciliter les relations économiques entre les deux pays, et ayant décidé de conclure un accord tendant à éviter la double imposition et à prévenir l'évasion fiscale en matière d'impôts sur le revenu,

Sont convenus de ce qui suit :

Article premier. Personnes visées

Le présent Accord s'applique aux personnes qui sont des résidents de l'un des États contractants ou des deux.

Article 2. Impôts visés

1. Les impôts auxquels s'applique le présent Accord sont :

a) En Pologne :

   i)   L'impôt sur le revenu (« podatek dochodowy »);

   ii) L'impôt sur les traitements et salaires (« podatek of wynagrodzeń »);

   iii) L'impôt de péréquation (« podatek wyrównawczy »); et

   iv) L'impôt agricole (« podatek rolny »);

(ci-après dénommés « l'impôt polonais »).

b) En Inde :

   i)   L'impôt sur le revenu, y compris toute surtaxe appliquée sur celui-ci en vertu de la loi de 1961 relative à l'impôt sur le revenu;

   ii) La surtaxe appliquée en vertu de la loi de 1964 relative à la surtaxe sur les bénéfices des sociétés;

(ci-après dénommés « l'impôt indien »).

2. Le présent Accord s'applique aussi aux impôts de nature identique ou analogue de l'un ou l'autre des États contractants qui seraient établis après la signature du présent Accord et qui s'ajouteraient aux impôts visés au paragraphe 1 ou les remplaceraient. Les autorités compétentes des États contractants se communiquent les modifications significatives apportées à leur législation fiscale visée par le présent Accord.

Article 3. Définitions générales

1. Au sens du présent Accord, à moins que le contexte n'exige une interprétation différente :

a) Le terme « Pologne » désigne la République populaire de Pologne et, lorsqu'il est employé dans un sens géographique, le territoire de la République populaire de Pologne et toutes les zones maritimes adjacentes à ses eaux territoriales sur lesquelles elle exerce sa souveraineté ou ses droits souverains et exclusifs en vertu de sa législation et conformément au droit international;

b) Le terme « Inde » désigne la République de l'Inde et, lorsqu'il est employé dans un sens géographique, le territoire de la République de l'Inde et toutes les zones maritimes adjacentes à ses eaux territoriales sur lesquelles elle exerce sa souveraineté ou ses droits souverains et exclusifs en vertu de sa législation et conformément au droit international;

c) Les expressions « un État contractant » et « l'autre État contractant » désignent, selon le contexte, la Pologne ou l'Inde;

d) Le terme « impôt » désigne l'impôt polonais ou l'impôt indien selon le contexte, mais ne comprend aucune somme payable par suite d'une omission ou d'un manquement à l'égard des impôts qui font l'objet du présent Accord ou qui constitue une amende se rapportant auxdits impôts;

e) Le terme « personne » comprend les personnes physiques, les sociétés et les autres groupements de personnes que la législation fiscale en vigueur dans les États contractants considère comme étant imposable;

f) Le terme « société » désigne toute personne morale ou toute entité que la législation fiscale en vigueur dans les États contractants considère comme une société ou une personne morale;

g) Les expressions « entreprise d'un État contractant » et « entreprise de l'autre État contractant » désignent respectivement une entreprise exploitée par un résident d'un État contractant et une entreprise exploitée par un résident de l'autre État contractant;

h) L'expression « autorités compétentes » désigne, pour la Pologne, le Ministre des finances ou son représentant autorisé et, pour l'Inde, l'Administration centrale du Ministère des finances (Département fiscal) ou son représentant autorisé;

i) Le terme « ressortissant » désigne toute personne physique qui possède la nationalité d'un État contractant et toute personne morale, société de personnes ou association constituée conformément à la législation en vigueur dans l'État contractant;

j) Le terme « trafic international » désigne tout transport effectué par un navire ou un aéronef exploité par une entreprise d'un État contractant, sauf lorsque le navire ou l'aéronef n'est exploité qu'entre des points situés dans l'autre État contractant.

2.   En ce qui concerne l'application du présent Accord par un État contractant, tout terme ou expression qui n'y est pas défini a, à moins que le contexte exige une interprétation différente, le sens que lui attribue la législation fiscale de cet État à laquelle s'applique l'Accord.

Article 4. Résidence

1.   Au sens du présent Accord, l'expression « résident d'un État contractant » désigne toute personne qui, en vertu de la législation de cet État, y est assujettie à l'impôt en raison de son domicile, de sa résidence, de son siège de direction ou de tout autre critère de nature analogue.

2.   Lorsque, selon les dispositions du paragraphe 1, une personne physique est un résident des deux États contractants, sa situation est réglée de la manière suivante :

a) Cette personne est considérée comme résidente de l'État où elle dispose d'un foyer d'habitation permanent. Si elle dispose d'un foyer d'habitation permanent dans les deux États, elle est considérée comme un résident de l'État avec lequel ses liens personnels et économiques sont les plus étroits (centre des intérêts vitaux);

b) Si l'État où cette personne a le centre de ses intérêts vitaux ne peut pas être déterminé, ou si elle ne dispose d'un foyer d'habitation permanent dans aucun des États, elle est considérée comme résidente de l'État où elle séjourne de façon habituelle;

c) Si cette personne séjourne de façon habituelle dans les deux États ou si elle ne séjourne de façon habituelle dans aucun d'eux, elle est considérée comme résidente de l'État dont elle possède la nationalité;

d) Si la question de la résidence ne peut être tranchée selon les dispositions des alinéas a) à c), les autorités compétentes des États contractants la tranchent d'un commun accord.

3. Lorsque, selon les dispositions du paragraphe 1, une personne autre qu'une personne physique est résidente des deux États contractants, elle est considérée comme résidente seulement de l'État où son siège de direction effective est situé.

Article 5. Établissement stable

1. Au sens du présent Accord, l'expression « établissement stable » désigne une installation fixe d'affaires par l'intermédiaire de laquelle l'entreprise exerce tout ou partie de son activité.

2. L'expression « établissement stable » comprend notamment :

a) Un siège de direction;

b) Une succursale;

c) Un bureau;

d) Une usine;

e) Un atelier;

f) Une mine, un puits de pétrole ou de gaz, une carrière ou tout autre lieu d'extraction de ressources naturelles;

g) Un entrepôt qu'une personne utilise pour offrir des services d'entreposage à des tiers;

h) Une ferme, une plantation ou un autre lieu où des activités agricoles, forestières, de plantation ou d'autres activités similaires sont exercées;

i) Un local utilisé comme point de vente ou pour recevoir ou solliciter des commandes;

j) Une installation ou une structure utilisée aux fins d'exploration de ressources naturelles;

k) Un chantier de construction, un projet de montage ou d'installation ou des activités de supervision liées à ce projet, mais seulement si ce chantier de construction, ce projet ou ces activités durent plus de six mois.

3. Nonobstant les dispositions précédentes du présent article, on considère que l'expression « établissement stable » ne comprend pas :

a) L'utilisation d'installations pour le stockage ou l'exposition de biens ou de marchandises appartenant à l'entreprise;

b) L'exploitation d'un stock de biens ou de marchandises appartenant à l'entreprise aux seules fins de stockage ou d'exposition;

c) L'exploitation d'un stock de biens ou de marchandises appartenant à l'entreprise aux seules fins de transformation par une autre entreprise;

d) L'exploitation d'une installation fixe d'affaires aux seules fins d'acheter des marchandises ou de réunir des informations pour l'entreprise;

e) L'exploitation d'une installation fixe d'affaires aux seules fins d'exercer, pour l'entreprise, toute autre activité de caractère préparatoire ou auxiliaire.

Toutefois, les dispositions des alinéas a) à e) ne s'appliquent pas si l'entreprise possède une autre installation fixe d'affaire dans l'autre État contractant pour toute fin autre que les fins énoncées auxdits alinéas.

4. Nonobstant les dispositions des paragraphes 1 et 2, lorsqu'une personne, autre qu'un agent jouissant d'un statut indépendant auquel s'applique le paragraphe 5, agit dans un État contractant pour le compte d'une entreprise de l'autre État contractant, cette entreprise est considérée comme ayant un établissement stable dans le premier État si cette personne :

a) Dispose dans cet État de pouvoirs qu'elle y exerce habituellement lui permettant de conclure des contrats au nom de l'entreprise, sauf si ses activités se limitent à l'achat de biens ou de marchandise pour l'entreprise; ou

b) Ne dispose pas de tels pouvoirs, mais exploite habituellement dans cet État un stock de biens ou de marchandises pour le compte de l'entreprise.

5. Une entreprise d'un État contractant n'est pas considérée comme ayant un établissement stable dans l'autre État contractant du seul fait qu'elle y exerce une activité par l'entremise d'un courtier, d'un commissionnaire général ou de tout autre agent jouissant d'un statut indépendant, à condition que ces personnes agissent dans le cadre ordinaire de leurs activités. Toutefois, lorsqu'il agit totalement ou presque totalement pour le compte de cette entreprise et qu'entre cette entreprise et l'agent sont établies ou imposées, dans leurs relations commerciales et financières, des conditions qui diffèrent de celles qui auraient été établies entre des entreprises indépendantes, cet agent n'est pas considéré comme un agent jouissant d'un statut indépendant au sens du présent paragraphe.

6. Le fait qu'une société qui est résidente d'un État contractant contrôle ou est contrôlée par une société qui est résidente de l'autre État contractant ou qui y exerce son activité (que ce soit par l'intermédiaire d'un établissement stable ou non) ne suffit pas, en lui-même, à faire de l'une quelconque de ces sociétés un établissement stable de l'autre.

Article 6. Revenus immobiliers

1. Les revenus qu'un résident d'un État contractant tire de biens immobiliers (y compris les revenus des exploitations agricoles ou forestières) situés dans l'autre État contractant sont imposables dans cet autre État.

2. L'expression « biens immobiliers » a le sens que lui attribue le droit de l'État contractant où les biens considérés sont situés. L'expression comprend en tout cas les accessoires, le cheptel mort ou vif des exploitations agricoles et forestières, les droits auxquels s'appliquent les dispositions du droit privé concernant la propriété foncière, l'usufruit des biens immobiliers et les droits à des paiements variables ou fixes pour l'exploitation ou la concession de l'exploitation de gisements minéraux, sources et autres ressources naturelles. Les navires, bateaux et aéronefs ne sont pas considérés comme des biens immobiliers.

3.   Les dispositions du paragraphe 1 s'appliquent aux revenus provenant de l'exploitation directe, de la location et de toute autre forme d'exploitation de biens immobiliers.

4.   Les dispositions des paragraphes 1 et 3 s'appliquent également aux revenus provenant des biens immobiliers d'une entreprise ainsi que des biens immobiliers utilisés pour l'exercice d'une profession indépendante.

Article 7. Bénéfices des entreprises

1.   Les bénéfices d'une entreprise d'un État contractant ne sont imposables que dans cet État, à moins que l'entreprise n'exerce son activité dans l'autre État contractant par l'intermédiaire d'un établissement stable qui y est situé. Si l'entreprise exerce son activité d'une telle façon, ses bénéfices sont imposables dans l'autre État, mais uniquement dans la mesure où ils sont imputables : a) audit établissement stable; b) aux ventes, dans cet autre État, de marchandises de même nature que celles qui sont vendues par l'établissement stable, ou de nature analogue; ou c) à d'autres activités industrielles ou commerciales exercées dans cet autre État et de même nature que celles qui sont exercées par l'établissement, ou de nature analogue.

2.   Sous réserve des dispositions du paragraphe 3, lorsqu'une entreprise d'un État contractant exerce son activité dans l'autre État contractant par l'intermédiaire d'un établissement stable qui y est situé, on impute à cet établissement stable, dans chaque État contractant, les bénéfices qu'il aurait pu réaliser s'il avait constitué une entreprise distincte exerçant des activités identiques ou analogues dans des conditions identiques ou analogues et traitant en toute indépendance avec l'entreprise dont il constitue un établissement stable. Dans les cas où le montant réel des bénéfices imputables à un établissement stable ne peut être déterminé ou lorsque le calcul dudit montant présente des difficultés exceptionnelles, les bénéfices imputables à l'établissement stable peuvent être estimés de façon raisonnable.

3.   Pour déterminer les bénéfices d'un établissement stable, sont admises en déduction les dépenses relatives aux fins poursuivies par cet établissement stable, y compris les dépenses de direction et les frais généraux d'administration ainsi enregistrés, soit dans l'État où est situé cet établissement stable, soit ailleurs, conformément aux dispositions et sous réserve des limites de la législation fiscale de cet État. Toutefois, aucune déduction n'est admise pour les sommes qui seraient, le cas échéant, versées (à d'autres titres que le remboursement des frais) par l'établissement stable au siège central de l'entreprise ou à l'un quelconque de ses bureaux, comme redevances, honoraires ou autres paiements similaires, pour l'usage de brevets, de savoir-faire ou d'autres droits ou comme commission ou autres frais, pour des services précis fournis ou pour une activité de direction ou, sauf dans le cas d'une entreprise bancaire, comme intérêts sur des sommes prêtées à l'établissement stable. De même, il n'est pas tenu compte, dans le calcul des bénéfices d'un établissement stable, des sommes (autres que le remboursement des frais) portées par l'établissement stable au débit du siège central de l'entreprise ou de l'un quelconque de ses autres bureaux, comme redevances, honoraires ou autres paiements similaires, pour l'usage de brevets, du savoir-faire ou d'autres droits ou comme commission ou autres frais pour des services précis fournis ou pour une activité de direction ou, sauf dans le cas d'une entreprise bancaire, comme intérêts sur des sommes prêtées au siège central de l'entreprise ou à l'un quelconque de ses autres bureaux.

4.   Aucun bénéfice n'est imputable à un établissement stable du fait qu'il a simplement acheté des marchandises pour l'entreprise.

5.   Aux fins des paragraphes précédents, les bénéfices à imputer à l'établissement stable sont déterminés chaque année selon la même méthode, sauf s'il existe des motifs valables et suffisants de procéder autrement.

6.   Lorsque les bénéfices comprennent des éléments de revenu traités séparément dans d'autres articles du présent Accord, les dispositions de ces articles ne sont pas touchées par les dispositions du présent article.

Article 8. *Transport aérien*

1.   Les bénéfices qu'une entreprise d'un État contractant tire de l'exploitation d'aéronefs en trafic international ne sont imposables que dans cet État.

2.   Les dispositions du paragraphe 1 s'appliquent aussi aux bénéfices provenant de la participation à un consortium, une coentreprise ou un organisme international d'exploitation.

3.   Aux fins du présent article, les intérêts provenant de fonds qui se rattachent à l'exploitation d'aéronefs en trafic international sont considérés comme des bénéfices tirés de l'exploitation de tels aéronefs et les dispositions de l'article 12 ne s'appliquent pas auxdits intérêts.

4.   Le terme « exploitation d'aéronefs » s'entend de l'exploitation de service de transport par voie aérienne de passagers, de poste, de cheptel ou de biens, qui sont transportés par les propriétaires ou les affréteurs des aéronefs, ainsi que la vente de billets pour ces services de transport pour le compte d'autres entreprises, la location occasionnelle d'aéronefs et toute autre activité directement liée à ces services de transport.

Article 9. *Transport maritime*

1.   Les bénéfices tirés de l'exploitation de navire en trafic international ne sont imposables que dans l'État contractant où le siège de direction effective de l'entreprise est situé.

2.   Si le siège de direction effective d'une entreprise de transport maritime en trafic international se trouve à bord d'un navire, il est considéré comme situé dans l'État contractant où se trouve le port d'attache de ce navire ou, à défaut de port d'attache, dans l'État contractant dont l'exploitant du navire est un résident.

3.   Les dispositions du paragraphe 1 s'appliquent aussi aux bénéfices provenant de la participation à un consortium, une coentreprise ou un organisme international d'exploitation.

4.   Nonobstant les dispositions du paragraphe 1 et de l'article VIII de l'Accord en date du 27 juin 1960 entre le Gouvernement de la République populaire de Pologne et le Gouvernement de l'Inde concernant la coopération en matière de transport maritime, les revenus qu'une entreprise d'un État contractant tire de l'exploitation de navires en provenance des ports de l'autre État contractant et en direction des ports de pays tiers et des ports de pays tiers en direction des ports de l'autre État contractant sont imposables dans l'autre État contractant, mais la redevance imposée dans cet autre État est réduite d'un montant égal à 50 % de celle-ci.

Article 10. Entreprises associées

Lorsque :

a) Une entreprise d'un État contractant participe directement ou indirectement à la direction, au contrôle ou au capital d'une entreprise de l'autre État contractant; ou que

b) Les mêmes personnes participent, directement ou indirectement, à la direction, au contrôle ou au capital d'une entreprise d'un État contractant et d'une entreprise de l'autre État contractant,

Et que, dans l'un et l'autre cas, les deux entreprises sont, dans leurs relations commerciales ou financières, liées par des conditions convenues ou imposées qui diffèrent de celles qui seraient convenues entre des entreprises indépendantes, les bénéfices qui, sans ces conditions, auraient été réalisés par l'une des entreprises mais n'ont pu l'être à cause de ces conditions, peuvent être inclus dans les bénéfices de cette entreprise et imposés en conséquence.

Article 11. Dividendes

1.   Les dividendes payés par une société résidente d'un État contractant à un résident de l'autre État contractant sont imposables dans cet autre État.

2.   Toutefois, ces dividendes sont aussi imposables dans l'État contractant dont la société qui paie les dividendes est résidente, et selon la législation de cet État, mais si la personne qui reçoit les dividendes en est le bénéficiaire effectif, l'impôt ainsi établi ne peut excéder 15 % du montant brut des dividendes lorsque ceux-ci se rapportent à des apports versés après l'entrée en vigueur du présent Accord.

Les dispositions du présent paragraphe n'ont pas d'incidence sur l'imposition des bénéfices de la société qui servent au paiement des dividendes.

3.   Le terme « dividendes » employé dans le présent article désigne les revenus provenant d'actions ou d'autres parts bénéficiaires, à l'exception des créances, ainsi que les revenus d'autres parts sociales soumis au même régime fiscal que les revenus d'actions par la législation de l'État dont la société distributrice est résidente.

4.   Les dispositions des paragraphes 1 et 2 ne s'appliquent pas lorsque le bénéficiaire effectif des dividendes, résident d'un État contractant, exerce dans l'autre État contractant dont la société qui paie les dividendes est résidente, soit une activité industrielle ou commerciale par l'intermédiaire d'un établissement stable qui y est situé, soit une profession indépendante au moyen d'une base fixe qui y est située, et que la participation génératrice des dividendes s'y rattache effectivement. Dans ce cas, les dispositions de l'article 7 ou de l'article 15, suivant le cas, sont applicables.

5.   Lorsqu'une société résidente d'un État contractant tire des bénéfices ou des revenus de l'autre État contractant, cet autre État ne peut percevoir aucun impôt sur les dividendes payés par la société, sauf dans la mesure où ces dividendes sont payés à un résident de cet autre État ou dans la mesure où la participation génératrice des dividendes se rattache effectivement à un établissement stable ou à une base fixe situés dans cet autre État, ni prélever aucun impôt, au titre de l'imposition des bénéfices non distribués, sur les bénéfices non distribués de la société, même si les dividendes payés ou les bénéfices non distribués consistent en tout ou en partie en bénéfices ou revenus provenant de cet autre État.

Article 12. Intérêts

1.   Les intérêts provenant d'un État contractant et payés à un résident de l'autre État contractant sont imposables dans cet autre État.

2.   Toutefois, ces intérêts sont aussi imposables dans l'État contractant d'où ils proviennent et selon la législation de cet État, mais si la personne qui reçoit les intérêts en est le bénéficiaire effectif, l'impôt ainsi établi ne peut excéder 15 % du montant brut des intérêts.

3.   Nonobstant les dispositions du paragraphe 2,

   a) Les intérêts provenant d'un État contractant sont exonérés d'impôts dans cet État s'ils proviennent et sont la propriété effective :

      i)   Du Gouvernement, d'une subdivision politique ou d'une autorité locale de l'autre État contractant; ou

      ii) De la Banque centrale de l'autre État contractant;

   b) Les intérêts provenant d'un État contractant sont exonérés d'impôts dans cet État s'ils sont la propriété effective d'un résident de l'autre État contractant et proviennent d'un prêt ou d'un crédit accordé ou garanti :

      i)   Pour la Pologne, la « Bank Handlowy w Warszawie SA », dans la mesure où ces intérêts sont uniquement attribuables au financement d'activités d'import-export;

      ii) Pour l'Inde, la Banque d'import-export de l'Inde (« Exim Bank »), dans la mesure où ces intérêts sont uniquement attribuables au financement d'activités d'import-export;

      iii) Par toute institution d'un État contractant responsable du financement public du commerce extérieur;

      iv) Par toute autre personne, pourvu que le prêt ou le crédit soit approuvé par le Gouvernement du premier État contractant mentionné.

4.   Le terme « intérêts » employé dans le présent article désigne les revenus des créances de toute nature, assorties ou non de garanties hypothécaires ou d'une clause de participation aux bénéfices du débiteur, et notamment les revenus des fonds publics et des obligations d'emprunts, y compris les primes et lots attachés à ces titres. Les pénalisations pour paiement tardif ne sont pas considérées comme des intérêts au sens du présent article.

5.   Les dispositions des paragraphes 1 et 2 ne s'appliquent pas lorsque le bénéficiaire effectif des intérêts, résident d'un État contractant, exerce dans l'autre État contractant d'où proviennent les intérêts, soit une activité industrielle ou commerciale par l'intermédiaire d'un établissement stable qui y est situé, soit une profession indépendante au moyen d'une base fixe qui y est située, et que la créance génératrice des intérêts s'y rattache effectivement. Dans ce cas, les dispositions de l'article 7 ou de l'article 15, suivant le cas, sont applicables.

6.   Les intérêts sont considérés comme provenant d'un État contractant lorsque le débiteur est cet État lui-même, ou une subdivision politique, une autorité locale ou un résident de cet État. Toutefois, lorsque le débiteur des intérêts, qu'il soit ou non résident d'un État contractant, a dans un État contractant un établissement stable ou une base fixe pour lequel la dette donnant lieu au paiement des intérêts a été contractée et qui supportent la charge de ces intérêts, ceux-ci sont considérés comme provenant de l'État contractant où l'établissement stable, ou la base fixe, est situé.

7.   Lorsque, en raison de relations spéciales entre le débiteur et le bénéficiaire effectif ou entre l'un et l'autre et quelque autre personne, le montant des intérêts, compte tenu de la créance pour

laquelle ils sont payés, excède celui dont seraient convenus le débiteur et le bénéficiaire effectif en l'absence de pareilles relations, les dispositions du présent article ne s'appliquent qu'à ce dernier montant. Dans ce cas, la partie excédentaire des paiements reste imposable selon la législation de chaque État contractant et compte tenu des autres dispositions applicables du présent Accord.

Article 13. *Redevances et honoraires pour services techniques*

1.   Les redevances et les honoraires pour services techniques générés dans un État contractant et payés à un résident de l'autre État contractant sont imposables dans cet autre État.

2.   Toutefois, ces redevances et honoraires pour services techniques sont également imposables dans l'État d'où ils proviennent et selon la législation de cet État, mais si la personne qui touche les redevances ou honoraires en est le bénéficiaire effectif, l'impôt ainsi établi ne peut excéder 22,5 % du montant brut des redevances ou honoraires.

3.   Le terme « redevances » employé dans le présent article désigne les rémunérations de toute nature payées pour l'usage ou la concession de l'usage d'un droit d'auteur sur une œuvre littéraire, artistique ou scientifique, y compris les films cinématographiques, ou les films ou bandes utilisés pour les émissions radiophoniques ou télévisées, d'un brevet, d'une marque de fabrique ou de commerce, d'un dessin ou d'un modèle, d'un plan, d'une formule ou d'un procédé secrets, ainsi que pour l'usage ou la concession de l'usage d'un équipement industriel, commercial ou scientifique et pour des renseignements ayant trait à une expérience acquise dans le domaine industriel, commercial ou scientifique.

4.   L'expression « honoraires pour services techniques » employée dans le présent article désigne le paiement de toute somme à toute personne, à l'exception des paiements à un employé d'une personne effectuant les paiements, en contrepartie de la prestation de services de gestion, techniques ou consultatifs, y compris la prestation de services par du personnel technique ou autre.

5.   Les dispositions des paragraphes 1 et 2 ne s'appliquent pas lorsque le bénéficiaire effectif des redevances ou honoraires pour services techniques, résident d'un État contractant, exerce dans l'autre État contractant source des redevances ou honoraires pour services techniques, soit une activité industrielle ou commerciale par l'intermédiaire d'un établissement stable qui y est situé, soit une profession indépendante au moyen d'une base fixe qui y est située, et que le droit, le bien ou le contrat générateur des redevances ou honoraires pour services techniques s'y rattache effectivement. Dans ce cas, les dispositions de l'article 7 ou de l'article 15, suivant le cas, sont applicables.

6.   Les redevances et honoraires de services techniques sont considérés comme provenant d'un État contractant lorsque le débiteur est cet État lui-même ou bien une subdivision politique, une collectivité locale ou un résident de cet État. Toutefois, lorsque le débiteur des redevances ou honoraires de services techniques, qu'il soit ou non un résident d'un État contractant, a dans un État contractant un établissement stable ou une base fixe, pour lesquels la dette donnant lieu au paiement des redevances ou honoraires de services techniques a été contractée et qui supportent la charge de ces redevances ou honoraires de services techniques, ceux-ci sont considérés comme provenant de l'État où se trouve l'établissement stable ou la base fixe.

7.   Lorsque, en raison de relations spéciales entre le débiteur et le bénéficiaire effectif ou entre l'un et l'autre et quelque autre personne, le montant des redevances ou honoraires de services techniques payés excède celui qui aurait été payé en l'absence de pareilles relations, les dispositions du présent article ne s'appliquent qu'à ce dernier montant. Dans ce cas, la partie excédentaire des

paiements reste imposable selon la législation de chaque État contractant et compte tenu des autres dispositions applicables du présent Accord.

Article 14. Gains en capital

1. Les gains qu'un résident d'un État contractant tire de l'aliénation de biens immobiliers visés à l'article 6 et situés dans l'autre État contractant sont imposables dans cet autre État.

2. Les gains issus de l'aliénation de biens mobiliers faisant partie des biens d'entreprise d'un établissement stable qu'une entreprise d'un État contractant possède dans l'autre État contractant ou de biens mobiliers appartenant à une base fixe dont dispose un résident d'un État contractant dans l'autre État contractant pour l'exercice d'une profession indépendante, y compris tels gains dégagés par l'aliénation dudit établissement stable (seul ou avec l'ensemble de l'entreprise) ou de ladite base fixe sont imposables dans cet autre État.

3. Les gains provenant de l'aliénation de navires ou d'aéronefs exploités en trafic international, ou de biens mobiliers affectés à l'exploitation de ces navires ou aéronefs, ne sont imposables que dans l'État contractant dont le cédant est résident.

4. Les gains tirés de l'aliénation d'actions du capital d'une société qui tire sa valeur ou la plus grande partie de sa valeur, directement ou indirectement, de biens immobiliers situés dans un État contractant sont imposables dans cet autre État.

5. Les gains provenant de l'aliénation de participations autres que celles visées au paragraphe 4 dans une société qui est un résident d'un État contractant sont imposables dans cet État.

6. Les gains provenant de l'aliénation de tout bien autre que ceux visés aux paragraphes 1, 2, 3, 4 et 5 ne sont imposables que dans l'État contractant dont le cédant est résident.

Article 15. Professions indépendantes

1. Les revenus qu'une personne physique résidente d'un État contractant tire de l'exercice d'une profession libérale ou d'une activité indépendante de nature analogue ne sont imposables que dans cet État, sauf dans les cas suivants, où lesdits revenus peuvent également être imposables dans l'autre État contractant :

   a) S'il dispose de façon habituelle dans l'autre État contractant d'une base fixe pour l'exercice de ses activités; dans ce cas, seule la fraction des revenus qui est imputable à ladite base fixe est imposable dans cet autre État; ou

   b) Si son séjour dans l'autre État contractant s'étend sur une période ou des périodes d'une durée totale égale ou supérieure à 183 jours au cours de « l'année précédente » en cause ou de « l'année d'imposition » en cause, suivant le cas; dans ce cas, seule la fraction des revenus provenant des activités exercées dans cet autre État est imposable dans cet autre État.

2. L'expression « profession indépendante » se rapporte aux activités indépendantes d'ordre scientifique, littéraire, artistique, éducatif ou pédagogique, ainsi qu'aux activités indépendantes des médecins, chirurgiens, avocats, ingénieurs, architectes, dentistes et comptables.

Article 16. Professions dépendantes

1. Sous réserve des dispositions des articles 17, 18, 19, 20, 21 et 22, les salaires, traitements et autres rémunérations similaires qu'un résident d'un État contractant reçoit au titre d'un emploi salarié ne sont imposables que dans cet État, à moins que l'emploi ne soit exercé dans l'autre État contractant. Si l'emploi y est exercé, les rémunérations reçues à ce titre sont imposables dans cet autre État.

2. Nonobstant les dispositions du paragraphe 1, les rémunérations qu'un résident d'un État contractant reçoit au titre d'un emploi salarié exercé dans l'autre État contractant ne sont imposables que dans le premier État si :

a) Le bénéficiaire est présent dans l'autre État pendant une période ou des périodes d'une durée totale égale ou inférieure à 183 jours au cours de « l'année précédente » en cause ou de « l'année d'imposition » en cause, suivant le cas; et

b) Les rémunérations sont payées par un employeur ou pour le compte d'un employeur qui n'est pas un résident de l'autre État; et

c) La charge de ces rémunérations n'est pas supportée par un établissement stable ou une base fixe que l'employeur a dans l'autre État.

3. Nonobstant les dispositions précédentes du présent article, les rémunérations tirées d'un emploi salarié exercé à bord d'un navire ou d'un aéronef exploité en trafic international par une entreprise d'un État contractant sont imposables dans cet État.

Article 17. Tantièmes et rémunération du personnel de direction de haut niveau

1. Les tantièmes, jetons de présence et autres rétributions similaires qu'un résident d'un État contractant reçoit en sa qualité de membre du conseil d'administration d'une société qui est résidente de l'autre État contractant sont imposables dans cet autre État.

2. Les traitements, salaires et autres rémunérations similaires qu'un résident d'un État contractant reçoit en sa qualité de dirigeant occupant un poste de direction de haut niveau dans une société qui est résidente de l'autre État contractant sont imposables dans cet autre État.

Article 18. Revenus gagnés par les artistes du spectacle et les athlètes

1. Nonobstant les dispositions des articles 15 et 16, les revenus qu'un résident d'un État contractant tire de ses activités personnelles exercées dans l'autre État contractant en tant qu'artiste du spectacle, artiste de théâtre, de cinéma, de la radio ou de la télévision ou musicien, ou en tant qu'athlète, sont imposables dans cet autre État.

2. Lorsque les revenus d'activités qu'un artiste du spectacle ou un athlète exerce personnellement et en cette qualité sont attribués non pas à l'artiste du spectacle ou à l'athlète lui-même mais à une autre personne, ces revenus sont imposables, nonobstant les dispositions des articles 7, 15 et 16, dans l'État contractant où les activités de l'artiste ou de l'athlète sont exercées.

3. Nonobstant les dispositions du paragraphe 1, les revenus qu'un artiste du spectacle ou un athlète qui est résident d'un État contractant tire des activités qu'il exerce personnellement et en cette qualité dans l'autre État contractant ne sont imposables que dans le premier État contractant si les activités exercées dans l'autre État contractant le sont dans le cadre d'un programme d'échange culturel ou sportif convenu par les deux États contractants et qu'elles sont entièrement ou largement

financées par les fonds publics du premier État contractant, ou d'une subdivision politique ou d'une collectivité locale de cet État.

4. Nonobstant les dispositions du paragraphe 2 et des articles 7, 15 et 16, lorsque les revenus d'activités qu'un artiste du spectacle ou un athlète exerce personnellement et en cette qualité dans un État contractant sont attribués non pas à l'artiste du spectacle ou à l'athlète lui-même mais à une autre personne, ces revenus ne sont imposables que dans l'autre État contractant si les activités de cette autre personne sont exercées dans le cadre d'un programme d'échange culturel ou sportif convenu par les deux États contractants et qu'elles sont entièrement ou largement financées par les fonds publics de cet autre État, ou d'une subdivision politique ou d'une collectivité locale de cet autre État.

Article 19. Rémunération et pensions afférents à la fonction publique

1. a) Les rémunérations, autres que les pensions, payées par un État contractant ou par l'une de ses subdivisions politiques ou collectivités locales à une personne physique au titre de services fournis à cet État contractant ou à l'une de ses subdivisions politiques ou collectivités locales dans l'exercice de fonctions de caractère public ne sont imposables que dans cet État contractant.

b) Toutefois, ces rémunérations sont imposables uniquement dans l'autre État contractant si les services sont exécutés dans cet État et si la personne physique est un résident de cet État qui :

i) Possède la nationalité de cet État; ou

ii) N'est pas devenu résident de cet État à seule fin d'exécuter les services.

2. a) Les pensions versées à une personne physique par un État contractant ou par l'une de ses subdivisions politiques ou collectivités locales, soit directement, soit par prélèvement sur des fonds qu'ils ont constitués, au titre de services fournis à cet État ou à l'une de ses subdivisions politiques ou collectivités locales ne sont imposables que dans cet État.

b) Toutefois, ces pensions ne sont imposables que dans l'autre État contractant si la personne physique est un résident de cet autre État et en possède la nationalité.

3. Les dispositions des articles 16, 17 et 18 s'appliquent aux rémunérations et aux pensions payées au titre de services rendus dans le cadre d'une activité commerciale exercée par un État contractant ou par l'une de ses subdivisions politiques ou collectivités locales.

Article 20. Pensions et rentes non publiques

1. Les pensions, autres que celles visées à l'article 19, et les rentes qu'un résident d'un État contractant reçoit en provenance de l'autre État contractant ne sont imposables que dans le premier État contractant.

2. Le terme « pension » s'entend d'un paiement périodique effectué en contrepartie de services antérieurs ou à titre d'indemnité pour des blessures subies pendant la prestation des services.

3. Le terme « rente » désigne une somme déterminée payable périodiquement à échéances fixes, la vie durant ou pendant une période qui est spécifiée ou peut être établie, en vertu d'une obligation d'effectuer des versements en contrepartie d'un capital suffisant intégralement versé en espèces ou en valeurs appréciables en espèces.

Article 21. Paiements reçus par les étudiants et les stagiaires

1.   Les sommes qu'un étudiant ou stagiaire, qui est ou qui était immédiatement avant de se rendre dans un État contractant un résident de l'autre État contractant et qui séjourne dans le premier État à seule fin d'y poursuivre ses études ou sa formation, reçoit pour couvrir ses frais d'entretien, d'études ou de formation ne sont pas imposables dans cet État, à condition qu'elles proviennent de sources situées en dehors de cet État.

2.   Les revenus qu'un étudiant ou un stagiaire tire d'activités exercées dans un État contractant dans lequel il est présent uniquement pour ses études ou sa formation ne sont pas imposables dans cet État, sauf s'ils excèdent la somme nécessaire à son entretien, à ses études ou à sa formation.

3.   Les avantages du présent article ne s'appliquent que pendant une période qui peut être raisonnablement ou habituellement considérée comme nécessaire pour compléter les études ou la formation entreprises, et une personne physique ne peut en aucun cas bénéficier des avantages du présent article pendant plus de cinq années consécutives à compter de la date de la première arrivée dans cet autre État contractant.

4.   Aux fins du présent article et de l'article 22, une personne physique est réputée être un résident d'un État contractant si elle réside dans cet État contractant au cours de « l'année précédente » ou de « l'année d'imposition », suivant le cas, pendant laquelle elle se rend dans l'autre État contractant ou au cours de « l'année précédente » ou de « l'année d'imposition » qui précède immédiatement.

Article 22. Paiements reçus par les professeurs, les enseignants et les chercheurs

1.   Un professeur ou enseignant qui est ou qui était résident d'un État contractant immédiatement avant de se rendre dans l'autre État contractant dans le seul but d'enseigner ou d'effectuer de la recherche, ou les deux, dans une université, un collège ou un autre établissement approuvé dans ledit autre État contractant, est exonéré d'impôt dans cet autre État en ce qui concerne les rémunérations correspondant à cet enseignement ou à ces recherches, durant une période n'excédant pas deux ans à compter de la date de sa première arrivée dans cet autre État.

2.   Le présent article ne s'applique pas aux revenus tirés de travaux de recherche si ces travaux sont menés non pas dans l'intérêt public, mais essentiellement dans l'intérêt privé d'une ou de plusieurs personnes déterminées.

3.   Aux fins du paragraphe 1, l'expression « établissement reconnu » s'entend d'un établissement qui a été approuvé à cette fin par l'autorité compétente de l'État contractant intéressé.

Article 23. Autres revenus

1.   Sous réserve des dispositions du paragraphe 2, les éléments du revenu d'un résident d'un État contractant, d'où qu'ils proviennent, qui ne sont pas expressément visés par les articles précédents du présent Accord ne sont imposables que dans cet État contractant.

2.   Les dispositions du paragraphe 1 ne s'appliquent pas aux revenus autres que les revenus provenant de biens immobiliers, tels que définis au paragraphe 2 de l'article 6, lorsque le bénéficiaire de tels revenus, résident d'un État contractant, exerce dans l'autre État contractant soit une activité commerciale par l'intermédiaire d'un établissement stable qui y est situé, soit une profession indépendante au moyen d'une base fixe qui y est située, et que le droit ou le bien générateur des

revenus s'y rattache effectivement. Dans ce cas, les dispositions de l'article 7 ou de l'article 15, suivant le cas, sont applicables.

3.   Nonobstant les dispositions des paragraphes 1 et 2 du présent article, les éléments de revenu d'un résident d'un État contractant qui ne sont pas visés dans les articles précédents du présent Accord et qui proviennent de l'autre État contractant sont imposables dans cet autre État.

4.   Les autorités compétentes des États contractants peuvent communiquer directement entre elles en vue de parvenir à un accord au sens des paragraphes précédents. Les autorités compétentes instituent, par voie de consultations, des procédures, des conditions, des méthodes et des techniques bilatérales appropriées pour mettre en œuvre la procédure amiable prévue dans le présent article.

Article 24. Élimination de la double imposition

1.   Sauf dispositions contraires contenues dans le présent Accord, l'imposition continuera d'être réglée dans chaque État contractant par la législation en vigueur dans cet État.

2.   Dans les deux États contractants, la double imposition sera évitée de la façon suivante :

a) Lorsqu'un résident d'un État contractant reçoit des revenus qui, conformément aux dispositions du présent Accord, sont imposables dans l'autre État contractant, le premier État contractant exempte ces revenus de l'impôt, sous réserve des dispositions de l'alinéa b) du présent paragraphe, mais peut, pour calculer le montant de l'impôt sur le reste des revenus de ce résident, appliquer le même taux que si les revenus en question n'avaient pas été exemptés.

b) Lorsqu'il impose ses résidents, chaque État contractant peut faire figurer dans la base d'imposition les éléments du revenu qui, conformément aux dispositions des articles 11, 12 et 13 du présent Accord, sont également imposables dans l'autre État, mais il déduit du montant d'impôt calculé sur cette base une somme égale à l'impôt payé dans l'autre État contractant. Toutefois, cette déduction ne saurait excéder la partie de l'impôt exigible par le premier État, tel que calculé avant l'octroi de la déduction, qui correspond au revenu imposable dans l'autre État conformément aux dispositions des articles 11, 12 et 13 du présent Accord.

3.   Aux fins de l'alinéa b) du paragraphe 2, le terme « impôt payé dans l'autre État contractant » est réputé inclure toute somme qui aurait été payable à titre d'impôt n'eût été un allègement sous forme d'élément déductible lors du calcul du revenu imposable, d'exonération ou de dégrèvement, ou sous une autre forme en vertu de la législation sur l'imposition du revenu en vigueur dans cet autre État contractant.

Article 25. Non-discrimination

1.   Les ressortissants d'un État contractant ne sont soumis dans l'autre État contractant à aucune imposition ou obligation correspondante qui soit autre ou plus lourde que celles auxquelles sont ou peuvent être assujettis les ressortissants de cet autre État qui se trouvent dans la même situation et sont soumis aux mêmes conditions.

2.   L'établissement stable qu'une entreprise de l'un des États contractants a dans l'autre État contractant n'est pas imposé selon des modalités moins favorables dans cet autre État que les entreprises de ce dernier qui exercent les mêmes activités dans les mêmes circonstances ou selon les mêmes conditions.

3. Aucune disposition du présent article ne saurait être interprétée comme obligeant un État contractant à accorder à des personnes qui ne sont pas résidents de cet État des déductions, allègements, réductions et dégrèvements fiscaux qui, en vertu de la loi, ne peuvent être octroyés qu'aux personnes qui en sont résidents.

4. Les entreprises d'un État contractant dont le capital est en totalité ou en partie, directement ou indirectement, détenu ou contrôlé par un ou plusieurs résidents de l'autre État contractant, ne sont soumises dans le premier État contractant à aucune imposition ou obligation correspondante, qui est autre ou plus lourde que celles auxquelles sont ou peuvent être assujetties les autres entreprises similaires du premier État dans les mêmes circonstances et selon les mêmes conditions.

5. Dans le présent article, le terme « imposition » s'entend des impôts visés par le présent Accord.

6. À moins que les dispositions de l'article 11, du paragraphe 7 de l'article 12 ou du paragraphe 7 de l'article 13 du présent Accord ne s'appliquent, les intérêts, redevances et autres montants payés par une entreprise d'un État contractant à un résident de l'autre État contractant sont déductibles, pour la détermination des bénéfices imposables de cette entreprise, dans les mêmes conditions que s'ils avaient été payés à un résident du premier État. De même, les dettes d'une entreprise d'un État contractant envers un résident de l'autre État contractant sont déductibles, pour la détermination de la fortune imposable de cette entreprise, dans les mêmes conditions que si elles avaient été contractées envers un résident du premier État.

7. Aucune des dispositions du présent Accord n'a d'effet défavorable sur les exonérations, allègements, réductions, déductions et dégrèvements fiscaux prévus par la législation interne des deux États contractants.

Article 26. Procédure amiable

1. Lorsqu'un résident d'un État contractant estime que les mesures prises par un État contractant ou par les deux États contractants entraînent ou entraîneront pour lui une imposition non conforme aux dispositions du présent Accord, il peut, indépendamment des recours prévus par la législation nationale de ces États, soumettre son cas à l'autorité compétente de l'État contractant duquel il est résident. Le cas doit être soumis dans un délai de trois ans suivant la date de réception de l'avis portant sur la mesure qui entraîne une imposition non conforme aux dispositions du présent Accord.

2. L'autorité compétente s'efforce, si la réclamation lui paraît fondée et si elle n'est pas elle-même en mesure d'y apporter une solution appropriée, de régler le cas par voie d'accord amiable avec l'autorité compétente de l'autre État contractant, en vue d'éviter une imposition non conforme au présent Accord. Tout accord ainsi convenu est appliqué quels que soient les délais prévus par la législation nationale des États contractants.

3. Les autorités compétentes des États contractants s'efforcent de régler par voie d'accord amiable les difficultés ou les doutes auxquels peuvent donner lieu l'interprétation ou l'application du présent Accord. Elles peuvent également se concerter en vue d'éliminer la double imposition dans les cas non prévus par le présent Accord.

4. Les autorités compétentes des États contractants peuvent communiquer directement entre elles en vue de parvenir à un accord au sens des paragraphes précédents. Lorsqu'il paraît souhaitable, pour parvenir à un accord, d'avoir un échange verbal de vues, cet échange peut avoir lieu par le biais d'une commission composée de représentants des autorités compétentes des États contractants.

Article 27. Échange de renseignements

1.   Les autorités compétentes des États contractants échangent les renseignements (y compris les documents) nécessaires pour appliquer les dispositions du présent Accord ou celles de la législation interne des États contractants relatives aux impôts visés par le présent Accord dans la mesure où l'imposition prévue par cette législation n'est pas contraire aux dispositions du présent Accord, en particulier afin de lutter contre la fraude ou l'évasion de ces impôts. Les renseignements reçus par un État contractant sont tenus secrets de la même manière que les renseignements obtenus en application de la législation interne de cet État. Toutefois, si ces renseignements sont considérés à l'origine comme secrets dans l'État qui les transmet, ils ne sont communiqués qu'aux personnes ou autorités (y compris les tribunaux et organes administratifs) concernées par l'établissement ou le recouvrement des impôts visés par le présent Accord, par les procédures ou poursuites s'y rapportant ou par les décisions sur les recours y afférents. Ces personnes ou autorités n'utilisent ces renseignements qu'à ces fins, mais peuvent les révéler au cours d'audiences publiques de tribunaux ou dans des jugements. Les autorités compétentes instituent, par voie de consultations, des conditions, des méthodes et des techniques appropriées pour les questions faisant l'objet de tels échanges de renseignements, y compris, le cas échéant, des renseignements sur l'évitement fiscal.

2.   L'échange de renseignements ou de documents peut être fait d'office, sur demande à propos de cas particuliers, ou des deux façons. Les autorités compétentes des États contractants se mettent de temps à autre d'accord sur la liste des renseignements ou documents qui sont communiqués d'office.

3.   Les dispositions du paragraphe 1 ne peuvent en aucun cas être interprétées comme imposant à un État contractant l'obligation :

a)   De prendre des mesures administratives dérogeant à sa propre législation ou à sa pratique administrative ou à celles de l'autre État contractant;

b)   De fournir des renseignements ou des documents qui ne pourraient être obtenus sur la base de sa législation ou dans le cours normal de sa pratique administrative ou de celles de l'autre État contractant;

c)   De fournir des renseignements ou des documents qui révéleraient un secret commercial, industriel ou professionnel ou un procédé ou renseignement commercial dont la communication serait contraire à l'ordre public.

Article 28. Assistance en matière de recouvrement

1.   Les États contractants conviennent de se prêter mutuellement assistance et appui pour la perception des impôts visés par le présent Accord dans les cas où les impôts sont définitivement exigibles selon la législation des États qui en font la demande.

2.   Pour ce qui est d'une demande de recouvrement, les créances fiscales de l'un ou l'autre des États contractants qui ont été établies définitivement seront acceptées aux fins de recouvrement par l'autre État contractant à qui la demande est adressée et perçues dans cet État conformément à la législation applicable au recouvrement et à la perception de ses impôts.

3.   Dans le cas de l'impôt polonais, la demande est envoyée par le Ministre des finances de la Pologne ou son représentant autorisé au Conseil d'administration des impôts directs du Département fiscal du Ministère des finances de l'Inde et est accompagnée du certificat exigé par la législation

de la Pologne pour attester que les impôts ont été établis définitivement et sont exigibles du contribuable.

4.   Dans le cas de l'impôt indien, la demande est envoyée par le Conseil d'administration des impôts directs du Département fiscal du Ministère des finances de l'Inde au Ministre des finances de la Pologne ou à son représentant autorisé et est accompagnée du certificat exigé par la législation de l'Inde pour attester que les impôts ont été établis définitivement et sont exigibles du contribuable.

5.   Lorsque la créance fiscale n'a pas été déterminée de façon définitive parce qu'elle fait l'objet d'un recours ou autre procédure, un État contractant peut, en vue de protéger ses recettes, demander à l'autre État de prendre en son nom des mesures provisoires dans la mesure permise par la législation de l'autre État contractant.

6.   Une demande d'assistance en matière de recouvrement ne peut être faite qu'en l'absence d'actifs suffisants du contribuable aux fins du recouvrement des impôts dans l'État contractant qui fait la demande.

7.   L'État contractant dans lequel les impôts sont recouvrés conformément aux paragraphes 1, 2 et 5 du présent article remet immédiatement le montant ainsi recouvré à l'État contractant qui a fait la demande.

Article 29. *Activités diplomatiques et consulaires*

Rien dans le présent Accord ne porte atteinte aux privilèges fiscaux dont bénéficient les fonctionnaires diplomatiques ou consulaires en vertu des règles générales du droit international ou des dispositions d'accords particuliers.

Article 30. *Entrée en vigueur*

Les États contractants se notifient mutuellement l'accomplissement des formalités exigées par leurs législations respectives pour l'entrée en vigueur du présent Accord. Le présent Accord entre en vigueur à la date de réception de la dernière de ces notifications et s'applique :

a) En Pologne, aux revenus générés au cours de toute année d'imposition commençant à partir du 1er janvier suivant l'année civile au cours de laquelle la dernière des notifications a été donnée;

b) En Inde, aux revenus générés au cours de toute année d'imposition commençant à partir du 1er avril suivant l'année civile au cours de laquelle la dernière des notifications a été donnée.

Article 31. *Dénonciation*

Le présent Accord reste en vigueur indéfiniment, mais chaque État contractant peut, jusqu'au 30 juin de chaque année civile suivant la cinquième année civile au cours de laquelle le présent Accord est entré en vigueur, le dénoncer moyennant une notification écrite adressée à l'autre État contractant par la voie diplomatique, auquel cas l'Accord cesse de produire ses effets :

a) En Pologne, aux revenus générés au cours de toute année d'imposition commençant à partir du 1er janvier suivant l'année civile au cours de laquelle la notification a été donnée;

b) En Inde, aux revenus générés au cours de toute année d'imposition commençant à partir du 1ᵉʳ avril suivant l'année civile au cours de laquelle la notification a été donnée.

EN FOI DE QUOI, les soussignés, à ce dûment autorisés, ont signé le présent Accord.

FAIT à Varsovie, le 21 juin 1989, en deux exemplaires, en langues anglaise, hindi et polonaise, tous les textes faisant également foi.

En cas de divergence entre les textes polonais et hindi, le texte anglais prévaut.

Pour le Gouvernement de la République populaire de Pologne :
[SIGNÉ]

Pour le Gouvernement de la République de l'Inde :
[SIGNÉ]

No. 52094

International Bank for Reconstruction and Development
and
Indonesia

Loan Agreement (Coral Reef Rehabilitation and Management Program – Coral Triangle Initiative (COREMAP-CTI) Project) between the Republic of Indonesia and the International Bank for Reconstruction and Development (with schedules, appendix and International Bank for Reconstruction and Development General Conditions for Loans, dated 12 March 2012). Jakarta, 17 March 2014

Entry into force: *5 June 2014 by notification*

Authentic text: *English*

Registration with the Secretariat of the United Nations: *International Bank for Reconstruction and Development, 26 August 2014*

Not published in print, in accordance with article 12(2) of the General Assembly regulations to give effect to Article 102 of the Charter of the United Nations, as amended.

Banque internationale pour la reconstruction et le développement
et
Indonésie

Accord de prêt (Programme de réhabilitation et de gestion des récifs coralliens – Projet concernant l'initiative du triangle de corail) entre la République d'Indonésie et la Banque internationale pour la reconstruction et le développement (avec annexes, appendice et Conditions générales applicables aux prêts de la Banque internationale pour la reconstruction et le développement, en date du 12 mars 2012). Jakarta, 17 mars 2014

Entrée en vigueur : *5 juin 2014 par notification*

Texte authentique : *anglais*

Enregistrement auprès du Secrétariat de l'Organisation des Nations Unies : *Banque internationale pour la reconstruction et le développement, 26 août 2014*

Non disponible en version imprimée, conformément au paragraphe 2 de l'article 12 du règlement de l'Assemblée générale destiné à mettre en application l'Article 102 de la Charte des Nations Unies, tel qu'amendé.

No. 52095

International Bank for Reconstruction and Development
and
Indonesia

Global Environment Facility Grant Agreement (Coral Reef Rehabilitation and Management Program – Coral Triangle Initiative (COREMAP-CTI) Project) between the Republic of Indonesia and the International Bank for Reconstruction and Development (acting as an implementing agency of the global environment facility) (with schedules, appendix and Standard Conditions for Grants made by the World Bank out of various funds, dated 15 February 2012). Jakarta, 17 March 2014

Entry into force: *5 June 2014 by notification*

Authentic text: *English*

Registration with the Secretariat of the United Nations: *International Bank for Reconstruction and Development, 26 August 2014*

Not published in print, in accordance with article 12(2) of the General Assembly regulations to give effect to Article 102 of the Charter of the United Nations, as amended.

Banque internationale pour la reconstruction et le développement
et
Indonésie

Accord de don du Fonds pour l'environnement mondial (Programme de réhabilitation et de gestion des récifs coralliens – Projet concernant l'initiative du triangle de corail) entre la République d'Indonésie et la Banque internationale pour la reconstruction et le développement (agissant en qualité d'agence d'exécution du Fonds pour l'environnement mondial) (avec annexes, appendice et Conditions standard pour les dons consentis par la Banque mondiale sur divers fonds, en date du 15 février 2012). Jakarta, 17 mars 2014

Entrée en vigueur : *5 juin 2014 par notification*

Texte authentique : *anglais*

Enregistrement auprès du Secrétariat de l'Organisation des Nations Unies : *Banque internationale pour la reconstruction et le développement, 26 août 2014*

Non disponible en version imprimée, conformément au paragraphe 2 de l'article 12 du règlement de l'Assemblée générale destiné à mettre en application l'Article 102 de la Charte des Nations Unies, tel qu'amendé.

No. 52096

International Development Association
and
Gambia

Financing Agreement (Maternal and Child Nutrition and Health Results Project) between the Republic of the Gambia and the International Development Association (with schedules, appendix and International Development Association General Conditions for Credits and Grants, dated 31 July 2010). Washington, 9 April 2014

Entry into force: *20 May 2014 by notification*

Authentic text: *English*

Registration with the Secretariat of the United Nations: *International Development Association, 26 August 2014*

Not published in print, in accordance with article 12(2) of the General Assembly regulations to give effect to Article 102 of the Charter of the United Nations, as amended.

Association internationale de développement
et
Gambie

Accord de financement (Projet concernant les résultats de santé et la nutrition maternelle et infantile) entre la République de Gambie et l'Association internationale de développement (avec annexes, appendice et Conditions générales applicables aux crédits et aux dons de l'Association internationale de développement, en date du 31 juillet 2010). Washington, 9 avril 2014

Entrée en vigueur : *20 mai 2014 par notification*

Texte authentique : *anglais*

Enregistrement auprès du Secrétariat de l'Organisation des Nations Unies : *Association internationale de développement, 26 août 2014*

Non disponible en version imprimée, conformément au paragraphe 2 de l'article 12 du règlement de l'Assemblée générale destiné à mettre en application l'Article 102 de la Charte des Nations Unies, tel qu'amendé.

No. 52097

World Bank (International Bank for Reconstruction and Development and International Development Association) and Gambia

Multi-donor Trust Fund for Health Results Innovation Grant Agreement (Maternal and Child Nutrition and Health Results Project) between the Republic of the Gambia and the International Bank for Reconstruction and Development and the International Development Association, acting as Administrator of the Multi-Donor Trust Fund for Health Results Innovation (with schedules, appendix and Standard Conditions for Grants made by the World Bank out of various funds, dated 15 February 2012). Washington, 9 April 2014

Entry into force: *20 May 2014 by notification*

Authentic text: *English*

Registration with the Secretariat of the United Nations: *World Bank (International Bank for Reconstruction and Development and International Development Association), 26 August 2014*

Not published in print, in accordance with article 12(2) of the General Assembly regulations to give effect to Article 102 of the Charter of the United Nations, as amended.

Banque mondiale (Banque internationale pour la reconstruction et le développement et Association internationale de développement) et Gambie

Accord de don du Fonds fiduciaire multidonateurs pour l'innovation en matière de résultats sanitaires (Projet concernant les résultats de santé et de nutrition maternelle et infantile) entre la République de Gambie et la Banque internationale pour la reconstruction et le développement et l'Association internationale de développement, agissant en tant qu'administrateur du Fonds fiduciaire multidonateurs pour l'innovation en matière de résultats sanitaires (avec annexes, appendice et Conditions standard pour les dons consentis par la Banque mondiale sur divers fonds, en date du 15 février 2012). Washington, 9 avril 2014

Entrée en vigueur : *20 mai 2014 par notification*

Texte authentique : *anglais*

Enregistrement auprès du Secrétariat de l'Organisation des Nations Unies : *Banque mondiale (Banque internationale pour la reconstruction et le développement et Association internationale de développement), 26 août 2014*

Non disponible en version imprimée, conformément au paragraphe 2 de l'article 12 du règlement de l'Assemblée générale destiné à mettre en application l'Article 102 de la Charte des Nations Unies, tel qu'amendé.

No. 52098

Argentina
and
Ecuador

Exchange of notes constituting an Agreement between the Government of the Argentine Republic and the Government of the Republic of Ecuador on recognition of primary and secondary education (with annex). Quito, 13 May 1993

Entry into force: *13 May 1993 by the exchange of the said notes, in accordance with their provisions*

Authentic text: *Spanish*

Registration with the Secretariat of the United Nations: *Argentina, 7 August 2014*

Not published in print, in accordance with article 12(2) of the General Assembly regulations to give effect to Article 102 of the Charter of the United Nations, as amended.

Argentine
et
Équateur

Échange de notes constituant un accord entre le Gouvernement de la République argentine et le Gouvernement de la République de l'Équateur sur la reconnaissance de l'enseignement primaire et secondaire (avec annexe). Quito, 13 mai 1993

Entrée en vigueur : *13 mai 1993 par l'échange desdites notes, conformément à leurs dispositions*

Texte authentique : *espagnol*

Enregistrement auprès du Secrétariat de l'Organisation des Nations Unies : *Argentine, 7 août 2014*

Non disponible en version imprimée, conformément au paragraphe 2 de l'article 12 du règlement de l'Assemblée générale destiné à mettre en application l'Article 102 de la Charte des Nations Unies, tel qu'amendé.

No. 52099

_____

International Development Association
and
Senegal

Financing Agreement (Health and Nutrition Financing Project) between the Republic of Senegal and the International Development Association (with schedules, appendix and International Development Association General Conditions for Credits and Grants, dated 31 July 2010). Dakar, 28 March 2014

Entry into force: *13 May 2014 by notification*

Authentic text: *English*

Registration with the Secretariat of the United Nations: *International Development Association, 26 August 2014*

Not published in print, in accordance with article 12(2) of the General Assembly regulations to give effect to Article 102 of the Charter of the United Nations, as amended.

_____

Association internationale de développement
et
Sénégal

Accord de financement (Projet de financement pour la santé et la nutrition) entre la République du Sénégal et l'Association internationale de développement (avec annexes, appendice et Conditions générales applicables aux crédits et aux dons de l'Association internationale de développement, en date du 31 juillet 2010). Dakar, 28 mars 2014

Entrée en vigueur : *13 mai 2014 par notification*

Texte authentique : *anglais*

Enregistrement auprès du Secrétariat de l'Organisation des Nations Unies : *Association internationale de développement, 26 août 2014*

Non disponible en version imprimée, conformément au paragraphe 2 de l'article 12 du règlement de l'Assemblée générale destiné à mettre en application l'Article 102 de la Charte des Nations Unies, tel qu'amendé.

No. 52100

World Bank (International Bank for Reconstruction and Development and International Development Association) and Senegal

Multi-donor Trust Fund for Health Results Innovation Grant Agreement (Health and Nutrition Financing Project) between the Republic of Senegal and the International Bank for Reconstruction and Development and the International Development Association, both acting as Administrator of the Multi-Donor Trust Fund for Health Results Innovation (with schedules, appendix and International Development Association General Conditions for Credits and Grants, dated 31 July 2010). Dakar, 28 March 2014

Entry into force: *13 May 2014 by notification*

Authentic text: *English*

Registration with the Secretariat of the United Nations: *World Bank (International Bank for Reconstruction and Development and International Development Association), 26 August 2014*

Not published in print, in accordance with article 12(2) of the General Assembly regulations to give effect to Article 102 of the Charter of the United Nations, as amended.

Banque mondiale (Banque internationale pour la reconstruction et le développement et Association internationale de développement) et Sénégal

Accord de don du Fonds fiduciaire multidonateurs pour l'innovation en matière de résultats sanitaires (Projet de financement pour la santé et la nutrition) entre la République du Sénégal et la Banque internationale pour la reconstruction et le développement et l'Association internationale de développement, agissant en tant qu'administrateur du Fonds fiduciaire multidonateurs pour l'innovation en matière de résultats sanitaires (avec annexes, appendice et Conditions générales applicables aux crédits et aux dons de l'Association internationale de développement, en date du 31 juillet 2010). Dakar, 28 mars 2014

Entrée en vigueur : *13 mai 2014 par notification*

Texte authentique : *anglais*

Enregistrement auprès du Secrétariat de l'Organisation des Nations Unies : *Banque mondiale (Banque internationale pour la reconstruction et le développement et Association internationale de développement), 26 août 2014*

Non disponible en version imprimée, conformément au paragraphe 2 de l'article 12 du règlement de l'Assemblée générale destiné à mettre en application l'Article 102 de la Charte des Nations Unies, tel qu'amendé.